Uncertain Unions

Uncertain Unions

MARRIAGE IN ENGLAND 1660–1753

—

By
Lawrence Stone

OXFORD UNIVERSITY PRESS
1992

Oxford University Press, Walton Street, Oxford OX2 6DP

Oxford New York Toronto
Delhi Bombay Calcutta Madras Karachi
Petaling Jaya Singapore Hong Kong Tokyo
Nairobi Dar es Salaam Cape Town
Melbourne Auckland

and associated companies in
Berlin Ibadan

Oxford is a trade mark of Oxford University Press

Published in the United States
by Oxford University Press, New York

British Library Cataloguing in Publication Data
Data available

Library of Congress Cataloging in Publication Data
Stone, Lawrence.
Uncertain unions : marriage in England, 1660–1753 | by Lawrence
Stone.
p. cm.
1. Marriage—England—History—17th century. 2. Marriage—
England—History—18th century. 3. Marriage law—England—
History—17th century. 4. Marriage law—England—History—18th
century. I. Title.
HQ728.S855 1992
306.81'0942'09032—dc20   91–33370
ISBN 0–19–820253–9

Typeset by Graphicraft Typesetters Ltd, Hong Kong
Printed and bound in
Great Britain by Biddles Ltd
Guildford and King's Lynn

No wise woman reckons on the performance of those extravagant things that are said to gain her.

Mary Delarivière Manley, *The New Atlantis*
(London, 1709), 240–1

I do not know a greater evil or one more productive of more misery and more mischief, than the uncertainty of the condition of the marriage tie; I speak now of uncertainty in way of proof.

Dr Stephen Lushington, *Royal Commission on Marriage* (1868), 28: xxi

To

Jeanne

for half-a-century
of certain union

Acknowledgements

Any book published today on the subject of marriage in early modern and modern England is inevitably constructed on the solid foundations of a large body of earlier work, mostly published in the last twenty years. This book would never have been written if some fifteen years ago Dr E. G. W. Bill, Librarian of Lambeth Palace Library, had not asked me to try to put together a consortium of American libraries to provide funds for a period of years, in order to microfilm the Process Books from the records of the Court of Arches. This was done, and microfiches of this enormous, invaluable, and hitherto inaccessible body of archival records, now augmented by microfilms of the bulk of the other records of the court, are deposited at the National Research Library and can be obtained on loan. For about eight years I was therefore able to consult these materials at leisure at Princeton. I am also indebted to Dr Bill and Miss Barber for their generous assistance while I was working on original records of the court in Lambeth Palace Library.

For a systematic survey of the records of some seven Consistory Courts, I am indebted to my research assistant, Dr Timothy Wales. Under my supervision, he spent two years examining selected samples of surviving records, tabulating matrimonial suits for statistical purposes, briefly noting all cases, and xeroxing or microfilming materials which he considered important. I am deeply grateful to him for his devotion to the task, and for the intelligence and historical imagination he exercised. The records of several of the cases in this volume were discovered by him in these Consistory Courts.

I am also grateful to Mr Geoffrey Clark. For two summers he combed the microfilm records of the Old Bailey for materials concerning bigamy and similar problems related to marriage.

My third invaluable helper has been my wife, Jeanne C. Fawtier Stone, who interrupted her own research in order to help me complete this book. She has put into the computer and edited all my handwritten drafts of this volume, has commented extensively on the text, and has spent many weeks on the thankless and dreary tasks of checking footnotes and compiling the index.

The fourth person upon whom I have relied heavily for assistance has been my long-suffering secretary, Mrs Joan Daviduk, who typed my almost illegible drafts of many case-studies, some of which are contained

vii

Acknowledgements

in this volume, and who also typed the flow of correspondence about the book as it took shape over the past nine years.

For financial support of this project I am indebted to the Rockefeller Foundation (G. A. Hum. 8116) and to the National Endowment for the Humanities (Grant R. O.-20220-82). I am also grateful to two semesters of paid leave from Princeton University, for a Rollins Research Grant from Princeton History Department, and for another grant from the Humanities Research Committee of Princeton University. A final revision of the MS was carried out when I was an Andrew W. Mellon Fellow at the National Center for the Humanities.

Among the staff of the many libraries and record offices visited for this project, all of whom were extremely helpful, I should like to single out those of the Bodleian Library, the Oxford University Law Library, and the British Library. For facilitating several days of intensive work on the extremely rich collection of printed pamphlet trial records in the Royal Irish Academy in Dublin, I am very grateful to Ms Brigid Dolan. I have also been helped by the staff of the following County and Local Record Offices: Cheshire, Devon, Hereford and Worcester County, Norfolk, Lichfield Joint Record Office, and Greater London.

I am extremely grateful for invaluable assistance in finding illustrations to Ms Betty B. Muirden of the Yale Center for British Art and to Mr Burton B. Fredericksen and Ms Libby Spatz of the Provenance Index at the J. Paul Getty Museum.

Finally I would like to thank the anonymous reader of this MS for the care and good judgement he exercised in suggesting cuts.

L.S.

Contents

List of Plates   xii

Abbreviations   xiii

I INTRODUCTION   1

   1. Case-Studies   3
   2. Legal Records   4
   3. Courtship   7
   4. The Making of Marriage   12
   5. Marriage, Property, and the Common Law   15
   6. Customary Unions and Concubinage   16
   7. Contract Marriage   17
      (i) The First Suppression 1540–1642   17
      (ii) The Revival 1642–1660   19
      (iii) The Second Suppression 1660–1753 21
   8. Clandestine Marriage   22
      (i) Definition and Development   22
      (ii) Demand from the Laity   23
      (iii) Supply by the Clergy   26
      (iv) Repressive Legislation and Actual Growth
         1666–1730   28
      (v) Reform and Abolition 1730–1753   29
   9. Conclusion   31

II CASE-STUDIES   33

   A. COURTSHIP AND CONTRACT   37

   1. *Troope* v. *Stenson* and *Henworth* v. *Stenson*,
     1652–1664   37
     Courtship among the minor gentry
   2. *Ryder* v. *Jones*, 1661   44
     Courtship among the provincial middling sort
   3. *Harris* v. *Lingard*, 1699–1701   48
     Courtship among the London middling sort

Contents

4. *Moseley* v. *Collier*, 1746–1747 68
    Cross-class courtship in the Bath marriage market

5. *Brace* v. *Cudworth*, 1680–1682 78
    A written contract

B. FORCED MARRIAGE 83

(a) Forced Marriage by the Parish 83

Introduction 83

6. *Preston* v. *Matthews*, 1695 85

7. *The Churchwardens of Hingham* v. *The Churchwardens of Snettisham*, 1713 88

(b) Forced Marriage by the Seducer or Suitor 92

8. *Houghton* v. *Cash*, 1703 92

9. *Hooper* v. *Fazas*, 1690 96

C. CLANDESTINE MARRIAGE 105

(a) A Fleet Parson 105

10. The Revd John Vyse, 1691–1714 105

(b) A Valid Clandestine Marriage 113

11. *Elmes* v. *Elmes*, 1706–1709 113

12. *Northmore* v. *Northmore*, 1664 118

13. *Morland* v. *Morland*, 1686 126

14. *Echard* v. *Townshend*, 1704 135

15. *Harcourt* v. *Harcourt*, 1707 147

16. *Beaumont* v. *Hurnard*, 1706–1712 153

17. *Rudd* v. *Rudd*, 1720–1730 158

18. *Griffin* v. *Griffin*, 1712–1714 161

19. *Phillips* v. *Cresse*, 1738 170

20. *Osborne* v. *Williams*, 1714–1716 175

(c) A Forged Clandestine Marriage 203

21. *Bentley* v. *Bentley*, 1715–1727 203

22. *Mordaunt* v. *Mordaunt*, 1707–1711 217

Contents

(d) A Bigamous Marriage   232

  23. *Tipping* v. *Roberts*, 1704–1733   232

  24. *Muilman* v. *Muilman*, 1722–1748   236
       Con Phillips, serial bigamist

    (i) Introduction   236
   (ii) Life   236
  (iii) *An Apology*   244
  (iv) Matrimonial Litigation   247

List of Plates

Between pages 178 and 179

1. Redgrave Hall, Suffolk
   (National Buildings Record)
2. Peregrine Osborne, 2nd Duke of Leeds
   (National Portrait Gallery)
3. Kiveton Park, Yorks.
   (J. Badeslade and J. Rocque, *Vitruvius Britannicus*, iv (1739))
4. Peregrine Hyde-Osborne, Marquis of Carmarthen and 3rd Duke of Leeds
   (Christie's)
5. Bridget Hyde, 2nd Duchess of Leeds, and her sister
   (In the collection of the Duke of Buccleuch and Queensberry KT)
6. Mary Osborne, 2nd Duchess of Beaufort, later Countess of Dundonald
   (Courtauld Institute of Art)
7. Teresia Constantia Phillips
   (National Portrait Gallery)
8. Genealogy of Lady Bridget Osborne

Abbreviations

CC	Consistory Court
DNB	*Dictionary of National Biography* (Oxford)
GLRO	Greater London Record Office
HMC	Historical Manuscript Commission
HWRO	Hereford and Worcester County Record Office
Lichfield JRO, LCC	Lichfield Joint Record Office, Lichfield Consistory Court
LPCA	Lambeth Palace, Court of Arches MSS
OB Proc.	*Old Bailey Proceedings* (London, 1714–1834)
Peerage	G. E. Cokayne, *Complete Peerage of England*, 14 vols. (London, 1910–65)
T & C Mag.	*Town and Country Magazine* (London, 1769 93)

I
Introduction

This book consists of a series of case-studies about the ambiguities and uncertainties surrounding the making of marriage in early modern England. The stories range in date from the Restoration of the authority of the church and its courts in 1660 to the passage of the Marriage Act of 1753. They illustrate the extraordinary variety of legal but hard to prove, quasi-legal, and illegal ways of making a marriage, ranging from customary concubinage to verbal marriage contracts to clandestine marriages to bigamous or incestuous marriages. As a result of glaring defects in the laws of marriage, very large numbers of perfectly respectable people in the seventeenth and early eighteenth centuries could never be quite sure whether they were married or not.

An earlier volume, entitled *Road to Divorce: England 1530–1987*, deals with these questions in greater detail in a general analysis of the legal, economic, social, and cultural aspects of the making and breaking of marriage. This volume, and a third entitled *Broken Lives: Separation and Divorce in England 1570–1857*, are composed of case-studies. Both are designed to be read quite independently, without reference either to each other or to the first analytical volume. Each is therefore provided with an introduction which explains as much of the legal, cultural, and social background as is needed to understand the unfolding of the stories. Those who have already read *Road to Divorce* can omit this introduction and go straight to the case-studies themselves.[1]

1. Case-Studies

Telling stories should require no justification from the historian. After all, literature is nothing but fictional narratives, which are avidly read for the light they throw both on the changeless qualities of human nature and on the very different types of values, behaviour, and conditions of life prevailing at the time and place in which they are set. Freud wrote:

It still strikes me myself as strange that the case histories I write should read like short stories and that, as one might say, they lack the serious stamp of science. I

---

[1] Only matters not included in *Road to Divorce* are here footnoted.

3

must console myself with the reflection that the nature of the subject is evidently responsible for this, rather than any preference of my own.

If the historian's prime task is to explain change over time, another equally important function is surely to bring the past alive. As any anthropologist who has done field-work will testify, other people are other. If Marc Bloch was right when he asserted that 'in the last analysis it is the human consciousness which is the subject matter of history', then the case-study has an irreplaceable role to play. As John Aubrey wrote in the seventeenth century:

The retrieving of these forgotten things from oblivion in some sort resembles the art of the conjuror, who makes those walk and appear that have been in their graves many hundreds of years; and represents as it were to the eye the places, customs, and fashions that were of the old time.[2]

2. Legal Records

Before the middle of the nineteenth century, the prime, but not sole, jurisdictional responsibility for all matters concerning sexual behaviour, marriage, and separation lay with the ecclesiastical courts. Most marital cases were begun in the Consistory Courts, one for each diocese, run by a Chancellor and staff appointed by the bishop. In the province of Canterbury, which covered all of southern England and of Wales, appeals from these courts were made to the Court of Arches in London, from whose huge, uniquely rich, and hitherto untapped records most of the case-studies for this volume are drawn.

The law of marriage administered by these courts was the medieval canon law, which had been left unaltered at the Reformation, except for a drastic reduction in the number of forbidden degrees of incest. In this respect, England was unique in Europe, since it preserved the lax medieval canon laws about marriage, which had been swept away in Catholic Europe by the Council of Trent, and had been severely modified in most parts of Protestant Europe. England thus had the worst of all worlds: marriage was far too easy to enter into, but extremely difficult to get out of.

It is not pretended that stories derived from ecclesiastical court records reveal the full and unvarnished truth, although the claim can be made that they offer a deeper and more intimate insight into the psychology,

---

[2] S. Freud, *Studies on Hysteria* (London, 1956), 160–1; M. Bloch, *The Historian's Craft*, trans, P. Putnam (London, 1949), 151; J. Aubrey, *Wiltshire: The Topographical Collection*, ed. J. E. Jackson (Devizes, 1862), 4.

behaviour, and even speech of actors in the past than can be obtained from any other source. This is because it was the practice in these courts both to deal only with written accusations and answers, and to write down, if only in somewhat summarized form, everything which was said before the court by either the litigants or their witnesses.

In recording the depositions and answers of witnesses, the clerks of the court usually, but not always, turned direct speech in the present tense into indirect speech in the past tense. For example, one record reads: 'the deponent said that she was married to Mr Williams, and that he was her husband.' In cases where a brisk exchange of dialogue is recorded, this indirect speech formula has sometimes been converted back into direct, but only when there is no possibility of ambiguity. Thus in the case-study, the recorded statement is adjusted to read: 'I am married to Mr Williams and he is my husband.' The purpose of this conversion is to recapture the immediacy and sharpness of the dialogue, much of which is so like that in a contemporary novel or play. It can be claimed with a very high degree of certainty that the statement as presented in the case-study now reads more or less exactly as the witness spoke it before the clerk, and before he had turned it into indirect speech in the past tense. The case-study in which this procedure has been used most extensively is that of *Osborne* v. *Williams*, where many witnesses gave identical detailed evidence about many long and very passionate conversations.

It has to be admitted, however, that even the reader of the original documents is one stage removed from the historian's ultimate goal, that elusive quarry the truth. First, the story of what really happened has to be pieced together from two semi-fictitious constructs created by the prosecution and the defence, each buttressed by the often coached, and occasionally false, sworn evidence by their respective posses of witnesses. Perjury, alas, was all too common in the early modern courtroom. For example, case-studies reveal that at least some clandestine marriage claims were based on nothing but forged documents and perjured testimony. They were the product of the desperation of a propertied family when faced with the situation of a daughter who was pregnant, but whose lover refused either to marry her, as promised, or to provide her with financial support. What is so astonishing about these extreme cases is the brazen fabrication of evidence based entirely on fraud, forgery, and perjury. Even more astonishing, however, is the high detective skill of the agents of the defendants in these cases, who somehow contrived to expose the frauds, identify the perpetrators, and even reconstruct their life histories. In doing so they reveal a seamy London underworld of venal and drunken clergymen and easily corrupted witnesses, all willing to swear to anything if they were adequately rewarded. These were men and women on the very edge of destitution, and driven by a combination of poverty, greed, and a total absence of moral principle.

But if we assume, as I think we must, that in most cases most sworn statements were perhaps evasive but at least not downright lies, then it can plausibly be argued that the truth emerges as clearly as it does in any court of law today.

A second qualifier is that some of the testimony has been tailored to fit the law, and some things we would like to know, or witnesses we would like to hear from, are therefore often missing. Witnesses could not be forced to incriminate themselves, although one can draw one's own conclusions from the questions they refused to answer. The third qualifier is that, although we have detailed records of the evidence of the litigants, we usually do not have the speech of the judge, giving his reasons for his verdict.

On the other hand, the mass of accusations, answers, and testimony of witnesses is often of enormous bulk, sometimes amounting to as much as a quarter of a million words for a single case. This huge, chaotic, and often repetitive outpouring of raw data has had to be compared, sorted out, rearranged, reorganized, and compressed into a coherent narrative, with allowances made for possible alternative interpretations. Some comfort may be derived from the fact that the interpretations of the evidence presented by me in these secondary narratives are usually—not always—supported by the opinions of at least the appeal judges. But of course other readers of the same documents might come to different conclusions.

Every effort has been made to avoid applying twentieth-century moral judgements to episodes occurring in a pre-modern society. The exact speech of witnesses, whether for praise or blame, has been carefully cited, since the precise meaning of words has often changed over the last 200 years. Modern words have to be used to describe situations, but authorial manipulation has been reduced to the minimum possible. In some stories, for example that of the behaviour of the Harris girls in *Harris* v. *Lingard*, many witnesses all agree both about the facts and about the moral conclusions. Mrs Harris and her daughter Abigail were over-ambitious fools, who were playing with fire in an attempt to provide the latter with a husband of higher status and income. Other episodes remain more ambiguous, both factually and ethically.

The central questions of concern in this volume are first to illustrate the significant changes in how marriages were made in the late seventeenth and early eighteenth centuries; and second to tease out from recorded behaviour the moral attitudes both towards courtship, including the display of female physical attractions, and towards irregular marriages or types of concubinage based on no more than vague verbal promises. This was a situation commonly known as 'married in the eyes of God', as opposed to marriage in the eyes of the church, the law, and the community.

Unfortunately, it is in the nature of evidence drawn from records of the courts of law that the resulting accounts of the lives of the protagonists are both partial and episodic. The actors in the drama emerge from the shadows; strut a while upon the stage; expose in intimate detail a story which may cover only a few years or decades of their lives up to that moment; and then, once the trial is over, abruptly vanish into the darkness of unrecorded history. What we have, therefore, are slices out of people's lives, illuminated for an instant in the beam of an immensely powerful searchlight. For a little while we can cavesdrop upon our forebears, listen to them and watch them travelling, drinking, courting, making love; and negotiating, threatening, and manoeuvring in order to make or unmake a marriage.

3. Courtship

There were three modes of courtship in early modern England, each of which was characteristic of, but not peculiar to, one of the three groupings into which contemporaries tended to divide the population. Among the quality, courtship before the middle of the seventeenth century was usually, but by no means always, a stilted and formal affair of short duration and limited significance. The procedure took two forms. The first was the selection of a possible spouse by the parents or 'friends', after careful examination of his or her economic prospects. If the results were satisfactory, a preliminary agreement was reached with the other set of parents and 'friends' about the terms of the financial settlement. The couple were then brought together, in order to discover whether or not they found each other personally obnoxious. If no strong feelings were aroused, the couple normally consented, the marriage settlement was signed, and the arrangements for a formal church wedding went forward. Alternatively, a man might meet or see a woman in a public place, in church, or at a ball or party. If he was attracted to her, he would approach her parents and friends, and formally ask their permission to court her. If investigation proved that he was financially and personally suitable, permission was granted and courting went forward, with all the usual rituals of visits, conversation, gifts, and expressions of love and devotion.

Occasionally, of course, and increasingly throughout the eighteenth century, unsupervised couples from propertied families would meet at court, or at Bath as in *Moseley* v. *Collier*, or on the hunting-field, and conduct their own courtship in complete secrecy. Sooner or later, however, they were obliged to face up to the necessity of obtaining consent of parents or friends. Negotiations and haggling over the settlement now became the last step instead of the first, as the father of the bride decided upon the size of the marriage portion, and the father of the groom upon the appropriate current maintenance for the couple, as well as the jointure for the bride in the event of her widowhood.

In the sixteenth and seventeenth centuries, the pressure of parents, 'friends', and kin in the highest circles of society was all but irresistible, especially because of the financial pressures which could be, and often were, brought to bear. By the eighteenth century, however, the concept of affective individualism was penetrating even these elevated circles, and thanks to the romantic movement, the tables had been largely turned by the end of the century. By this time, there had emerged a world in which, even in a social group for whom large estates and ancient titles were the stakes in the game, the complex calculations of scheming parents and artful lawyers took equal, or even occasionally second, place to the wishes of the couple. The only provisos were that the decision should be based on long-standing affection rather than on either mere physical lust or romantic passion; and second that the family of the proposed spouse should be of roughly similar status and wealth. After 1660 the increasingly rare cases of brutal patriarchal control of marriage are confined to Tory aristocratic families, as in the case of *Osborne* v. *Williams*. In *Moseley* v. *Collier* a rich baronet and his wife shifted in their treatment of their middle-aged daughter from the grant of almost total freedom in social contacts and courtship, to the most ruthless exercise of patriarchal power when it came to preventing her marriage with a person of inferior income and status with whom she had fallen deeply in love.

These case-studies make absolutely clear that among the middling and lower gentry social classes, unmarried English women enjoyed what was by European standards a quite exceptional freedom to conduct their own courtship rituals, if not necessarily to select their own spouses. It was this exceptional freedom which made the use of professional marriage-brokers so relatively rare, compared with France, at all levels below the squirarchy. Not only were young unmarried women permitted to go about alone in the streets of London and other towns, and even to go out to taverns with men, and to attend dances, fairs, and other festivities without chaperones. It was also customary, apparently up to the small gentry, for unmarried girls to grant limited or even full sexual favours to their suitors. This is shown in the case of *Troope* v. *Stenson*, and among the free-wheeling Norfolk parish gentry who figure in the case of *Harcourt* v. *Harcourt*. The same behaviour is also found among the middling sort at the beginning of the eighteenth century, as shown in the cases of *Bentley* v. *Bentley*, *Harris* v. *Lingard*, and *Ryder* v. *Jones*.

These case-studies leave no doubt that in all social strata except the highest, British courting rituals normally involved the custom of bundling, by which is meant the practice of staying up all night together in the woman's place of residence, after the old folks had gone to bed, either without their knowledge or with their tacit consent. This took place either in the kitchen beside the fire or in a bedroom on or in the bed. Sometimes such all-night sessions occurred at weekly intervals for months or years on end, and yet, in the seventeenth century—unlike the eighteenth—only in a minority of cases did they result in pregnancy. Although the rules are nowhere explicitly stated, one has to conclude that there were strong built-in conventions surrounding the practice of bundling in the seventeenth century, which dictated that full intercourse should be avoided, although it is equally hard to escape the conclusion that there must often have taken place an exchange of other forms of sexual gratification.

It has long been known that bundling was common in Wales and Scotland, as well as New England and Scandinavia. It is now certain that it was also very common throughout England in the seventeenth and eighteenth centuries. Moreover it seems possible that the procedure was more widespread throughout Europe than has hitherto been suspected, since it has recently been shown to have been common among the Russian peasantry in the late nineteenth century, as well as in Switzerland, and in parts of France. As in early modern England, some of this 'night courting' was carried out in public, and some of it in private. The penalties for getting pregnant, however, were even more severe in Russia than in England.[3]

---

[3] M. Drake, *Population and Society in Norway 1735–1865* (Cambridge, 1969), 138–45; P. Caspard, 'Conceptions prénuptiales et développement du capitalisme dans la principauté de Neuchatel, 1678–1820', *Annales E. S. C.* 29 (1974); J.-L. Flandrin, 'Repression and Change in Sexual Life of Young People in Medieval and Early Modern Times', *Journal of Family History*, 2 (1977); B. A. Engel, 'Peasant Morality and Premarital Sexual Relations in Late 19th Century Russia', *Journal of Social History*, 23 (1990).

In England this procedure was usually only indulged in after an exchange of verbal promises of marriage, which put the couple in a state generally known as 'married in the eyes of God'. Case after case involved these unwitnessed, and therefore unprovable, promises, accompanied by an exchange of gifts, especially a ring or a bent or broken coin, which for some reason was popularly believed to carry special symbolic meaning. This courtship tended to be prolonged, rarely lasting less than four months and sometimes continuing for several years. What is surprising is how often the mother played a critical role in stage-managing the court-ship of her daughter, acting without the knowledge or consent of the father. Examples are the cases of *Harris* v. *Lingard* and *Harcourt* v. *Harcourt*.

As a result, situations could and did arise in which courting and bundling were first permitted by the mother, and then suddenly forbidden by one or both the fathers, usually because of a quarrel over the financial arrangements for marriage or because of a discrepancy in social status. If the parents forcibly separated the lovers, this could lead to a suit in the ecclesiastical courts, as one of them sued the other on the grounds that a contract existed between them, as in case of *Ryder* v. *Jones*. Alternatively, it could lead to an elopement and a clandestine marriage, as happened with the connivance of the bride's mother in *Bridgen* v. *Pigeon*.[4]

What is so remarkable about these courting procedures in the early seventeenth century is that they involved three features which at first sight seem wholly incompatible, and indeed were to prove to be so in the eighteenth century. One was the delay of marriage to a decade after puberty (and for the poor a decade after leaving home), that is to about 26 to 28 for men and 24 to 26 for women; the second was this all but universal practice of bundling among the lower and the middling sort, right up to and including at least some of the small gentry; and the third was the very low level of both bastardy and pre-nuptial conceptions which resulted. One has to conclude that England in the seventeenth century was sexually an extraordinarily restrained society.

It is reasonable to assume that usually the parents or 'friends' were informed of what was going forward and were asked for their advice, consent, and financial help. If a satisfactory financial arrangement could not be worked out, the couple frequently abandoned the whole affair, sometimes with great grief, sometimes with resignation. Detailed accounts of hundreds of such episodes show clearly that love and material

---

[4] LPCA, D. 247.

interest were inextricably interwoven in the minds of most participants in the courting ritual. As the moment of decision came closer, 'interest' tended to loom larger. Sometimes the two issues became polar opposites, facing the couple with a hard choice between love or money. More often, however, the two remained closely interlocked, since the courting process had itself involved not merely the choice of a congenial and sexually attractive companion but also a shrewd calculation of economic benefits.

Among the propertyless poor, who comprised perhaps the bottom third of the population, freedom of choice among children was almost absolute, if only because the parents lacked the economic resources to exercise effective control. In any case, since courtship and marriage came so late, one or both sets of parents were often already dead by the time their children reached a decision to marry. Parental power was further reduced in this class by the fact that most young people had left home to become agricultural or domestic servants before the time they became seriously interested in the opposite sex. As a result, poor boys and girls were free to meet unchaperoned, as fellow-servants in the same house, or at village fairs and festivals, dances, and church services. Thereafter they made their own arrangements for courting and bundling, subject only to the prurient curiosity and gossip of neighbours and fellow-servants.

One of the most difficult problems facing young English girls in the early eighteenth century was how far they could prudently go in advertising their physical attractions during 'bundling', now that the legal mechanisms of social control had collapsed and the Puritan moral inhibitions upon full penetration had evaporated. This led to an explosion of pre-nuptial pregnancies and bastardies, since there were few guidelines to steer a young girl between the Scylla of prudishness which might deter prospective suitors, and the Charybdis of too easy compliance which might lead to loss of virginity and pregnancy before a binding contract had been made. One way in which some girls tried to protect themselves at this time was to conduct their courting, often including fairly heavy petting, in the presence of other women, usually their sisters, their maids, or sometimes their mothers, relying on these eye-witnesses to prevent things from going too far. All these aspects of the courting scene of eighteenth-century England are well brought out by the story of the two sisters in *Harris* v. *Lingard*.

When bundling resulted in pregnancy, the high level of pre-nuptial pregnancy in the eighteenth century proves that the normal suitor honoured his promises and married the girl. On the relatively rare occasions when the suitor either could not or would not marry the pregnant girl, the results could be catastrophic for the latter. These are the cases which wound up in the courts, as the family of the woman tried to prove a binding contract or clandestine marriage. These court records suggest that bastardy was in most cases a product, not of sexual promiscuity, but of thwarted expectations of marriage.

4. The Making of Marriage

If marriage is regarded in social rather than legal terms, it is a complex and often lengthy process and not merely a single formal public event. This has become evident in the last few years, when the Western world has become full of young couples in various stages of coming together. Some are courting, often including a good deal of physical intimacy; some are temporarily or semi-permanently cohabiting; some are secretly becoming engaged; and some are getting married. If they do marry, the ceremony is performed either in private at a registrar's office, or openly in a field or garden or private house, or formally and publicly in a grand ceremony in a church. The traditional sequence used to be a more or less chaste courtship, followed by a formal publicly announced engagement, followed by a public wedding in a church, followed by consummation, followed by pregnancy. This is now no longer the norm, and many produce children in or out of wedlock at any of these various stages. There are no longer any rules for an orderly progression from one stage to the next, nor even for a single socially accepted mode of formal marital bonding. In this respect we have—quite suddenly and perhaps only temporarily—drifted into a situation not dissimilar from that which prevailed in early modern England.

At that time far more people and institutions had a vested interest in the process of marriage than merely the man and woman involved, their rivals, and their competitors. There were also the 'friends',—that is influential kin, masters, or patrons—who often assumed the right of control or veto and were in a position to enforce their will by the granting or withholding of favours, be it money, house, property, or good will. The higher the social status and wealth of the family, the more likely it was to exercise overwhelming pressure, as can be seen in the case of *Osborne* v. *Williams*. Lower down the social scale, there were the neighbours, who had to be persuaded to accept the couple into their midst as a morally bonded domestic unit.

The following case-studies prove conclusively that the period 1680 to 1710 was one of acute crisis in many propertied families, from the lowest to the highest. The clash between the conflicting ideals of patriarchy and individualism in the choice of a spouse reached an acute stage at this time, just as the rival motives of affection or interest also came into serious conflict. To make matters worse, this was a period when fortune-hunting male, and occasionally female, predators and impostors were both peculiarly common and peculiarly ruthless in their tactics. Sometimes, as in the case of Sir Samuel Morland, the hunter became the hunted. *Caveat emptor* should have been the guiding principle of those men and women from the propertied classes who entered the London marriage market in the late seventeenth and early eighteenth centuries.

The major institutions of society were also concerned with marriage in the seventeenth and eighteenth centuries. The church was closely concerned, in part because it had for centuries enjoyed prime legal control over matrimonial affairs, and in part because it was increasingly insisting upon the active participation in the ceremony of the parish clergyman. The state was also concerned in a variety of ways. At the theoretical level, a host of writers in the seventeenth century tried to base the divine right of kings upon the patriarchal principle embedded in the structure of the family. At a more mundane level, the state became directly concerned in the 1690s, when it tried first to raise money by putting a tax on marriages, and then imposed a heavy stamp duty on marriage licences and certificates. It therefore suddenly developed a vested interest in making everyone go through a regular wedding in church. But it was not until 1753 that the political will could be mustered in Parliament to effect a radical tightening up of the law of marriage.

All three branches of the law—ecclesiastical, common, and equity— had control over some aspect of marriage. The medieval canon law determined the rules of marriage, which were revised and restated in the Canons of 1604 and enforced by the church courts. The criminal courts could also become involved if either of the parties chose to sue the other for such statutory penal offences as bigamy or sodomy, as in *Rudd* v. *Rudd*. Con Phillips's story in *Muilman* v. *Muilman* shows how these various courts interlocked, overlapped, and not infrequently returned contradictory verdicts, about what did or did not constitute a legally valid marriage.

The equity law of Chancery, which had jurisdiction over trust deeds, became deeply involved in marriage in two ways. First, Chancery was the court where litigation took place concerning marriage settlements to trustees of the estates of husbands, which always included provision of jointures for widows. Second, after about 1730, Chancery became involved in the enforcement of the growing numbers of trust deeds made by wealthy women about to be married. By these deeds they conveyed their property to trustees on their behalf, in order to keep it under their

13

own control after marriage, thereby thwarting the common law doctrine that a wife's property passed at marriage under the control of her husband. A third type of trust deeds took the form of maintenance contracts for wives who had been privately separated from their husbands. These last two types of trusts, which were the first steps towards a married woman's property law, became increasingly common in the eighteenth century, especially among the more opulent classes of society.[5] In addition, since Chancery also exercised wardship over orphans and lunatics, it insisted, not always successfully, upon its consent being obtained for their marriage.[6]

Problems of money and property, or lack of it, also loomed large among the poor because of the peculiarities of the English Poor Law and Law of Settlement. Each parish was responsible—under the supervision of the local JPs—for raising taxes on the richer third of the village population to keep the indigent from starvation. The key to a claim for relief on a particular parish was settlement, acquired either by place of birth or place of domicile. Since illegitimate children were becoming an increasing burden on the community by the eighteenth century, every effort was made by the parish to identify the father by prior interrogation of the mother, either by a JP before the birth, or during her labour by the midwife under threat of withholding assistance. Once paternity was ascertained, a filiation order was issued by a JP against the father, who was required to give bonds and provide sureties to pay an annual sum sufficient to cover the cost to the parish of maintaining the child for the first seven years of its life (if it lived that long, which a majority did not). But if the father ran away, or was himself nearly destitute, the burden would necessarily fall upon the parish itself. Every effort was therefore made by the village authorities to bully the alleged father into marrying the mother. But the father might run away even after marriage, so the most reliable solution of all was somehow to transfer the legal settlement of mother and child to another parish. The easiest way to do that was to persuade or bribe a man with a settlement elsewhere to marry the woman, since by marriage the wife and child acquired settlement in the parish of the husband.

Disputes about paternity were decided by the JPs based on the sole testimony, often unsworn, of the pregnant mother. Any JP had the power

---

[5] A. L. Erickson, 'Common Law versus Common Practice: The Use of Marriage Settlements in Early Modern England', *Economic History Review*, 43 (1990); unfortunately, Dr Erickson confuses these two very different types of trust deeds. S. Staves, *Married Women's Separate Property in England, 1660–1833* (Cambridge, Mass., 1990).

[6] LPCA, D. 883.

to demand sureties of an accused father to appear at Quarter Sessions, or to commit him to gaol to await trial there, if he refused to marry the woman at once. The pressures for a shotgun marriage were therefore great, and sometimes whole villages were involved in criminal conspiracies to achieve this end. Examples of such inter-parochial disputes are revealed in cases of litigation between the churchwardens of rival villages,[7] and in *Preston* v. *Matthews*.

5. Marriage, Property, and the Common Law

After inheritance, marriage was probably the single most important method for the transmission of property. In consequence, a great deal of litigation about marriage was, in reality, litigation about property, over which the common law courts had legal jurisdiction. On her marriage, the family of the bride paid a cash dowry to the family of the groom, in return for which the latter settled property for the current maintenance of the couple and for a future jointure, which was an annuity for the widow for the rest of her days. By marriage, all the wife's property which had not been previously conveyed to trustees passed to the husband. The latter could do what he liked with the personal estate, including furniture, jewels, and money, and could enjoy the income of any real estate.

But although the husband could use any or all of this property to pay off his own debts, at marriage he also became liable for all the outstanding debts of his wife. The importance of this responsibility can hardly be exaggerated, since it gave a powerful weapon to an abandoned wife. They could spend money for necessaries appropriate to her station in life, and then urge a creditor to sue her errant husband for the debt. Case after case involves this obligation of a husband to pay his wife's debts for necessaries. This issue of debt loomed so very large in eighteenth-century English life, since the penalty for non-payment was arrest and imprisonment. It is hardly surprising, therefore, that there are many cases of men marrying women merely in order to seize their property and use it to pay their own debts, as in *Morland* v. *Morland*. On the other hand, some unscrupulous women played the same game. Thus a woman could arrange for a clandestine marriage to be faked in order to oblige a cast-off lover to pay her debts.[8] For a woman enmeshed in debt, marriage was often a solution to her difficulties, as exemplified by Con Phillips's

---

[7] See below *Churchwardens of Hingham* v. *Churchwardens of Snettisham*; see also Norfolk CRO, Norwich CC Records, Con/44, 52; Con/39, 90, 45, 59, 62; Dep/56, fos. 353–67; Dep/58, Con/45.

[8] *Smith* v. *Constantine*, LPCA, D. 1929; Eee. 11/28–40, 44–62, 65–7.

clandestine marriage of convenience to a married man, as described in *Muilman* v. *Muilman*. Her creditors were no longer able to arrest her, since she was now a married woman whose debts were henceforward the responsibility of this alleged husband.

Since the common law had jurisdiction over questions of credit, and since a husband was responsible for his wife's debts, the common law courts inevitably found themselves drawn into deciding upon whether or not a woman sued by her creditors for debt was legally married. Clandestine marriage thus offered endless possibilities for deceit and duplicity by fortune-hunters of both sexes: by men, as in *Morland* v. *Morland*, *Hooper* v. *Fazas*, and *Graves* v. *Smith*;[9] and by women as in *Muilman* v. *Muilman*.

6. Customary Unions and Concubinage

As a result of the legal confusion which prevailed before 1753, large numbers of persons were living together in situations of varying uncertainty. Some of the poor undoubtedly set up customary unions, which were strictly illegal but were accepted by the neighbours; many rich and respectable men, like Pepys, lived for decades with a mistress; some, of all classes, were tied by unwitnessed verbal contracts whose legal standing was becoming increasingly dubious; some, by no means confined entirely to the poor, took part in clandestine marriages that later might be hard to prove; others went through a regular church wedding, but were marrying bigamously; a few, of all classes, were married to their uncles or aunts or to a deceased wife's sister, marriages which, if ever discovered and brought to court, would be declared incestuous and null and void.

Some scholars of the family now believe that in the early modern period, and more especially in the late eighteenth and nineteenth centuries, considerable numbers of English men and women lived in a condition of customary concubinage, illegal according to the laws of church or state, but recognized by the neighbourhood. It seems more than likely that, especially in remote areas such as Wales where there were few resident landlords or educated clergymen to exercise control, such customs may have been generally accepted, and concubinage may have been frequent. But just how frequent we have no idea. There is good reason to think that in most of England, especially the south and east, the all-important problem of legal property transfer was sufficient to

[9] LPCA, D. 1915.

restrict mere concubinage largely to the propertyless poor, and to the very rich who were indifferent to public opinion. Moreover, from the late sixteenth to the late seventeenth century there was combined pressure by community, church, and state, acting through churchwardens, constables, JPs, apparitors, and church courts, to regularize sexual and marital behaviour and punish deviants, which certainly reduced the amount of bastardy and pre-nuptial conceptions to an astonishingly low level, and which must have made mere concubinage by folk custom uncomfortable and fairly rare.

By the eighteenth century, however, the old moral controls on bundling were clearly breaking down, the proof being the rise in the bastardy rate between 1690 and 1790 from 6 to 20 per cent of all first births, and the even more startling explosion of pre-nuptial conceptions. By the late eighteenth century consummation and conception normally preceded—and indeed precipitated—marriage, as shown by the fact that a third of all brides were pregnant on their wedding-day, and over half of all first births were conceived out of wedlock. Contract marriages may have been legally dead, but these forms of 'marriages in the sight of God' were clearly widely accepted among the lower sort in the eighteenth century as a moral justification for starting sexual relations, on the assumption, usually justified, that the man would marry the woman if and when she became pregnant.

7. Contract Marriage

(i) *The First Suppression 1540–1642*

In order to be legally binding, marriages before 1753 did not have to be performed in church, by a clergyman of the Church of England, according to the rites laid down in the Book of Common Prayer. In the thirteenth century Pope Innocent III had decreed that the free consent of both spouses, not the formal solemnities by a priest or in a church, was the sole essence of marriage. Consequently a valid and binding marriage was created by a mere verbal contract, performed by an exchange of vows to this effect between a man and a woman over the age of consent (14 and 12), witnessed by two persons, and expressed in the present tense. A promise in the future tense, however, was only binding if it was followed by consummation, which was taken to be evidence of consent in the present. Thus the statement 'I take you for my wife/husband' was fully binding, since it implied present consent, but the statement 'I shall take you for my wife/husband' was only binding if followed by consummation (see the cases of *Butler* v. *Ingelbright*[10] and *Harris* v. *Lingard*). By the mid-eighteenth century these verbal exchanges in the future, even if followed by consummation, were not necessarily any longer considered by the ecclesiastical courts to be binding. In the case of *Fuller* v. *Sheppard* in 1747, the woman claiming marriage in this way lost in the Consistory Court, won on appeal to the Chancellor, but finally lost on the man's appeal to the Court of Arches.[11]

The third and most common type of verbal contract was conditional: 'I do contract matrimony with thee, if my father (or 'friends') consents.' If the parent or 'friends' refused, this conditional contract was clearly not binding. Similarly the conditional nature of the contract was unambiguous if it ran: 'I will marry you if your brother will give me £200 with you.'

Thus in church law a verbal contract, if duly performed in the present tense before witnesses, was complete in substance, though not in ceremony, and was indissoluble. This made any later marriage—even one performed in church—voidable by a court sentence as bigamous. In common law, however, and therefore in all matters relating to property, the contract had no standing whatever. It gave the husband no rights over his wife's property; it imposed on the wife none of the disabilities of 'coverture', such as being unable to make contracts, or write a will, or run up debts; it gave the wife no right to dower (the use for life of a third of her husband's property after his death); it gave the children no claim on their parents' property as legitimate heirs; and a subsequent church marriage was recognized as valid unless proved otherwise in a church court. Few of the lower sort, however, were aware of these serious drawbacks to a contract marriage, or if they were, some of them were so poor that these questions of property were of no concern to them.

By adopting this position, the medieval canon law had put itself in direct conflict with the generally accepted practice among persons of property, that marriage was made largely by parents and kin, with a view to family advantage not personal pleasure. The case of *Preston* v. *Matthews* offers an example of a man successfully using a contract marriage to resist a forced marriage against his consent.

This gap between the church law and the laity was widened by the latter's faith in rituals which had little or no validity in a court of law. One was the gift by a man to a woman of a ring, the acceptance of which was popularly believed to imply a formal contract. Another very common

---

[10] Ibid. D. 338; B. 9/7.   [11] Ibid. D. 797; B. 17/196.

ritual involved an exchange of what were regarded as significant tokens, either the gift of a bent or 'bowed' coin, or the breaking of a coin in two, each party keeping one half, or the gift of a ring. The symbolism of the broken coin is obvious, but exactly why the bent coin carried such heavy meaning in the seventeenth and early eighteenth centuries is not clear. But there is no doubt that it did so, even in genteel circles, as in the case of *Osborne* v. *Williams*.

Other gifts, predominantly from a man to a woman, were normal accompaniments to virtually every courtship of which we have record. The regular citation of these gifts in court to bolster an argument for a valid contract indicates that contemporaries regarded such gift exchanges as more than mere tokens of esteem. Both the gift and its acceptance constituted, it was believed, evidence certainly of a courtship relationship, and possibly of a contractual one. The fact that when the woman wished to break off the engagement she nearly always scrupulously returned all the gifts she had received adds weight to this argument that even quite trivial presents had significance to contemporaries. The church courts, however, paid no attention to any gift apart from a ring.

By the sixteenth century the church courts found themselves trying to do justice in cases of contract marriages without witnesses, often accompanied by the exchange of symbolically significant gifts, thanks to which the man assured the woman that they were now 'married in the eyes of God'. In these cases enormous pressure was often brought by his parents and kin to persuade the man to repudiate the contract. While he hesitated and procrastinated, it often happened that the woman became pregnant. The pressure from his parents and kin then intensified, and the man often reluctantly, or cynically, went back on his alleged promise to marry.

The courts responded in the sixteenth and early seventeenth centuries by slowly but surely tightening the rules of evidence in all contract litigation which came before them. By adopting this policy, the courts were both responding to the wishes and interests of propertied parents and kin, and strengthening the control of the church over marriage. It was by no means an unpopular policy, and it shifted a significant proportion of the population from being 'married in the eyes of God' to 'being married in the eyes of God and the Church'.

(ii) *The Revival 1642–1660*

After the outbreak of civil war in 1642, the ecclesiastical courts virtually ceased to function, the old marriage service in church according to the Book of Common Prayer was denounced as 'popish', and it was no longer clear just how a legal marriage should be conducted. Many took to being married clandestinely by clergymen, and many others openly by laymen, so much so that in 1643 the House of Commons instructed the Westminster Assembly to take steps to stop such disorderly proceedings. But neither the Parliament nor the clergy could agree on a new policy on marriage, and although many efforts were made to clear up the confusion, nothing was achieved throughout the 1640s. It was not until 1653 that legislation about marriage was finally passed by the Barebones Parliament. The legislation was hotly disputed and was generally unpopular, since it was characterized by a strong anti-clericalism which was not shared by the bulk of the population.

The legislation ordered each parish to elect a 'register', whose job it was to keep a record of all marriages. Prospective marrying couples were instructed to declare their intentions to the register; to have banns read three times in church; to produce a certificate from the register that there had been no objections; and if under 21 to provide proof of parental consent. Armed with these documents, the couple were to present themselves to a JP, who would perform a simple secular ceremony in a private house. All other forms of marriage were declared illegal, especially any performed by clergymen or in a church.

Enforcement of these new rules was virtually impossible. Information about them took time to spread, and when it did many refused to accept them. This purely secular form of marriage was very unpopular, and doubts persisted about its legality, since it violated the traditional customs and habits of most of the population. The result was chaos. Some were married by a JP as ordered; some persisted in being married by a clergyman in a church; a significant number seem to have gone through two marriages, one by a JP and one by a clergyman, just to be on the safe side; some resorted to clandestine marriages in private houses. These were conducted by clergymen, who might have been ejected from their livings because of loyalty to the Church of England, or merely be vagrants whose prime object was to obtain a fee; some couples made simple promises before the congregation in an independent sectarian chapel; and some went back to private verbal contracts. How many fell into each category, it is impossible to tell.

In 1657 there was a long and angry debate in Parliament on the whole subject, the result of which was merely to make matters worse. Unable to agree on what to do, Parliament prolonged the existing legislation for another six months, but abolished the clause which invalidated all forms of marriage other than that prescribed in 1653. This appeared to mean that almost any form of marriage was now legal. At the Restoration, the Convention Parliament tried to tidy up the mess by retroactively legitimating all marriages carried out by JPs since 1642, leaving all the other kinds of marriage, including contracts and clandestine marriages, to be sorted out by the newly restored ecclesiastical courts.[12]

(iii) *The Second Suppression 1660–1753*

The result was an avalanche of matrimonial suits which fell upon these courts in 1660, the majority of which, however, never came to sentence and were presumably settled by arbitration. The central problems that faced the courts after 1660 were therefore first how to roll back the revival of private verbal contracts, and second how to persuade the population to abandon clandestine marriages in private houses and return to regular public weddings in church. Despite the persistently sceptical attitude of the church courts towards poorly supported claims of contract marriages, the laity continued, if in diminishing numbers, to come to court with claims of ambiguous and unproven promises, supported by ritual exchanges of gifts, public bedding, recognition in the neighbourhood as a married couple, and calling each other 'husband' and 'wife'. But none of these pieces of evidence were accorded much respect by the canon lawyers who ran the church courts. The latter were looking for some certainty and proof in the morass of unverifiable claims, vague assumptions, and tokens with indeterminate meaning. Such poorly attested suits were peculiarly common in the Consistory Court of Exeter, where there were no fewer than 87 of them between 1660 and 1730. Many are more like suits for breach of promise than for marriage contracts.

A few exceptionally well-attested contract marriages certainly continued to be upheld by the church courts into the late seventeenth century, as in the case of *Brace* v. *Cudworth*. But contract suits died away to almost nothing between 1680 and 1733, largely because of this generally hostile attitude of the courts. In the early 1730s there were three bitterly contested and very expensive contract cases, which were fought to a finish up through the ecclesiastical courts. They seem to have made legal history as the last of their kind. All three were cases of women who gave birth as a result of sexual relations with a suitor, entered into on the basis of an alleged contract which was later repudiated.

By 1753 laymen in general, and especially lawyers and judges, had

---

[12] This account of developments during the 1640s and 1650s is taken from C. Durston, *The Family and the English Revolution* (Oxford, 1989), and C. Durston, ' "Unhallowed Wedlocks": The Regulation of Marriage during the English Revolution', *Historical Journal*, 31 (1988).

become exasperated by the cases before the courts brought by women who had been seduced and impregnated on promise of what proved to be unenforcable contracts. By the Marriage Act of 1753, all marriage contracts were therefore declared invalid, regardless of tense or the reliability of the witnesses.

8. Clandestine Marriage

(i) *Definition and Development*

An official marriage ceremony was conducted in church by a clergyman in regular orders, according to the Book of Common Prayer. The Canons of 1604 prescribed that the ceremony had to take place within canonical hours, in a church within the parish in which one of the parties was a resident, and following either the public reading in church of banns on three successive Sundays or the presentation of a licence from a surrogate. After 1660 virtually all the middling sort and above were married by licence, but the cost put it out of reach of the lower classes.

The closing ritual was the public bedding of bride and groom before numerous witnesses, a ceremony which included ancient folk customs such as the throwing of the stocking, as in *Muilman* v. *Muilman* and in the account of the Revd John Vyse. This symbolic ritual was intended to signify the consummation of the marriage, but in fact there were occasions when no consummation actually occurred. In the case of *Brace* v. *Cudworth*, the fact that the bride had run away within fifteen minutes of the bedding enabled the court to void the marriage in favour of another suitor to whom she had earlier contracted herself in due form. The laity, particularly the poor, were very confused about the legally binding nature of this public bedding ritual, as is shown in *Sergeant* v. *Sergeant*,[13] when it was thought prudent for the pregnant clandestinely-wed wife to share her husband's deathbed, in order to make up for the fact that there had been no public bedding on their marriage.

A clandestine marriage was a ceremony conducted by a man who at least purported to be a clergyman (although often one not holding a cure) and which followed the ritual prescribed by the Book of Common Prayer. But it could be irregular and in violation of canon law in a number of ways, the central one being that it was done in secret rather than in public: it was a *clandestine* marriage. First, it was performed without either the prior reading of banns or the procuring of a valid licence from

[13] Lichfield JRO, LCC, BSC/1663: depositions for Anne Sergeant, fos. 18–19; depositions for Rowland Sergeant, fos. 15ᵛ–16.

a church official. Second, it took place anywhere but in the parish church of one of the spouses. It might be performed in a 'Peculiar', that is in a church which, for historical reasons, was accidentally exempt from episcopal jurisdiction; or in a church in another diocese, especially in a busy church in the City of London, where it was impossible for the clerk to check whether the residential requirement for calling the banns was being fulfilled. But it could equally well take place in a private house, an alehouse, a coffee shop, a prison, or even a brothel. Third, it could, and usually did, take place outside the canonical hours of 8 to 12 a.m., often in the middle of the night. Fourth, it was usually not recorded in any official parish register, and sometimes—though rarely—not even in the grubby personal notebook or private register kept by the officiating clergyman. And fifth, it might involve the marriage of a minor without the consent of parent or guardian.

After 1597 a clergyman conducting a clandestine marriage became liable to prosecution in an ecclesiastical court and suspension from all clerical functions for three years, thus forcing him into unemployment. In 1696 the state added a £100 fine to the penalties imposed on the clergyman. The only penalty for the bride and groom and witnesses was excommunication, but this had no teeth, and anyway seems only rarely to have been used, and hardly at all after about 1680.

Despite the success of the church before 1640 in suppressing contract marriages, scattered evidence suggests that clandestine marriages were already becoming an increasingly serious problem. The restored church courts in the 1660s faced an even more difficult situation. As we have seen, during the Interregnum, Church of England weddings had been forbidden, so that it had become a pious duty for ejected Anglican clergymen to conduct clandestine marriages of the faithful in private houses. At the same time, the control of the church over marriage had been weakened by the creation of a system of secular marriages by JPs, and there had sprung up a substantial body of Dissenters who often conducted their own marriage ceremonies in their own chapels, using their own rituals.

(ii) *Demand from the Laity*

A clandestine marriage performed by some sort of clergyman offered five great advantages over a mere contract marriage. The first was the participation of a clergyman, whose presence gave it the appearance of respectability. The second was that the ceremony, however sordid, was recognized by both the canon law and the common law as legally binding and as carrying with it full property rights. This was a by-product of the shift from marriage by consent to marriage by religious ceremony. The third was that it was easier to prove, since there were witnesses, usually a written entry in a marriage register, even if a private one, and often a written certificate.

The fourth advantage of a clandestine marriage over a regular one was that it provided secrecy: it was clandestine. The fifth was that it was considerably cheaper than an official church marriage service, which was a major attraction to the poor. On the other hand, it was more expensive than a contract, which cost nothing; it had some, but not all, of the same uncertainties about proof; and the behaviour of the officiating clergyman and the nature of the surroundings were both often extremely squalid.

There were several very common practical reasons why couples from the middling sort should want the secrecy of a clandestine marriage. Many wished to thwart the known or feared opposition to the marriage of parents, kin, and 'friends', usually because of a status or financial difference between the bride and groom. Many of these couples were minors under the age of 21 or apprentices, who wanted the marriage kept secret until they came of age or their terms were up. Many others were couples where one of the partners—usually the man—had or professed to have expectations from a wealthy but cantankerous parent or relative. On the grounds that this benefactor would cut him out of his or her will if it became known that he had married without consent, he insisted that the marriage be kept secret until his aged benefactor should die.

Others had their own special reasons for secrecy. Some were maidservants fearful of dismissal if they were known to be married. Others were apprentices who would be in breach of their articles if they married before their seven-year term was out, or college fellows who would be obliged to resign from their fellowships if their marriage were known. Others were widows who, if their remarriage became common knowledge, would lose the copyholds or annuities which they enjoyed as jointures from their first husbands. Others were in a hurry to use a secret marriage in order to thwart contract litigation against them by a discarded lover. Perhaps a majority were marrying in haste and secrecy pregnant women to whom they were contracted, in order to legitimize their children. Some of the very poor wished to get married, but were afraid of opposition from the parish authorities on the grounds that they had no visible means to support a family and were therefore likely to produce children who would be a burden on the parish poor-rate.

A handful of men sought secrecy since they were incestuously marrying their deceased wife's sister or a niece. Others, who were committing bigamy after abandoning their first wife, were naturally anxious to keep the marriage as secret as possible, even if they felt reasonably secure from a prosecution for felony. Taken all together, there were thus a sizeable number of couples from all walks of life and economic levels who had their own perfectly legitimate reasons for seeking secret marriage. Others, however, had evil intentions, and this minority was one of the reasons why clandestine marriages got such a bad name in the eighteenth century. A few patrons of clandestine marriage shops were ruthless and scheming adventurers who had either kidnapped or procured the love of rich heiresses, and now wanted to marry them for their money without the knowledge or consent of their parents or 'friends'. Sir Samuel Morland in *Morland* v. *Morland* had just such a scheme in mind, but he was caught in a counterplot to marry him to a penniless prostitute instead. The forcible abduction of heiresses, however, had long been a penal offence, and more common were ambiguous episodes involving half-drugged female victims, especially rich widows like Mrs Hooper.

In addition to all these groups with strong practical reasons to seek clandestine marriage, there were large numbers of others who were motivated by sheer modesty. The most obvious evidence of this widespread desire to avoid publicity in marriage was the growth in the numbers willing to pay the substantial fees for a licence rather than have to have banns called publicly three times in the local church. By the eighteenth century at least a fifth, and possibly a third, of the population were being married by licence.

This long-standing and widespread aversion to the publicity involved in putting up the banns is probably to be explained by the unusual freedom of social contacts accorded to young people in England, which extended through the 'bundling' procedure to some degree of sexual experimentation. It is understandable that a couple about to be married would not wish to expose their intention before a congregation with some of whom they had had previous sexual contacts. Another reason for secrecy was that a clandestine marriage, or one performed by licence in an unknown church, avoided the need to endure the often boisterous rituals of treating, feasting, practical jokes, and ribald songs, culminating in public bedding and the throwing of the bride's stocking across the bed. All this was not merely expensive but could be acutely embarassing to the shy.

Last but not least, there were increasing numbers, running into thousands, who were not seeking so much secrecy or speed as economy.

Introduction

In the early eighteenth century the fees for a clandestine marriage—especially for a Fleet marriage—were only about a third of those charged by a qualified clergyman for a regular public church service.

There were thus important and persistent practical and psychological reasons, which lasted from the late seventeenth to the late nineteenth century, why there was a very high and apparently increasing demand for secret marriage. It met a strongly felt need among all classes of society from peer to pauper. Between 1660 and 1753 clandestine marriage served as a safety-valve in the pressure-cooker system of legalized official church marriage, still largely controlled by parents and 'friends', regulated by church, state, and parish, and delayed a decade or more after sexual maturity. There was therefore a huge demand for clandestine marriage, and in so poorly policed a society as England, the supply to meet it was not slow in springing up.

(iii) *Supply by the Clergy*

A key group who catered for this demand were the surrogates, beneficed clergymen scattered about the countryside who were authorized to issue marriage licences. A substantial amount of the income of church officials came from these licences, which were sold in blank by the bishops' registrars to surrogates, who resold them at a profit to the laity. The surrogates had a very strong financial incentive to sell as many licences as possible, and not to enquire too closely about the truth of the sworn statements of the applicants concerning their age, consent of parents or guardians, or place of residence, nor to pay too much attention to the quality of the persons who acted as bondsmen that the statements were all true. Many were willing to leave the place of marriage blank, to be filled in by the purchaser, and a few could even be bribed to leave the names blank. Indeed some of them were said to hold weekly 'markets' to drum up business.

Once the licence had been procured from a surrogate, by whatever means, there were plenty of clergy who were living so close to the poverty line that they were willing to run the risk of a three-year suspension from office in order to conduct a clandestine ceremony. No questions were asked, and the clerk and the sexton were often employed as witnesses in return for a tip. The safest churches were 'Peculiars', outside the jurisdiction of any bishop, and in the late seventeenth century such a place was known as 'a lawless church'. Many clergymen were even willing to run the risk of marrying couples without a licence, and indeed before the government put a stamp tax on licences in 1696, the majority of the poor seem to have dispensed with this expensive preliminary.

Clandestine marriage was certainly very common in the countryside after the Restoration in 1660, but church officials made every effort to stamp it out. In the course of twenty-three years from 1676 to 1699 in the small Archdeaconry of Chester no fewer than 58 clergymen were prosecuted for this offence. By 1720, however, in most dioceses the ecclesiastical court system had virtually collapsed. Official prosecutions petered out, and churchwardens now routinely returned *omnia bene* at visitations. This meant that despite the increase of the statutory penalties, the chances of a clergyman being detected for operating a marriage shop in the countryside, and punished for doing so, were much smaller in the early eighteenth century than they had been in the 1670s and 1680s.

There can be little doubt that in most instances it was poverty rather than greed which drove these rural clergymen into breaking the law. Rich laity often tempted them with large rewards, and some offered them bonds to pay all fees and expenses in case there were any legal problems later—bonds which in fact always turned out to be worthless. A real dilemma facing the church authorities was that by suspending a clergyman for three years for conducting a clandestine marriage, they virtually forced him into conducting more in order to survive.

In addition to these country parsons and curates busy adding to their income on the side, mostly in a small way, there also sprang up some very busy professional marrying shops in London, located either in 'Peculiars', outside the reach of episcopal control, or in or around the Fleet Prison. In the late seventeenth century the three 'Peculiar' churches most active in the London marriage business were St James's Duke's Place, the Holy Trinity Minories, and St James-on-the-Wall, commonly called Lamb's Chapel. Not only were their incumbents exempt from episcopal jurisdiction, but they were also authorized to issue marriage licences, a situation which was tantamount to a permit to print money. An educated guess from the surviving registers is that in the late seventeenth century these three London churches were responsible for between 2,500 and 3,000 marriages a year, which was not far off the total of official marriages in all of London.

Another major centre for clandestine marriages in the late seventeenth century was the chapel inside the Fleet Prison, where 50 to 60 couples were being married every week. This arose from the fact that clergymen who were suspended for three years for performing a clandestine marriage often found themselves imprisoned for debt in county gaols. From there they could get themselves transferred to the Fleet Prison by writs of habeas corpus. Once in the Fleet, they were able to set up in the business of marrying all comers in the chapel of the prison, no questions asked, and before the new legislation in 1696 without licences.

(iv) *Repressive Legislation and Actual Growth 1666–1730*

In the 1690s the need to find money to finance the wars with France drove the government first in 1695 to place a tax on all marriages (which largely failed), and then to impose a substantial 5s. stamp tax on marriage licences and marriage certificates. This at once drew official attention to the loss of revenue to the Crown from the widespread practice of clandestine marriages, and as a result a series of Acts were passed to try to close them down. As so often happens, these Acts had both expected and unexpected consequences. Some, but not all, professional marriage shops in various 'Peculiars' in London were certainly shut down, such as St James's Duke's Place. An Act of 1712 also stopped the performance of clandestine marriages inside the Fleet Prison. In the countryside, however, clandestine marriages continued to be performed, despite the penalties, and false licences continued to be issued. Although the tax on official licences may have frightened off the more respectable clergy, it also increased the financial incentive to fraud by the unscrupulous.

In London the trade simply moved elsewhere, and between 1710 and 1753 it expanded at a tremendous rate into the Rules of the Fleet Prison, a sanctuary area just outside the prison where clergymen imprisoned for debt could obtain licence to live. As these parsons were already in prison for debt, they could not be imprisoned to force them to pay the £100 fine imposed on them; and as they held no cure or were already suspended from one, they could not be suspended again. They were therefore immune from punishment and were free to marry customers freely and cheaply, at any time of day or night, anywhere within the Rules of the Fleet. Many issued official-looking certificates, mostly on unstamped paper. The story of the sordid life of the Revd Vyse vividly illustrates the quality and background of these Fleet parsons.

Fraud was rampant in all aspects of Fleet marriages. For a fee, false entries in the grimy private registers could be inserted, genuine ones erased, and entries backdated to cover a pregnancy or 'to please their parents'. If it came to proving a marriage, perjured witnesses were easy to find in these dingy lanes and courtyards, and the ecclesiastical courts, King's Bench, and Chancery were kept busy dealing with the frustrating legal consequences of this dubious trade. It was hardly surprising that one of the busiest of the Fleet parsons in the 1720s and 1730s was known as 'the Bishop of Hell'.

Despite the laws, more than one enterprising clergyman still managed to carry on a lucrative trade outside the Rules of the Fleet. One set up shop in the Savoy Chapel, while an even more successful and longer-lasting clandestine marriage business was established in 1730 by the Revd Alexander Keith in Mayfair Chapel off Piccadilly, where he 'constructed a very bishopric for revenue' as Horace Walpole put it. He advertised widely in the newspapers, offering to marry all comers for a guinea, including a 5s. stamped official licence and a certificate, and was patronized by a far higher class of clientele than those who crowded around the drunken clergymen in the Rules of the Fleet.

The astonishing scale of the clandestine marriage business in London can be estimated by combining the figures of those performed in the Rules of the Fleet with those of the other marriage shops in London. A reasonable guess would be that in the middle of the eighteenth century between 15 and 20 per cent of the marriages in all of England were conducted in these clandestine ways.

In the decades before 1753, there is clear evidence of a trend towards ever greater variety in the range of trickery, falsification, and perjury. The guile and ingenuity of suitors, witnesses, lawyers, and clergymen had now stretched beyond exploiting the ambiguities in the medieval marriage system to include the wholesale manufacture and manipulation of evidence to prove whatever was needed to create or void a marriage. Thus a false entry in a register of a prior marriage could be used to invalidate an existing marriage on grounds of bigamy. Or fake marriages could be performed, backdated in the register, and used, along with witnesses bribed to give false evidence, in order to invalidate a later one, as in *Mordaunt* v. *Mordaunt*. Or a victim could be tricked into committing bigamy, by counterfeiting the death of one of the spouses and thus inveigling the survivor into marrying a second time, as in *Rudd* v. *Rudd*.

(v) *Reform and Abolition 1730–1753*

By the 1730s elite public opinion was beginning to turn against the continued toleration of the clandestine marriage system, as shown by growing complaints in the London newspapers. The laity were becoming increasingly exasperated by these scandalous marriage procedures, especially since they served occasionally to facilitate secret runaway marriages of upper-class heiresses.

The judges were also exasperated by the unreliability of the evidence for clandestine marriages, and on one celebrated occasion Lord Chancellor Hardwicke is said to have seized a Fleet Register produced in Court, and torn it in pieces with his own hands to show what he thought of it. The judges were also disgusted at the scandalous way surrogates were issuing blank licences. As a crowning absurdity, 'proctors sometimes stand at the door of the Doctors' Commons [the official building housing the London ecclesiastical courts], and solicit persons to take out licences, just in the same manner as the runners to Fleet parsons do.' These protests by judges were supported by essays by moral reformers in the public press, and by a barrage of satirical comment by novelists and playwrights.

The story of this extraordinary explosion of clandestine marriages between 1660 and 1753, first all over the country and then mainly in professional London marriage shops, reveals several things about the relationship between the law, law enforcement, and public opinion. Demand for secret private marriages was so intense among all classes of society that it flooded in like a rising tide, seeping into the cracks and crannies of the precarious sea-wall of legislation, ecclesiastical court prosecutions, and punishment. When one passage was blocked, another was soon found to meet the apparently almost insatiable demand. Although the problem existed in the early seventeenth century, when it was exacerbated by contract marriages, it seems to have been the collapse of church weddings during the Interregnum which triggered the large-scale development of this extraordinary and curious social phenomenon. So long as the countryside was full of half-starved curates, and so long as penniless clergymen were imprisoned for debt in the Fleet Prison, poverty drove many of them to make a living by supplying this insatiable public demand for secret weddings.

What is strange is why the repeated efforts in Parliament to pass a bill to put a stop to the trade failed again and again, sometime in the Lords, and always before 1753 in the Commons. The abuses were obvious enough, but many thought that the remedy would be worse than the disease. Only in 1753 was elite lay, legal, and religious opinion sufficiently aroused to be powerful enough to push through an Act, the Hardwicke Marriage Act, which subjected clergymen convicted of performing clandestine marriages to a penalty of transportation for fourteen years to America, and invalidated any marriage of any kind of a minor without the written consent of parents or guardians. As a result of these two clauses, the huge clandestine marriage business ground to a halt. But the options of flight to the marriage shops in Gretna Green, just over the Scottish border, and marriage in the anonymity of a crowded City church still remained for those seeking speed, secrecy, and legality.

9. Conclusion

It is not too much to say that the marriage law as it operated in practice in England from the fourteenth to the nineteenth century was a mess. The root cause of the trouble was that there was no consensus within the society at large about how a legally binding marriage should be carried out. Popular custom took one position, the church another, and the state and the propertied laity a third. Village opinion seems to have been satisfied by the outward signs and gestures of marriage, without enquiring too closely into the hard evidence of a legal ceremony. The church was satisfied by a mere verbal contract, if properly witnessed, but the common law denied that these had any effect on the transmission of property. The church also took the position that any ceremony performed between two persons of almost any age, and taking place anywhere and at any time, if performed by an ordained clergyman was legally valid, although a punishable offence for the officiating clergyman. The propertied laity objected strongly to these secret ways by which their children could legally marry without their consent. Parliament was at odds within itself, the House of Commons and the House of Lords repeatedly taking different sides on proposals to reform the law of marriage. The Lords naturally favoured parental veto over marriage of minors, while the Commons, which contained many heiress-seeking younger sons and small gentry, just as naturally opposed it. Legal and clerical vested interests grew up to protect the status quo, however scandalous it might seem. And to make matters worse, after 1753 Scotland and Ireland were out of step with England.

The result was a condition of moral and legal confusion which appeared to many thoughtful contemporaries from the sixteenth to the nineteenth centuries to maximize insecurity, misery, and disappointment. The explosion of the clandestine marriage business between 1660 and 1763 was inexplicable, except in terms of an endless confused conflict between deeply entrenched vested interests. The public almost always found a way to get around the law for their own purposes, but the cost in wasted lives was very high, as is shown in the following case histories.

It is curious and comforting to find that most of the themes illustrated by the case histories in this book also crop up in Defoe's novel, *Moll Flanders*, published in 1722. There is the endless conflict between money, love, and 'sincere affection' as motives for marriage. Defoe took the cynical view that 'nothing but money now recommends a woman', but it has to be remembered that he was writing at the end of a thirty-year period of extremely cynical matchmaking.[14] At that time 'men made no scruple to set themselves out, and go a fortune-hunting, as they call it.' Indeed there is a story of two fraudulent fortune-hunters pursuing and marrying each other.[15] The courting process is exclusively controlled by the mother and sisters. 'And as for the father, he was a man in a hurry of public affairs, and getting money, seldom at home, thoughtful of the main chance, but left all those things to his wife.'[16]

In the novel as in life, unmarried women normally sleep together in the same bed as a form of protection.[17] A verbal assurance of marriage is a well-known ploy by a man to get a woman into bed with him, assuring her that 'I was your husband intentionally and that was as effectual a marriage that had passed between us as if we had been publicly wedded by the parson of the parish'.[18] There is a clandestine marriage at night in a country inn, performed by a clergyman not the parson of the parish, but only after the production of a licence.[19] There is mention of the need of an unmarried pregnant woman to fend off 'the parish impertinences' of a demand to know the name of the father.[20] Bath is a place 'where men find a mistress sometimes, but very rarely look for a wife'.[21] Thus the middle-class world that Defoe described in 1722 is identical down to minor details to that exposed in these case-studies.

[14] D. Defoe, *Moll Flanders*, ed. J. Sutherland (Cambridge, Mass., (1959), 20, 59–60.
[15] Ibid. 60, 128–33. [16] Ibid. 48, 51. [17] Ibid. 30. [18] Ibid. 36.
[19] Ibid. 156, 158–9. [20] Ibid. 141. [21] Ibid. 93.

II

Case-studies

There are three ways in which these could be arranged. The first is according to topics, such as courting and contract marriages, forced marriages, valid clandestine marriages, and faked clandestine marriages. There are, however, two objections to such an arrangement. The first is that it destroys any sense of change over time, so that the peculiar brutality of marital relationships in the period 1690 to 1710 is lost sight of, and other significant changes in language, values, and behaviour are also obscured. The second objection is that many of these cases cover many topics at once. For example, under what heading should one put the case of *Mordaunt* v. *Mordaunt*, which involves bigamous marriage, several faked marriages, and blackmail by marriage?

A second possible arrangement would be according to the social and economic status of the leading protagonists, loosely grouped into the poor, the middling sort, and the elite. But this too is unsatisfactory for two reasons. First, so many cases cut across status lines. For example, *Osborne* v. *Williams* involves the high aristocracy and the middling professional sort, while *Mordaunt* v. *Mordaunt* runs from the high aristocracy to the scum of the London underworld. Second, the great majority of the litigants belong to the middling sort, so that such an arrangement offers few benefits.

The third solution, which is in fact the one adopted, is to group the cases by topic, but to arrange them within each topic in chronological order. This preserves the thematic framework, but allows the legal and cultural peculiarities of different periods to be observed. Thus cases about contract marriage are naturally grouped together in the late seventeenth century. Cases about forced marriages by the parish or by the kin fall naturally into the 1680 to 1720 period, as do most cases of faked marriages, while cases about clandestine marriage all occur in the early eighteenth century. Thus by shifting a very few cases out of strict chronological order, it is possible to group them roughly by topic.

35

A. COURTSHIP AND CONTRACT

I

Troope v. *Stenson* and *Henworth* v. *Stenson*, 1652–1664

Courtship among the minor gentry

Between 1652 and 1663 a young woman called Mary Stenson lived with her aged and ailing maternal grandfather, Robert Walker, in a substantial country house in Breadsall, near Derby.[1] She came from a good gentry family, but had no fortune of her own, being entirely dependent for a marriage portion upon what her grandfather might choose to leave her in his will. Until he died, therefore, she was severely circumscribed in her search for, and reception of, potential suitors. According to her, she always made it clear to the latter that whatever contracts she might enter into with them were conditional upon waiting until her grandfather died and her legacy was at last irrevocably her own. The suitors, however, did not recall her promises as conditional, although they agreed that her several engagements were to be kept secret until the old man had died.

Her first suitor, Jonathan Troope of Nottingham, was 'so mean a person' that Mary was afraid that if her grandfather got to know that she had given him any encouragement, he would cut her out of his will. None the less she consorted with Jonathan for a year from May 1652 until June 1653, and in the autumn of 1652 they verbally contracted themselves in marriage before two witnesses. According to a much later claim by Jonathan (but not according to Mary), the contract was unconditional and in the present tense; however by then the witnesses could not be found, so there is no proof of what was actually said. Jonathan declared that Mary held his hand and said: 'I, Mary, do take my bed-fellow Jonathan Troope to be my husband, and I do here seriously, in the presence of God, vow, promise and engage never to have any other to be my husband, so long as we do live.' Jonathan then reciprocated. Mary's alleged use of the word 'bedfellow' presumably implied that they had

---

[1] Lichfield JRO, LCC B/C/5/1664: *Troope* v. *Stenson* and *Henworth* v. *Stenson*.

already begun sleeping together, even before they were engaged. Along with the verbal promise, Jonathan said that he gave Mary a gold ring 'as a token and pledge of contract'. Soon afterwards, 'in confirmation of their unseparable love and of friendship between them' they exchanged 'letters, tokens and things of weight', including two or three more gold rings from Jonathan.

The engagement lasted until June 1653, when there was a great quarrel between them in a private room at an inn in Derby, in the presence of Neville Lacock, who was both a relative of Jonathan, and a former schoolfellow of Mary. Mary accused Jonathan of spreading stories about their 'familiarity' which had come to the ears of her friends—meaning her grandfather—'whereby I am likely to cause their displeasure'.

In reply, Jonathan several times asked Mary: 'Are you not my wife? Did you not acknowledge it' before two witnesses, an alewife and a trooper? 'Did you not then at my bidding rise up and come and kiss me?' When Mary did not answer a word, Jonathan lost his temper. He 'clapped his foot upon the ground' and said: 'I wish it might open and I sink into it, if you are not my wife and you did not acknowledge it before the witnesses.' Mary still did not reply, but left the room, saying to her ex-schoolfellow: 'I durst not come near him for fear of displeasing my friends.' When Miss Lacock remarked that Jonathan must have some reason for such vehement protestations, Mary replied: 'Surely he is in drink'—which he patently was not, but only very angry.

Jonathan was so distressed by Mary's renunciation of the engagement that he joined Lambert's regiment as a trooper on the Parliamentary side and went off to the wars. Before he left, however, he took the precaution of instructing a friend to put a stop to any attempts by Mary to marry someone else while he was away, swearing: 'I will be the death of any that shall marry her, for she is my wife and would be but the other's whore.'

Even after he was posted back to Nottingham three years later, Jonathan made no attempt to get in touch with Mary. He clearly took the position that, if there was to be a reconciliation between them, it was up to her to make the first move. In May 1656 Mary heard a sermon by the local parson about the keeping of 'vows, promises and engagements' and was struck with guilt about her behaviour to Jonathan. She wrote him three letters in terms of increasing warmth, inviting him to visit her again. Finally they arranged to meet in secret in her grandfather's house.

Mary met him in the dark at the back door of the house, took him by the hand, and led him up to her bedroom, trembling with fear and emotion. When asked by Jonathan what was the matter, she said—

according to him—that she had not been able to sleep at night, since she was so 'troubled in her mind' about her false denial of their contract at Derby three years before. She offered to renew the contract again, using the same words, and assured him that this time her decision was taken as a result of 'long and serious consideration and for the discharge of a good conscience'.

The contract was duly renewed, and Jonathan stayed in her bedroom until four in the morning. When not called away on military duties, he continued to visit her secretly at her grandfather's house almost every two weeks for the next four years, choosing nights when the servants were busy brewing the beer. He always stayed with Mary until dawn, and there is little doubt that full sexual relations regularly took place. Jonathan claimed that he once asked Mary what she thought about the propriety of 'the familiar actions and passages betwixt us'. She replied: 'If I did not seriously believe and know that we are really man and wife in the presence of God, (nothing being wanting but the outward ceremonies), I would fear that we did offend God in our too familiar actions.' She always explained that she could not marry him until her grandfather died, because of her financial expectations from him, and her fear of his disapproval. Jonathan was reluctantly content to wait, despite his complaint in 1657 that 'I am in great want of a wife to look to my house'.

Inevitably, there were several persons in or about the house who knew all about this protracted secret sexual liaison. One was a relative of Mary, Ellen Walker, who lived with her in her grandfather's house. She and Mary normally slept in the same bed together, as a normal protection against sexual assault, and as proof of innocence. Ellen testified that on nights when Jonathan visited Mary, they 'were private together till towards morning', when Mary got up and went into Ellen's bed. Jonathan would sometimes stay concealed in the house for two full nights, but never more.

Another person who knew all about the liaison was an elderly husbandman, Robert Jackson. It was he who had carried the three letters from Mary, who had led Jonathan to the back door to meet her in 1656, and who had come into the room at dawn the next morning to warn him to get up and go 'because folks were stirring' and to smuggle him out of the house again. He continued to carry letters to and fro between them, and it was he who was told by Mary that Jonathan had given her another ring.

Yet another person in on the secret was of course Neville Lacock, who had been present during the breaking off of the first engagement in 1653.

When she met Mary again in 1656 or 1657, the latter told her about her fears lest her bundling sessions with Jonathan would come to the ears of her grandfather, especially since she was closely watched by one Reginald Pindar 'who lived in the town and made love to her, and was likely to discover it to her grandfather if he had any suspicions that anybody came from (Jonathan)'.

Given these circumstances, it is quite extraordinary that rumours of this protracted liaison, regularly carried on under his own roof every week or two over a period of four years, never reached old Robert Walker. The servants must have been heavily bribed to keep their mouths shut, and he may have been hard of sight and hearing.

It can surely be no accident that Mary's final turning away from Jonathan Troope and the eager welcome she offered to a new suitor coincided with the Restoration of Charles II in the spring of 1660 and the disbandment of the old republican regiments. In the new conservative era of the Restoration, Jonathan Troope became particularly unsuitable as a prospective husband, for he had been a trooper for seven years in the regiment of Major-General Lambert, although at least he did not stay with him to the bitter end in his futile efforts to fight Monck's advance on London and the Restoration of the King. Added to which each passing year only brought nearer Mary's chances of becoming a well-endowed heiress, while Jonathan remained, in her own words, 'a mean person'.

By March 1661 Mary was distancing herself from Jonathan, and encouraging courtship by another suitor, William Henworth, a maltster of Derby. According to her own story, William at first acted entirely by the rules of etiquette. He openly visited Mary in her grandfather's house, and asked her if she was already pre-contracted to anyone else. To this she replied effusively: 'I am not engaged to any man and you could never have come to me at a better time, I being so free from engagements to anyone.' Thereafter William began secretly courting Mary, and before long she had contracted herself to him, and was receiving him in her bedroom at night. At their first such encounter Mary met William at the back door and taking him by the hand (just as she had done with Jonathan, eight years before) led him up to a room. This time she merely talked with him in the great chamber (which may or may not have had a bed in it) 'all or most part of the night until morning'. On later occasions, he was led up to a room with a fire and a bed. Mary lay down with him in or upon the bed for part of the night.

He, like Jonathan before him, suggested to Mary that 'her grandfather might be acquainted with their proceedings as concerned their marriage', but she only answered as usual: 'If he knew, I would cause his displeasure.' William was so disturbed by this that he threatened to break off relations, but she explained that 'my grandfather will do well for me if we can keep him from knowing of our affections towards (one) another so long as he lives'. Later, to soothe his feelings, Mary sent him a love-letter, but William still was not satisfied, arguing that he earned enough money in the malting trade to keep them both, so that they did not need her grandfather's money in order to get married. But Mary had higher ambitions and continued to play for time until her grandfather died and she got her hands on his fortune.

William stuck to his guns, pointing out the impropriety, when they were not married, of their bundling together once a week, which clearly included a lot of sexual play if not full intercourse. But all the satisfaction he got was her angry retort: 'What, do you think I make no conscience of what I do?' So the couple continued with their weekly nocturnal assignations, stimulated by bottles of wine and sweetmeats (paid for by William). He also presented her with gloves, scarves, and gold rings, all of which she accepted gladly, saying: 'were it not upon the account that I love you dearly, I would scorn to receive any such things from you or anyone in the world else'. Once when he was ill she hugged him around the neck, kissed him, and told him: 'I am resolved to be your wife though all the friends I have were against it.'

By these tactics, Mary successfully held William in thrall until in about February 1662 her grandfather finally died and she came into her fortune, which apparently was a large one. On 18 March William appeared on her doorstep, accompanied by a minister the Revd John Mott and other friends, and demanded that she fulfil her promise and marry him forthwith. They all sat down and Mary acknowledged before them that she had promised to marry him, which she intended to do. But she now argued that her grandfather had made her his sole executrix, and therefore asked for a year's delay in the marriage so that she could prove the will and clear up the estate.

William agreed to this new delay, but the Revd Mott took advantage of the occasion to make Mary enter into a legally-binding contract with William, in front of himself and other witnesses. Using the present tense, she said: 'I do accept and take you for my husband.' They then kissed and Mary promised to go through the ceremony of a marriage in church with him that same day one year later.

In confirmation of the seriousness of her intentions towards him— and revealing her innate snobbery as the granddaughter of a gentleman towards a mere tradesman—she offered William £300 for maintenance if he would wind up his business as a maltster before midsummer and live thereafter as a gentleman of leisure until they were married. He accepted her offer and abandoned his trade. According to William, he often visited Mary openly at her late grandfather's house in the following months and they stayed together all night on most occasions.

The first slightly disturbing thing that happened was that when riding pillion behind a friend one day, Mary remarked: 'Now I have a fine time to play me in, and to see my friends.' Although she reiterated her intention of marrying William, it sounded as if she was savouring her new-found freedom on the death of her grandfather, and was in no hurry to tie herself down again under a husband.

William must have seen very clear signs that Mary was growing cool towards him long before the year was up. On 17 March 1663 he sent her a letter, reminding her of her promise to marry him the next day, but was mortified to have it returned unopened. The next day he came to the house of a JP where she was staying, accompanied by a clergyman, his plan being to confront her and demand that she fulfil her solemn promise made the year before, and go with him to church to be married. But Mary sent word that she would neither see nor speak with him.

Meanwhile, what of Jonathan Troope, who had been dropped by Mary back in 1660? He still had claims on her in view of their long relationship, frequent intimate sexual relations, and two verbal contracts of marriage, although he admitted in 1661 that since the latter were not witnessed they were probably not 'worth a rush'.

The last meeting to discuss the matter had taken place in Derby on 29 May 1662, almost three months after Mary's grandfather's death, the only person present besides the two of them being Mary's friend Neville Lacock. Miss Lacock reminded Mary of her long engagement to Jonathan, pointed out that because of it he had refused many 'considerable matches', and urged that in now casting him off she did him 'a great deal of wrong'. Mary merely retorted that she freely 'gave him leave to take his fortune and his best match'. Miss Lacock replied that it was not in her power to give any such leave 'for you are his wife in the presence of God'. She told Mary she must know it in her conscience, and that she could marry no other but Jonathan. Forced on to the defensive, Mary retorted: 'I will live unmarried and so may he.'

Six months later, in September 1662, Mary returned by a messenger the three gold rings Jonathan had given her, with the verbal message that she would have nothing more to do with him or his tokens, and that she would like to have returned the case with her bodkin and scissors she had left with him. But Jonathan refused to take back the rings, and when the messenger came back with them to Mary, she too refused to accept them, so that at the time of the trial in 1663–4 the messenger still had the rings in his possession.

In the spring of 1663, Mary took a step which galvanized into action her two rejected suitors: she married in church yet another, hitherto unknown, suitor, Gilbert Mundy. This marriage took place in the middle of a lawsuit begun by Jonathan Troope to establish his right to her hand by contract, and it probably triggered a second lawsuit by William Henworth, also claiming his right to her by contract, which began in June that year. Marriage during a trial concerning the validity of a previous contract was a favourite device of litigants seeking to put pressure on the courts to declare a contract invalid. Everyone knew that the courts were now generally very reluctant to break up a freely undertaken legal marriage in church in order to force an unwilling spouse into an earlier contract marriage with someone he or she now rejected. Their reluctance was particularly great when the woman was with child by her new husband. The courts rightly concluded that rigidly to enforce the law of contract would only result in adultery and bastardy, which were not socially or morally desirable ends.

One could therefore easily predict that Jonathan Troope would lose his case, as indeed he did in October 1664. He could prove long association, exchange of rings and other gifts, and intimate sexual relations with Mary, but he had no witnesses for either of the two verbal contracts. William Henworth's case, on the other hand, was witnessed and legally watertight, and it must have presented the court with a much greater dilemma in making a decision. But as usual the court flew in the face of the letter of the law, and in December 1664 gave sentence for Mary. Her marriage with Gilbert Mundy was finally confirmed as legally valid, and both Jonathan and William lost all claims upon her.

2

Ryder v. Jones, 1661
Courtship among the provincial middling sort

In 1660 George Ryder was a busy and successful young attorney and solicitor in Shrewsbury. He was rapidly building up a lucrative practice in the local area by acting not only as a lawyer, but as an investment adviser and financial trouble-shooter to a growing middle-class clientele.[1] His field of activities included Chester, where he settled for a while to do some business involving a goldsmith and alderman of the town, Samuel Jones. He fell in love with Mr Jones's daughter Priscilla; the attraction was mutual, and the young couple were soon courting.

By the time George left on a business trip to Ireland, they had become very fond of each other, and while he was away letters were exchanged. The Jones household was run by Priscilla's mother, and her father the alderman appears in this story as no more than an easygoing old gentleman who left all serious domestic decisions to his wife. Priscilla, however, had not told her mother about the courtship, and the correspondence with George was therefore secretly exchanged through a friend, the goldsmith apprentice in her father's shop. By this means, she contrived to send George a lock of her hair, while in return he sent her a gold ring 'for a token', a piece of gold, and a watch.

While George was still in Ireland, Mrs Jones cross-questioned Priscilla about her matrimonial preferences, asking her whom she liked best as a possible suitor: George Ryder, Mr Gamull of Crabball, or a third gentleman. Priscilla expressed a strong preference for George, saying she would have him 'though it were but in his shirt', in other words even if he were penniless. Since George was alleged to have an estate of some £80 a year or more, as well as his growing income as an attorney, Mrs Jones provisionally encouraged Priscilla to entertain him as a suitor in marriage, while she made more enquiries about his estate. It seemed at the time to be financially a perfectly suitable match, as well as one that Priscilla had already more or less set her heart on. Both interest and affection seemed to be working in harmony in this case.

---

[1] Chester RO, CC Papers, EDC 5/1661/31.

On his return from Ireland to Chester, in about midsummer 1660, George took lodgings with a couple who had rented part of the Jones's house, so that he now lived under the same roof as Priscilla. He was warmly received by the Jones parents, and treated as a provisionally accepted suitor. Priscilla said that, in view of her parents' behaviour, 'she took it for done', that is that they had accepted George as her prospective husband.

The young couple indulged in a lot of 'bundling', staying up 'very late till far in the night' after the old people had gone to bed, either in the Jones' house, or in George's lodgings next door, thanks to the tolerant complicity of the servants and lodgers. There was, as usual, a lot of love talk and some mild sexual play, sometimes lying fully clothed on a bed. Although Priscilla was still a virgin, she felt a little guilty about these bundling sessions, and finally urged George to declare his intentions to her mother and discuss the possible financial terms for a marriage.

Advised by Priscilla as to when would be a suitable occasion, George went to Mrs Jones and they had a long talk about money. Mrs Jones made two stipulations: first that he would give her the full particulars of his estate, and second that he would promise to live in Chester and not carry Priscilla off to Shrewsbury, since she was unwilling to be parted from her daughter. She went on to say that if things worked out, 'there was room enough for them', and they could 'live altogether in that house', by which she seems to have meant that George and Priscilla could take over the part of the house that was then let out.

It must have been a somewhat daunting prospect for George to have to live in such close proximity to his strong-minded mother-in-law. But he kept to himself any qualms he may have felt, and told Mrs Jones that he was about to leave for London to negotiate the purchase of an Exchequer office in Chester. If he was successful, he proposed to establish his business there rather than among his friends and relations in Shrewsbury.

Mrs Jones then turned to the crucial question of money. 'Suppose I should give my daughter £400, what would you lay down to it?' After a pause to consider, George replied: 'Three' (presumably meaning £300). He said he had an estate in Shrewsbury worth about £100 a year, and it was agreed that Mrs Jones should investigate the truth of this claim while he was away in London. Mrs Jones seemed reasonably pleased, and encouraged George to continue his courtship of Priscilla, contingent always upon the truth of his claims about his estate, and full assurance that he would move to Chester.

As a result, Priscilla was sufficiently encouraged openly to begin wearing the gold ring George had sent her months before from Ireland, saying

'I may wear it without danger of anger', since 'I take it for done'. She thought—mistakenly as things turned out—that all was settled. George explained these arrangements to a friend, who advised him to have it all put in writing before he left for London. But nothing could be done until he had bought his Exchequer office at Chester, and Mrs Jones had satisfied herself about his estate.

So George went off to London, with matters still hanging fire. While in London he wrote two letters to Priscilla, and on the day of his return the Joneses invited him to dinner, when Mr Jones gave him a gold ring in return for some business he had done for him in Wales. Five days later, however, the blow fell. He had returned empty-handed from London, without the Exchequer job, and meanwhile Mrs Jones had discovered that he owned no land at all. George was obliged to confess that his 'estate' was only 'a good place at Shrewsbury'; that he would after all have to return there; and that for the time being, if he married Priscilla, he was not in a position to make her a jointure for her widowhood. On the other hand, he argued that he was a young man with very good professional prospects as an attorney, and was likely to become prosperous within a few years.

Under these circumstances, Mrs Jones broke off the negotiations and rescinded her provisional consent for the courtship. To soften the blow, she pointed out to him that Priscilla was young and could well wait three to four years, and told him to 'go home and settle himself in his employment there, and if he had any money to lay it out upon something'. The suggestion seems to have been that if he succeeded in obtaining an estate within three or four years, the negotiations could be resumed. On the other hand, no promise was made to keep other suitors away from Priscilla; and in the mean time George was forbidden the house and Priscilla was ordered not to see or communicate with him in any way.

On hearing the bad news, Priscilla at first wept and remained loyal to her lover. In view of her continued devotion to George, a family friend suggested that Mrs Jones distract her mind by producing another suitor. It was hoped that this might work, since Priscilla had once confessed to a friend that her affection for George was real, but 'it was only such as she could take off when she would, if her parents were not content therewith'. Three weeks later, there turned up on the doorstep a Mr Townsend, whom Mrs Jones clearly regarded as a much more suitable candidate for her daughter's hand. His father said that if the Joneses put up £500 with her, he would put up £1,000, and if they put up £1,000, he would put up £2,000, which was financially a much more attractive offer than any poor George Ryder could make.

Priscilla was now totally cut off from George, and surrounded by her parents and the friends of Mr Townsend, who were persistently running down the former and urging the merits of the latter. In view of all this, George asked for the appointment of arbitrators, to assess the validity of his prior claims on Priscilla, whom he alleged was contracted to him. When the arbitrators met, they established very clearly where Priscilla's preference lay, and discovered that for several months she and George had been given every encouragement by Mrs Jones. On the other hand, they found not a hint of evidence of any formal contract. George and Priscilla had merely been courting with the consent of her parents, but with marriage dependent on a financial agreement which had fallen through. The arbitrators therefore advised George 'to desist, for God has put an end to it'.

But George would not give up, and in late 1661 he launched a suit in the Chester Consistory Court, claiming a verbal marriage contract, and asking the court to sequester Priscilla from her parents and from friends of Townsend, who were poisoning her mind against him. The court issued a sequestration order, but to George's frustration, it failed to enforce it, being no doubt fearful of offending a respected alderman of the city. Meanwhile George's legal harassment backfired, for it annoyed Priscilla, who found herself in the position of a defendant accused of reneging on a formal contract, and unable to speak her own mind.

The case dragged on, and by 1662 Priscilla had become entirely alienated from George. She declared that 'if I might have a room piled high full of gold with him, I will never have him', that 'I will beg my bread before I will have him', and that 'I hate the sight of him and if there were no more men in the world than he, I would not have him'. She now 'hated him for his base carriage towards her', first by falsely accusing her of fickleness when in fact she had remained loyal to him even after the parental veto, and then by falsely accusing her in court of making a verbal contract of marriage and then denying it. There can be little doubt that Priscilla maried Mr Townsend.

3
Harris v. *Lingard*, 1699–1701
Courtship among the London middling sort

At the very end of the seventeenth century, an organ-maker called René Harris lived in the City of London, together with his wife, one son, and two daughters. This story concerns the elder daughter, Abigail, who in 1699 was about 18, and her sister Clarissa, who was two years younger. Both Mr Harris and his daughters were Catholics, although Mrs Harris was a Protestant. Some twenty years back, in 1677, Mr Harris had been convicted in King's Bench of trying to shift responsibility on to a Mr Jacobson for a bastard child whom he had fathered.[1] In other respects, however, his life appears to have been uneventful. He travelled a good deal, setting up organs in churches around the country, and so was often away from home for long periods, leaving the running of the household and management of the children to his wife. Like most Londoners of the middling sort and above in the seventeenth and eighteenth centuries, he removed his family from the heat and stench of the city every summer, and took lodgings for them in the fashionable town of Richmond. Although not a rich man, Mr Harris was prepared to give £500 as marriage portions with each of his daughters, so he was clearly quite comfortably off.[2] He was a patron, as well as a supplier, of culture. For example, he once took the family out on the river to Mortlake to hear some music, and he hired an artist to paint his wife's portrait.[3]

Mr Harris had long been on very friendly terms with John Lingard, a vintner and master of the Bell Tavern in Nicholas Lane in the City. The Lingards had much more money and status than the Harrises. John Lingard senior was 'a person of a considerable estate', thought to be worth between £150 and £800 a year in property and £2,000 to £3,000 in goods.[4] He was a Protestant like all his family, a citizen of London, and a churchwarden of St Clement's Eastcheap. His only child and heir Jack was 24 in 1699, and lived in chambers in the Inner Temple, where he was training for a career as a barrister.

[1] LPCA, D. 972: 84, 355, 357, 359, 446–7, 519.   [2] Ibid. 283, 357, 548, 573, 591.
[3] Ibid. 519, 311–12.   [4] Ibid. 84.

It was not until August 1698 that the two families met, after Mr Lingard as churchwarden had commissioned Mr Harris to set up an organ in St Clement's. One Sunday soon afterwards the three ladies of the Harris family went to the church to hear Mr Baptist play on the new organ, and then were invited back to the Lingard house in Nicholas Lane. The young law student, Jack Lingard, escorted Abigail Harris from the church to the house, which was the first time they met. Soon afterwards Mrs Harris, accompanied once again by her two daughters, visited the Lingard house to collect the money due for her husband's work on the organ. This time they stayed till nightfall and Jack escorted them home. The relationship was further cemented by a visit of Mrs Lingard to Mrs Harris, followed by a return visit by Mrs Harris and her two daughters. This time Jack took them home in a coach, was importunately invited in, and stayed until one or two in the morning in animated conversation with the two young women. The next day he came again to apologize for staying so late.

Soon afterwards, Mrs Harris asked Mrs Lingard's permission for Jack 'to come and spend an evening sometimes at her house'. The permission was promptly granted, and thereafter he became an almost daily visitor from his chambers in the Inner Temple to the Harrises, a circumstance which he thought it prudent to keep from his parents, especially his mother. The fact is that Jack was not just paying friendly visits; he was actively courting Abigail Harris. According to Clarissa, after six months he 'became so passionately in love with Abigail that for near two years together he came almost every day to see her, and at length did gain her affections, and he wrote several endearing letters to her and she returned answers thereto'. When the Harrises were lodging at Richmond during the summers of 1699 and 1700, Jack visited them and stayed for several days at a time. Jack also often took Abigail out, and 'showed as much love for her as 'twas possible for him to express'. He showered presents upon her—'a ring which his own mother gave him with some of her own hair worked into it with a crystal round it', a medal, a snuff box, a fine fan, and a tortoiseshell comb.[5]

Abigail later claimed that Jack told her 'he thought he had been too old [at 24] to have been in love, and that he did not think he could have loved any woman so well as he found he loved her'. After about a year or more of courting, Abigail claimed that he said to her 'By God I will marry you and no other woman'. He persuaded her to make the same promise, and they shook hands on it. She also claimed that on another

[5] Ibid. 71, 339–52, 411–18, 452, 74, 597–9.

occasion he said 'By God and all that is sacred I will marry you and no other woman, and I do look upon you to be my wife before God', and they again shook hands on it. If spoken, the words were ambiguous, and could be taken either as a promise for the future, or just possibly, as the Harrises later claimed, as a contract 'in words of the present'.

These claims by Abigail about a marriage contract were supported by Clarissa, who testified that both Abigail and Jack had told her about them at the time, and that Jack also told her that Abigail 'was his wife before God and that he would never marry any other woman'. It is noticeable that the expression was always 'before God' rather than 'before the law', a distinction all parties seemed to recognize. It was no more than a vague moral commitment, and since it was not witnessed even that could not be proved. It is also suspicious that although Abigail later claimed that the contract was made in about August 1699, she admitted that she and Jack did not publicly acknowledge it to her sister or any of the neighbours until April or May 1700, which is when she first realized that she was pregnant.[6] The version Jack told the court eighteen months later was very different and equally unconvincing. He said that Abigail and Clarissa 'being brisk airy women, their company was diverting enough to serve an idle amusement'. He admitted his regular visits, especially all day on Sundays, but claimed that they were made to the whole family, especially to the brother 'who plays upon the harpsichord, which I also play upon'. He flatly denied ever acting the role of the romantic lover, asserting that he often told Mrs Harris and Abigail that in his opinion 'they are fools who marry for love, and I will never marry any woman except she has a good portion with her'. He denied that his presents were tokens of love, and unchivalrously suggested that Abigail had wheedled the ring out of him, and had actually filched the medal from his pocket while sitting on his lap one day. As for making Abigail a formal promise of marriage, he flatly denied it.[7]

A 20-year-old servant, Elizabeth Shirley, who had been with the Harrises for five months in the latter end of 1699, testified, perhaps falsely, that Clarissa told her that she had never heard Jack 'say anything of marriage to Abigail in her life', and that in her opinion Jack would no more marry Abigail than he would marry herself. Jack claimed that when Mrs Harris first visited him in his chambers in September 1700 to discuss Abigail's pregnancy and to ask him to marry her, she never made any reference to the existence of a marriage contract.[8]

[6] Ibid. 74–7, 271–2, 336–7, 349–52, 373.   [7] Ibid. 419–26, 482.
[8] Ibid. 576–672.

What comes out very clearly from a welter of confusing and contradictory evidence is two things. The first is that for a period of over a year from early 1699 to mid-1700 Jack and Abigail were undoubtedly in love, and that Mrs Harris did everything she could to encourage the romance, often watching with satisfaction while Jack took Abigail on his knee and kissed her. Since Mrs Harris was so actively encouraging Jack, people assumed that the two were secretly contracted to each other. After all, a young man does not sleep in the house of a young lady on fifty occasions without a certain amount of gossip. The second is that no formal, legally binding, and duly witnessed, contract had been made between them, but only an exchange of vague assurances about being contracted in the eyes of God.

The seduction of a young woman, under vague promises of marriage, is common enough. This case is unusual, however, in two respects. The first is that the man seems to have been the seduced rather than the seducer. The second is the extraordinary freedom in their social and sexual lives allowed by their mother to the 18-year-old Abigail and her younger sister in a respectable middling sort London family in 1699–1700.

Jack never denied that, so far as he could tell, he had taken Abigail's virginity; but he insisted that he was systematically lured into it by Mrs Harris, Abigail, and Clarissa. He was constantly being invited to the house, and then pressed importunately by all three to stay the night there. A maid (whose veracity is not above suspicion) claimed that Clarissa used to lock the front door and put the key in her pocket, while Abigail, in her mother's presence 'would hang about his neck and kiss him, and tell him he should not go'. The two sisters slept together in the same bed in a room on the top floor, and a maid who served in the house from September 1698 to the summer of 1699 testified that every night she locked the two girls in their room, and unlocked them in the morning. This practice of locking women in their rooms at night, as well as having them sleep two to a bed, were common precautions against fornication or rape. At first Jack slept on a different floor from that of the girls, but after September 1699 he was moved, on Mrs Harris's instructions, to a room on the top floor beside theirs, with a communicating door blocked only by a large chest. Soon afterwards, the chest was removed, again on Mrs Harris's instructions, 'to the end that Abigail and Mr Lingard might have better access to each other's chambers'. Several times, Mrs Harris personally 'conveyed him out of the house privately in the morning'. Thus what had begun as a perfectly respectable courtship, with sexual access carefully blocked by two women sleeping in a bed behind a locked door, slowly turned into an open invitation by Mrs Harris to bundle with one of her daughters.[9]

The evidence suggests that Abigail took the initiative in the seduction of Jack, at first in the presence of her mother, her sister, or maid. Thanks to her mother giving Jack an adjacent room with a communicating door, she would come with Clarissa into his chamber in the evening to say goodnight and there undress herself, which gave her a chance to display her naked breasts to him; she would lie on top of the bed he was in and kiss him; she would unbutton his waistcoat and put her hands into his bosom and pockets. She and Clarissa would come again to his bedroom early in the morning, as soon as he signalled to the girls that he was awake by knocking on a chair with his snuffbox, and on Sundays they would stay there sitting on his bed for the best part of the morning.[10]

Mrs Harris's motive in encouraging all these goings-on was presumably in order to catch a wealthy barrister husband for her daughter. According to a not too trustworthy account, one day when Jack called at the house, Mrs Harris came down to the kitchen, where Abigail and Clarissa were, and announced: 'Mr Lingard is come. He can as well be hanged as keep away, but we'll make it up as soon as we can. The old folks [meaning Jack's parents] will be plaguey mad when they know it, for he is the only child and they have a considerable estate, but we'll do well enough with them.'[11]

Matters came to a head in late 1699 or early 1700. According to Jack, he and Abigail were walking in Lincoln's Inn Gardens one day when she told him she wanted him to come to her house and go to bed with her. He 'looking upon the same as an extravagant proposal, laughed at it'. But Abigail insisted, and when they got to the house he found Mrs Harris in the kitchen airing the sheets for his bed. She too invited him to stay for the night. That evening Abigail slipped into his room and lay on his bed, giving him the opportunity to sleep with her. He resisted the temptation, however, which so annoyed Abigail that the next day she 'sang an immodest song to him', which ran as follows:

> High Hoe, my heart is light.
> I lay with a young man all last night
> All the night and all the day,

[9] Ibid. 366–7, 456–75, 566, 578–81.   [10] Ibid. 582–3, 612–15.
[11] Ibid. 531–2.

And yet I came a maid away.
Sure he was drunk or sure he was mad,
Or else he'd have given me such as he had.

On another occasion she slipped into bed with him, clad only in an underpetticoat and a night-gown. It is hardly surprising that in the end Jack succumbed to these repeated temptations: by May 1700 Abigail was pregnant, and the fat was in the fire.[12]

What is strange is the way Mrs Harris behaved as though she were unaware of the dangers to which she was exposing her daughters because of her casual indifference to the most elementary rules of modesty and prudence. A charitable view of Abigail would be that she looked far more mature than she was, that she was not so much a knowing tease as a hoyden, revelling in her own emerging sexuality, but with little understanding of, and no instruction in, the dangers inherent in an over-enthusiastic approach to bundling. The practice had been relatively safe in the sixteenth century, when it was governed by strict and well-understood codes of behaviour. But it had become extremely unsafe by the mid-eighteenth century, when the codes had broken down, with the result that about a half of all first children were conceived out of wedlock. The Harris girls were caught in the transition.

More surprising than this elaborate, long-drawn process of the seduction of a young man by a young girl, using her mother and sister as active accomplices, is the fact, which Jack only found out later and then used with devastating effect in court, that he was by no means the only man with whom Abigail had been carrying on a flirtatious courtship. Indeed one of the points made by the Harrises themselves was that during this period of courtship by Jack, Abigail 'had several good offers of matches suitable to her quality'.[13]

During late 1698, 1699, and early 1700 when the affair with Jack was in full swing, Abigail was simultaneously being courted by, or was flirting with, no fewer than five other men. One was a 17-year-old clerk named Thomas Bewick, who lodged a few doors down the street. He lost his heart to Abigail in 1698 to 1699, and hung around her for a long time, being encouraged by her sitting on his lap, kissing him, and allegedly urging him to marry her secretly. When he first saw her sporting a ring that Jack had given her, he went into shock: 'I saw Abigail at Mrs

---

[12] Ibid. 428–33.   [13] Ibid. 84, 326, 335, 380.

Lewis's dancing school in Wine Office Court with a ring on her thumb, and was so surprised at it that my nose burst out a bleeding, for fear she was married.'[14] But he went on courting her assiduously, wrote her love-letters, gave her a pair of earrings, and told his cousin and landlady that she was 'a pretty woman'. In May 1699 he wrote a barely literate letter to Abigail's brother about his frustrated love for her: 'I think I am an unfortunate lover as for to displease that dear creature whom I love so passionately, I knowing her to be one of that infinite goodness that she will pass all these blind things by, for Cupid is the occasion of it.'

With Mrs Harris's encouragement, he concealed from his landlady his frequent visits to the Harris house by sneaking surreptitiously in and out. Mrs Harris and Abigail seem to have kept him stringing along as a cover for the more serious pursuit of Jack Lingard. On the other hand, Mr Harris went to the length of interviewing Thomas's kinsman, an attorney, to enquire about his estate, but the report was not satisfactory, and anyway his relatives in Northumberland were urging him to drop his suit. At last, when the Harrises left for Richmond in the summer of 1699, Abigail curtly 'forbade him keeping company with her any more, telling him that he was too young to have thoughts of marriage, and that he had no estate at present to maintain a wife'. Exit Thomas Bewick.[15]

But there were plenty of others to fill the breach. A young artist named Thomas Forster, who came to the house to draw her father's and mother's portraits, was immediately attracted to Abigail, and 'made addresses to her in the way of marriage'. But Mrs Harris was 'very indifferent' to him, and Abigail 'did use me very ill and ridiculed and spoke very contemptibly of me', several times 'reflecting upon my person'. She told him that 'she could not fancy him or abide him, and that he was a proud fellow and that he looked like a boy'. He never did get much encouragement from anyone except Mr Harris.[16]

A more serious suitor was William Barlow, a young Irish law student at the Middle Temple, who first met Abigail in the summer of 1699, and made an immediate hit with her. She freely allowed a great deal of kissing and embracing, all of which took place with one or more women witnesses, her mother, her sister, or her maid. For example, Barlow once sang to Abigail 'a song which carried a bawdy meaning with it'. In the presence of her mother or sister, Abigail allowed him to embrace her, squeeze her hand, sit her on his lap, and feel her naked breasts, and once

---

[14] Ibid. 571.
[15] Ibid. 335, 328–33, 396–8, 543–5, 620, 650–1, 662–3.
[16] Ibid. 309–14, 391–2.

to take up her skirts and see her stockinged leg. It was thus a public courtship, encouraged by and carried on within the familial world of women, concurrently with the more serious pursuit of Jack. Mr Harris, as usual, knew nothing about it. It is not clear whether the flirtation was carried on as an insurance policy in case Jack dropped out, but the evidence suggests that it was largely sheer sexual fun.

The critical episode took place in February 1700, when his fellow law student and friend, Mr Pierson, who was also a friend of Abigail's brother, lost his room-mate, who suddenly died. Pierson was therefore invited to stay at the Harrises for a week. William Barlow visited him there and was invited to stay the night with him, sharing the same room adjoining that of the girls which was used by Jack Lingard. William's story is that early in the morning he went into the girls' room, bade them good morning, and sat on the side of their bed. 'After some jocular discourse I asked them if I should come into bed to them, which they absolutely denied. And after some further discourse, I leapt into bed by surprise between them, at which they were very uneasy, but upon my promise that I would not offer any further incivility,' they let him stay there for half an hour. William admitted he kissed Abigail, but denied, probably truthfully, that 'I did touch or feel her privy parts'.[17]

William returned with Mr Pierson the next evening to talk to Mr Harris, and they were only too glad to accept an invitation to stay a second night. Soon after they had all gone to bed, Abigail and Clarissa came in to talk to them, and then Abigail returned to her own room, followed soon after by William Barlow. So there was now one daughter and one law student in each bedroom. William stayed sitting or lying on Abigail's bed for half an hour, trying to persuade her to let him get into bed with her, promising to 'make no attempt of her chastity', and assuring her that 'I only design it as a frolic'. Abigail adamantly refused, until her maid Margaret Carey came into the room. Margaret said to her, 'What should you be so afraid of? My honey [i.e. William] would not meddle with you.' Reassured by these words, and by Margaret's presence in the room and in the bed, she allowed William to climb into bed with her and stay there all night.

During most of the night her sister Clarissa and/or the maid Margaret Carey were also in the bed with them, but there were times when Abigail and William were alone in the bed with the curtains partly drawn. Both admitted that they kissed and that he had fondled her breasts, but denied

---

[17] Ibid. 290, 293–5.

that she lost her virginity. William swore that she had let him 'feel her belly and thighs, and I have attempted to feel her privy parts, but she has resisted and not suffered me.' Abigail was thus careful to maintain the well-defined limits, beyond which she would not allow bundling to go.

This flirtation with William Barlow continued through July and August 1700, by which time, unknown to William, Abigail was already pregnant by Jack Lingard. William and Mr Pierson took the two girls on a trip to Vauxhall, and entertained them several times at the Middle Temple, twice in William's chamber, once in Mr Pierson's. It seems certain that William was telling the truth when he said that the two young men went with the Harris girls 'only for recreation and diversion', and with no intention of marriage. Abigail's motives seems to have been the same.

When he discovered late that summer that Abigail was pregnant, Barlow naturally panicked, afraid that he might be accused of being the father because of that imprudent night when he bundled with her. He therefore went to the trouble to track down the maid Margaret Carey, and promised her money to keep her mouth shut about seeing him in bed with Abigail. But the birth of the child in January 1701 occurred eleven months after the bundling episode, so that he could not be the father. He therefore withdrew his promise of a bribe.[18]

Abigail's most faithful suitor during all this period of intense multiple courtship was an elderly gentleman called Mr Rogers, whom she kept dangling, just in case he might one day come in useful. He 'made honourable love to her', and she boasted that 'I may marry Mr Rogers when I please'. Her mother's interest in Mr Rogers was frankly social and mercenary. She boasted that Rogers 'would be knighted and have some place or preferment, and that Sir John Rogers would give or leave him a good estate if Sir John's son died'. He courted Abigail seriously, with Mr Harris's consent, and gave her 'a handkerchief wrought with gold', which she first accepted, but then returned in a fit of remorse some six weeks later. He also sent Abigail love poems, which she observed cynically 'he wrote or caused to be copied'. Although she said 'he is too old for me', she kept him on a string for some time, although she never allowed him the familiarities she granted to her younger suitors. This was not the end of the affair however, since, as we will see, his name came up again in July 1700, when Abigail's pregnancy first became known.

So far the story makes a rough kind of sense: two young girls, the eldest of whom was eager for mild sexual experimentation and looking

[18] Ibid. 297–305, 307, 401–5, 480, 513–21, 585–7, 622–6.

for a suitable husband, but careful to preserve their virginity; a scheming and foolish mother anxious to display the physical attractions of her daughter in order to drum up offers of marriage; a husband away most of the time on business, and kept ignorant of much of what was going on, but anxious to obtain for his daughters the highest price on the market; and a common practice of close sexual contact, which was supposed to stay just within conventionally established limits, and stop short of full intercourse.

Much more surprising, however, is that, along with all these flirtations and sexual tumblings with a range of potential suitors, Abigail and her sister were for some reason allowed by their mother to be taken out and entertained by wealthy members of the social elite, knights and others. These were men who were much older than the Harris girls, who concealed their true names and went under pseudonyms, and whose dishonourable intentions cannot have been in doubt. It remains a mystery why Mrs Harris allowed her daughters to take part in this extraordinarily dangerous social activity, which could easily have ended in seduction or even rape. Respectable unmarried women were free to roam the streets in eighteenth-century England, but not in such disreputable company.

It all began in the summer of 1698 when Abigail met at a dance at Richmond Wells an elderly gentleman who gave himself the nickname of 'Thames', and who later turned out to be Sir Charles Sedley, Bt. Sir Charles was a 60-year-old poet and playwright, who in the 1660s and 1670s had been one of the most debauched men-about-town in London. He was now a broken-down roué whose interest in young girls must have been a last effort to revive the flagging lusts of his youth. He was a married man, a fact that he carefully concealed from the Harrises. Abigail and Clarissa were invited by Sir Charles to several very expensive private suppers at the Roebuck in Suffolk Street, or the Blue Post in the Haymarket, but on these occasions he did nothing more than kiss Abigail and put his arm round her waist. Once Abigail, Clarissa, and their maid stayed out dancing with 'Thames' and other gentlemen, one of whom was known as 'Chelsea', and did not get home until two in the morning. Only once was there trouble, when after a supper at the Roebuck, Clarissa was foolish enough to go home alone in a coach with one of the gentlemen in the company. He stopped the coach at a chocolate house near Covent Garden and escorted her inside. As she explained it, 'he offering some rudeness and indecencies—I thereupon threw a dish of chocolate in his face and on his clothes', a story she had to tell her mother since she came home all splashed with chocolate.

Abigail, who was clearly intoxicated with her own powers of attraction for men, once went down on her knees before her mother, and drank to three or four of her gentlemen suitors, one of whom was 'Thames'. Her mother did not even reprove her for being so silly. When challenged by the suspicious neighbours, Abigail tried to pass off the association as a purely commercial one, saying that she made linen for Sir Charles, while he gave her a dozen pairs of gloves in return.[19]

But in fact their relations were rather more intimate than that. During the weeks in late 1698 when they were going around together, before it became known that 'Thames' was married, Abigail and her mother committed the supreme indiscretion of inviting him for the night on about eight occasions and putting him in the usual guest bedroom adjacent to that of the girls, isolated from the family on an upper floor of the house. Abigail admitted that she had visited him in his room in the morning, in the company of her mother and sister, and that he had once kissed her as she sat on the side of his bed. One servant, whose evidence is admittedly suspect, said that 'Thames' often kissed and embraced Abigail and put his hand into her bosom on these occasions, while she whetted his jaded appetite by undressing herself in front of him. Another servant said that Abigail let him 'kiss and tumble her' on the bed in the presence of her mother and sister.[20]

No one suggested that anything more serious took place, and all of it was done in public, but this Lolita-like relationship with an elderly baronet of deplorable reputation, carried on with the full knowledge of the mother (but not of the father) is very odd, to say the least. Abigail and her mother may have been toying with the idea of captivating and then luring into marriage a rich old baronet worn out by a lifetime of dissipation, and of inheriting his estate on his death (he died three years later in 1701). But if so, they were playing with fire. They were lucky that Sir Charles's sexual powers were not what they had been thirty years before, and that they learned in good time that he was still married.

So far, the three elements in this story have been first the courtship of Abigail by Jack Lingard, leading up to the alleged contract and then to Abigail's loss of virginity and pregnancy in early 1770; second, the extraordinarily free and varied courting and sexual play with numerous suitors, entered into during the same period by the two teenage girls, Abigail and her sister Clarissa, with their mother's active encouragement; and third, their gadding about the streets and taverns of London, unchaperoned, with elderly rich debauchees.

---

[19] Ibid. 380–7, 533–4, 537–8, 552–3.   [20] Ibid. 380–90, 525–34, 552–5, 451–2.

The fourth and last part of the story is the response of the two families to the news that Abigail Harris was pregnant by Jack Lingard. Several possible options were open to the Harrises: the best was to persuade Mr and Mrs Lingard to agree to a marriage; failing that, which seemed unlikely, the next best solution was to induce Jack to perform a clandestine marriage with Abigail at once, without the knowledge or consent of his parents. This might be done by an appeal to his love of Abigail and his sense of obligation to fulfil his somewhat equivocal private promises of future marriage; or by threats of public exposure; or by the offer of a substantial dowry. Another possible option was to arrange a hasty clandestine marriage with the still devoted Mr Rogers before he learned that Abigail was pregnant. If all else failed, Abigail could sue Jack in an ecclesiastical court, in the hope of getting it to order the pair to regularize their situation by a church wedding. The Harrises tried all these alternatives.

Abigail concealed her condition as long as she could. Although she must have conceived in May, it was not until late July that she consulted a midwife, who took her to see a 37-year-old doctor living in Westminster, called Hope Chamberlain, who confirmed that she was pregnant. Abigail told him that she was not married but she was sure that the gentleman responsible would marry her as soon as she asked him to do so. She asked Dr Chamberlain if he knew of a clergyman who was willing to marry them clandestinely without banns or licence, the idea being to keep the matter secret both from her own father and from the Lingard parents. Dr Chamberlain obligingly said he did.[21]

Abigail's plan was not only to arrange for a clandestine marriage, but also to backdate the marriage certificate, to make it appear, both to her father and to the Lingard parents, that she had been married before she became pregnant. The clergyman was an elderly Frenchman called Peter Berault who had been a minister of the Church of England for thirty years. He lived on the fringes of respectable society, earning a precarious living 'by teaching the Latin and French tongues and writing some books and being Chaplain in the ships'. He admitted that at the age of 61 he was still penniless, which was why he was willing to perform an illegal but legally binding clandestine marriage without banns or licence.[22]

Abigail then revealed her condition to her mother, who hurried off to see Jack Lingard in his chambers in the Inner Temple, in order to break the bad news to him and to ask him to marry her daughter. Jack denied

---

[21] Ibid. 275–7, 285.   [22] Ibid. 255, 266–8, 277.

neither the paternity nor that it was he who had taken her virginity. He was, however, extremely distressed by the news, saying: 'I shall be ruined if it is known to my father before I am called to the bar and have something settled on me.' He explained that he was still wholly dependent upon the good will of his father, who was just then looking for an office in the lawcourts to buy for him, for which he was willing to spend £1,800. He 'cried and wept very much', trapped as he was between his love and obligation to Abigail on the one hand, and his dependence on his father for his future career on the other.

For the next few days the young man was in an agony of indecision. Sometimes he told Abigail, 'I will marry you and sell my plate and chambers and go and live in some retired place until my friends [meaning his parents] will be reconciled to me.' At other times, worldly prudence prevailed, and he drew back, merely promising that 'he would do his utmost to obtain his friends' [meaning his parents'] consent very speedily'. Later he became so distraught that he told Abigail that 'he loved her above all creatures in the world', and that rather than let her marry Mr Rogers or anyone else, 'he would first stab her, and then himself'. The pregnancy could not have occurred at a worse moment for him.[23]

Faced with the catastrophic results of her machinations, Mrs Harris had a near breakdown, while Abigail in desperation said that rather than ruin Jack's career, she would try to marry Mr Rogers instead. The Harris parents also saw this as one way out of the dilemma, especially since Abigail's pregnancy was not yet visible, and in July Mr Harris told Mr Rogers that he could have her if Abigail would agree. By August, however, this plan was no longer practical, since Abigail 'was so far gone with child that his [Mr Roger's] friends would find it out, and perceive that she was with child before she married him'. Indeed, as soon as Mr Rogers got to hear about the pregnancy, he promptly abandoned his courtship.[24]

Meanwhile Mrs Harris was obliged to tell the story of his daughter's pregnancy to her hitherto unsuspecting husband, who was—not unreasonably—furious with her and Clarissa for allowing Jack to sleep in the room next door to Abigail on some fifty occasions without his knowledge or consent. He was even angrier with his wife when he learned about the scandalous 'Thames' episode, and called all three women, his wife and his two daughters 'several ill names'. At first he threatened to

[23] Ibid. 79, 80, 616–18, 627–33, 639–40.
[24] Ibid. 316–18, 392–5, 548, 584, 617, 621, 636, 653, 663–5.

turn Abigail out of doors, then cooled down and turned his attention into
trying to bribe, persuade, or bully Jack into marrying her.[25]

Soon afterwards he visited his lawyer, Mr Castlemaine, looking very
pleased with himself. He explained:

I have been the last night in the City, drinking a bottle of wine with old Mr
Lingard, and among other discourse Mr Lingard said that he designed to lay out
two thousand pounds for an employment for his son and to marry him; and I
believe that when Jack has something to subsist on, he will then declare himself
to his father.

Mr Castlemaine remarked that 'it would be more generous to tell Mr
Lingard before he lays out his money than afterwards', but Mr Harris
retorted: 'Jack knows best when to declare himself.'[26]

If this story is true, it seems clear that both the Harris parents knew
about the pregnancy in July, but at Jack's urgent request kept it secret
from old Mr Lingard until late August or early September, in the hope
that by then the latter would have bought Jack the office. Jack was said to
have suggested asking Mr Harris's Catholic confessor to advise him to
delay pressing for an immediate marriage.[27]

But Mr Lingard delayed making the purchase, and eventually Jack was
obliged to tell his parents what had happened. They, and especially his
mother, were very angry. They immediately forced him to make a solemn
promise not to marry without their consent, and since they held the
purse-strings, he was obliged to agree. They also promptly moved him
out of chambers to a friend's house, so as to cut all contacts with Abigail.

In this isolation, Jack wrote Abigail a letter, which is a masterpiece
of guilty evasion. It is addressed 'Dear child'—appropriately enough
considering Abigail's age. He asked her 'to make yourself as easy as you
can, since you may be sure my thoughts and inclinations are with you,
though I am forced to submit at present to avoid greater inconveniences.
I am very much afflicted at your poor mother's illness, being sensible of
the occasion of it.' He urged Abigail to stop worrying, since 'it will be
necessary to put a good face upon the matter to avoid suspicions—in
short, if you are dejected and cast down all will be ruined, whilst courage
and prudence will restore us all to our quiets again, and I do not doubt
but this cloud will blow over and we shall recover our former tranquility.
I am not very good at thinking at present' (which was clearly true). He
concluded 'if wishes would bring you happiness you would certainly

---

[25] Ibid. 375–7, 390.   [26] Ibid. 553–64, 610.   [27] Ibid. 638, 644, 668.

enjoy it', and added: 'Say you are absolutely sure I will marry you, but tell her [Mrs Harris] you are sure of my affections, that I will do anything that is reasonable. And if I can do it without ruining us both, you are sure I will do it.'[28]

This last line was the give-away; it meant that Jack was convinced that, if he married Abigail, his father would refuse to buy him the legal office, and so blast his future career as a lawyer. He was therefore beginning to make private promises to marry Abigail conditional upon his father's consent. A second, private, letter was said to have stated frankly that there was no hope of a marriage, since Jack's mother, Mrs Lingard, was utterly opposed to it.

Mrs Harris, who was now frantic to repair the damage she had done, tried to provide something which might possibly soften the objections of the Lingard parents to a marriage. She gave Jack Lingard two tickets in Sydenham's Lottery, the prize for which was £600 a year, and she promised that if he won, he could keep the prize as a major addition to Abigail's portion. Jack had also been given two tickets by his parents, which he gave to Abigail. His plan was that if any one of these four tickets won the prize, he would pretend to his parents that it was hers, hoping that this very substantial dowry would induce them to consent to him marrying her.[29]

On 16 September there was a meeting between Mr and Mrs Harris and Jack Lingard at Dr Chamberlain's office. Jack there admitted 'that he had her maidenhead—and had gotten her with child', and promised to try to get his parents' permission to marry, since 'he loved her above all creatures in the world, and never could be happy without her'. To encourage him, Mr Harris first offered to give with Abigail as a marriage portion £500, and then raised it to £600 and possibly higher still—Abigail said up to £1,000—'rather than have any blot in his family'.

A few days later the Revd Peter Berault was discussing the project for a clandestine marriage with Dr Chamberlain and Mr Harris at the Globe Tavern in Fleet Street, when news arrived that Jack Lingard was at the Harris's house. According to Berault, whose version is no doubt somewhat embroidered in his own favour, he said: 'Gentlemen, if you think it fit, I'll go and talk with the gentleman [Jack] and do what I can to persuade him to marry her.' When they got to the Harris's house, Mr Harris waited downstairs, while Berault went upstairs to talk to Jack. The following exchange took place about the ethics of marrying a pregnant young woman:

[28] Ibid. 86–7, 629.
[29] Ibid. 78, 84, 283, 357, 375–7, 548, 603, 640–1, 673.

PETER BERAULT. Sir, I am told that this gentlewoman is got with child, and that it is by you, but before you give me an answer, I desire to know whether you had her virginity.

JOHN LINGARD. I think so.

PETER BERAULT. Well sir, since you think so, and grant it to be so, I tell you that in honour and conscience you are bound to marry her.

JOHN LINGARD. I have promised my parents never to marry any woman without their consent.

PETER BERAULT. Sir, you should have promised also your parents never to kiss a woman without their consent. If I were a King, and had done what you have done, I would marry her.

JOHN LINGARD. And so would I, if I were a King.

PETER BERAULT. And since you are not a King, I think you have the greater reason to marry her, especially she being not inferior to you in quality, as I am told.

Jack made no answer to this last point, took up his sword, and went downstairs.[30] What is interesting about the conversation is the stress Berault laid on two points: on Abigail being a virgin when Jack first slept with her; and on her being of the same social status as himself. Both were matters which, in the eighteenth-century system of values, argued strongly for marriage. The second point, however, was doubtful, especially since Jack sported a sword like a gentleman.

As Jack was proceeding downstairs, Berault warned him 'If you will not give me a better answer, you will find somebody below to whom you must answer.' He then went down and told Mr Harris the gist of the conversation, namely that Jack had admitted that he had had Abigail's maidenhead, but refused to marry her without his parents' consent. Mr Harris lost his temper, locked the front door to prevent Jack from escaping, and then tried to seize him by the throat, shouting: 'God damn your soul, I will pistol you if you will not marry her.' But Peter Berault intervened, and anyway Jack had little to fear, since he had a sword and Mr Harris was unarmed.

Mr Harris then turned his fury on his wife, accusing her of knowing that Jack had been lying with Abigail. 'What', he exclaimed to her, 'would you turn bawd to your daughter?' The situation was saved by Jack falling on his knees and swearing, not entirely truthfully, that neither Mrs Harris nor Clarissa had known anything about it. After this Mr Harris cooled down, and said that he expected Jack to marry Abigail; and that he would give her a portion exceeding £500 in view of the

[30] Ibid. 256–62, 436–7.

63

superior financial position of the Lingards. Jack promised to do what he could to get his parents' consent, and Mr Harris, now quite friendly, said he could go and talk alone to Abigail for a while. Jack again told Abigail that he would never be happy till he married her and went off to discuss the matter with his parents.[31]

Everything now hinged on the reaction of the Lingards, but both of them, especially the mother, still strongly opposed the match, as Jack had foreseen. They did so partly because the Harrises were socially and economically inferior to them; partly because Mr Lingard wanted John to marry a Miss Green, the daughter of a wealthy vintner for whom Jack said 'he had no inclination or fancy';[32] and partly also, no doubt, since they were reluctant to let their son marry a pregnant teenage girl, especially since it was clear that he had made no legally binding promise of marriage. Curiously enough, they never openly raised the other possible objection, that Abigail was a Catholic.

In the following weeks, Jack was under inexorable pressure from his parents to refuse marriage, reinforced by the threat of the ruin of his career if his father did not buy him the office; and now there came to light the flood of revelations, from a former maid of the Harrises, hired by Mr Lingard, about Abigail's flirtations with other men—including the disreputable Sir John Sedley, who was old enough to be her father—at the very time that she was engaging herself to him. As a result of the new information, John's passion for Abigail began at last to ebb, so that by October the Lingards were presenting a common front.

In that month several grand family consultations were held in the chambers in the Inner Temple of the lawyer, Mr Castlemaine.

At one of these meetings Mrs Frances Sheppard (a friend of the Lingards) pointed out to Mrs Harris the way she had deliberately concealed the courtship from the Lingard parents.

MRS SHEPPARD. You did design to make Jack your cully to marry your daughter, for when you went to see Mrs Lingard and found Jack with her you asked him why he was so great a stranger to you and why he would not come and see you and your daughter now and then; [and this was] when Jack had been at your house but the night or some very short time before.

JACK [*to Mrs Harris*]. Did I ever desire you to say any such thing or to do so?

MRS HARRIS. No, but I did it because I knew you had a mind your mother should not know it.

---

[31] Ibid. 262–5, 272–3, 281, 434–8, 482–4.   [32] Ibid. 372.

As time went on, the discussions between the two families took on an increasingly bitter tone, since the Lingards were now convinced that the Harrises had set out to entrap their son so that Abigail would make a 'good' marriage in terms of social and financial advantage. At one meeting Abigail addressed Jack as 'Mr Lingard' rather than her usual terms of endearment. Jack asked, 'Is it come to this, to be called plain Mr Lingard by you?', to which Abigail retorted sharply ''Tis your fault not mine'.

By late October negotiations broke down, and both sides began collecting evidence for the inevitable lawsuit. Abigail gave birth on 28 January 1701[33] and in March the case came to trial in the London Consistory Court. Abigail sued Jack to get the alleged contract confirmed by the court as a valid marriage, but Jack flatly denied that he had entered into any such contract. He now knew all about Abigail's flirtations and physical dalliance on and in beds with a variety of suitors. In court, under the guidance of his proctor, he went so far as to call his former mistress and love 'a person of ill reputation, and of a loose carriage and behaviour, and of a vicious life and conversation'. To prove the point, he described to the court all the details of Abigail's sexual flirtations with her various suitors, her cynical manipulation of the affection of the elderly Mr Rogers, and her reckless behaviour with the old lecher Sir John Sedley.[34]

Abigail could not deny the accusations of improper behaviour, and had no witnesses to back up her claim of a contract, except accounts by her mother and sister of what she had told them. Moreover, the evidence of her sister Clarissa did her more harm than good, for she denied any direct knowledge of the contract and added more details about Abigail's promiscuous flirtations and physical contacts on the third floor of the Harris house. Since there were no witnesses to the contract, Abigail's suit was rejected by the Consistory Court, and on appeal it was also rejected by the Court of Arches in June 1702.[35] At this point darkness falls, and she disappears once more from history, a victim of her own imprudence and her mother's gross folly in encouraging her. The latter's motive was to catch for her pretty daughter a rich and socially elevated husband, but the result was an unmarried teenage mother.

The prime interest of this story lies in the light it sheds on courting procedures among the middling sort in about the year 1700. What is remarkable is the almost complete freedom allowed to two teenage

---

[33] Ibid. 352.   [34] Ibid. 426, 449, 460–1, 656.   [35] Ibid. B. 13/123, 128.

daughters of a respectable London tradesman. Even more surprising is that the mother of the sisters was constantly inviting their suitors and young male friends to stay for the night; odder still was that the guests were put in a bedroom on the isolated top floor adjacent to that of the sisters; and strangest of all was that, after a period when the girls were locked into their bedroom all night, access between the two bedrooms was deliberately made easy, so that the guests were positively encouraged to bundle with the girls. What made things so difficult for young girls in the period 1680 to 1720 is that the moral codes of the Puritan ethic regarding pre-marital sexuality were breaking down, resulting by 1750 in a massive increase of pre-marital conceptions and bastards. The inherited practice of bundling as a recognized courtship procedure would only work if strict moral codes prevented impregnation. At the same time, the number and ruthlessness of male predators in the London marriage market, who were only looking for money or sex, seems to have been increasing. The world described on the stage by Otway, Shadwell, and Vanbrugh, reflected a reality of which Sir John Sedley was a classic example.

The evidence in this case allows us to find out exactly what happened during these all-night bundling sessions. A clear code of conduct was supposed to apply. Men were allowed to lie on the beds of women, but not to get into bed with them without their permission. Once there, the men were allowed to fondle the women's breasts, and even their bellies, but not to touch their genitals. Much, if not all, of this activity took place in public, with sister, maid, and sometimes mother looking on, and occasionally in the same bed. This is not unusual for the period, and crops up in other cases. This group participation allowed a woman to expose herself in front of a man, for example by undressing to her smock and exposing her breasts, as Abigail did before several suitors, without running the risk of rape.

The story again illustrates the extreme importance of mothers in matters of courtship. The whole courtship and bundling procedure was stagemanaged by women, and the two fathers were kept entirely ignorant of what was going on until the very last minute. But they had the last word, since it was they who controlled the money.

When Abigail became pregnant, and the question of a formal marriage became critical, it was material considerations which immediately came to the fore. In the end the parental power over money exercised by the Lingard parents forced Jack to abandon Abigail to her fate, while the revelations about her many other flirtations provided him with ample justification for doing so. Even so, one witness, a maid, thought that Jack was 'a villain' to abandon her.[36] Abigail was the victim of a pre-marital sexual culture in transition between the austerity of the Puritan seventeenth century and the more tolerant attitudes of the eighteenth. But it was recklessly foolish encouragement from her mother, and a lack of common sense about knowing when to stop on her own part, which led to the pregnancy and so to her ruin. The family must have spent on the two lawsuits much of the money Mr Harris had vainly offered with Abigail.

[36] Ibid. D. 972: 659–60.

4
Moseley v. Collier, 1746–1747
Cross-class courtship in the Bath marriage market

In the spring of 1745 there arrived in Bath two middle-aged single persons, both anxious to find a mate in that great national marriage market.[1] The first to arrive was Arthur Collier, the 37-year-old son of an intellectually distinguished but financially unsuccessful metaphysician and clergyman of the same name.[2] Arthur earned a modest living as a civil lawyer in London at Doctors' Commons, where the ecclesiastical courts were located, and he came to Bath during the Easter vacation. The second was Elizabeth Moseley, the 36-year-old only daughter of Sir Oswald Moseley, 1st Bt., of Rolleston in Staffordshire. The Moseleys were not a particularly distinguished family, but they were ranked among the county elite, and their descendants in the late nineteenth century owned over 3,000 acres.[3] Elizabeth had two brothers, but both had long since left home and do not appear in this story. She accompanied to Bath her elderly and sickly parents, the baronet and his formidable wife, who came from an old Nottinghamshire family, the Thornhaughs.[4] Elizabeth Moseley was without a doubt in a much higher social and economic bracket than Arthur Collier, but both were of genteel birth and education and therefore could associate together in Bath without discomfort.

Arthur was clearly looking for a wife, or failing that an intrigue; and Elizabeth, who hated her mother, was desperate to get away from her aged and unlikeable parents and find a suitable husband before it was too late. She was 36, and within a few years would be too old to bear children. Arthur was lodged in a single bedchamber over the shop of a haberdasher, John Bowden, while the Moseleys lived in some grandeur with perhaps four to six servants at the house of an attorney.[5]

---

[1] LPCA, D. 453.   [2] *DNB*, s.n. Arthur Collier.

[3] In 1873 the Moseleys of Rolleston owned 3,700 acres with a rental income of £7,500 a year (J. Bateman, *The Great Landowners of England* (London, 1879), 315).

[4] For the Moseleys, see Sir Oswald Moseley, *Family Memoirs* (London, 1849); J. and J. B. Burke, *Extinct and Dormant Baronetcies of England* (London, 1838), s.n. Mosley.

[5] LPCA, D. 453: 49–51.

On account of their age and infirmity, the Moseley parents did not go out much, and Elizabeth was therefore left to circulate unchaperoned in the frenetic social whirl of Bath. Within a few days of her arrival she had met Arthur in the public rooms and on the public walks. He took to her at once, and invited her to a breakfast at Lycombe Spaw House a mile out of town, to which they walked together, in the company of other friends. A few days later, Elizabeth returned the hospitality by inviting Arthur to drop by one evening to make up a party at cards with her parents, herself, and three other guests, all old friends of the Moseleys.

The affair blossomed, and the couple began to meet privately, away from the crowds, either in the Abbey Church or walking together in the fields. Things moved so fast that on 24 April Arthur asked her 'if she liked him well enough to make him her husband', and she replied that she did. Arthur said he proposed to ask her father the baronet for her hand that very afternoon, but after initial acquiescence, Elizabeth suggested that this was something best done later on, by letter, to avoid 'public talk'. She therefore urged that it be deferred until he had gone back to work in London at the end of the month.[6]

April 30, which was Arthur's last day in Bath, was a busy one. Early in the morning he met Elizabeth in the Pump Room, took her across the ferry to Bathwick, and then spent three hours walking with her up to Clerkendown. They talked all the while of marriage and promised to be 'ever faithful and constant to each other at all events'. They also agreed to keep in touch by letter after Arthur had gone back to London, and at Elizabeth's instigation he arranged to send his letters for her addressed to his landlady Mrs Bowden, with a coded mark on them to indicate that they were intended for Elizabeth. Only in this way could they correspond privately, unknown to her parents.

That same evening, there was to be a ball in the public rooms, to which they were both going, and Arthur invited Elizabeth to have tea with him in his rooms beforehand. They returned to Bath by two in the afternoon, and at four Elizabeth came to his lodgings in a chaise. To preserve the proprieties, Arthur persuaded his landlady to sit with them as chaperone, and obtained the use of the dining-room from another lodger, to avoid having to invite Elizabeth into his bedroom. She left for the ball in her chaise at six, followed soon after on foot by Arthur. They stayed at the ball till nine in the evening, when Arthur led her home on foot, and they parted after more mutual promises of fidelity. At first

[6] Ibid. 52–65.

dawn he set out for London in the stage-coach. They were not due to meet again until mid-September.[7]

Throughout the next two weeks the lovers exchanged letters every few days. Elizabeth kept reiterating her love 'so long as I live', and told him that she was 'determined in my mind and shall from this time imagine myself entered into that state which I hope in God will be happy for us both'. 'Its impossible for anything to alter the steady resolution I have taken of being one day yours.' She kept him amused with stories of a disastrous trip taken by her and some women friends to Bristol, when the coachman got so drunk that they dared not let him drive them home, but also dared not take beds for the night in an inn for fear of contracting smallpox from the sheets.

On 13 May she told him that the fortune she expected from her father was £5,000, and an uncertain amount more from others, including her mother. What she failed to make clear, however, was that the £5,000 was not legally settled on her, but was dependent on the good will of her father.[8] This information should have been a warning to Arthur that he was moving in circles way above him, not only in status but also in money. But he seems to have missed its significance.

The same day he sent Elizabeth an undated letter to her father Sir Oswald, asking for her hand in marriage, leaving it to be presented by her when she thought the moment most fit. But her reply set the precedent for a pattern that was to be repeated again and again for the next eighteen months. She said she was afraid to show her father the letter lest he reject the proposal out of hand. But she was especially afraid of her mother, who she was sure would refuse to 'accept anything less than a Smithfield bargain', that is to say an arranged marriage for money.

So a decision was postponed indefinitely, and the sickly Moseley family made its painful way back to Rolleston in late May. Elizabeth managed to keep up an active secret correspondence with Arthur, by taking into her confidence an old Bath acquaintance Mrs Gripwell, and by gaining the loyalty and silence of her personal maid. In her letters, she continued to harp on the terrible risks of asking the permission of her parents, and especially of her mother, and finally made it clear that the £5,000 she expected from her father depended entirely on his good will, since there had been no strict settlement of the estate. In short, if her parents objected to the marriage, Arthur would have only his modest legal income to live on, and she would bring nothing at all. The financial

---

[7] Ibid. 67–88.   [8] Ibid. 89–96, 419–30.

obstacle to marriage between them at last became clear, even if Elizabeth continued to declare that 'I will never renounce you while I live'.[9]

The weekly correspondence continued all summer long, with Elizabeth asking Arthur for advice regarding books to improve her mind, but jibbing at his suggestion that she take notes on them. At his instigation, she read the first book of Milton's *Paradise Lost, The True Patriot*, and *The Fable of the Bees* by Arthur's late friend Bernard Mandeville. Meanwhile she occupied herself in concocting 'romantick' schemes by which they might be lodged in adjoining bedrooms in an inn at Birmingham or Gloucester en route again for Bath in September. Elizabeth remained convinced that it would be fatal to tell her mother about their plans, but expressed hopes that 'a winter may bring great alterations', meaning that there was reason to hope that the old lady might die.[10]

The couple did indeed meet at Gloucester as Elizabeth had planned, and with the complicity of the footman and her maid managed to get adjacent bedrooms, which allowed them to have a two-hour private talk in the morning. On arrival at Bath, the problem of keeping their connection secret from the gossip-mongers became acute. Elizabeth once tried to visit Arthur in his room over the haberdasher's shop, only to find the shop full of quality, including 'the tip top of all gossips...chattering and grinning like an ape'. In the end it turned out to be safer for Arthur to visit Elizabeth in her bedroom late at night, after her aged parents had retired to bed, being let in quietly by her maid or the footman, and for Elizabeth to visit Arthur in the mornings from eleven to one in his chambers—he had now rented a dining-room as well as a bedroom.

In very late September, the gossip-mongers in the goldfish bowl of Bath society at last began to get wind of the affair. Elizabeth's maid reported in agitation to Elizabeth that she had met a woman in a shop, who asked if her mistress was married, to which she replied: 'No, why do you ask?'. The woman said: 'A certain person is come down with that design. The affair began in the spring, and they have been seen to walk alone together in the fields several times. To be sure, the old people know nothing about it, or she his character. For as to his fortune, he is worse than nothing, and as to women, there is not a man in the world that loves a pretty girl in a corner more than he, and would marry anyone who has money.' The gossip concluded with dark references to 'how matters were between him and Bowden' (his landlady).[11]

The story naturally alarmed Elizabeth, for two reasons: she was upset

[9] Ibid. 104–27, 444–80.   [10] Ibid. 128–65, 484–511, 627.   [11] Ibid. 196–7.

by the accusations against Arthur's character, and afraid lest their connection might become public knowledge. She stuck firmly to her opinion
that if their relationship ever reached the ears of her parents 'I am ruined
forever'—a position she clung to until the end. She sincerely loved
Arthur, took great risks in keeping in touch with him, and genuinely
wished to marry him. But she was very doubtful whether she would be
able to stand up to the combined bullying of her father and mother if, as
she anticipated, they strongly opposed the match. She once admitted that
'I fear the violence of my mother's temper would make her insist upon
my making promises, which I never will. Till this time they have found
me all obedience'. Furthermore there is detectable a slight hint of
condescension showing through her always warm and affectionate letters.
He was her 'dear Dr Collier', but in more informal moments he became
'poor little man', 'little sir', 'the dear little man'—presumably all references to his diminutive stature.[12]

Finally, one may suspect that, having been brought up in the lap of
luxury, living in big houses, and waited on hand and foot by servants, she
was deep down determined not to lose her promised marriage portion of
£5,000, and be condemned to the constricted life of the wife of a not very
successful lawyer without either capital or a private income. She told
Arthur uncertainly: 'I own I long for the time you are to speak [to Sir
Oswald], and dread it. They can't alter the steady resolutions I have
taken, but their approbation would make my happiness complete.' Since
she always made it clear she had no affection for either of her parents, the
thing that would complete her happiness was clearly not their approbation but her £5,000 portion.

What worried her was the not unreasonable fear lest she be cut off
by her parents without a farthing, and then left penniless in the world
if Arthur should die suddenly or change his mind about marrying her.
She declared: 'Was I independant [financially] I would as soon choose
to-morrow as to put it off any longer. As that is not the case, and everything in this world is very uncertain, what must become of me if
anything should happen to you?' On the other hand, she kept telling
herself and Arthur that 'I thank God neither my temper nor my
education incline me to set my heart on the trifling vanities of the age'.
'Honour and riches I give you my word I don't regard, where virtue is
wanting.' On another occasion she wrote that she was pleased to hear that
his brother had had a stroke of good fortune, but sorry it was not his:
'not that it would in the least add to the affection I bear you or the want

<hr />

[12] Ibid. 116, 119, 319, 328, 490, 516, 534.

of fortune make me love you less. You know very well all the merit in the world signify nothing with the old people if there be not what they call the one thing needful.'

She reported an inauspicious conversation with her mother on the subject of marriage, in which the latter said 'many bitter things on the folly of our own sex, and made it plain that the jointure was the thing only could make people happy'. When Elizabeth ventured mildly to disagree, 'the old lady gave me a look that struck me dumb'. She concluded that if her parents ever suspected anything of the affair with Arthur, 'they would leave me a farthing'.[13]

All these warning flags run up by Elizabeth would have been visible to anyone less deeply in love and with a more sensitive ear for what was being said to him than was Arthur. But he possessed a straightforward legalistic mind, had rather unworldly opinions about money, no doubt inherited from his father, and was curiously oblivious to the social distance between the middle-class professional Colliers and the elitist landed Moseleys. The latter might mix socially with Arthur on the neutral ground of Bath, but they never invited him to visit their country seat at Rolleston, and their daughter rightly anticipated their outraged reaction to any suggestion of marriage between them.

So the affair was secretly resumed again through September and October 1745 in Bath, Arthur pressing Elizabeth for a confrontation with her father, and she obstinately resisting and postponing. He left Bath to return to his work in London in late October, leaving behind the Moseleys, who had decided to stay in Bath for the winter. Elizabeth warned Arthur not to return to Bath before Christmas, since otherwise 'it will set the tongues of idle people a going'. So Arthur postponed his return to Bath until 10 January 1746. Ten days later, according to him, they made a verbal contract of marriage, without witnesses 'to take, acknowledge and behave towards each other as man and wife'. Four days later Arthur left for London, swearing to inform her father on his next visit.[14]

This issue of whether or not to tell her parents continued to play a prominent role in their correspondence during the early months of 1746, he insisting upon it and she arguing that 'nothing but misery can follow'. Arthur was back in Bath by the middle of April, and this time stayed until June, the lovers resuming their routine of daily meetings in his room during the day from eleven to one, and at night from seven to

---

[13] Ibid. 108, 109, 263, 307, 311, 319, 328.   [14] Ibid. 203–55.

twelve. Once he had conceded that they were now 'husband and wife', he was willing to postpone the interview with her parents, she relaxed, and their love affair proceeded smoothly. It seems almost certain that they were now sleeping together.

To prepare the way for the prospective interview, Arthur did his best to cultivate the friendship of the baronet and his wife. There was a scare in late April when Elizabeth reported that, according to her friend Mrs Gripwell, 'our affair is now become so public, and everybody talks of it so openly, that she was surprised my father had not heard of it'. Mrs Gripwell added that 'she believed it would be in the papers soon', the Bath newspapers being full of sexual gossip and innuendo. But the scare blew over for the time being.[15]

Arthur planned to come back to Bath in September and finally have it out with Sir Oswald, but Elizabeth begged him to do no such thing, warning him that it would be hopeless and would merely destroy the relationship. She added that 'everybody in this place looks on me as married', which raised the question of how long the Moseley parents would be the only people in Bath not to know about it. Arthur did not come until 1 October, but this time he was determined to regularize the relationship once and for all. Elizabeth told him to come to the Moseleys' house the night after his arrival at nine, after her parents had gone to bed. He knocked gently on the front door, and was let in by Elizabeth's maid, who led him to her mistress's bedroom, where he stayed till one in the morning.

During these four hours they had a big quarrel about what to do next. Arthur said he would not be 'vexed and teased any more' about her fears of telling her father, and said he would definitely do it the very next day. Elizabeth begged him not to, 'for if you do I am ruined'. He raised the stakes by saying that the only way for her to stop him was by marrying him in church that morning. She replied she would do it if he insisted, but suggested that a written marriage contract, properly drawn up by an ecclesiastical lawyer like himself would serve the same purpose and avoid the inevitable publicity of a marriage in a church. He agreed to her proposal, and on 4 October drew one up in his own name on stamped paper, signed it, and sent it to her, with a blank sheet of stamped paper for her to copy it out, substituting her own name and signature. It looked as if he had finally coaxed a legally binding marriage contract out of her, although still without her father's consent.

Two days later disaster struck. At ten in the morning, Sir Oswald's

15 Ibid. 256–303.

steward and upper servant came to Arthur's lodgings with a verbal message. The effect was that Sir Oswald knew of the relationship, and 'took it very ill of him that he should carry on an affair of that nature with his daughter without acquainting him'. The servant also brought a message from Elizabeth that the marriage 'would be very inconvenient to them both', that 'her father would never be brought to consent', and asking Arthur 'to think no more about her'. When asked, the servant volunteered the information that Sir Oswald was in a towering rage with Elizabeth and that the latter was 'crying bitterly'. Arthur told the servant that he would reply either in writing or in person to defend himself from the charge of having acted dishonourably.[16]

Arthur spent the day drafting a long, dignified, and fairly convincing defence of his behaviour, explaining that the failure to consult Sir Oswald was entirely the fault of Elizabeth and not himself; he pointed out that he could not be accused of having any 'mercenary view', since Elizabeth was entirely dependent on Sir Oswald's good will for her marriage portion, and that he had never concealed from her his modest financial circumstances. He declared himself to be born and bred a gentleman and therefore socially worthy of her hand. He pointed out that long correspondence and conversation and the exchange of solemn and sure engagements could not be broken by a mere verbal message sent through a servant. He therefore demanded a personal interview with Elizabeth to find out her real wishes, for he suspected her rejection of him arose from 'some sudden terror and apprehension of mind and not from the real purpose of her heart'.[17]

He sent this long and carefully worded letter to Sir Oswald by a messenger, who promptly returned with it unopened, saying that the baronet had refused to receive it. Arthur then wrote a covering letter to Elizabeth, enclosing the letter to her father, and personally pushed it under the front door of the Moseley lodgings. It asked her whether she would put her integrity before her interest, and suggested that if her father proved inexorable, she should 'immediately come away to me, who will pledge you all the sanction the church and the law can give, and if that will satisfy you (though you may not have the most opulent) yet will assure you the most faithful and affectionate husband'. Arthur had—too late —realized at last the dilemma Elizabeth had always been facing, torn between her love of him and her fear of losing her £5,000 portion. If forced to choose, what would she do? This was something Arthur was never given a chance to find out, for within half an hour his letter to her

<hr>

[16] Ibid. 356–65.   [17] Ibid. 367–78.

was returned unopened, and he was never allowed to set eyes on her again.[18]

Arthur took the only course left open to him: he sued Elizabeth in the London Consistory Court for restitution of conjugal rights. He argued that they had had a long and intimate courtship, with repeated pledges of fidelity by her, as shown by the 59 letters of hers he produced in court. He claimed that she was prevented from following her natural inclinations by the 'threats and menaces' of her parents; he argued that they were formally contracted as 'lawful husband and wife'; and he asked that the court order Elizabeth to solemnize the marriage in church.

The trouble was that Arthur did not possess Elizabeth's signed contract, nor even his own (of which he had only a copy), and could produce no witnesses to prove their earlier verbal engagement. Nor did he have a single letter from Elizabeth which called him 'husband' or herself 'wife'. He nevertheless won his case in the lower court, no doubt thanks to his professional connections.

But the Moseleys appealed the sentence to the Court of Arches, where Elizabeth's proctor flatly denied that there had been any contract, although he admitted that Arthur had frequently suggested that he meet with her father to ask his consent to a marriage between them. He stated that he was unable to produce Arthur's signed contract, since Elizabeth had thrown it at once into the fire! Finally he declared that her refusal to correspond further with him 'proceeded entirely from her own voluntary inclination'. For lack of any proof of a contract, except the copy of that of Arthur to Elizabeth, and despite the 59 affectionate letters protesting eternal fidelity, the Court of Arches upheld the appeal, which under existing precedents was certainly the correct verdict.[19]

It will never be known whether Elizabeth would have signed the written contract, or even whether it was she who leaked the secret in order to avoid having to do so. The fact that the Moseleys refused to let her set eyes on Arthur again suggests that they were fearful that she might change her mind once more and throw in her lot with his. At all events, they gave her no such opportunity: they removed her to their country seat in Staffordshire, and quickly married her off very suitably, no doubt with the £5,000 portion she had been so reluctant to be parted from, to the heir of another ancient and wealthy local family, Humphrey Trafford of Trafford. Given her age, it was naturally a childless marriage. Since both Elizabeth's brothers failed to marry, the direct line of the Moseleys ran out, and all the estates and money so carefully hoarded by Sir Oswald

---

[18] Ibid. 378–91. [19] Ibid. Ee. 10, fo. 91; B. 17/178.

and his wife passed to a distant cousin. It is a melancholy story of the barren rewards of greed and heartlessness.

It is sometimes argued that the conflict of love versus 'interest' which loomed so large in the writings of eighteenth-century novelists, dramatists, and pamphleteers, is a false and exaggerated dichotomy. It is also sometimes argued that the strict settlement, which provided fixed portions on children yet unborn, out of the control of the parents, did not make much difference to people's lives. But this story should effectively dispose of both these revisionist myths. Here is a vivid example of a woman torn between love for a man of relatively humble means, and a desire to continue to live the life of ease and plenty to which she was accustomed. If the Moseley family had only executed a strict settlement, she could have had her cake and eaten it, that is married Arthur Collier and brought her £5,000 marriage portion with her, regardless of whether or not her parents approved the match. There is great poignancy in her lament: 'if I were independant'.

The story throws a dazzling light upon the peculiar advantages and disadvantages of Bath as a marriage market and as a place of intrigue. Here it was possible for members of both sexes to mingle easily in the public rooms, the extensive public walks, and even in the fields which pressed up against the city on all sides. Elizabeth had a freedom in Bath that she could not possibly have enjoyed in the country seat at Rolleston. On the other hand, since the town was full of the quality, with nothing to do all day but gossip, intrigue, and play cards, it was extremely difficult to carry on an affair without it becoming common knowledge. The public rooms and parades were filled with people, and there were always sharp eyes to observe a couple walking together in the fields or along the river. As a result gossip soon began to circulate about them, and there was a serious risk of a malicious item appearing in a newspaper gossip column. Thus Bath offered special opportunities for a love affair, but also special risks of publicity.

5
Brace v. Cudworth, 1680–1682
A written contract

Mary Cudworth was the daughter of the well-to-do Rector of Kinwarton in Warwickshire.[1] In 1680–2 she lived much as she pleased, sometimes at her father's rectory at Kinwarton, and sometimes in lodgings in the nearby little town of Alcester. It was there that she kept all her personal estate, presumably a legacy of her deceased mother, including a considerable sum of money in cash. This was to be her marriage portion, and was entirely under her own control, and not that of her male relatives. She thus enjoyed a freedom of choice denied to most young women of her estate and time. And yet, as we shall see, that freedom had its limits, for she was still exposed to considerable psychological pressure from her 'friends', especially from her father and brothers.

Her first provisional choice of a suitor was a Mr Robert Harbach, the son of a yeoman farmer from a nearby village. In about November 1680 she sent a message to Robert and his father to meet her at an inn at the town of Evesham to discuss marriage. The following dialogue was alleged by the Harbachs to have taken place:

MR HARBACH SENIOR. I understand you have a kindness and love for my son Robert. I think it is fitter for you to be married to a gentleman.

MARY CUDWORTH. I will not be married to a gentleman, for gentlemen usually live extravagant, damning [sic] and sinking, and when they die leave their wives in poor conditions.

MR HARBACH. If you do not like a gentleman, what say you to a tradesman?

MARY CUDWORTH. I will not have a tradesman, for if I should, my fortune will be put into his trade, and when he dies, his creditors may turn me out of all.

MR HARBACH. Why, then, if you do not like a gentleman nor a tradesman, what think you of a clergyman, you being a clergyman's daughter yourself?

MARY CUDWORTH. I will not have a clergyman, for they usually have nothing but their parsonages to live upon, and when they die leave their wives in mean conditions. My desire is to be married to an honest plain country-man, who

---

[1] HWRO, Worcester CC Records, G 795.02 B.A. 2273/1–3; 2102/Box 14 (i); 3202/7347–8.

78

has an estate of his own, or [is] in a probability of having an estate, and one whose house stands by itself.

MR HARBACH. Mistress Mary, if you should have a countryman, you cannot away with such coarse diet as we in the country eat.

MARY CUDWORTH. But I can, and will eat pudding without salt, and brown bread, and do delight to eat such victuals as they have in the country.

From this dialogue, Mr Harbach concluded that Mary really wanted his son, whose condition and prospects exactly fitted her prescription. He therefore told her: ' "I wish my son Robert and you all happiness together", and then seeing his son and Mary in a very loving position together, he went forth of the room and left them together for three, two, or at least one hour.' When he returned 'he did bestow a very good treat [a feast] upon Mary at his own proper cost and charges.'

It is hard to know what to make of this piece of dialogue, which sounds suspiciously like a rehash of traditional folk wisdom, perhaps with some classical roots, rather than a real exchange. If the dialogue really occurred, Mary is revealed as a very calculating and money-minded young lady, which is not at all the way she appears later on.

On the other hand, there is no doubt that some such meeting took place. Mary admitted that it occurred and that she spent three hours drinking small beer in the Harbachs' company. What is most remarkable about the episode is that although Robert was accompanied by his father, Mary negotiated alone, without either her father or her brother. This is a sign of the independence she enjoyed because of her control over the personal property that made up her marriage portion.

However by November 1681, a year after the meeting with the Harbachs at Evesham, Mary had fallen head-over-heels in love with John Brace, the son of the Rector of Doverdale, close by in Worcestershire. Mary was a very businesslike and well-educated young woman, and as the daughter of a Rector she clearly knew her canon law. On 8 November she drew up a written marriage contract, with all the right wording in the present tense, properly witnessed, and duly signed and sealed. It read as follows:

I, Mary Cudworth...do hereby declare that from a faithful resolution and great affection, I have and ever do take Mr John Brace...to be my wedded husband, to have and to hold, for better or for worse, to love, cherish and obey according to God's holy ordinance, and thereto plight thee my troth never to marry or be a wife to any other person. This I do with my own great desire and free consent, as appears under my own hand and seal...written by me Mary Cudworth. And in the aforesaid contract in confirmation thereof, I do also declare that I give to my husband Mr John Brace, all my money and goods: £200 in a red trunk; and three chests, a fair large box and a large black trunk and all that is in them; a new bed and all belonging to it; a new dressing table with a drawer and all things belonging to it, being at Mr Ryland's house in care and custody at Alcester.

> In witness hereof, I put my hand and seal,
> Mary Cudworth, sealed and delivered in the
> presence of John Croley, his mark.

This remarkable document not only irrevocably committed Mary in marriage to John, but also surrendered to him all her marriage portion, and yet he neither signed a similar contract with her, nor offered her any jointure in return, which indeed he was not in a position to do, since he was still dependent on his father. Mary had thus committed herself to John, without him committing himself to her. To make things even more legally binding she later executed a deed conveying all her goods and chattels to John, under a bond of forfeiture for non-execution of at least £1,300. She was now entirely in John's power, since she had surrendered to him her marriage portion, without which she would be unable to contract another marriage, if she changed her mind and wanted to do so.

There can be little doubt that the marriage contract and this transfer of all her property were made in order to protect both her and it from forcible seizure by her father and brothers. Five months later, in March 1682 Mary wrote John an affectionate letter telling him to visit her at Kinwarton, so that she could inform him 'where her money and goods were, that so he might not be juggled out of them in case she should die'.

Soon after she wrote the letter, her father and brothers urged her to marry a well-to-do and prominent clergyman enjoying a rich living, a proposal she resolutely refused, much to their disgust. To give herself even more protection from the growing family pressure against marriage with John Brace, Mary showed her contract with him to several persons in the city of Worcester, one of whom strongly advised her to get a similar document from John. This she did, but although the document was signed it was neither dated nor witnessed, which demonstrates that it was not drawn up at the same time as hers. It also meant that its legal status was moot. Mary told all her friends that John was 'the only man I love in the world', and in July she was still writing to him as 'my husband before God'.

As she feared, throughout the summer of 1682 her father and brothers kept putting more and more pressure on her not to marry John Brace, whom they accused of being extravagant and unreliable, but rather to marry Robert Harbach. By late July Mary was desperate, and tried to save herself from her relatives by carrying out a clandestine marriage with John. She arranged to meet him early one morning at an inn three miles out of Alcester, where a local curate, Mr Shelton, had promised to meet them and marry them. But although they waited all day, the curate never turned up. So that evening they went to his house, where they spent the night trying to persuade him to marry them. He explained that he was afraid to do it for fear of the anger of Mary's brothers, but eventually he promised to marry them on the following Thursday at an inn in Worcester.

Meanwhile Mary did her best to postpone the proposed marriage with Robert Harbach, on the unconvincing plea that she had no horse. She also haggled over the details of the marriage contract with Robert, tearing up the first draft and demanding a clause giving her sole disposal of her personal clothes and goods and £100 of her portion if she should die before him. The Harbachs agreed, and in return old Mr Harbach settled on her a jointure of £40 a year for her widowhood.

On 1 August a marriage licence was procured, and Mary was taken to church, riding behind Robert Harbach on his horse. It was a very private wedding, attended by none of the relatives of either family except one of Mary's brothers. Even inside the church Mary later claimed that she protested that she was already pre-contracted to John Brace. But it was no good, and the marriage service took place, conducted by the same curate whom Mary had tried a few weeks before to persuade to marry her to John Brace. But she never claimed that she did anything but make the correct responses during the marriage service. She seems to have been either thoroughly cowed or thoroughly confused.

After the service, the small party returned to the Harbach's house— not the Cudworths—for the marriage feast and ritual bedding. Mary gave the curate Mr Shelton a guinea, not (according to her), out of gratitude for what he had just done, but because she had promised it to him a week before if he would carry out the abortive clandestine marriage to John Brace. After dinner a female servant of Robert Harbach senior took Mary upstairs, undressed her, and put her to bed. Soon after, her new husband, Robert Harbach, came up and got into bed beside her. While they were there Robert's sister came into the room and sat for a while talking to Mary, presumably trying to soothe her and persuade her to go through with the consummation. But after a quarter of an hour, Mary burst into tears, jumped out of bed, and ran downstairs, where she obstinately remained for the rest of the night.

Early next morning Mary left the Harbachs' house for good with the marriage still unconsummated, and a month later John Brace launched a collusive suit against Mary claiming a prior marriage contract with her, which invalidated her church marriage with Robert Harbach. Thanks to the careful wording of the contract, the fact that it was duly witnessed, and had been shown by Mary to several respectable citizens, the issue could hardly be in doubt, and the court gave its verdict that the contract marriage with John Brace was legally binding. The Harbachs did not appeal the verdict, so Mary was presumably finally united with John Brace. This is one of the rare occasions when the story of a marriage contract has a happy ending.

Or did it? What happened to Mary's goods and marriage portion is not at all clear. In view of her contract, indenture and bond giving it all to John Brace, it is difficult to see what the Harbachs had to gain in return for the £40 per annum jointure they had settled upon her. Their story is that in fact Mary deposited most of her portion in their hands before the marriage took place. If this is true, John Brace would have had to sue the Harbachs in the secular courts to recover it. If he lost, which was possible, Mary's bond of forfeiture of £1,300 would not have done him any good, since she was now his wife and all her worldly goods were therefore his anyway.

From the legal point of view, the main interest of the story is the degree of independence conferred on Mary by control of her own marriage portion, and her skill in drafting an ironclad marriage contract, which even the ecclesiastical courts were obliged to honour, something which by 1720 they were hardly ever willing to do.

From the psychological point of view, the story shows in an acute form the clash between individualism and freedom of choice of a spouse on the one hand, and deference to kin and conformity to the principle of patriarchy on the other. Mary twisted and turned, uncertain up to the last minute whether she ought to follow her instincts and choose her own marriage partner or follow the advice of her family.

B. FORCED MARRIAGE

(a) Forced Marriage by the Parish

Introduction

In 1597, Parliament first instituted a nation-wide system of poor relief by which each parish was ordered to raise money by taxation of property-owners in order to pay for those indigents who were 'settled' within the parish. Settlement could be acquired by either birth or residence, which opened the way to ambiguity, and to disputes between parishes, which were settled by the JPs. The parish officers responsible, the overseers of the poor and the churchwardens, were naturally extremely concerned to keep the costs down. They were therefore particularly anxious to prevent any poor unmarried woman from giving birth in the parish, or if she did to make her identify the father. Their purpose was to force the latter either to marry the girl, or else to provide bonds from sureties that he would pay for the maintenance of the child until it reached the age of 7, or died, whichever came first. Whenever a poor unmarried woman in the village was found to be pregnant, there was therefore a flurry of activity by the parish officers.

Up to the late seventeenth century this financial concern of the parish officers had been accompanied by strong moral disapproval of fornication as a sin, which was punished by the church courts. Those found guilty there were sentenced to the humiliating shame punishment of confessing the sin in the parish church on a Sunday in service time before the full congregation, while carrying a candle and clad only in a white sheet. Before about 1680, the JPs displayed the same concern for moral order, sentencing fornicators of both sexes to whipping or the stocks.

Between 1690 and 1750, however, the church courts largely, but not completely, ceased to impose shame punishments, and the JPs became interested in suppressing sexual deviance only if it cost money. Pregnant unmarried women and the men who had got them with child were therefore still energetically pursued by the parish officers and the JPs, whose concern was now exclusively money not morals. Many JPs routinely offered the alleged father of the unborn child the choice between

83

marriage or gaol. Their object was to pass the financial burden of maintaining the child on to someone other than the parish, preferably an alleged father who had settlement in another parish. Sometimes, however, the real father tried to cover his shame by putting the blame on someone else, or even offered a bribe to a poor man to marry the pregnant girl. If the latter had settlement elsewhere, this was likely to lead to litigation between the parishes. Sometimes the mother was induced falsely to father the child on a rich member of the village, thinking to improve its financial prospects, an act of duplicity which was very hard to disprove. A series of lawsuits, all confined to the period 1690–1730, illustrates how these ethical and financial conflicts worked themselves out at a time of growing financial pressures on the parish.

6

Preston v. *Matthews, 1695*

In Warwickshire in 1695 an attempt was made by a pregnant unmarried mother and the father of her child, with the active complicity of the parish officers and the local JP, to transfer financial responsibility for it to an innocent man from another parish. Throughout the year from Michaelmas 1693 to Michaelmas 1694, Farmer Hibbert of Salford in Warwickshire had employed at least two living-in servants, one maid-servant Mary Matthews, and one male agricultural labourer, Richard Preston.[1] At Michaelmas 1694 Richard's annual contract expired and he moved to another employer at the nearby village of South Littleton in Worcestershire, where again he worked as a living-in agricultural labourer. As such he received board and lodging, perhaps some clothing, but very little as an annual money wage.

Some time in January 1695, Richard was astonished to receive a verbal message from his former fellow-servant Mary Matthews, telling him that 'she was with child and would have him take some care about it'. He immediately went to his parents, explained the situation, and declared his total innocence of any sexual relations with Mary. Soon afterwards the Salford parish officials came to Richard and urged him to marry Mary, which he absolutely refused to do. He therefore found himself summoned by a warrant to appear before a JP on a paternity charge brought by the churchwardens and the overseer of the poor of the parish of Salford.

On 8 February 1695 the case was heard before Sergeant Rawlins, JP. On the one side there were Mary, the Salford officials, and many other villagers; on the other were Richard, his parents, his brother, and his brother-in-law. Under examination (but not under oath) Mary declared Richard to be the father of her child, and Richard protested his innocence. Justice Rawlins—no doubt prompted behind the scenes by the Salford officials—refused the offers of sureties for bail from Richard's relatives, on the grounds that they were not worth £100.

To increase the pressure on Richard, Justice Rawlins told him that if he refused to marry Mary, 'he should be sent to a gaol and put into a dungeon where he should lie and rot and that he should never come out

---

[1] HWRO, CC Records, b 795.02 B.A. 2237/1; b 797.51 B.A. 2637.

of gaol or have liberty to work for his subsistance'. Since Richard still refused, and insisted on his innocence, Justice Rawlins made out an order to send him at once to gaol. The Salford officials prepared to take him off to prison, and he bade a sad farewell to his parents and brothers.

On the way to gaol, the Salford officials kept up the pressure, partly by renewed warnings about Richard rotting in a dungeon for life, and partly by suggesting that 'he might run away and leave her as soon as he had married her'. Their sole concern was to transfer the financial responsibility for the child away from the parish of Salford. That evening at nine, alone and cowed by all these threats and promises, Richard gave way and reluctantly consented to marry Mary. The Salford parson was promptly summoned, and a hasty clandestine marriage took place, in a private house not the church, without any banns or licence, after canonical hours, and with the groom under the threat of immediate gaol if he refused. The next day the triumphant officials of the village of Salford took Mary with them and handed her over to the officials of South Littleton, which because of her marriage was now her place of settlement. Salford had successfully got rid of responsibility for her and for the baby in her womb.

But the Salford officials had reckoned without the obstinacy of Richard and the moral qualms of Mary. Richard flatly refused to have anything whatever to do with his new wife, and neither slept with her nor lived in the same house with her. A fortnight after the marriage he consulted another JP, Sir Francis Russell, for he was now convinced that the whole affair, perhaps including Mary's initial accusation, was a plot concocted by the Salford authorities to shift on to others the financial responsibility for Mary and her child.

Richard now knew that Justice Rawlins's threats of leaving him to rot in a dungeon for life were all bluff. He made an official deposition of his story before Sir Francis, and no doubt on his advice made an affidavit to the same effect before a notary public and several witnesses on 26 February, just under three weeks after the marriage. By March he had started a suit against Mary in the Consistory Court at Worcester, in order to get the marriage annulled on the grounds that he had not been a free agent.

Meanwhile Mary had also been having second thoughts. Seven weeks after her marriage but before she gave birth, she confessed to some female friends that she had 'abused and wronged' Richard in accusing him of being the father, a statement she repeated under semi-official interrogation by the midwife during labour. The true father, she now said, was a man named Nicholas Harris of Salford, who had had intercourse with her three times, once in a barn and twice 'in a ground where pulse growed'.

What happened next is not known. The Worcester Consistory Court officials were so perplexed that they asked for technical advice from the Court of Arches in London. But the advice is not preserved, so we do not know whether or not the marriage was annulled. Although totally irregular, it was legally binding, except that the degree of coercion applied to Richard did appear to have been severe.

7
The Churchwardens of Hingham v. The Churchwardens of Snettisham, 1713

If the cost of maintaining the bastard children of the poor was a constant source of anxiety for parish officers in the early eighteenth century, so also was the maintenance of the mental defectives of the parish. This problem occurred less frequently, but it was likely to be of longer duration. One case, regarding the maintenance of a retarded woman and her bastard child, involved an attempt to solve both problems through a forced marriage.[1]

In the summer of 1713 there was living in the tiny hamlet of Snettisham in central Norfolk a mentally retarded young woman called Margaret Cooper, generally known as Peg. She was, it appears, capable of looking after herself, doing housework, minding children, and running errands, but not much else. She could not earn her own living and apparently had no relatives, so the parish was obliged to pay her 1s. 6d. a week for her support.

In the same village was 'a loose idle fellow', named Edward Buck, who had been born and grew up in the nearby parish of Hingham, and who worked as a servant and assistant to a thatcher on the usual one-year contract. He had generally a bad reputation in the village, especially where women were concerned. The seventh of July 1713 was a day of public festivities to celebrate the signing of the Treaty of Utrecht, which at last put an end to the interminable wars with France. Mary Lacy, 'a poor foolish wench, was overtaken with drink that day', and lay down under a hedge in a pasture in the nearby village of Larling to sleep it off, 'with her clothes turned up above her knees'. She was found in this exposed position by Edward Buck, who seized his chance and tried to rape her. But he was interrupted and dragged off by the owner of the pasture, who happened to be going by.

Later that month a farm-worker who lived in the house where both Buck and Peg Cooper lodged went up to the former's chamber after dinner at about 12.30 in the afternoon. There he found Peg 'lying flat on

[1] Norfolk CRO, CC Records, Con/45, 59, 62; Dep/56, fos. 253–67.

her back upon the bed with her petticoats up to her middle and Edward Buck upon his knees by her with his breeches down'. Under questioning, Peg said that he 'had put a long thing into her', and that he had done the same two weeks before. Immediately after the discovery, Buck leapt to his feet and ran away, thereby breaking his contract with his master the thatcher.

After looking for Buck in vain for two or three days, the thatcher got a warrant from a JP to warn all parish constables in the vicinity to be on the look-out for him, and to arrest him for deserting his service before his time had expired. On 29 December he at last discovered that Buck was working as an itinerant chimney-sweep. He personally arrested him, and handed him over to the Snettisham constable to be kept in custody overnight, before being taken before a JP the next morning.

In the mean time, Peg had several times said that she was pregnant, although there was no clear evidence that she knew what the word meant or, if she did, that she was telling the truth. But the rumour was enough to alarm the churchwardens and overseer of the poor of the village, who now feared that they would have to assume the cost of upkeep of Peg's baby as well as that of its mentally defective mother. Overnight, under the leadership of Parson Neech, who had been vicar of the parish for forty years, they hatched a plot to rid themselves once and for all of this burden on the parish poor-rate.

The next morning, 30 December, Buck was brought before Justice Harvey to be punished for running away from his master the thatcher. But the parish officers led by Parson Neech also turned up with a second charge of fathering the child of Peg Cooper—a fact which Edward could hardly deny. He was told that he had three options: he could find sureties for payment of maintenance for Peg and her child; he could marry her and thereby become legally liable to support her and her child; or he would be sent to gaol. When Buck asked for time to send to his home village of Hingham some miles away to see what they would do for him, he was told that there was no messenger available. He admitted he could not provide sureties, and so was faced with the option of marriage or gaol. Alone and penniless, without friends or money, and under heavy pressure from Parson Neech and the parish officers, Edward soon caved in and agreed to marry Peg. His only stipulation was that he should have some respectable clothes for the occasion, instead of the sooty rags of a chimney-sweep which he was wearing, and that he should be given a little money. His master promised some old clothes, and the agreement to marry was ratified before the justice.

Everything had evidently been carefully prepared. Parson Neech was too crafty to run the risk of marrying them clandestinely himself, or to let it be done in the parish church of Snettisham. So Buck was promptly hurried off to New Buckingham, a village a few miles away, where a minister—probably the curate—was waiting to marry them, although he had neither read the banns nor obtained a licence. The ceremony went off satisfactorily, although Peg had to be prompted in her responses now and then. Thus when asked her name, she replied 'Peg', which Parson Neech translated as Margaret.

After the wedding, Peg was taken back alone to the local alehouse, while Buck was hurried off a few miles to go before two JPs, one of whom was the influential Sir Edward Bacon, to determine his legal place of settlement. This was agreed to be Buck's birthplace of Hingham, so a warrant was made out and signed by the JPs, ordering the removal thither of Edward and his new wife. Buck and his captors then returned to the alehouse at New Buckingham, where the Snettisham officials treated the bride and groom to a dinner, before being publicly put to bed in the usual manner. The only memorable incident was that 'some idle young people falling upon the bed and upon his wife, he [Buck] fell into a great passion and said "What do ye mean to do? Consider the condition my wife is in."' He at least was convinced that Peg was pregnant.

Early the next morning the overseer of the poor of Snettisham woke up Buck and Peg and took them off to Hingham, after first paying Buck 2s. 6d. which was due to Peg as her last allowance from Snettisham. When the party got to Hingham, they dumped Edward and his pregnant retarded wife on the authorities there, showed them the settlement order signed by the two JPs and the certificate of marriage, and returned home in triumph.

Not unnaturally, the authorities of Hingham were outraged by this trick played on them by the hamlet of Snettisham, and within a couple of months had started litigation in the Norwich Consistory Court. The two churchwardens and the overseer of the poor of Hingham, along with Edward Buck, sued Parson Neech and the churchwardens and the Overseer of Snettisham, along with Margaret Cooper. The object of the suit was to obtain a nullity of the marriage on the double grounds of coercion and idiocy. They claimed first that Edward had acted under duress by having been offered the choice of marriage or gaol and had been given no opportunity to look for sureties; and second that Margaret was so mentally deficient that she was unable to understand the meaning of marriage.

There is no doubt that Edward was pressured into consent, and also no doubt that Peg was mentally retarded. The clinching evidence of her incapacity came from a local parson who was asked by the Hingham authorities to examine her. He testified that she could not tell a half-crown piece from a half-penny piece, she could not count her fingers, and she could not tell the day of the week. He concluded that she was 'a very fool or idiot', incapable of understanding the meaning of marriage. Who won this battle is unknown, since the sentence book is defective, but the case for nullity sounds a strong one. It seems likely that Peg ended up back at Snettisham and that Buck went free. Parson Neech and his friends may have been been a little too clever.[2]

[2] An even more gruesome episode occurred in 1723—again in Norfolk—in which in order to get rid of her, an idiot female child was passed from parish to parish like a football—from St Mary's Norwich to Hingham, from Hingham to Guist, from Guist to Gunthorpe, and from Gunthorpe back again to Guist. The two last transfers were only accomplished by an illegal farce of a marriage of an under-age imbecile to a man whose sole object was to lay hands on a wife of some sort in order to claim settlement, and therefore poor relief, in another village. See Ibid. Con/45; Dep/58.

(b) FORCED MARRIAGE BY THE SEDUCER OR SUITOR

8

Houghton v. Cash, 1703

Not infrequently it was not the parish officers but the true father who took the initiative in trying to transfer the financial responsibility for a bastard child to another man. During the years 1702–3 a disputed paternity case put the little village of Winwick in south-west Lancashire in an uproar, caused a reversal of the judgment of the Petty Sessions on appeal to the Quarter Sessions, and led to two lawsuits in the ecclesiastical courts.[1] Ellen Greenhalgh was a poor young woman without any economic resources whatsoever, who worked as a menial domestic servant in the house of Mr James Cash, who was one of the 'better sort' of the village and held the office of constable. As so often happened, Cash, who was married and aged 42, pursued and finally seduced Ellen, who after a while became pregnant. In order to save both his reputation in the village and his money, Cash persuaded Ellen to attribute the paternity to Thomas Houghton, a young bachelor blacksmith down the road who was the son of another member of the village elite.

Cash therefore concocted a plausible-sounding story about how Thomas had frequently visited Ellen at his house and had courted her at night. He said 'they sat up several nights together as lovers...till twelve or one of the clock.' He claimed that he had suspected 'that Thomas had no real design to marry her but to debauch her, he being in condition or circumstances as to estate above her'. He clearly took it for granted that a reasonably prosperous blacksmith would never marry a penniless maidservant.

As proof of Thomas's responsibility for Ellen's pregnancy, Cash further claimed that at 5 a.m. on Shrove Tuesday 1702, he called to Ellen to get up, but found that she was not in her bedroom. Suspecting that she was at the smithy with Thomas Houghton, he went down there, knocked on the door in order to wake him up, told him of his suspicions,

---

[1] Chester CRO, CC Records, EDC 5/1793/3; 1704/7.

and by the authority of his office as parish constable threatened to break the door down if he did not open it.

Cash reported that he went in and found Ellen in Thomas's bed, dressed in nothing but her shift, though hastily trying to put on her petticoat. He said that Thomas was in great distress and begged him to say nothing. He promised to marry Ellen later, but explained that he could not do so at once, since he would lose his inheritance if his father got to hear of it. But Cash, 'considering that his father was a good neighbour and had a pretty estate to leave him and might justly take it ill of him if he did not acquaint him of the matter, and suffer his son to marry such a mean and low person, he told him the whole passages; and his father then said if he married her he should never have anything of his'.

According to his own self-serving story, Cash had behaved with impeccable propriety: as a householder careful of the welfare of his maid-servant, though tolerant of her habit of 'bundling' at night with a young man; as a constable zealous to detect fornication; and as a member of the 'better sort' of the village with an obligation to warn a father from the same social group of his son's secret intention to make a socially unsuitable marriage. On all counts, he appeared to be a model citizen.

Ellen confirmed Cash's story, and obtained from a JP a warrant against Thomas Houghton, whom she identified as the father of her unborn child. Cash's wife also abetted her husband, adding that in his virtuous indignation at Ellen's behaviour, he had sometimes refused to let her back into the house when she returned from a late-night assignation with Thomas. She also alleged that Thomas Houghton had at first said that 'if there is any faith or belief in any Christian, I will marry her', but later broke his promise.

In October 1702, exactly forty weeks after the episode in the blacksmith's shop, Ellen fell into labour, during which she again confessed to the midwife and female neighbours that Thomas Houghton was the father of her bastard child. After the birth she took a position with a 55-year-old 'badger' or itinerant corn-dealer, to nurse his child, 'putting her own child out to nurse' in order to save her milk.

In January 1703 her paternity case against Thomas Houghton came before the Petty Sessions at Wigan. When she left to give evidence, the badger urged her 'to father the child aright, to do justice, and tell the truth before God and the world and set the saddle on the right horse'. On oath before the court, Ellen again fathered the child on Houghton. Although the latter denied responsibility for the conception of the child, he admitted that he had lain with her once in his smithy—and the court consequently made out a maintenance order against him.

The JPs and most of the villagers were satisfied that justice had been done, and some even convinced themselves that the baby looked like Thomas Houghton. But there were a few who still suspected that James Cash might in fact have been the father, even though Ellen continued to swear that she 'knew not whether he was a man or woman'. When questioned by a maidservant who shared her bed at the badger's house, she still stuck to her story. The only evidence to the contrary was provided by a 73-year-old woman who was a near neighbour of the Cashes. She testified that before she became pregnant Ellen had often complained to her that her master James Cash 'was very often following or teasing her', so much so that she was resolved to leave his service.

Thomas Houghton appealed the decision of the Petty Sessions at Wigan to the full Quarter Sessions at Ormskirk, where he asked that both James Cash and Ellen be summoned, in order to be examined on oath. He put his case so strongly that the Justices ordered them both to appear at the next sessions. Meanwhile, the local JP began to have doubts. He called Ellen before him and pressed her very hard indeed 'not to incur the guilt of perjury, but to do justice to the two persons suspected as to the filiation of her child'. Ellen broke down, burst into tears, and blurted out: 'My child is my master's child.'

In an effort to get Ellen to recant this confession, James Cash took the risk of going to the house of a husbandman, summoning Ellen, and withdrawing with her into a dark bedroom. It so happened that the bedroom lay just beyond a room where the constables were at that moment meeting on business. Pushing through the crowd of village constables, the mistress of the house flung open the door of the bedroom, to find Cash and Ellen on the bed 'in a familiar loving manner, kissing and snuggling together'. After this episode, public opinion shifted and it was generally believed in the village that James Cash was in fact the father of Ellen's bastard.

At the next Quarter Sessions, Ellen seems to have recanted her confession, but the truth nevertheless came out. It was proved to the satisfaction of the Bench that the ascription of the paternity to Thomas Houghton was the result of an ingenious seduction plot planned by Cash and carried out by Ellen, either for love or money. As soon as she knew she was pregnant, Cash had arranged for her 'late one evening to go with his plow irons to Houghton's shop, and improve that occasion to draw Houghton into the snare; which taking effect according the design and contrivance he had formed, Cash earlier than usual next morning went directly to Houghton's shop and lodging, and there found Ellen in bed with him'. The assembled Justices dismissed the case against Houghton, who was clearly the victim of a conspiracy orchestrated by James Cash.

But Thomas Houghton had his revenge, not on the real villain, Cash, but on Ellen. The Quarter Sessions not only dismissed the case against him, but also ordered her to be whipped for perjury. Later he sued Ellen in the Consistory Court for defamation and bastardy, and had little trouble getting a conviction, since she was by now pregnant again by somebody else. She was sentenced to do public penance in church on a Sunday, dressed in a white sheet, a humiliating ceremony which he presumably attended with pleasure.

9
Hooper v. *Fazas*, 1690

Between 1675 and 1710 relations between the sexes seem to have been at their most brutal. A specialized sub-branch of the ruthless pursuit of rich wives for the sake of their money and not for their persons, was the abduction and marriage of well-to-do widows, sometimes with the help of drugs or alcohol.

One such case is that of Mrs Lucy Hooper.[1] In 1688 she was an energetic, attractive, and out-going middle-aged widow of a prosperous west London coach-maker. Her servant said she was 'of a generous and free spirit, and a good housekeeper'. After her husband's death some six years before, she had taken over the business with the help of an apprentice and was clearly doing well. As such she was a natural prey to the sexual-financial predators of London. Many suitors circled around her, but she rebuffed them all, declaring that she would never marry. She also continued to wear a 'habit of second mourning' to make it clear that she was only recently widowed.[2]

One of her suitors was a 52-year-old brewer, with £14,000, who eventually gave up; another was a young Frenchman, Jean-Jacques Fazas. He was the son of a large landowner near Guines in France, who as a Huguenot had been forced into exile by the Revocation of the Edict of Nantes in 1685, and had lost all his estates. Jean-Jacques claimed that his father had managed to get out of the country his personal property worth some £2,000 to £3,000; and that he had enjoyed 'a very genteel and liberal education' at Bordeaux. The first seems unlikely, since although his cousin confirmed the gentility of the family and the breadth of the estates in France, he said that Jean-Jacques himself was 'penniless'. By 1688 he was certainly down on his luck, having recently been discharged for neglect from his position as domestic tutor to the son of Sir Levinus Bennett. Sir Levinus did say, however, that Jean-Jacques had 'carried himself very civilly'.[3]

As a result of this set-back, in 1688 Jean-Jacques was looking around

[1] LPCA, D. 734.
[2] Ibid. E. 10/28; D. 734: 185; Eee. 7, fo. 235.
[3] Ibid. D. 734: 20–1; E. 10/15; Eee. 7, fos. 178, 228.

desperately for some way to retrieve his shattered fortunes, and his greatest hope seemed to lie in marriage with a rich woman. He first got to hear of Mrs Hooper when he was commissioned to act as the agent for the purchase of a chariot for a Huguenot relative of his named Madame Berty, who was engaged to marry a merchant in the City. He and Mrs Hooper agreed on a price of £80, and Jean-Jacques brought Madame Berty to inspect the chariot. But next time he came alone, explaining that the deal was off since the merchant had unexpectedly died, but offering to buy the chariot for himself instead. It later emerged that this was an excuse to allow him to cultivate the further acquaintance of Mrs Hooper, rather than a serious business proposition.[4]

Leisurely financial negotiations continued for some fifteen months, while Jean-Jacques pursued his courtship of the generous and hospitable Mrs Hooper. Jean-Jacques's story, which is highly suspect, was that Mrs Hooper was far more ambivalent in her attitude towards her ardent young suitor than she later admitted. He alleged she said: 'I know him to be a gentleman, and I verily believe he loves me.' She contrasted him favourably with her other suitors who had 'exposed her and laughed at her', whereas Jean-Jacques 'had a kindness for her'.[5] Fazas claimed to have visited her three or four times a week for months on end, to have given her rich gifts such as a gold watch worth £18, dozens of bottles of wine, many pounds of tea, and many barrels of oysters. He also claimed that he and Mrs Hooper 'used much dalliance together and much mutual delight, complacence and satisfaction with each other's company and society'.[6] There is little doubt that he kept coming to the house for months, but no evidence that Mrs Hooper had any intention of marrying him, as even he grudgingly admitted. The most he ever claimed was that she said 'whenever I marry it shall be to yourself'.

Mrs Hooper and her friends, however, told a different story, claiming that she said: 'I scorn him. He is a pitiful fellow and a Frenchman, and he durst not speak to me about any such thing.' A fairly objective witness revealed that Mrs Hooper liked him well enough, but had grave doubts about marriage: 'I think him a very good-humoured man, but all the world will blame me if I marry so young a man.'[7] As for the gifts, she admitted that once he gave her a quarter of a pound of tea, but insisted that this was the only one she accepted.[8] Later two barrels of oysters were

<hr />

[4] Ibid. Ee. 7, fos. 85–6; E. 10/30.
[5] Ibid. D. 734: 70–1; Eee. 7, fos. 172–4.
[6] Ibid. D. 734: 23, 30.
[7] Ibid. E. 10/27; Eee. 7, fos. 187–8, 200–1; D. 734: 22–31.
[8] Ibid. Ee. 7, fo. 86.

delivered at the house, closely followed by Jean-Jacques, who ate one barrel with Mrs Hooper, but the other went bad. Then one day a porter staggered into the house carrying a hamper of three or four dozen quart bottles of sherry, a gift from an unknown donor in the City. Mrs Hooper ordered the porter to remove the load at once, but he refused to do so, so the hamper stayed in the house. Three days later Fazas came by and confessed that the hamper was a present from him. Mrs Hooper ordered him to remove it at once, but it remained sitting in her hall. Later still Fazas sent her a watch, at which she was very angry, since she was clearly being manoeuvred into a courtship situation. She flatly refused to accept the watch, and told Fazas never to return to the house, and to send her a bill for the wine, which he did.[9]

Thereafter Mrs Hooper heard nothing more from Fazas until late August or early September 1690, when a messenger brought a letter from him, which she threw into the fire unopened. Soon afterwards he turned up in person, saying that he was now acting as agent for Lady Fairfax, who was about to leave for Scotland to join her husband and wanted to buy a second-hand calash. He looked at one in Mrs Hooper's shop, which was priced at £13, and went away to tell Lady Fairfax. Later he returned, saying that Lady Fairfax had postponed her trip to Scotland and now wanted a new coach, and that she would come and see Mrs Hooper in person shortly. Three days later he came back, saying that Lady Fairfax was confined to bed in her house, but would see her. He and Mrs Hooper walked together to St James's, went into a house, and were sent upstairs, where a gentlewoman told them that Lady Fairfax was asleep, but asked them to wait. Mrs Hooper waited with Fazas for an hour, then said she was busy and got up to go.

When she got downstairs she was met by another gentlewoman, who asked her to wait a little longer and showed her into a room with candles and a table laid for a meal. She was asked to sit down with the two gentlewomen and Fazas, the latter saying cheerfully: 'Come, let us eat. The lady shall have her coach more the cheaper for this.' Mrs Hooper said she was busy and tried to leave, but was asked by one of the gentlewomen to go into a room next door. She told Mrs Hooper: 'You can't but be sensible [that] this gentleman [Fazas] has a great love for you. Do not you say you love him?' Mrs Hooper replied indignantly that she did not nor ever would love him, protested that 'I find this to be a trick and an artifice', and tried to leave the room.

Fazas now came into the open, and said to her: 'This is a design I had

_____

[9] Ibid. Ee. 7, fos. 87–8.

upon you. You are or must be my wife. You must have nobody but I.' Mrs Hooper was 'highly provoked' by this impertinent claim, and retorted angrily: 'Are these your French tricks? They shall do you no good. I am sorry I have stayed so long in this house.' Tis time for me to be gone.' As she tried to leave, Jean-Jacques barred the way, saying: 'you shall stay with me this night. You are my wife.' Mrs Hooper replied: 'Open the door. I must and will be gone,' only to be told by one of the women that Fazas had locked the door and pocketed the key. Mrs Hooper rushed to the window, which opened out to the street, and threatened: 'I will break this glass and cry out "murder".' At this, Fazas gave way, unlocked the door, and Mrs Hooper escaped from the house and took a coach home. It was a narrow escape from rape, and one which makes it unthinkable that Mrs Hooper would ever again willingly have entrusted herself to the company of Fazas.

After this alarming episode in early September 1690, nothing happened until October, when there came into Mrs Hooper's shop a woman (whom she later got to know as Mrs Carpenter) who said she knew a lady who wanted to buy a new coach in a hurry, and offered to serve as inter-mediary. On 6 November, Mrs Hooper returned home after spending the morning consulting a lawyer about a Chancery suit, to find Mrs Carpenter waiting for her, with an invitation to come at once to see the lady about the coach. Mrs Hooper said she was busy, as she had arranged with her lawyer to come back that afternoon to make her answer to the bill against her. But she was finally persuaded by Mrs Carpenter to get into the coach with her to go to discuss the purchase of a new coach. They went to a house in Pall Mall where the lady lived. Mrs Carpenter introduced Mrs Hooper as 'a very good friend of mine whom I bring to discourse with you about making your coach'. The lady replied graciously: 'Oh, a friend of yours shall make it before anybody...in three or four days my husband will come to town and then bespeak a coach.'

Mrs Hooper was irritated to find that there was therefore no hurry about the business, but before she could leave she was invited to drink a dish of chocolate brought up by a footman in livery. Mrs Hooper tasted it and complained that it was too thick. The lady disagreed, and the foot-man refilled her cup and stirred the contents with a knife. The lady finally agreed that the chocolate stuck in her throat, and called for a glass of wine, of which they each drank one small glass. Very soon afterwards, Mrs Hooper began to feel giddy and dizzy, her vision became blurred, her speech slurred, and she could hardly stand. She still had just enough control of herself to say: 'Oh, what ails me. I'll go home. Let a coach be called.'

The lady advised her to lie down for a while, but Mrs Hooper insisted on going home, a coach was called, and she was helped downstairs and into it. The last thing she remembered before she lost consciousness and slumped in the bottom of the coach was to tell the coachman to drive her to her home at The White Lyon in Long Acre. It was now one o'clock in the afternoon and another thirteen hours were to go by before she recovered her senses. Mrs Hooper had been given a powerful soporific drug, probably in the chocolate.[10] Later investigations eventually revealed what had really happened, and what was to happen while Mrs Hooper was drugged.

By the summer of 1690, Fazas was desperate, and determined somehow or other to force a marriage with Mrs Hooper, with the assistance of a sinister figure called Captain George Hilton, 'a tall, thin-faced man with a dent in the middle of his nose and one blear eye', who was the master-mind of the whole conspiracy, being hired by Fazas for the purpose.[11]

The two 'gentlewomen' involved in the plot, 'Mrs Carpenter' and the lady negotiating to buy the coach, turned out to be sisters, Anne and Ursula Bennett, daughters of a Dublin schoolteacher who was a recipient of a charity from the Commissioners for the Relief of Irish Protestants.[12] They lodged together in Pall Mall, along with a parson called the Revd Moody. Anne Bennett had been on the stage in Dublin, had moved to Bristol, and had recently arrived in London in the company of a mountebank. By November 1690 she had shed the mountebank and was living with Captain Hilton and passing as Mrs Carpenter, or Mrs Hilton. Her sister Ursula seems to have been a high-class courtesan, who lived in style with a maid and a liveried footman. It was her apartment which was chosen as the place for the drugged marriage of Mrs Hooper.

On the morning of 6 November, while Mrs Hooper was consulting her lawyer about her Chancery suit, Fazas was at a writer's house, where he signed and sealed two bonds, which were given to Captain Hilton in payment for the proposed conspiracy to drug and then marry off Mrs Hooper. Fazas spent the rest of the morning until one o'clock in the house of the writer, waiting for Mrs Hooper to be lured to Ursula Bennett's lodgings and drugged.[13]

When we left Mrs Hooper, she was in a coach, having just had the energy to order the coachman to take her home before she passed out.

---

[10] Ibid. Ee. 7, fos. 88–90, 175, 181, 226, 231, 241; E. 10/30; D. 734: 13.
[11] Ibid. Eee. 7, fo. 222.   [12] Ibid. Eee. 7, fos. 274, 276.
[13] Ibid. Eee. 7, fos. 116, 271.

The coachman noticed that she was 'very much stupified and I could hardly understand what she said'. As soon as Mrs Hooper was fully insensible, Mrs Carpenter, who had got into the coach with her, countermanded Mrs Hooper's instructions, and told the coachman to drive to Knightsbridge instead. Soon after they set off, the coach was overtaken by another containing two men, one of whom was Captain Hilton. Both stopped, and messages were carried to and from the two coaches, while Mrs Hooper lay, according to the coachman, 'in a senseless manner in the bottom of the coach, not able to speak or help herself'. Finally Mrs Carpenter told the coachman to drive back to Ursula Bennett's lodgings in Pall Mall, which he did, being followed by second coach. When they reached Pall Mall, Captain Hilton from other coach and Mrs Carpenter together carried Mrs Hooper into entrance hall of the house 'and let her fall down within the door'. After a rest, they dragged Mrs Hooper up the stairs, paid off the coachman, and shut the front door.

So far the story is fully attested by the evidence of the drivers of the two coaches. What happened next has to be reconstructed from bits and pieces. As soon as they had got the body of Mrs Hooper into Ursula Bennett's apartment, the conspirators summoned the Revd Alexander Moody. He was a 37-year-old MA from Edinburgh, currently a clergyman at St Mary Le Bow. Since he later claimed to be an old suitor of Mrs Hooper, and admitted having met Captain Hilton before at a coffee-house, he was probably a participant in the plot. He certainly raised no objections when Fazas asked him to perform the marriage ceremony between him and the now more or less insensible Mrs Hooper. With the two Bennett sisters acting as witnesses, the Revd Moody married them according to the rites prescribed by the Prayer Book. No one ever claimed, however, that Mrs Hooper was sufficiently conscious to make the correct responses.[14]

The next step was to get the couple into bed and allow Fazas to consummate the marriage. According to him the following implausibly high-minded exchange took place about an hour after the marriage. Fazas said to Mrs Hooper—now Mrs Fazas—:

My dearest, now we are man and wife, and I will not part with you without bedding you, for I can't bed you at home at your house (every bedroom in [her] house being then full, and she having a young gentlewoman then her bedfellow)

In this predicament he turned to Ursula Bennett and said:

[14] Ibid. D. 734: 32–6, 46–7; Eee. 7, fos. 170, 176, 181.

Madam, since you have granted us the favour to be married in your lodging, I hope you will give me leave to perfect it and bed my wife there also, and I beg it of you.

To this, Ursula Bennett primly replied:

Sir, this is a thing I cannot grant, or I know not how to grant it, but I'll leave you here if you please and my man to wait on you.

So at about three in the afternoon Mrs Hooper was undressed and put into bed with Fazas, where they stayed until about six, during which time, according to the latter, the marriage was indeed consummated.[15]

Meanwhile, however, rescue was on the way. The coachman remembered the address Mrs Hooper had first given him and was convinced that she was the victim of some kind of foul play. As soon as he was paid, he therefore drove straight to Long Acre and informed the Hooper household of what he had seen.[16] A friend of Mrs Hooper, named Mrs Woodward, immediately took the coach and went back to the house in Pall Mall. There the maid admitted that Mrs Hooper had indeed been there, but asserted that she had recently left, 'very much in drink'. But Mrs Woodward noticed Mrs Hooper's pattens in the hall and so pushed her way into the house and refused to move, since she was sure that Mrs Hooper was still there. The servant then said that Mrs Hooper was there but asleep. Mrs Woodward still refused to leave, and waited in the hall for three hours, while another servant from the Hooper household came from time to time to keep her company. She threatened to get a search warrant from a magistrate and to return with it and a constable.

Eventually, at about six in the evening she was allowed upstairs and shown into a bedroom where she found Fazas and Mrs Hooper lying in bed together, stripped respectively to their shirt and shift, which was what was known at the time as 'in naked bed together'. Mrs Hooper was still quite insensible, and Mrs Woodward exclaimed to Fazas: 'What! Have you murdered her? She is a dead woman.' Even he was alarmed, and helped Mrs Woodward to try to bring Mrs Hooper round, first with cold water, then coffee, and finally spirits. Nothing worked, but between them they at last managed to dress her, carry her downstairs, and put her into a coach. Mrs Woodward took her home, where she arrived at about ten in the evening, still dazed and incoherent and unable to recognize anyone. Her apprentice testified that she was 'dragged like a dead woman out of the coach'.[17]

[15] Ibid. D. 734: 37–9; Eee. 7, fo. 176.
[16] Ibid. E. 10/30; Eee. 7, fos. 222, 236, 243.
[17] Ibid. E. 10/30; Eee. 7, fos. 226, 232–3, 243–5.

Mrs Hooper did not come round sufficiently to recognize anybody until 'after the watchman cried in the streets past two o'clock'. Suddenly Mrs Woodward noticed something disturbing, and the following exchange took place:

MRS WOODWARD. What have you been doing?
MRS HOOPER. Why?
MRS WOODWARD. Do you see a wedding ring on your finger?
MRS HOOPER. Oh! I know nothing of it, nor how I came by it.

She then tore the ring off her finger and threw it on the ground 'in great passion and anger'.[18] To add insult to injury, Fazas had the gall to turn up at Mrs Hooper's shop the next morning, give her servants money to drink their mistress's health, and tell them that she was now his wife.[19] He was clearly attempting to establish his legal credentials as Mrs Hooper's husband.

The abduction and forced marriage on 6 November touched off an immediate flurry of litigation. Mrs Hooper sued Fazas, the Revd Moody, and the Bennett sisters in the Lord Mayor's Court, presumably for conspiracy, and instituted a hunt for Captain Hilton, who had prudently disappeared. It was not until six weeks later that an informer told Mrs Hooper where he was hiding, and she had him arrested. The upshot of the suit is unknown. There was also a hearing in the house of Lord Chief Justice Holt, to which witnesses on both sides were summoned, and a suit in King's Bench was launched by Mrs Hooper to deny the legality of the bonds given by Fazas to Hilton, on the grounds that they were used to pay for a criminal conspiracy.[20]

Meanwhile, Fazas had the audacity to sue Mrs Hooper in the London Consistory Court for restitution of conjugal rights, in order to prove the marriage and to obtain an order for her to return to her wifely duties. Since Mrs Hooper was taken by surprise, and unable to locate the key witnesses, Fazas won. She then appealed the sentence to the Court of Arches, asking for jactitation of the alleged marriage, that is a legal declaration that it was invalid.

This time, she took care to arrange for all her witnesses to be present to testify to exactly what had happened on 6 November. The most valuable were the two coachmen, who had been instrumental in informing Mrs Hooper's household that she had been kidnapped, and could testify that she was already insensible and slumped down in the bottom of the

18 Ibid. Eee. 7, fos, 226, 233–4, 236–7, 245; E. 10/30.
19 Ibid. Ee. 7, fo. 92.
20 Ibid. Eee. 7, fos. 180, 184, 228, 266, 271–2.

coach by one o'clock in the afternoon, before the marriage had taken place. Faced with a barrage of evidence about the drugging, the testimony of two witnesses of Captain Hilton's previous offer of a drugged marriage to another suitor, and the exposure of the Bennett sisters as prostitutes or courtesans, the defence collapsed and Mrs Hooper won her case. The marriage was declared null and void, since carried out by force.[21]

It is not known what happened to the perpetrators of this brutal kidnapping, that is Hilton, Fazas, and the Bennett sisters. Mrs Hooper had at least preserved her person, her business, and her fortune. On the other hand, she had been kidnapped, drugged, subjected to a parody of a marriage, and raped while still unconscious. All this would have been enough for a criminal charge of conspiracy and assault in King's Bench, but whether Mrs Hooper launched such a suit is not known. She may well have been deterred by the inevitable publicity.

[21] Ibid. B. 12/27.

C. CLANDESTINE MARRIAGE

(a) A FLEET PARSON

10
The Revd John Vyse, 1691–1714

In the first half of the eighteenth century, many obscure parsons earned a living—usually precarious, occasionally comfortable—by conducting a clandestine marriage business in the Rules of the Fleet Prison. One or two of them have left sufficient evidence in the records for a reasonably complete story of their lives and times to be put together.[1] John Vyse was born at Eccleshall in Staffordshire in about 1674. His father owned land in the county worth at least £100 a year and possibly more, and so was probably a yeoman farmer or small gentleman. He intended John for the church, and in 1689 put the boy, now aged about 15 or 16, as boarder in the house of Mr Hawkins, a respectable citizen at Trentham, where he studied classics at the grammar school. While there, John fell in love with the daughter of the house, Mary Hawkins, who was about 21 years old, and before long she became pregnant, giving birth in April 1690.

There were rumours at the time that the father of the child might have been another lodger in the house, one of the schoolmasters. But it was John whom Mary publicly declared to be the father, and it was therefore John's father who was obliged to give bond to the parish for the maintenance of the child. An admittedly interested party in the case remembered over twenty years later hearing the schoolmaster say that 'he was very afraid that Moll Hawkins would have fathered her child upon him, but she fathered it on Johnny Vyse'. For the latter, it was a bad start to a clerical career, but not an irreparable one, for such accidents were always happening, and anyway the infant soon died while out at wet-nurse, as such children so often did (and were intended to do). The episode was quickly forgotten.[2]

---

[1] The equally unedifying life of another, William Clewer, can be reconstructed from LPCA, E. 8/15; Ee. 2, fos. 57–9, 67, 70, 80, 86; Eee. 1, fos. 31–2; Eee. 7, fos. 670–2, 676; Eee. 8, fos. 32–5, 55–9, 67–70, 80–7, 90–100, 111–12, 144–51, 149; Eee. 10, fos. 675, 677–8, 694–705.
[2] LPCA, D. 2153: 138, 186–7, 189, 345–50, 385–6, 417–20, 431–2.

To separate him from Mary, his father removed Johnny from the Hawkins house at Trentham and put him to school elsewhere for another six months, before sending him on to Cambridge University. But Johnny had still not forgotten Moll Hawkins, and in April 1691, while still no more than 18 and an undergraduate, he was foolish enough to ask her to marry him in Lichfield Cathedral. The marriage had to be a clandestine one, without banns or licence, since Johnny was still under age and would never get the permission of his father for so hare-brained a scheme.

Mary accepted the offer, her father bought her a new suit of clothes, and she set off for Lichfield riding pillion behind her brother. When they arrived, Johnny Vyse was there to welcome them, and sent at once for the sacrist. He explained to the latter that he wanted a distinctly unusual wedding performed in the greatest secrecy. He claimed (falsely) that he was a graduate of Cambridge 'and designed for a very good living of one hundred and fifty pounds a year', left him in his grandfather's will, and that he was fearful that, in case his marriage came to be known, 'his degrees might be stopped and his preferment hindered'. Had his situation been as he described it, this would indeed have been a real possibility. He therefore asked the sacrist to arrange for him 'to be married in the greatest secrecy imaginable, and not insert it in the registry till such time as he should give him orders'.

The sacrist prepared to issue the licence, but Mary's brother, who was clearly unused to perjury, refused to give the necessary bond that there was no impediment 'because he knew not the consent of friends on both sides'. In fact he knew only too well that Johnny was still under age, and that he did not have his parents' consent to the marriage. So the resourceful sacrist summoned an illiterate ostler whom he knew would be willing to sign the bond, and then filled in the licence, which was made out for a marriage at Trentham, not Lichfield. Mary Vyse later alleged that it was quite normal to marry persons in Lichfield Cathedral on the basis of licences directed to other churches.

After these preliminaries had been settled, the sacrist, the bride and groom, the bride's brother, and the daughter of the master of the inn where they were staying all went into the Cathedral, where the marriage service took place. For these illegal services, including the licence, the fee, a formal certificate of marriage, and the insertion of a written memo of the marriage in his notebook but not in the marriage register, the sacrist only charged one guinea.[3]

[3] Ibid. 138–41, 168–75, 194–5, 204–5, 350–1, 350–5, 438.

With all the ardour of a newly-married man, Johnny asked for the consummation to take place that night, but in view of what had happened before when she had slept with him, Moll refused 'by reason she might prove with child, and so that marriage come to be discovered sooner than it might be convenient it should'. So Johnny slept with his new brother-in-law, Edward Hawkins, in one room of the inn, and Mary in another, although Johnny later told Edward that while the latter was asleep he had in fact slipped out and made love to Moll.[4]

The next morning Edward took his sister Moll back home to Trentham, leaving Johnny Vyse to go back to Cambridge. But two days later Moll disappeared and was found with Johnny in a neighbour's house. So the Hawkins family made the best of it, took them both home, and duly performed the consummation ritual over them. Moll's sister Jane 'with others after they were so in bed, threw a stocking at them, as is customary upon such occasions of brides and bridegrooms first bedding together'.[5] As a result of this cohabitation, the news of the marriage soon leaked out. Presumably expelled from his College, Johnny abandoned his Cambridge education and settled down for the next four years with his new wife in the Hawkins house. For the sake of Moll, he had lost the chance of getting a university degree, had substantially reduced his career opportunities in the church, and had presumably alienated his father.

In 1696 the couple moved away and set up house at Stone in Staffordshire, where they gave a huge house-warming feast with 200 guests, each of whom brought a present in cash, 'according to the custom of the country, when married persons first take to housekeeping'. The gross take for the day was between £10 and £20.[6]

But they only stayed at Stone for two years, at the end of which Johnny left for Ireland in search of a church living, and Moll and the children returned once more to her father's house in Trentham. In 1697 Johnny Vyse persuaded the Bishop of Cork to ordain him as a priest, despite his lack of a degree, but it was not until five years later, in 1702, that he could find a living near Cork, and returned to Trentham to collect his family.[7]

Within two years Johnny and Moll had quarrelled, and in 1704 Johnny returned to England alone. He informed the Hawkins family that he was separating himself from Moll, but promised to make her an allowance

---

[4] Ibid. 176–7.   [5] Ibid. 140–2, 177–8.
[6] Ibid. 180.   [7] Ibid. 143–50, 176–83.

appropriate to one who was 'a gentlewoman and his wife'. It seems certain that the allowance for Moll was never paid, and within a year she and the three children were once more back in her father's house at Trentham.[8] After a brief stay locally as a curate, Johnny went off to London, where by early 1705 he was courting a girl whom he had known back in Trentham. Her name was Jane Robins, the daughter of a gentleman who had left her the handsome portion of £200, which was probably not the least of her attractions for Johnny. In April 1705 he committed bigamy by going through a clandestine Fleet marriage with her. It took place at a public house called The Sign of the Bricklayers' Arms in the Rules of the Fleet and was conducted by the Revd John Ogle, one of the professional marrying parsons there.[9]

Jane was a little distressed that her certificate of marriage was not on stamped paper, as by law it should have been, the reason being that she had not thought to bring a stamped sheet with her. By 1707 she knew enough about her husband's previous marriage to be worried about the legality of her own. So she went back to the Revd Ogle to obtain a new certificate. By now Ogle was very ill, but he told her to bring some stamped paper, on which he promised to sign another certificate. When she came back, however, Ogle was too ill to sign his name. Three years later still, in 1710, foreseeing trouble ahead, Jane persuaded three of the witnesses to her marriage to make affidavits to that effect before a judge in his chambers. The second Mrs Vyse had thus done everything possible to allow her to prove her clandestine marriage in a court of law.[10]

Between 1705 and 1707 Johnny and Jane had lived at many different addresses, probably moving just one step ahead of the bailiffs. In the first seven years after the marriage, Jane claimed to have lived in no fewer than 22 places.[11] In 1707, however, the bailiffs finally caught up with Johnny, and he found himself arrested for debt. He seems to have been imprisoned in a county gaol, but like many others he managed to turn disaster into some kind of victory. He 'bought his *Habeas Corpus*', that is to say he paid for a writ of habeas corpus, which served to transfer him from a prison in the provinces to the Fleet Prison in London. Once there, he bought from the Marshal of the prison the right to live and work outside in the Rules of the Fleet, where he settled down to make a living conducting clandestine marriages.

In 1709, however, the Revd Vyse almost found himself in serious

---

[8] Ibid. 184–5.   [9] Ibid. 223, 229, 241–2, 250–5.
[10] Ibid. 226–7, 244, 260–2, 264, 270, 273.   [11] Ibid. 268, 277.

trouble by conducting a marriage without banns or licence, which was such a scandalous aspect of the Fleet marriage business.[12] This narrow escape may explain his reluctance in 1712 to marry Edward Griffin without a licence[13] What happened was this. For some six months, from October 1708, William Warren, a well-to-do timber merchant in Blackfriars, had been keeping as his mistress a widow, Ann Meadows, and by March 1709 she was pregnant. Since her lover was unwilling either to marry her or to support her and her baby, she concocted a plot by which to blackmail him into buying her off. She found someone willing to impersonate Warren, and together with a witness—an old childhood friend of hers called Richard Cooke—they turned up at ten in the morning on 5 April 1709 at the Bull and Garter, a notorious marriage shop just by the entrance to the Fleet Prison. They asked the keeper to find them a parson, and he sent for Johnny Vyse. Ann explained to the Revd Vyse that the alleged William Warren wanted a private marriage 'for that he was rich, and his friends, if they knew it, would deprive him of what he had'. They all went into the Fleet Chapel, where Johnny performed the ceremony, without either a licence or publication of banns. Under later interrogation in court, he could not remember whether he was 'in his priest's habits or in his night gown', but denied that he was 'drunk or intoxicated or disordered', although he did admit that he had been drinking. Indeed quite a lot of drink must have been consumed that morning, since even the witness Mr Cooke admitted to absorbing two quarts of beer.

Drunk or sober, the Revd Vyse performed the ceremony without a hitch. The keeper of the Bull and Garter served as the second witness and an entry was made in the marriage register of the chapel. A certificate of marriage was prepared in the name of 'William Warren, gentleman', but when they had all returned to the Bull and Garter for another drink, the new bride made the clerk alter the certificate to read 'William Warren, deal merchant' rather than 'gentleman'. The party then broke up, the so-called William Warren leaving first, and then Ann and Mr Cooke, who parted company in the Strand, the former remarking that 'they would take some other opportunity to be merry in'. The abrupt disappearance of the bridegroom without the bride seems to have put something of a damper on the proceedings.

Armed with two witnesses and a certificate of marriage, Ann prepared for battle, sending her landlord to ask William Warren 'why he never

[12] *Warren* v. *Warren* (1710), LPCA, D. 9641.
[13] See *Griffin* v. *Griffin*, pp. 162–3 below.

came near her since his marriage'. William hotly denied that he was married to anyone, but a visit to the Fleet showed an entry in one of the marriage registers. William declared angrily: 'It is a trick or cheat', but Ann's landlord suggested that it would be 'better for you to make it up and give Ann Warren some money and so to be rid of her, and not expose yourself.'

Although Mr Cooke prudently refused to swear that William Warren was the man whose marriage he had witnessed, Ann first asked for £100 to hush things up, then came down to £50. But William Warren called the whole thing 'a cheat' and threatened to prosecute Ann unless she dropped the matter. He pointed out that one witness, the keeper of the Bull and Garter, was in debt and penniless, and therefore a man 'easily seduced' to lie, while the other, Mr Cooke, would not even swear that William was the bridegroom. He himself had a cast-iron alibi, since he had been drinking with a group of friends in a kitchen from eight in the morning until one in the afternoon, as many could testify.

This did not stop Ann from suing William in the London Consistory Court in order to prove the marriage. She lost, then appealed her case to the Court of Arches, and lost again. John Vyse appeared in court, revealed some more of his unedifying life history, admitted he was 'worth nothing', and disappeared. It is difficult not to believe that he was a member of the conspiracy, and had been promised by Ann a reward for marrying her without banns or licence. It seems unlikely, however, that he knew that the bridegroom was not the man he pretended to be. Johnny Vyse was lucky not to be prosecuted for this criminal offence.

Despite this one brush with the law, for the first time in his chequered career Johnny Vyse was by all accounts earning a tolerable income. He needed it, for Jane had produced four children, so he had a large second family to look after, besides having to satisfy a growing taste for alcohol. He was said to be living 'very handsomely and genteely' by marrying couples without banns or licence, first in the chapel in the prison, and, when that was made illegal in 1712, in public houses in the Rules.[14]

News of the Revd Vyse's new prosperity eventually found its way back to Staffordshire, and in June 1711 Edward Hawkins, the brother of Johnny's first wife Moll and now himself a clergyman, turned up in the Rules of the Fleet. He was looking for Johnny Vyse, to whom he wanted to talk, in order to force him to give a separation allowance for Moll and her children. He was advised that the best place to find Johnny was in

[14] LPCA, D. 2153: 282–3, 401–4.

the prison chapel on a Sunday morning, when he performed many of his clandestine marriages.

Edward went into the prison courtyard on a Sunday, spotted Johnny, and followed him into the chapel along with some couples come to be married. He settled himself down in the front pew beside the communion-table and watched Johnny marry several of them. When it was all over, Edward approached Johnny, shook his hand, and said: 'How do you do, brother Vyse?' Presumably they discussed Johnny's failure to supply maintenance for his first wife Moll Hawkins and her children, and arrangements for making such an allowance in the future.[15]

But whatever Johnny promised he did not perform for long, since about eighteen months later, in 1713, Mary began a suit in an ecclesiastical court against her husband. She asked for separation on the grounds of his adultery with Jane Robins, and for the award of a maintenance allowance for herself and her children. Since Jane had long ago taken steps to collect evidence about her Fleet marriage with Johnny in 1705, the latter was liable to be charged with bigamy. His line of defence was therefore to insist that he and Mary Hawkins were never married, but to admit that he had lived with her, that he had fathered children by her, as recorded in his own hand in the family Bible which she possessed, and that they had passed both in Staffordshire and in Ireland as man and wife.

He claimed that the story of the marriage in Lichfield Cathedral was a fabrication. He pointed to the absence of any entry in the marriage register, despite the fact that the sacrist was known to have been 'a very exact and careful man in the entry and registering of all marriages'. There was also the puzzling fact that the licence was made out for a marriage at Trentham not Lichfield, and that it was an illiterate ostler who had put his mark to the bond. On the other hand, Mary Vyse proved that a licence had been made out and signed by the sacrist. She also produced a marriage certificate (which Johnny had made the mistake of leaving behind him when he abandoned Mary in Ireland), the signature on which was certified as genuine by the sacrist's widow.[16]

Mary Vyse's account of the Lichfield wedding was accepted by the Consistory Court, which issued a sentence in her favour. Johnny appealed the sentence to the Court of Arches, but did not pursue the matter to the end, no doubt preferring to settle out of court rather than

[15] Ibid. 165, 190, 407–15, 444–8.   [16] Ibid. 109–31.

run the risk of prosecution for bigamy as a result of the publicity. If he did commit the criminal offence of bigamy, as the Consistory Court sentence implied, he was never put on trial for it, presumably because the Hawkins family had no interest in prosecuting him so long as he paid the court-ordered alimony to Moll. He is last heard of in 1718, still pursuing his trade as a Fleet parson.[17] Thus the clandestine marriage business proved first the undoing and finally the partial salvation of Johnny Vyse.

[17] J. S. Burn, *The Fleet Registers* (London, 1833), 36; Burn is wrong to say that Vyse was a Fleet parson from 1689 (LPCA, D. 2153: 404, 428).

(b) A VALID CLANDESTINE MARRIAGE

11

Elmes v. Elmes, 1706–1709

Henry Elmes was a poor widower of uncertain occupation, who in 1706 was living in a lodging-house run by a Mrs Jordan at White Horse Yard, Drury Lane, in London.[1] Among his fellow-lodgers were four young women, Mary Wise and three sisters, Jane, Ellen, and Anne Ordway. Mary Wise was 20 years old, originally from the country. But she must have come up to London as a very small child, since she could barely remember Stow-on-the-Wold in Gloucestershire, where she was born. Anne Ordway was presumably the eldest of the three sisters, probably in her early or middle twenties. Both their parents would appear to have already died.[2]

Mary Wise had already given birth to an illegitimate child, fathered on her by a sailor, when some time after May 1706 Henry Elmes first took her as his mistress. They lived together for the next two years or more, and when it suited him Henry claimed that they were married on 8 January 1707, within the Rules of the Queen's Bench Prison in Southwark, another of those privileged areas around a prison where cheap and dubious marriages took place. Whether the marriage ever in fact happened was to be the main issue in dispute in the coming years. Henry alleged that he had a certificate to prove it, but he seems never to have produced it in court.[3]

By 1707 Anne Ordway had left the lodging-house at White Horse Yard and taken a room with a cordwainer, Mr and Mrs Thomas Ly, in Rose Street, Covent Garden, where she stayed for about six months. She then left to become a servant to Mr Jones, a cook in Russell Street, near Drury Lane. Henry Elmes had kept in touch with her, however, and in the summer of 1708 he began pressing her to marry him. One day in July Mrs Ly accidentally met Anne in the street and remarked that she had heard that she was 'going to be married to a man who I hear has lived a lewd life for near three years with another woman'. She warned Anne not

---

[1] LPCA, D. 677.   [2] Ibid. 128, 104, 115.   [3] Ibid. 68, 129.

to commit herself to marriage without consulting her, advice which the girl promised to follow.[4] Mrs Ly seems to have been the only elderly woman in whom Anne could confide in this crisis in her life.

On or before 26 July 1708, Anne Ordway agreed to marry Henry Elmes, and the latter, in a boastful or truculent mood, told his ex-mistress Mary that if she came to the Fleet the next morning, she would see him married to Anne.[5] Early the next day he and Anne turned up on the doorstep of the Lys, along with Anne's two sisters. Henry and Anne announced that they intended to get married and asked the Lys to accompany them, and in particular Anne asked Mr Ly to act as her father and give her away.

They had all settled down to two pots of ale and some bread and cheese, when in came Mary Wise. Immediately a row broke out between Henry and Mary, since the latter insisted on joining the wedding party. Eventually they all set off for the Fleet with Mary trailing after them, and at Somerset stairs they took a boat for Blackfriars. Henry forcibly prevented Mary from getting into the boat, but she hurried along on foot and met them again when they reached the Fleet.[6]

All seven of them—Henry Elmes the bridegroom, Anne Ordway the bride, Mary Wise the bridegroom's mistress, Ellen and Mary Ordway the two sisters of the bride, and Thomas and Margaret Ly the substitutes for the bride's parents—went upstairs to a room over a distiller's shop near the gate to the Fleet Prison. A clergyman was summoned, who came bustling up and, wasting no time, asked which couple he was to join. The ceremony was about to begin when the following conversation took place:

MARY WISE. Sir, there is no occasion for a wedding, for he is my husband before God, though not before man.
MINISTER. Sweetheart, have you had any child by this man?
MARY WISE. Yes, Sir, two.
HENRY ELMES. You lie, you bitch, it was none of mine. Damn you for a bitch, you had one by a seaman, and got out of your bed in your shift when you had lain in but a week, and run after me to make me father of your child, and I took you and lived with you because the parish should not take you.[7]
MINISTER. Sweetheart, did he ever promise you any marriage?
MARY WISE. Yes.
MINISTER. Why were you not married?
MARY WISE. Because we had not money.

---

[4] Ibid. 79, 92.   [5] Ibid. 68, 106, 116.   [6] Ibid. 80–2, 93–5, 114–17.
[7] i.e. to prevent her from being arrested and put in the House of Correction by the parish authorities for burdening the rate with the maintenance of a bastard child.

HENRY ELMES. And the money shall still be wanting for I never designed to marry you.

Henry, who was by then very angry, took off his hat, said to the company: 'I am your humble servant till the next opportunity,' and ran off down the stairs, closely followed by Mary.[8]

After this unexpected turn of events, the others sat around for a while and drank a bottle of cider, while Anne announced that she intended to break off relations with Henry. They set off for home, but in Fleet Street they overtook Henry and Mary 'walking together arm in arm'. Henry left Mary, gave her a kick, and told her 'to be gone from him'. He caught Anne by the hand and said: 'Come, my dear, let us go back again.' Anne snatched her hand away and said she wanted nothing more to do with him. Mary meanwhile was trying to separate them and Henry turned on her, called her names, and threatened to kick her again. Finally Anne said: 'As you have lived together I think it would be convenient for you to live together still, and God bless you,' to which Mary added thankfully: 'God bless *you*.'[9]

But Henry was nothing if not persistent, and at noon he was back at the Lys's house, where he swore he was not married to Mary Wise, and begged Anne to relent and marry him at once. He called for a pot of ale and drank to her, but Anne refused to pledge him back and left the house to get away from him.

Henry returned the same evening, again importuning Anne to marry him. He swore that he was not married to Mary, and promised that in future he would have nothing more to do with her. Anne finally weakened under this barrage, and they hurried off again to the Fleet to get married, only to find that the minister had gone home for the night.

So at four o'clock the next morning (presumably in order to outwit Mary) they all got up again and were back at the distiller's house by the Fleet gate at dawn. This time the ceremony went off without a hitch, Anne being duly given away by Thomas Ly.[10] The marriage itself, however, only lasted three weeks, apparently because Henry found it impossible to give up the pleasure of sleeping with Mary Wise.

Five months later, in December of 1708, Henry's brother William died, and there was a lawsuit over his property. This seems to have accentuated the tension, since Henry now had some money, or the prospects of money, and was worth fighting for.[11] In the same month Anne sued Mary for assault and battery before first one JP and then the

---

[8] LPCA, D. 677; 96–7, 120.   [9] Ibid. 72–3, 98–9, 121.
[10] Ibid. 73–4, 87–8, 100–1, 123.   [11] Ibid. 75, 89.

full Bench of Justices at Quarter Sessions at Hick's Hall, and had Mary committed to the New Prison. The suit was 'on account of Mary rising out of bed from Henry Elmes and beating Anne'. In the course of the trial Anne forced Henry to admit before the justices that she was his lawful wife 'and that Mary Wise was only his servant'.[12]

Meanwhile, Mary, encouraged presumably by Henry Elmes's prospects of inheritance from his dead brother, now decided to try a little blackmail. She told a friend of Henry's, a shoemaker called Nicholas Hudson in Lincoln's Inn Fields, that if Henry would give her £100, she 'would go about her business and trouble him no more'. She made the offer in front of Anne, urging her to persuade Henry to agree, and allegedly admitting that she 'had so long lived in adultery with him, that she would be afraid to die'. This somewhat unexpected confession of a guilty conscience was not at all the way she put her hopes and plans to her ex-landlady at the White Horse Yard, Mrs Jordan, to whom she declared: 'I will make up a purse of two hundred pounds…and then be gone, and Henry and Anne may live together and be damned.' She added that if Henry did not pay up, she knew a man called Jackson who for £50 would provide testimony which would get him and Anne divorced.[13]

The story ends in a characteristically ambiguous and confused manner. Anne, who was now separated from Henry, followed the usual procedure to force the civil courts to decide upon the validity of a marriage. She ran up a bill for clothes and other necessaries and told the shopkeeper to sue her husband for the money. This he did before Lord Chief Justice Trevor in Westminster Hall, but a jury of solid citizens threw out the suit, on the grounds that Henry was not Anne's legal husband. Somehow or other, perhaps because of the bribed false testimony of the man called Jackson, the jury concluded that there had been a prior contract or marriage with Mary Wise.

Some months later a judge in the ecclesiastical court, in a suit by Anne for restitution of conjugal rights, took a different view, upholding the validity of the marriage, and making Henry responsible for her necessary debts. Henry appealed the sentence, but was rejected by the Court of Arches.[14]

The story peters out in this state of utter confusion, with the secular and ecclesiastical courts taking different positions about who was and was not the lawful wife of Henry Elmes. What remains a mystery is why Henry got himself into this tangle in the first place, if, as seems to be the case, he was satisfied with the sexual services of his mistress Mary Wise,

[12] Ibid. 89–90, 102–3.   [13] Ibid. 76–7, 103, 125–6.   [14] Ibid. 131–7; B. 14/205.

and had nothing to gain financially by marriage to a poor orphaned servant girl like Anne Ordway.

What seems fairly certain is that Mary and Anne would not have bothered to fight over their rights to him, if the death of his brother had not unexpectedly made him financially desirable as a husband. Among this section of the London poor, formal marriage only became important when there was money involved, and when it occurred it was usually done in a clandestine manner on the cheap in the Rules of the Fleet or elsewhere.

12
Northmore v. *Northmore*, 1664

In 1653 Edward Northmore was entered as a commoner on the books of Wadham College, Oxford. He was the son of a small Devonshire gentleman and landowner, apparently of conservative Anglican leanings. The father probably chose the college because of its close connections with the West Country, and perhaps also because its Head and Fellows, who had all been intruded into their positions by the revolutionary government, were better known for their scientific interests than for religious fanaticism. Seven years later, Edward emerged from Oxford with a Master's degree, an event which precisely coincided with the Restoration of Charles II, and the re-establishment of a persecuting Anglican Church, anxious to stamp out all signs of religious dissent.[1]

Unfortunately for his future prospects, during his period of education at Wadham Edward had picked up strong dissenting religious views. He called his fellow religionaries 'friends' and may perhaps have been a Quaker. At all events, he obstinately refused to conform to the new Anglican regime and therefore deprived himself of all chances of obtaining a church living. Instead he was obliged to adopt the insecure life of a dissenting preacher, dependent on the charity of his more affluent co-religionaries and liable at any time to run afoul of the law.

He seems to have settled down in the Oxfordshire–Berkshire area where his friends and patrons lived, although he also spent some time in London. In 1664 when things were at their most difficult for Dissenters, he began courting a young Oxford woman, possibly a member of his own religious sect. Elizabeth Locke was the widow of a barber, Leonard Locke, by whom she had had one or two children, and was existing on a very small income, barely adequate to maintain her family. But if she was not much of a financial catch, neither was Edward Northmore. He had neither a settled income nor a home and was entirely dependent on voluntary donations and hospitality from pious 'friends'.

His only hope of economic independence was to obtain a settlement

---

[1] J. Foster, *Alumni Oxonienses*, 4 vols. (Oxford, 1891–2), iii. 1078; R. B. Gardiner, *Registers of Wadham College, Oxford*, 2 vols. (Oxford, 1889), i. 201.

from his father, who was certain to be strongly opposed to the secret marriage to Mrs Locke, a woman of humble origins, without financial means, burdened with children, and probably not a member of the Church of England. His father was an Anglican supporter who claimed, truly or falsely, to have influence with the Archbishop of Canterbury. A country gentleman who had so enthusiastically climbed on board the Restoration bandwagon was unlikely to look favourably on either his son's dissenting principles and activities, or his marriage to an impoverished widow from the lower middling sort, who shared his son's religious beliefs.[2]

When in October 1664 the pair agreed on marriage, Edward therefore insisted that it be kept a secret from his father, which meant that it had to be a clandestine marriage in a private house. But it remains a mystery why he chose someone quite as disreputable as William Milner to perform the ceremony. Although even that fact was disputed, it seems likely that Milner had recently taken orders as a deacon, but not as a priest entitled to dispense the sacraments or conduct a marriage. Moreover his past history was deplorable. If he was indeed a friend of Edward, it suggests that the latter was not very particular about the company he kept. From about 1643 to 1654, during the siege of Oxford and after, Milner had served as a tapster at an alehouse in St Giles, where he became an alcoholic.

Years after, when Edward was anxious to undermine Milner's credibility, he alleged, in his priggish way, that Milner was not only a drunk, but also 'much given to prophaning the Lord's name by rash, untrue and frequent oaths'.[3] Under pressure from his wife and friends, Milner was finally persuaded to swear an oath to drink no more, written in his own blood. He took to schoolmastering, perhaps to remove himself from the proximity to alcohol, but it was no good. A former schoolgirl recalled that when his wife was out of sight he often sent one of his scholars to the alehouse 'for a pint of strong beer'. Neighbours joked to one another about this drunken abstainer saying 'if Mr Milner is so often drunk with drinking of water, we would advise him to drink strong drink again.'[4]

By the late 1650s he was using his literary skills for petty crime, and eventually fell into serious trouble. In about 1657 he met in an alehouse a family of Irish beggars and was persuaded to forge for them a 'brief', or licence to beg, on the grounds of losses by fire at Milford Haven, a

[2] LPCA, D. 1501: 96, 134, 150, 157; Eee. 3, fo. 694.
[3] Ibid. D. 1501: 169, 221, 268, 294.
[4] Ibid. 169–70, 262–4, 269–70.

document purportedly signed by three JPs and sealed. Armed with this imposing instrument, the Irish went begging for money in the streets of Oxford, until they were arrested and taken before a JP. They showed him their brief, but he at once suspected it to be fraudulent, and under pressure they soon confessed that it had been written by Milner at their dictation.

They and he were put in Bocardo (the town gaol), to await trial at Quarter Sessions. There the Irishmen were condemned to be whipped, and Milner to stand in the Oxford market on market-day mounted on top of the cage for all to see. He stood there 'to the public view of hundreds of people, with a note or paper on his breast, written in large characters and mentioning his offence'. A decade later there were many who remembered seeing him undergoing this humiliating shame punishment.

Even this experience did not teach Milner his lesson, and some time later the gaoler recalled that he was imprisoned again for the same offence. After he was ordained deacon in 1664, he continued this career of petty crime, issuing a false certificate of marriage with a forged signature in 1665 and another one in 1667, the second in return for the trivial sum of 2s. 6d. Everyone who knew him agreed that he was 'of an ill life', 'a man of ill fame', and 'a debauched liver'.[5]

Such was the man Edward Northmore chose in October 1664 to carry out a clandestine marriage between himself and Mrs Locke, in a private room in Carfax, before a single witness, at seven in the evening. Milner later said that he had at first refused to do it, but was persuaded by Edward's argument that the church allowed the sacrament of baptism to be carried out privately in a house, so why not marriage 'which is none'. If he found this sophistry convincing, Milner certainly did not know his canon law on the subject.

He read the Anglican marriage service, although there is some doubt whether the ceremony of the ring was carried out, which was often a sticking point with dissenters. But when it came to reading the exhortation to the newly married, Edward interrupted, saying 'hold, sir', since what he was about to say was 'popish'. He then took Elizabeth by the hand and led her upstairs to drink 'a sack posset together'. Two days later Edward paid Milner the modest fee of 6s. for his services.[6] It was all rather squalid, as well as being illegal by canon law, but it formed a binding and irrevocable contract, and for three years Edward never denied its validity.

[5] Ibid. 285–6, 290, 172–3, 239–43, 272, 277–80, 289.
[6] Ibid. 54–5, 666–8, 116, 221–5, 150–4, 162.

The next problem was where the consummation was to take place. Because of the need for secrecy, Elizabeth Locke's house—which was that of her elderly parents—could not be used, and Edward was homeless. They therefore borrowed for a couple of nights the room and bed shared by the witness, a young woman called Catherine Bishop, and her sister. Thereafter they could only sleep together in the houses of close friends who were in on the secret, such as a Mrs Greetham, a dissenting minister Mr Smith, both in Berkshire, and in a room in an inn at Marlborough.[7]

After the marriage, Elizabeth returned to her parents' house in Oxford and Edward resumed his peripatetic existence as a wandering dissenting preacher. But within a year two things forced the marriage into the open. Not only did the neighbours notice the cohabitation and begin gossiping, but Elizabeth became pregnant. She therefore insisted that their marriage be made public so as to preserve her reputation.[8] The second thing which precipitated a crisis was Elizabeth's growing suspicion about Edward's relations with a wealthy and pious dissenting lady, Mrs Goddard, who was providing him with free shelter at Marlborough.

Edward's letters to Elizabeth were full of complaints at the miserable conditions in which he lived; assertions that he was 'fully resolved never to comply' (that is to conform to the Anglican Church), 'though I starve'. He reminded her 'what a worldly man my father is, and what matches he hath profferred me lately', coupled with assurances none the less to be 'constant and faithful'. And he reiterated warnings that 'if matters be divulged there will be little hope of ever living together. I judge secrecy best till I see what my father will do for me.' In a postscript he added: 'If the gentlewoman be with child, the Lord bless it...Be careful.'[9]

But once Elizabeth was pregnant, all this insistence by Edward on secrecy became futile, and in late 1665 or early 1666 she openly proclaimed their marriage. The first Edward knew that his marriage was now public knowledge was a summons from his father to visit him in Devonshire. He wrote anxiously 'I am afraid you have discovered it to my father: pray inform me,' and he said he could easily imagine his father's 'cutting expressions'. He complained again and again that by telling his father of the marriage, Elizabeth had destroyed all chances that they would ever have a settled income. He claimed 'I scarcely have a farthing of my own at present,' and said that he feared that now his father 'will not give me a farthing'. He warned her that as a result 'we are

---

[7] Ibid. 76, 93–5, 55; Eee. 4, fo. 250.
[8] Ibid. D. 1501: 95, 178, 323; Eee. 3, fo. 394.
[9] Ibid. D. 1501: 92–6.

like to live in extreme misery together,' and added threateningly: 'I am not bound by law to do the least for your children [by Mr Locke].'

He complained that 'you have done me infinite injury and irreparable wrong. The infinite God forgive you. You have ashamed me in City and University and all the county over, to the pleasure of all enemies to me and my non-conformity.' He told her that 'tis commonly reported about Marlborough and Chalford that I am a barber's wife's husband [Mrs Locke's], and keep company with another woman [Mrs Goddard]. All this comes from you.'

Ignoring Elizabeth's pregnancy, in his egotistical way he went on and on about how 'you obliged your soul by sacred bonds and promises and oaths before God not to divulge it.' He reported that, on learning that he was married, Mrs Goddard 'is in a terrible rage, and intends to vindicate her honour publicly. She hath freely parted with my company for ever, so long as you and I live.' He insisted that Mrs Goddard was 'as religious and I believe as pious a woman as ever I was acquainted with'. He asked: 'what fault can you find than that she hath kept my company all this while ignorantly, as a friend. You consented to it too. I was in great neccessity, knew not where to go.'[10]

In another letter dated December 1665 he reproached her for calling him 'dog, knave, rogue…flatterer, cheat, dissembler'. He then tried a little moral blackmail, telling her that 'I am not fit to go into a pulpit.… You have made such a stir, you have deprived me of those means of living comfortably with you. People believe I am such as you relate.' The couple were even quarrelling over matters of religion, since Elizabeth apparently was pressing him to conform to the Church and settle down to a respectable life as an Anglican clergyman. He complained that 'you talked to my father like a high conformist'.

He also alleged that 'I was like to have some convenient way of living; [but] by your means and discourse 'tis lost.' The wealthy religious ladies who had supported him, and especially Mrs Goddard, now would not help him, and his father was about to disinherit him, partly for marrying without his permission and partly for his religious opinions. He concluded sanctimoniously 'God give us bread and water. I shall be satisfied.' Even so, 'I intend not for a thousand worlds to conform against conscience.'[11]

In fact, Elizabeth's disclosure of the marriage turned out to have been unnecessary, for she miscarried.[12] By July 1666, however, a new blow

---

[10] Ibid. 83–9.   [11] Ibid. 78–83.   [12] Ibid. Ee. 3, fo. 720.

fell, which reduced Edward to incoherent despair. On a charge of unlicensed preaching, he had been summoned before the bishop 'who is infinitely angry with me'. He was told 'I must never preach more, neither here nor in any other diocese,' and so was deprived of all means of livelihood; if he was found preaching again, he was in danger of a two and a half year gaol sentence at the Assizes, and his family was furious with him 'on your account'. He concluded miserably: 'You say I am condemned by all. Oh friend, I expect none other from the world.'[13]

In view of the combined pressure of acute poverty, public obloquy, abandonment by his wealthy female co-religionaries, threats of disinheritance from his father, angry accusation from his wife, and the lack of any other visible solution to his financial troubles, it is hardly surprising that in early 1667 Edward Northmore swallowed his words, stifled his conscience, conformed to the Anglican Church, and was ordained by a bishop. By September 1667, presumably thanks to the patronage of the local squire and the influence of his father with the Archbishop of Canterbury, he was comfortably installed as vicar of Newton St Cyres, in his native Devonshire, worth about £80 to £100 a year.[14]

Edward Northmore's wayward decade as a religious rebel was over, and over also, he decided, was his unfortunate clandestine marriage to the Oxford barber's widow, Mrs Locke. Elizabeth, however, had other ideas, and on hearing of her husband's good fortune, decided to leave the home of her parents and brother in Oxford, where she had been staying for several years, and to go down to Devonshire to join him. First she armed herself with a certificate of marriage, freshly obtained from William Milner, who was now a curate in a village near Oxford. In order to conceal the fact that the marriage had been a clandestine one, performed in a private room without a licence, which if known might seriously threaten Edward's position in the vicarage, she asked Milner to make it out as having occurred in Carfax Church. This he obligingly did, the signing of false marriage certificates never being much of a problem with him.

Later on, when the lawsuit began, Milner realized that he would have to appear in court and testify on oath to the marriage, along with the only other witness, Elizabeth Bishop, who would presumably tell the truth. He therefore hastily issued another certificate which omitted all reference to the place of marriage, which enabled him to swear to it without committing perjury.

[13] Ibid. D. 1501: 90–1; Ec. 3, fo. 720.
[14] Ibid. D. 1501: 103, 136, 318; Foster, *Alumni Oxonienses*, iii. 1078.

Meanwhile, Elizabeth went with the first certificate down to Newton St Cyres, but Edward refused to receive her. So she took lodgings in the village, showed her evidence to the local squire and others, and started a suit in the Consistory Court for restitution of conjugal rights, intending to prove the legality of her marriage. It seems likely that her real object was not to force Edward to take her back as his wife, but rather to obtain payment of old debts and a satisfactory maintenance allowance in the future. She had run up a debt of £24 to her brother during the time when she was living in Oxford without support from Edward, and this needed to be paid off.

Edward retorted by serving a warrant on Elizabeth—on what charges is unknown—and trying to suborn her chief witness.[15] He set out with a weaver from the village on a trip to Oxford to see what he could do to make William Milner change his story. They stayed at the George Inn, and Edward, under a false name, sent a message to Milner to meet him there. Milner's version of the story is that Edward told him that 'Mrs Locke had undone him', admitted that she was 'his wife before God', but said he 'had no way to secure himself but by denying the marriage'.

He therefore asked Milner to retract his two certificates and deny all knowledge of the marriage. First he threatened Milner that his father was 'a man that had great influence with the Archbishop of Canterbury', and that if Milner refused to do it, his father would use that influence 'to banish him out of this kingdom for breaking canon law by conducting a clandestine marriage in a room'.

When this rather implausible threat failed to dissuade Milner, Edward tried bribery, promising him 'a benefice worth £30 per annum', and that 'he would be a very good friend to his children'. In return, he asked Milner to make out an affidavit denying that the marriage ever took place, assuring him that he had nothing to worry about. As for Elizabeth, he claimed that the certificate of marriage 'was taken from her and torn to pieces', and that she 'was lying in gaol for being taken in the act of adultery with two watermen, and was never likely to come out of gaol'—both barefaced lies. By his own account, Milner continued to refuse all blandishments, and Edward then asked him for a specimen of his handwriting, which he also refused, suspecting that it would be used to forge some document in his name.[16]

Edward's very different version of the encounter was backed up by the evidently perjured testimony of the weaver he had brought up with him

---

[15] LPCA, D. 1501: 62, 135–7, 318–19, 324, 330; Ee. 3, fo. 720.
[16] Ibid. D. 1501: 70–6, 126–32.

from Devonshire and a 19-year-old student from Gloucester Hall, who both allegedly were secretly listening, 'standing behind a curtain in a chamber'. They claimed that Milner easily confessed that the certificate was false, and that 'Mrs Locke had seduced him therein', and that he said he was prepared to testify to this effect. Edward grudgingly admitted that he had dropped hints of his father's 'interest in public affairs'—in order to encourage Milner to tell the truth.[17]

Edward Northmore lost his case in the Consistory Court at Exeter in 1668 and again on appeal to the Court of Arches in London in 1669.[18] There were several reasons for these defeats. First, the testimony of his key witness for the interview with Milner at the George Inn at Oxford, the weaver from Newton St Cyres, was undermined by the evidence of the local squire. After hearing Elizabeth's story, he had convinced himself she was telling the truth, and he testified that a few years ago before he had caught the weaver forging a bond. He therefore thought his testimony was worthless, which meant that Edward was a liar too. He said he believed that Edward and Elizabeth had indeed been married clandestinely, just as William Milner and Elizabeth Bishop described.[19]

The second was Edward's failure either to intimidate or bribe Milner to change his story, and the third was the impression made by the production of Edward's letters to Elizabeth from 1665 to 1666. They showed him in a most unattractive light, and also proved that at that time he regarded himself as fully married to her.

Although they were now declared man and wife in the eyes of the law, it seems very unlikely that Edward and Elizabeth ever lived together again in the vicarage of Newton St Cyres. Relations must have been soured after this prolonged and bitter legal battle, and Edward's unscrupulous attempt to bully or bribe William Milner into denying the marriage. It is more likely that Edward was obliged to pay Elizabeth's debts and supply her with an annual maintenance allowance out of the proceeds of his vicarage, thus substantially reducing his net income. For the last four years, 1666–9, Mrs Locke had been reduced to going into domestic service in London, so she clearly needed the money badly. Moreover because the courts had upheld the validity of the marriage, neither was able to remarry and form a new legal family before the death of the other. The clandestine marriage system had proved to be a disaster for them both.

---

[17] Ibid. 104, 229–33, 313–17, 336–7.
[18] Ibid. B. 8/107.   [19] Ibid. D. 1501: 318–23.

13
Morland v. Morland, 1686

The playwrights of the 1680s and 1690s were unanimous in portraying the elite marriage market as a cold-blooded, treacherous, and ruthless struggle for sex and money. This grim picture is supported by the story of the matrimonial misfortunes of one of England's most fertile and famous technological inventors. Samuel Morland was educated at Winchester School and Magdelene College, Cambridge. After a stint as a College Fellow, he entered public life at the age of 28 in 1653, as a bright young man on the make in the new Cromwellian administration.[1] He was first attached to the important embassy to Sweden in 1653, and moved quickly to the position of chief clerk to Secretary Thurloe, who presided over the highly efficient Cromwellian secret service. In 1656 he was also appointed to the influential and lucrative post of Clerk of the Signet. On a mission to the Duke of Savoy on behalf of the Vaudois, he took the opportunity to make a good marriage to the attractive daughter of a French Protestant nobleman, Baron de Boissay. Morland was thus a conspicuously successful, affluent, and influential beneficiary of the revolutionary regime.

But at least by 1658 he had realized that the revolution was doomed, and began acting as a double agent. He supplied vital intelligence to Charles II and earned his passage to the royalist camp by revealing a Republican plot to kill the King. In order to cash in on this coup, in early 1660 he hurried over to Breda to meet the King, carrying with him a bundle of secret documents revealing which royalists had been betraying information to Secretary Thurloe. Charles greeted him warmly, knighted him, and gave him a pension of £500 a year for life and the profits from the sale of two baronetcies, one of which he took for himself.

---

[1] For Morland's biography, see H. W. Dickinson, *Sir Samuel Morland* (London, 1970). For his scientific activities, see the article on him in C. C. Gillispie (ed.), *The Dictionary of Scientific Biography* (New York, 1970–87) and his own publications: *Tuba Stentoro-phonica* (London, 1671); *Two Arithmetic Instruments* (London, 1673); *Élévation des eaux par toute sorte de machines* (Paris, 1685); *Hydrostatics, or Instructions concerning Water Works* (London, 1699). There is an example of his calculating machine in the History of Science Museum at Oxford, and one of his speaking trumpets in Trinity College, Cambridge.

Pepys, who knew Morland well from their college days at Cambridge, regarded him as a knave for his treacherous behaviour in the 1650s, and also as a fool.[2] In the 1660s he fell upon hard times, due partly to his own extravagance and the cost of his scientific experiments, but mainly to the incapacity of kings—especially English Kings—to fulfil their financial promises. During this decade he invented a variety of devices, such as a pump to raise water and a calculating machine, the latter of which Pepys described as 'pretty but not very useful'.[3]

He also drew on his experience in the 1650s in the service of the great spymaster Thurloe to design a device to open correspondence without being detected, and a circular cyphering machine. Some of his inventions, such as a capstan to raise heavy anchors and two kinds of barometers, were of direct interest to the Navy, which is probably why he kept in fairly close touch with Samuel Pepys over the years. It was a contact which was to come in very useful in the long run.

But all this technological activity brought little financial reward (he claimed he actually lost money from his post as Gentleman of the Privy Chamber), and from considerable affluence he slid into poverty, being forced to sell his royal pension in 1663.[4]

After 1668, however, his fortunes improved. He obtained some offices in Ireland and England and a patent to manufacture metal fire-hearths. After the death of his first French wife, he made a second good marriage to the daughter of a Knight. And he continued to turn out practical inventions, which included a speaking trumpet, which he claimed would carry three-quarters of a mile.

But above all Morland developed an improved water pump, one of which successfully raised large quantities of water. In a display to impress the King, he pumped water, mixed with red wine for visual effect, to the top of the tower of Windsor Castle, a height of 60 feet. Charles II was delighted, and gave him £250 in cash and a new annuity of £300 a year, and in 1681 appointed him to the high-sounding but empty title of Royal 'Master of Mechanics'. The next year Charles sent him over to Paris to advise Louis XIV on pumps for his waterworks in the gardens at Versailles. For this he devised a steam pump, recently described as one of the first to show the practical possibilities of steam power. Whether it was ever actually constructed is not known.

But late seventeenth-century kings were perennially short of cash, and Morland's close personal connections with Charles II and Louis XIV

---

[2] *Diary of Samuel Pepys*, ed. H. B. Wheatley, 10 vols. (London, 1913), i. 131; ii. 205.
[3] Ibid. ii. 337.   [4] Ibid. iii. 233; iv. 276, 284.

brought him much renown but little income. In 1684, three years after he had entered into the service of two of the greatest monarchs in Europe, neither of them had yet paid him very much. His pension from Charles II seems to have been nominally raised to £600 a year, but it was never paid regularly.

By 1686 Morland was desperate. He was heavily in debt, and fearful of going out of his house for fear of arrest by his many creditors, for the Lord Treasurer had cut £1,300 off his arrears of pension.[5] To raise a lot of money very fast, only two options were open to him. One was to intrigue at the Court for the grant of an office or pension from the new King, James II. As experience had shown, this was a very lengthy and uncertain process, although he did manage to get his pension restored. The other option was to marry a third wife, this time a really rich one. But Morland was now over 60 and dogged by creditors, so he was hardly the most attractive candidate for the hand of a young heiress. Only his influential court connections and genteel life-style worked in his favour.

What happened next is most succinctly described in Morland's own autobiographical sketch, written three years later:

As an addition to all these misfortunes, having charitably redeemed a certain woman (whose morals I then knew not at all) from perishing in a prison, [I] was inhumanly betrayed by her, under a pretence of gratitude, into a vain expectation of marrying an heiress of 20 thousand pounds. And swallowing too greedily the gilded bait, it proved my utter ruin.[6]

The woman's name was Barbara Bartlitt, who had indeed been helped by Morland, perhaps in return for sexual favours. Barbara had a younger sister Mary, who by 1686 had fallen upon very hard times. For almost two years, in 1684 and 1685, she had been the mistress of a gentleman called Thomas Cheeke, and in 1686 she had given birth to a daughter, the couple then passing as husband and wife. Soon after the birth, Cheeke abandoned her, and she was left with no means of livelihood but her wits. Such was her poverty that she was forced to pawn all her fine clothes in order to pay the rent, and eventually took refuge with her sister Barbara.[7]

Barbara knew all about Morland's elegant life-style and court connections, as well as his financial troubles and his urgent need to marry an

---

[5] *The Letters and Second Diary of Samuel Pepys*, ed. R. G. Howarth (London, 1933), 175–6.
[6] Dickinson, *Morland*, 18.
[7] GLRO, DL/C/145, fos. 36–8; *Pepys Letters*, 176.

heiress. She therefore concocted a scheme to pass off her sister Mary as a rich heiress, the virgin only daughter of a Sir John Ayliffe. The story was that her parents and sister had all died, leaving her an estate worth £500 a year and £4,000 in cash, but that she was being kept from her inheritance by her aunt, in whose London house she was living.[8] Barbara went to Morland, and explained that, as a return for all his former kindness to her, she could now arrange for him to marry a great heiress with whom she had been at school.

Three weeks later Morland confessed his gullibility to Pepys, in an agony of remorse: 'The devil himself could not contrive more probable circumstances than were laid before me. And when I had often a mind to enquire into the truth, I had no power, believing for certain reasons that there were some charms or witchcraft used upon me.' This was not a very a plausible story for a scientist to offer to a bureaucrat to explain an act of almost unbelievable folly.[9]

On Sunday 30 January 1686 the trap for Sir Samuel Morland was baited. Barbara and Mary 'Ayliffe' together visited him for the first time at his house in Old Spring Gardens. Mary was dressed in all her finery—redeemed from pawn by her landlady—and behaved impeccably. She suggested they all take a walk in Hyde Park, during which she had the opportunity to tell Morland who she was, how much she was worth, and how badly her aunt was treating her. Morland swallowed it all, ardently courted Mary, called her 'child', and asked her on the spot to marry him, to which she demurely agreed. On the Monday Barbara visited Morland, telling him that the next day, Tuesday, had to be the day, since the aunt was going to a feast in the City, leaving the coast clear for Mary to escape from the house and be married. She assured Morland that it was now or never.[10]

So on the next day, Tuesday 1 February, they all three went in Morland's coach to a well-known clandestine marriage chapel in Knightsbridge. There was an awkward moment when the clerk who was entering the marriage in the register asked how to spell 'Ayliffe'. Barbara and Mary fell into an argument about whether there was a 'y' in it, which seemed a little odd, but otherwise the marriage service passed off smoothly. The marriage was duly entered in the register, and the marriage certificate was made out, both entries in the names of Samuel Morland and Mary Ayliffe.[11]

Mary and Barbara must have been only too well aware that the fraud

---

[8] GLRO, DL/C/145, fos. 31–3. [9] *Pepys Letters*, 176.
[10] GLRO, DL/C/145, fo. 34. [11] Ibid. fos. 38–9.

was bound to be detected fairly soon. Mary had not gone into the marriage for love or lust for Morland, who was old enough to be her grandfather—he was 61 and she was still under 21—and she successfully persuaded the old man not to lie with her for a fortnight or so, until they knew each other better. As a result, consummation still had not taken place when the storm broke a week later.[12] Since Mary was still under the legal age of 21, Morland asked her to make him her official guardian and to introduce him to her lawyer, so that he could take steps to force her aunt to hand over her estate. Barbara said she would go to the lawyer the next day, but came back to announce that there was no estate—it was all mortgaged. Morland—still not quite realizing what had happened to him—asked about the £4,000 in cash. Mary tried to bluster it out and pretend it was safe, but under pressure she eventually confessed that it too did not exist.[13]

Morland at last understood the full enormity of what he had done. He lost his temper, threw both Mary and Barbara out of the house, and immediately used his experience in detective work to find out just who it was he had married. He soon discovered that Mary was Barbara's sister and that her real name was Bartlitt. He also learnt that, despite her immature age, she had already been another man's mistress for a couple of years and had given birth to an illegitimate child; and also that she was absolutely destitute.

Meanwhile Mary, who was no fool, was also busy. She realized that if she was to defend and prove the marriage in a court of law, it was essential that her name in the entry in the marriage register and on the marriage certificate be changed from Ayliffe to Bartlitt. On 16 February she went back to Knightsbridge, this time with her mother, and had a difficult interview with the curate Mr Watts. She explained that the name Ayliffe was that of her stepfather, a fact corroborated by her mother, and that she had given it by mistake. She therefore asked for a new marriage certificate to be made out in the names of Morland and Bartlitt, which Mr Watts duly prepared and signed, no doubt in return for a handsome bribe.

The next day Mr Watts told the parish Clerk, Mr Hipsley, about the change of name, and asked him to make the necessary alteration in the register. Mr Hipsley was naturally suspicious about the whole business, recalling how the two women had argued about how to spell the name Ayliffe before it was entered in the register. But he too was no doubt

---

[12] Ibid. fo. 39.   [13] Ibid. fo. 41.

bribed, and after some grumbling he crossed out 'Ayliffe' and wrote in 'Bartlitt'—a striking proof of the unreliability of the marriage registers of these clandestine marriage chapels.[14]

Meanwhile Morland was trying to annul the marriage he had made in such reckless haste and ignorance. Not only had he not acquired a fortune, but he was saddled with a wife of disreputable morals, and for whose maintenance and debts he was legally responsible until he could somehow repudiate the marriage or obtain a separation. Three weeks after the marriage, he appealed to his old college acquaintance Samuel Pepys, now high in the administration of the new King James, to get him out of the mess. He was launching a suit in the London Consistory Court to annul the marriage, on the grounds of a pre-contract made by Mary with her former keeper Mr Cheeke—for which there was not a shred of evidence except that she and Mr Cheeke had passed themselves off as man and wife to their landlady at the time of the birth of their illegitimate child. Morland implored Pepys to put in a word for him with James II to interfere in the trial: 'I presume that one word from His Majesty to his Proctor and Advocate and Judge would procure me speedy justice.'[15]

The suit for a nullity by Morland was stalled during the summer of 1687, since his evidence was so very thin.[16] Moreover Morland was himself in trouble with the court for obstinately refusing to pay Mary a penny of the temporary alimony awarded to her in order to allow her to fight her lawsuit. He was duly excommunicated for his contumacy, allowed the allotted forty days to go by, and was now threatened with arrest by 'rude fellows who threaten to take me dead or alive; so I am shut up as a prisoner in my own hut near Hyde Park Gate'.

He implored Pepys to persuade the King to give him £400, with which he could bribe enough witnesses to make his claim of a pre-contract stick, and so get the marriage annulled. Meanwhile Morland's matrimonial problems became the talk of the town, and as early as March Narcissus Luttrell recorded in his diary that 'Sir Samuel Morland the mathematician is lately married, and to not one of the best reputation.'[17]

What happened next behind the scenes is revealed in another letter of Morland to Pepys in the spring of 1688:

[14] Ibid. fos. 39–40.   [15] *Pepys Letters*, 176, 192.
[16] GLRO, DL/C/145, fos. 59–65.
[17] Ibid. fo. 405ᵛ; *Pepys Letters*, 184; N. Luttrell, *Brief Relation of State Affairs*, 6 vols. (Oxford, 1857), i. 396.

A little before Christmas last, being informed that she was willing, for a sum of money, to confess in open court a precontract with Mr Cheek; and being at the same time assured both by her, and my own lawyers, that such a confession would be sufficient for a sentence of nullity, I did deposit the money, and accordingly a day of trial was appointed. But after the cause had been pleaded, I was privately assured that the Judge was not at all satisfied with such a confession of hers, as to be a sufficient ground for him to anull the marriage, and so that design came to nothing.

Though Mary might be prepared to perjure herself in court in return for money, there were still some honest judges in England in 1687–8 who could be neither browbeaten by the court nor bribed by the litigants. Morland went on to explain to Pepys that, thwarted in the scheme to obtain a nullity, he had been advised by his lawyers to try to buy off Mary with a cash sum and a life annuity, in return for security 'never to trouble me more. But her demands were so high I could not consent to them.'[18]

In the spring of 1688, when some sort of financial accommodation seemed the only way that Morland might be able to get rid of Mary, he had a stroke of luck. He was unexpectedly informed that since the summer of 1687 Mary had been the mistress of a rich baronet who was providing her with the money for her lawsuit. His informant also alleged that Mary 'besides had the pox [i.e. gonorrhoea]'. Morland set to work and soon found proof of this new liaison. So he switched tactics and started a new suit against Mary for a separation from bed and board on grounds of adultery. If he won, he would at least not have to pay her alimony.

It is not hard to understand why Mary had entered into this relationship. Her chief problem in the autumn of 1687 and the spring of 1688 had been how to find the funds both to live in reasonable comfort and to fight her legal battles with Morland, especially since the latter was still refusing to pay her a penny in alimony. She therefore resorted to her usual solution, and looked around for a rich man who would make her his mistress. Her choice fell on a wealthy married but separated baronet, Sir Gilbert Gerard, Bt. Sir Gilbert, who enjoyed an estate worth between £2,500 and £4,000 a year, had married the daughter of the Earl of Falmouth in 1681, when he was only 20 years old. She had brought £8,000 with her as a marriage portion, so between them they were a very rich couple.

Two years later, however, in 1683, Lady Gerard sued her husband for

[18] *Pepys Letters*, 187–8.

separation on grounds of cruelty.[19] According to well-attested accounts, Gerard seems to have been almost deranged in his hatred of his wife. He was in the habit of going to bed with her with a naked sword in the bed beside him, and three or four loaded pistols behind the bed-head, which was enough to alarm the most trusting of wives. He also pinched and beat her so cruelly that she was obliged to leave home for the first time after only eighteen months of marriage. She soon returned, after a reconciliation, but the physical brutality was immediately renewed, and after a near-successful attempt by Sir Gilbert to suffocate her in bed with a pillow, she fled for her life and started a suit against him for separation from bed and board. Sir Gilbert had little to say in his defence, except that all the servant witnesses were liars, and that the real reason for his wife leaving him was that she would not accompany him from London to his estate in Yorkshire, saying 'I will go to Devilshire as soon as Yorkshire.' He accused his wife of gross extravagance and explained away all the weapons he took to bed with him on the grounds that this was 'usual for many persons of quality to have for defence of themselves and their families'. The Court of Arches issued no sentence on the case, and so the two presumably settled on a private out-of-court separation.

Such was the man whom Mary picked on as her protector and keeper two years later. It was a very risky venture, but her urgent need for money, left her little alternative. Discovery would inevitably expose her to a suit for separation from Morland, without alimony, leaving her as penniless as she had been before her marriage. But her new affair with Sir Gilbert paid off handsomely. From the summer of 1687 to the middle of 1688 Mary lived in comfort in a house in Piccadilly in a suite of rooms linked to those of Sir Gilbert. At first she passed as Madame Atkinson, the daughter of a person of quality who kept a coach and six horses. But in the spring of 1688, when they moved to a grand house in Leicester Fields, the couple brazenly passed themselves off as Sir Gilbert and Lady Gerard.

Sir Gilbert was plainly besotted with Mary, treating her as if she were his wife, and giving her money to support herself and to defend herself from Morland's lawsuits. In the first half of 1688 Morland pressed his suit in the London Consistory Court for separation without alimony on grounds of his wife's adultery, produced plenty of servant witnesses of Mary's open cohabitation with Sir Gilbert, and was duly awarded a sentence of separation.[20] Although he clearly neither liked nor respected

[19] LPCA, E. 7/67, 86, 89, 100; Ee. 5, fos. 50–63; Bodl. Rawlinson MS B. 382, fos. 42–6.

[20] GLRO, S/DL/C/242, fos. 136–41, 271–5.

Morland, Pepys may perhaps in the end have pulled strings on his behalf. The only evidence that Morland received royal help is that after she had lost the suit, Mary threatened to ask for a Commission of Appeal against the sentence, 'as pretending the King's Advocates and Proctor have proceeded illegally in this trial'. But nothing came of this, and all that Mary had to show for her plotting and scheming was that Morland had been made legally responsible for her debts and her maintenance from the day of her marriage on 1 February 1687 to that of the formal sentence of separation on 16 July 1688.[21] But it seems very doubtful whether she actually got any money out of him.

The story of Morland after he had got rid of Mary is soon told. He continued to have serious financial problems, not least due to the cost of these lawsuits with Mary, and in 1689, after the Glorious Revolution, he sent Archbishop Tenison a short autobiography, listing all his achievements for the State, stressing the value and expense of his inventions, and appealing to the new regime for support in his old age. This he seems to have received, for after he went blind in 1692 he continued to live in modest comfort in London, still inventing mechanical and arithmetical devices and experimenting with water pumps. He died in 1695.[22]

What happened to Mary is less certain. One would have supposed that in the normal course of events Sir Gilbert would eventually have tired of his new sexual toy and abandoned her. But it is said that after the death of Morland in 1695, Sir Gilbert, whose own wife had died two years before, actually married Mary.[23] This sounds implausible, and there is no hard evidence to back it up, but then almost everything about this tale is implausible. The period between 1660 and 1710 was an exciting but sinister age, when in the aftermath of the failed Puritan revolution high and low society appeared for a time to have lost their moral bearings. The villains appear larger than life, and the victims ridiculously gullible. Everyone was busy chasing everyone, in hot pursuit of money, sex, or power.

---

[21] *Pepys Letters*, 190.   [22] *DNB, s.n.* Samuel Morland.
[23] W. L. Chester, *Westminster Abbey Register, Harleian Soc.* 10 (1875), 20 n. 1, 198 n. 12.

14

Echard v. *Townshend*, 1704

The clandestine marriage system was mainly used by young couples seeking to arrange to marry without the knowledge or consent of their relatives and friends. On rare occasions, however, the device was used by parents to trap an unwary man or woman into an unwanted marriage alliance with their child.

One example, remarkable for the ruthlessness of the tactics employed, and the high social status of the participants, occurred in Norfolk in the last years of the seventeenth century. It involved the well-known baronet family of Bacon of Redgrave Hall, the impoverished minor gentry Townshend family and their grand cousins, the aristocratic family of Townshend of Raynham. Some were rich and powerful, others were poor and struggling to survive, but all the participants in the marriage plot were somehow related to the Townshends or the Bacons.[1]

George Townshend, a cousin of Lord Townshend of Raynham, had married the daughter of Sir Robert Baldock of Baldock Hall, and had produced three daughters, Mary, Kathleen, and Frances. George must have fallen upon hard times before the story began, since for ten years in the 1690s Mrs Townshend and two of her three daughters, Mary and Frances, were boarders with a Mr Dixon at Tacolneston Hall, a few miles south of Norwich. Other boarders at this establishment were Mr and Mrs Thatcher, the latter of whom was 'someway related' to the Townshends, and the Revd John Echard, the young Rector of the nearby parish of Wreningham, who was obliged to board out, since he lacked a parsonage in which to live.

John was a weak-willed and indecisive young man, who was easily persuaded by more cunning and determined people to say things he did not really mean, and do things he did not really want. Inevitably, the three young people, Mary and Frances Townshend and John Echard, were thrown closely together in this upper-class boarding-house. John soon fell head over heels in love with Mary, who was not only very pretty but also had a good marriage portion. John's income from the rectory

---

[1] LPCA, D. 653: 247, 254, 333.

was £150 a year, but it was heavily encumbered with debt and other obligations and expenses, so that he needed a wife who would bring with her a substantial marriage portion. John pursued Mary for two years from 1698 to 1700, but his ardour was not reciprocated: 'The more he endeavored to oblige her, the more she slighted him.'[2]

Throughout 1699 and 1700, Mary persisted in treating John with open disdain. On a trip to Stourbridge Fair she refused to allow him to hold her hand 'in the street and in company' and in general she 'used him very uncivilly and ungratefully', even to the point of using 'opprobrious and vilifying words of abuse' about him in the kitchen before the servants. She said that he 'was a lying blackhead, and ought to have his gown pulled over his ears', and hoped that someone 'might assault or fall on his person, and beat his eyes out or thrash or bang him soundly'. The final breach occurred at a Twelfth Night party in 1701, when Mary 'seemed perfectly to hate him and generally to treat him with great insolence and scorn'.

This persistent hostility of Mary was a great disappointment to John. The only alternative was Mary's sister Frances, but she was universally agreed to be ugly—John once unkindly called her 'crooked'. Moreover her marriage portion was only £20, and even that depended on the consent of her mother, who was said not to like her as well as her other two daughters.[3] But John became more and more grateful to Frances, who repeatedly upbraided her sister Mary for her harsh conduct, and who sided with him in some family quarrels.[4]

In the winter of 1700–1, John was confined to his room in Tacolneston Hall, since he had fallen off his horse and damaged his leg. Mary never came near him, but Frances was always there, full of sympathy and proffers of love. Although his heart was still set on the unrelenting Mary, he inevitably found himself attracted to Frances, who caught him on the rebound.[5] What John did not know, however, was that the 'friends' of Frances, including her parents the Townshends, the Thatchers, her uncle the Revd Baldock, and her remote kinsman Sir Robert Bacon of Redgrave Hall were all anxious to see her safely married. She was penniless and ugly, and if left a spinster was likely to become a burden to the family.[6]

In early 1701, things were brought to a head by Mr and Mrs

[2] Ibid. 103–6, 185, 382, 402–3.
[3] Ibid. 119, 131–2, 184, 203, 230, 256, 261–4, 301, 333, 380, 570.
[4] Ibid. 219–20, 393–6, 401–6, 409; Bodl. Rawlinson MS 382, fo. 330.
[5] Ibid. 106–7.   [6] Ibid. 334.

Thatcher, the only lodgers at Tacolneston Hall who were adults in their thirties, as opposed to adolescents aged about 19 to 20 like John and the two Townshend sisters. One day when they were sitting with Frances in John's sick-room, the Thatchers opened up the subject of the latter's intentions towards Mary and Frances, asking 'if he was in earnest or would have either of them—and particularly Miss Frances'. According to Mrs Thatcher, John was irritated by the question and gave an angry answer. But Mr Thatcher refused to be put off and asked him directly if he courted Frances, to which John replied vaguely 'I do design to marry her.' Taking advantage of that statement, Mr Thatcher said 'give me your hand.' He took John's hand, joined it to that of Frances and said: 'Now you are contracted to Miss Frances Townshend, and cannot marry any other woman but her; and if you marry anybody else, Miss Frances Townshend may sue you and recover any money of you for wife, and I am witness of your contract. Now I can swear I heard you promise Miss Frances marriage.'[7]

It looks very much as if the vacillating suitor had been trapped into making a contract out of what was intended to be no more than a vaguely expressed intention in the future. John himself did not deny that the episode took place, but argued that it was not serious. He claimed that Mr Thatcher was 'an airy frolicsome person' who 'in a merry and jocular way did propose a match between me and Miss Frances Townshend, and got our hands and put them together'. He firmly denied that this amounted to a 'contract or spousal' between Frances and himself, and professed himself still free of all marriage contracts.[8]

This was not a very plausible explanation of what had taken place, since it omitted all mention of the critical fact that John had told Thatcher that he intended to marry Frances. Since the Thatchers were kin and friends of the Townshends, it seems likely that they deliberately caught the rather weak-minded John Echard off-guard, at a moment when he was despairing of ever gaining Mary's affections and was deeply grateful to Frances for her attentions to him. By canon law the ritual was a contract in the future tense, freely entered into, and proved by two plausible witnesses, Mr and Mrs Thatcher. But since it was in the future tense, it was not legally binding unless followed by consummation, a point about which John appears to have been entirely ignorant.

In the spring of 1701, Frances Townshend left the boarding-house at Tacolneston and went a few miles south to live with her uncle the Revd

---

[7] Ibid. 72–4, 205–12.   [8] Ibid. 107–8.

John Baldock at his rectory at Redgrave, just across the Norfolk border into Suffolk. During that spring and early summer John often rode over to Redgrave. One reason was to pursue his courtship of Frances, especially when in March the Revd Baldock declared his intention to give his niece £2,000 as a marriage portion. This immediately made Frances much more attractive in John's eyes, even if his heart was still set on the unresponsive Mary. He wrote many letters to Frances, and in June he gave her a gold ring, which was always regarded as a significant sign of an engagement. Another reason for John's frequent visits to Redgrave was that in June the Revd Baldock fell sick, and on several Sundays John officiated for him in Redgrave Church.[9]

At Redgrave, Frances found two friends and enthusiastic supporters, Jane and Abigail Bacon, the young daughters of Sir Robert Bacon, 5th Baronet, of Redgrave Hall. The Hall had been built by Sir Nicholas Bacon in the middle of the sixteenth century, and was largely unaltered (Plate 1). As a result, the great hall, which measured about forty feet by twenty, was still the centre of domestic life.[10] The Bacon daughters, especially Jane, were eager to coax Frances's dilatory suitor into a more open declaration of his intentions. Some time in June they invited Frances over to dinner at Redgrave Hall, and John said that he would call in later to pick her up. When he arrived, he was shown into the great hall, where he found the three young women sitting in a window embrasure. Jane called for a bottle of wine and offered a toast to 'John Echard's mistress's health', and then enquired innocently who his mistress was, Mary or Fanny. John replied evasively 'It is not Miss Mary,' to which Jane came back with 'name your mistress and drink her health, whosoever she is'. With this pistol at his head, John weakly gave way and said 'Miss Fanny, your health', looking at and bowing to Frances.

Later in the same month, Frances, John, and Jane all went into the gardens of Redgrave Hall to pick strawberries. Jane soon tactfully withdrew, leaving the other two alone for an hour. Frances later testified that John 'among other courtships asked her when they should be so happy as to be married'. John's version was that they merely discussed Mary's 'scornful treatment' of him.[11]

The crisis came on 29 July 1701, when the Revd Baldock, John, and Frances were all invited by Sir Robert Bacon to dinner at Redgrave Hall. As it turned out, this was a trap, artfully laid by Sir Robert, to get the

---

[9] Ibid. 100, 135–6, 258, 267, 420, 587–8, 593, 600–2.
[10] E. R. Sandeen, 'The Building of Redgrave Hall', *Suffolk Institute of Archaeology Proceedings*, 29 (1964). I owe this reference to Dr Howard Colvin.
[11] Bodl. Rawlinson MS 382, fos. 75–9, 112, 159.

unattractive Fanny once and for all off the family hands and transferred to those of John. After dinner John and Frances retired first to a room and then to the garden for an hour, during which they discussed 'love and marriage'. When they rejoined the Bacon family and the Revd Baldock in the drawing-room, someone said 'the two lovers had best be married, and handsel the new common prayer book', which was lying conveniently on a table.[12]

Before he knew what was happening, John found himself standing with Fanny before the Revd Baldock, who began to read the marriage service over them. The only hitch occurred when John was asked if he would take Frances as his wife, to which he unexpectedly answered 'Nolo' (Latin for 'I will not'). The women, who knew no Latin, had no idea what he meant. Sir Robert Bacon, who was giving away the bride, sternly ordered John to 'recollect himself', at which his last flicker of resistance crumbled and he weakly replied 'Why, then, I will.' He was so agitated that at first he said 'I John take thee Price,' but then he changed it to 'I John take thee Frances.' The rest of the service, including the ceremony of the ring, supplied by John from his own finger, was duly performed without a hitch, except that the company laughed at the eagerness with which Frances said 'I will.'[13]

After it was all over, the company wished the couple joy, John kissed Fanny and all the women, and the women kissed Fanny. According to Abigail Bacon, John sat down and pulled Fanny on to his lap, saying 'Come, my dear, now you need not be afraid to sit down.' After a quarter of an hour, the couple retired to the house of the Revd Baldock.[14] Consummation did not take place, however, because Fanny 'did not think what was done was sufficient authority for doing so'.[15] Clearly, nobody had a very good grasp of the canon law on the subject of clandestine marriage.

Everyone later agreed that the Revd Baldock was very anxious to marry off his impecunious niece, and that Sir Robert Bacon was the master-mind behind the whole scenario. There were too many witnesses to the clandestine marriage for there to be any serious doubt that it happened exactly as described. Even John never absolutely denied it, merely claiming that he took the earlier talk of marriage as 'a banter, and laughed to hear it'. He implausibly claimed that he treated the marriage ceremony itself as 'a mere jest and joke to divert the company', in which

---

[12] 'handsel' is archaic for 'use for the first time'.
[13] Ibid. 83–6, 138–41, 150–1, 167–70, 235–47.
[14] Ibid. 170–82, 188–99.   [15] Ibid. 170–82, 188–99, 361–3.

he took part out of politeness because he was a guest in Sir Robert Bacon's house. He asserted that he was laughing all the time, and that the Revd Baldock was so convulsed with merriment that he had to put down the Book of Common Prayer.[16]

The real puzzle is why Sir Robert chose to plan a carefully orchestrated clandestine marriage, which was bound to cause trouble sooner or later, rather than to arrange for a proper marriage by licence in the parish church. The answer must be that he was afraid that, if given time to reflect, John would refuse to go through with it. The only hope was to catch him by surprise and then bully him into saying his part, which is exactly what happened.

Within a few days of 29 July, the Revd Baldock realized that he had done something very foolish and dangerous. Since the ceremony had been performed by a clergyman with the full rites of the church according to the book of Common Prayer, and attested by many witnesses, it was certainly binding for life at canon law. But by performing a clandestine marriage in a private house without banns or licence, the Revd Baldock had broken the law and rendered himself liable to suspension from performing the services of a minister for three years and to a fine of £100. To make matters worse, Sir Robert Bacon forced him to enter this clandestine marriage in the official register of Redgrave Church, so that there was official written evidence of what had happened.

To get himself out of this scrape, the Revd Baldock decided to try to legalize the situation. On 11 August, less than two weeks after the clandestine marriage at Redgrave Hall, he obtained a blank licence to marry from the surrogate (which itself was illegal), and proposed to John and Fanny to fill in the license in their names, and carry out a swift and private marriage in church at 8.30 the next morning. By backdating the licence and using it as a permit to perform another marriage in church, he hoped to exonerate himself from blame for having carried out the clandestine marriage.

His scheme was thwarted, however, since John refused to go through with a second marriage in church, and left the area immediately. But the Revd Baldock did not give up attempts to save himself from legal jeopardy, and six months later he paid the collector of taxes on births, marriages, and deaths for the parish of Redgrave £1. 2s. 6d. for the marriage in the register book. This did not save him from later being fined £100 for performing a clandestine marriage, but he seems to have

[16] Ibid. 115–17, 129–30, 257, 261, 272.

avoided suspension for three years, presumably due to the influence of Sir Robert Bacon.[17]

The bridegroom, John Echard, was the other person who within days —or perhaps hours—began to have qualms about what he had done on 29 July, 1701. He had gone through a marriage ceremony, but had no idea whether or not it was legally binding. His bride was an impecunious and ugly woman, and he still had his eye on her well-endowed and pretty elder sister. The marriage had not been consummated, because of moral doubts by Fanny about its legality, and by 12 August John had left her.

Between 9 August and 28 August, however, he received and replied to a string of letters from Fanny, all affectionate in tone and signed 'your sincere friend and humble servant till death'. It is significant that this phrase omits the key word 'wife', further suggesting that Fanny did not consider the clandestine marriage as valid. A month later, however, in late September, she changed her tune and was full of reproaches: 'Your denying any such thing as marrying of me proves yourself a very ill person, for had you been an honest man, I had demonstration of that which you now falsely assert not to be true.'

When John received the letter, he said that 'Fanny had sent him a letter which grieved him as much as if one had struck a dagger in his heart'. He claimed that he had not denied the marriage 'and if he had he would recant it'.[18]

At about this time, John met Mrs Thatcher at the Norwich Assizes and invited her to have a drink with him and his maidservant at the White Swan. He remarked that someone at the court 'had wished him joy' of his marriage. Mrs Thatcher asked him 'Are you married?', to which John replied: 'I cannot tell, but Revd Baldock read matrimony and Miss Fanny and I said after him.' Mrs Thatcher reminded him that earlier in the year she had warned him 'of your doing ill in case you pretend more than you intend towards Miss Fanny'. John assured Mrs Thatcher that 'Fanny shall never be the worse for loving me', and drank her health, crying 'Oh, dear Fanny'.[19]

It is clear from this and other testimony that during September and October John was not only uncertain whether he really wanted to be married to Fanny or not, but also whether the clandestine marriage was binding or not. At the same time Fanny at first thought that the marriage was insufficient to permit her to go to bed with John or to call him

---

[17] Ibid. 131, 152–3, 273, 307–9, 341–4, 355–7, 425, 459–60.
[18] Ibid. 616–27, 226–7, 584–8.   [19] Ibid. 213–15.

husband, but later began to claim to be his wife. On 2 October she told a friend that at first 'she did not look upon herself as married', but was later assured by others that 'it was a marriage'.

The reason for her change of tune was that the Townshend family was by now negotiating on her behalf for a financial settlement from John. They demanded an allowance for Fanny in return for a formal release from any matrimonial engagement with Fanny. This release was very unlikely to be found legally binding if tested in court, but it might be good enough as a bargaining counter. Whether it would free John and Fanny to remarry was an open question. John's (probably correct) interpretation of Fanny's change of attitude over the validity of the marriage was that 'she was instructed by some of her friends to make such pretensions to him, with design to get money, if it might be, of him for a release from her'.[20] Despairing of proving the clandestine marriage, the Townshend family were now trying their hand at blackmail instead.

The first meeting to discuss terms for a financial settlement was held in the Revd Baldock's house between Fanny and Baldock on one side and John's brother Thomas Echard on the other. Thomas Echard was strongly opposed to the marriage, presumably on the grounds of Fanny's poverty, and it is therefore unclear who was the first to propose negotiations to abandon it in return for compensation. The Revd Baldock (falsely) assured George Townshend that by mutual consent the clandestine marriage 'might be discharged or released', but Fanny herself was by now very uncertain about what to do. She was afraid that 'the noise and clamour' aroused by rumours of the clandestine marriage would prevent her from marrying again later.[21]

Nine days afterwards, however, on 11 October, Fanny allowed her father George Townshend to continue negotiations with John's brother Thomas Echard for 'a mutual and friendly agreement about the pretended marriage'. The negotiators met on 30 October, when Mr Townshend demanded £500 in cash, 'but seemed shy of declaring what it was for'. He had good reason for 'shyness' in coming out into the open, since the Townshend family was now plainly using the clandestine marriage as a bargaining chip to obtain future maintenance for Fanny. But this could not be stated openly because of its patent illegality, so Mr Townshend merely hinted that in return for the money he would arrange for 'mutual discharges and releases given to each other of the pretended marriage'.

---

[20] Ibid. 117.   [21] Ibid. 358–63, 427–8.

A few days later Mr Townshend repeated the demand for £500 in front of a witness, but admitted that he had no authority to promise a release 'so as both parties might marry elsewhere'. As a result, the negotiations were stalled, although Mr Townshend had not entirely given up hope. A day or two later, he met John and Thomas Echard in an alehouse and said to the former: 'You know what I propounded to you, that for thirty pounds a year or five hundred pounds you may have an end of it, or discharge.' Or, as he put it more clearly on another occasion, he would offer 'to free Mr Echard of all manner of claims to him as a husband, and by a good and lawful acquittance discharge him of all pretended matrimonial contracts or engagements whatsoever'.[22]

The trouble was, however, that even the cleverest of lawyers could not devise a document which would effect a binding release of both parties from the marriage, would allow them to remarry, and would prevent them from suing each other later in the church courts. John would therefore be paying good money for an unenforcible contract. Mr Townshend was advised by his lawyers that his proposal was illegal, and negotiations were therefore broken off. The blackmail had failed.[23]

While John's brother Thomas was actively negotiating with Fanny's father in an effort to annul the marriage, John himself was, as usual, having second thoughts. On 12 October he wrote a friendly letter to Fanny, telling her that his brother had made him promise not to see her, but asking for a secret assignation at Market Harling the following Tuesday. He wrote: 'I pray that God will direct us both to our mutual advantage and satisfaction, and I hope in this your prayers will be joined along with him who is, dear heart, your affectionate friend and humble servant, John Echard.' Fanny agreed, and they duly met, with what results are not clear. But the fact that John and Fanny were still anxious to keep the relationship alive as late as October 1701 helps to explain what happened next.[24]

The Townshend family, who knew nothing of this overture by John, were advised by their lawyer to get Fanny to sue John in the Norwich Consistory Court for 'restitution of conjugal rights' in other words to prove the legality of the marriage, the real object being to force John to pay a fixed maintenance for one who was his lawful but abandoned wife.[25] This was what John in court rightly described as a plot 'to shift off a burden from themselves and lay it upon me'. He told the court that

---

[22] Ibid. 117–18, 274, 276–88, 344–8, 360, 366–76.
[23] Ibid. 221, 276, 312–15, 346–7, 354, 366–76.
[24] Ibid. 430, 467.   [25] Ibid. 96, 280.

Fanny, when asked what she would do with him as a husband, if she won her suit, had replied: 'As soon as I have got maintenance of him, I will get rid of him as fast as I can, and if no other way will do it, I will endeavour it by brandy.' He also told the court that the suit was merely another blackmail device to force him to come to terms out of court and settle a life annuity on Fanny, in return for which he would be 'discharged of all manner of matrimonial contracts and matrimony between them', thus in theory leaving him free to choose another wife.

He complained that 'if her friends had given her more money and made her fortune, instead of spending money in suits, there should have been no disturbance in the Court; and if my Lord Townshend had made any proposal he [John] would not have been unreasonable'. He blamed Fanny's father George for not approaching Lord Townshend 'to see what he would have done'. John felt particularly bitter about the financial aspects of the marriage, since the Revd Baldock, who had formerly promised Fanny £2,000 as a portion, had withdrawn the offer and was now spending the money instead on litigation, first on this suit of his niece Fanny to prove her marriage, and second to defend himself from the suit by the church court officials against him for performing a clandestine marriage.

Fanny's father George Townshend was promoting her suit and her uncle the Revd Baldock was paying for it, and her influential relative Sir Robert Bacon was backing it, while Lord Townshend was hovering in the background.[26] Given this family support, it is hardly surprising that the suit dragged on from December 1701 until the spring of 1702, and that the breach widened between the Townshends and Bacon on the one hand and the Echards on the other. Harsh recriminations were exchanged in court, at the prompting of each party's proctor; lies were told and wild allegations were made on both sides.

John told the court that 'he could not love Fanny nor like her parts', and claimed that he had never had any intention of marrying her, since 'her portion is so small, and her fortune so slender and inconsiderable, and her person so disagreeable that if I would take her to wife, I must thereby be ruined in my estate and would probably be under a great temptation of treating her harshly. And because of our want to mutual affection our lives would be uncomfortable and the happiness of us both, now and hereafter, would be greatly endangered.'[27] But this was a later, and partly false, reconstruction of his original state of mind.

[26] Ibid. 258, 260, 274, 288, 335–8, 358, 437, 459, 582.
[27] LPCA, D. 653: 285–6.

But there is evidence that despite all this public show of animosity, John was still ambivalent in his feelings towards Fanny. By April 1702 she had fallen very ill at Mr Dixon's boarding-house at Tacolneston Hall, to which she had returned. John was worried, and told friends that 'if she grows worse I will see her myself, let what will come of it', adding that 'I love her very well, whatever people might say of me'. In May John visited Mr Dixon's boarding-house to see how she was getting on, and they had another meeting. John's abbreviated and probably biased account was that they met accidentally on the road, when Fanny was out walking with Mrs Dixon. He admitted he saluted her (i.e. kissed her) and congratulated her on her recovery. He went on to blame her for the lawsuit against him brought by her friends and to remind her of 'the unkindness of her sister Mary'. By his own account, he said: 'Since I was denied the eldest sister, Miss Mary Townshend, with so much scorn and insolence, I will never be so much babbled and culled as to have the youngest, Miss Frances Townshend, imposed upon me.' Fanny wept, and invited him in, but he refused.[28]

Other witnesses to the scene told a rather different story. They said that when they met, John got off his horse and kissed Fanny several times, holding her tightly in his arms. He said that, compared with Mary, 'Fanny has a better skin, a better forehead, and I am sure better hair, and in my opinion better wit.' Accused of telling the court that Fanny was 'crooked and he could never love her', he explained that his proctor had made him say it. All the witnesses agreed, however, that during their half-hour conversation John did say that if only her friends had settled a fortune on her, the lawsuit would have been unnecessary. As he left John said 'I hope no advantage will be taken on account of this meeting,' and some months later sent a man to offer a witness a guinea to keep her mouth shut and not describe to the court what had happened.[29]

After this meeting and semi-reconciliation, the suit ground on its inexorable way throughout the summer of 1702. Given the canon law about clandestine marriage, the conclusion of the court was predictable, and a Major Brown offered all comers odds of 3 to 1 in guineas that the court would give sentence for Frances and the validity of the marriage.

Since the judge's speech explaining the sentence of the court has not survived, one can only guess what were the legal considerations which induced such uncertainty as to cause an exceptionally long delay. The marriage seems to have been perfectly straightforward, except that John's first reply to the question whether he was willing to marry Fanny was

[28] Ibid. 476–9, 508.   [29] Ibid. 434–7, 533–60, 582.

'nolo', which he only changed to 'I will' after some verbal pressure put on him by Sir Robert Bacon. The legal issue was presumably whether the evidence of this change of mind indicated that John had not undertaken the marriage freely, but rather under duress.

In January 1703 the court issued the sentence, upholding the validity of the marriage. But John obstinately refused to concede defeat and appealed the case to the Court of Arches, thus greatly increasing the costs on both sides. In June 1705, two and a half years later, the Court of Arches upheld the original sentence and declared the marriage valid and binding.[30]

What happened next we do not know. John's moods had vacillated so wildly in 1701–2 for and against marriage with Frances that it is hard to predict how he must have reacted to the final verdict of 1705 that he was bound to Fanny for life. It seems most likely, however, that protracted and bitter litigation had long since destroyed what bonds of affection still existed between them in early 1702. If so, then John would have been obliged to agree to give Fanny a suitable maintenance allowance for life, while they continued to live apart. The calculating machinations of the Townshends and the Bacons may be said to have paid off, in the sense that Fanny was at least provided for financially.

But the result was to prevent either Fanny or John from remarrying, unless he or she chose to risk bigamy. At this fairly elevated social level, and after such a widely publicized series of lawsuits over the clandestine marriage, it seems likely that both were forced into a life of solitude or cohabitation. The efforts of the Townshends and Bacons to get rid of their responsibility for Fanny succeeded all too well for the happiness either of her or of her vacillating suitor John Echard.

[30] Ibid. 608; B. 14/58.

15

Harcourt v. *Harcourt*, 1707

In 1707 John Harcourt, the son of a fairly well-to-do Norfolk country gentleman, had just come down from Cambridge with a BA degree, had taken orders in the church, and was looking around for a suitable parsonage and a wife to go with it.[1] His first choice fell on a woman called Anne Jermy, whom he courted for several months, although how far they had become morally or legally committed to each other was a matter that was later disputed.

In February 1708 John switched his interest to Frances Hunt, the younger daughter of another country gentleman, and asked her mother for formal permission to court her. As is so common in these stories, her father was apparently not informed about what was going on. According to Mrs Hunt, whose evidence is highly suspect, she specifically questioned John about his relations with Anne Jermy, telling him that 'you have been a long time acquainted with Miss Jermy, and you must not pretend to my daughter if you mean anything there'. She alleged that John replied that 'he was not contracted to any other woman'.[2]

After permission to court was granted by Mrs Hunt, things moved fast, since the houses were only about eight miles apart, and the two families saw a great deal of one another. During February John frequently came on visits to the Hunt house for several days at a time, and he and Frances were observed by many witnesses to spend much time in each other's company, exhibiting all the signs of love and affection. But only one witness alleged that John ever called her 'spouse'. It later turned out that by late February Frances had allowed John to start sleeping with her, on the basis of nothing more substantial than a secret contract of marriage. Even that degree of commitment was later disputed, and one

---

[1] Norfolk CRO, Norwich CC Records, Con 49, 59, 62; Dep 55. These documents have been labelled as follows: Libel (L); Answer (A) Depositions and Interrogatories (D):

Revd Charles Preston	D. 1–2	Revd Bainbrig Dean	D. 9–10
Frances Hunt	D. 3–5	Mary Preston	D. 11–12
Wally Leigh	D. 6–6v	Miles Baispoole	D. 13–16
Mary Leigh	D. 7–8		

[2] A; D. 3, 5ᵛ.

witness asserted that John had always made it clear that marriage with Frances was conditional on the consent of his old father.[3]

Involved in this affair were a close-knit little group of friends, all living to the north of Norwich within ten miles of one another. All were either parish gentry or parsons; all lived in houses large enough to accommodate up to eight or nine overnight guests; and all were constantly riding over to visit each other for days on end. They seem to have lived a life of almost constant extended party-going. They included Mrs Hunt and her daughter Frances of Heveringham; the Leighs of Catton, who were the Hunts' other daughter and her husband; the Revd Charles Preston, vicar of Barton Turf, and his wife, who lived barely a mile away from John Harcourt and his old father at Neatishead. Finally, there were two bachelors, Miles Baispoole from Aylsham and the Revd Bainbrig Dean, Rector of Belaugh.

On 8 March 1708, a three-day party began at the Leighs of Catton, attended by Mrs Hunt and Frances, John Harcourt, Miles Baispoole, and the Prestons. Everyone observed the great love and affection shown towards each other by John and Frances, and Mr Baispoole took it upon himself to cross-question John about their relations. The latter explained that he regarded himself as 'contracted to her before God as his wife', and admitted that they were already sleeping together. Mr Baispoole strongly advised the young man that, since sexual relations had already begun, he was honour bound to tie himself more securely to Frances. His story, which may or may not be true, is that on the same evening he took Frances and John off into another room, locked the door, and privately read to them the marriage ceremony from the Book of Common Prayer, including the ritual of the ring. John and Frances made the appropriate responses and repeated all the words after Mr Baispoole.

If it ever happened, this ceremony was clearly a secret marriage contract, which if it had been witnessed would have been binding at law. But there were no witnesses, except that Mrs Hunt later alleged, almost certainly falsely, that she was looking through a hole in the door and saw and heard it all. Unfortunately, she spoilt her story by claiming to have spied through a door leading to a room different from that in which Mr Baispoole claimed to have conducted the ceremony. She testified that first Frances and then Mr Baispoole came into her bedroom, told her what had happened, and assured her that John had said he 'would be married regularly the next morning'. Frances then left her mother, and openly went to bed with John. She later told Mrs Preston that 'Mr Baispoole did

[3] D. 6, 9, 13.

marry me to John Harcourt and put us in bed together'. For the next three days, during which the party stayed on at Catton, Frances and John were openly sleeping together behind locked doors and addressing each other as 'love' and 'dear'. The Hunts claimed that they also addressed Mrs Hunt as 'mother' and the Leighs as 'brother' and 'sister'. But the party broke up on 13 March without any move by John to arrange a regular church marriage, although he made public promises to do so soon and never to marry anyone else.[4]

Ten days later, on 23 March, the whole group and the Revd Bainbrig Dean assembled again for another extended party, this time at the vicarage of the Prestons at Barton Turf. Early the next morning Mr Baispoole told John that 'it is necessary to marry regularly to avoid scandal', and John expressed his willingness to go to church to be married by the Revd Preston that morning—or so they later alleged. Preston refused to conduct a marriage without a licence, so his son was sent off to try to get a marriage licence from the local surrogate. But he returned empty-handed, since the latter had run out of blank licence forms. Because of this the whole party moved that same evening about eight miles to the Leighs' home at Catton, which was only two miles from Norwich, where it would be easy to procure a licence.[5]

Early in the morning of the 25th Mr Leigh and the Revd Dean rode into Norwich and obtained a marriage licence, paid for by Mrs Hunt, under seal from the bishop's clerk. But by the time they got back to Catton it was after the canonical hour of twelve, and John used this as an excuse once more to postpone the marriage until the next day. Hitherto the Revd Preston had been meticulous in fulfilling the canon law, but he unexpectedly caved in at eleven o'clock that night, perhaps in a moment of drunken good will. What happened was that the sleeping arrangement for the party had become confused. Two married women, Mrs Preston and Mrs Hunt, were supposed to be sharing a bed, but when they tried to get into their room, they found the door locked. Mr Baispoole set his foot against the door and forced it open, only to find John and Frances in bed together. The party, including the two Prestons, Mr Baispoole, and Mr Dean poured into the room, where John and Frances continued 'tumbling' in the bed. At the same time Mrs Hunt and her daughter Mrs Leigh stood outside on the landing and looked in. The Revd Preston sat on the bed, with the Book of Common Prayer in his hand, and said: 'How now Jack! You have got a very pretty lady. Will you marry her?' When John coolly replied 'yes, for this night' (or 'no, unless I can have

[4] D. 1, 3, 3ᵛ, 4, 11ᵛ, 12, 13.   [5] L; D. 4, 7, 7ᵛ, 11, 13ᵛ, 14.

her for one night'), Preston was taken aback and retorted: 'Pox, what do you mean? If you have her, you must have her forever.' Turning to Frances, he asked 'Frances, what say you, will you have him?', to which she replied: 'You hear? He says he won't have me.' Preston once again asked John if he would marry Frances, to which he replied firmly 'By God, no, parson, no matrimony for me except for one night.'[6]

Up to this point, all the witnesses are agreed about what happened, but there are two versions of what occurred next. Mrs Hunt and her daughter Mrs Leigh alleged that the Revd Preston pushed on with the marriage service, despite this unpromising beginning, and that both John and Frances said 'yes, yes, I will' or 'Ay, ay' at the appropriate moments. They also claimed that the ceremony of the ring was carried out, with John repeating the words. On the other hand, the more independent witnesses, not only the Revd Preston and his wife, but also Mr Leigh and the Revd Dean, ostentatiously avoided any mention of a marriage ceremony. They said that as soon as John had refused to take Frances except for the night, the two clergymen withdrew and went to bed.[7]

All the evidence suggests that the Revd Preston and the others had come into the room all ready to carry out a clandestine marriage ceremony there and then, with the couple already in bed together. But when John refused to take Frances except for the night, and flatly declined marriage, the party left them to it and dispersed to bed. It seems virtually certain that the story of the clandestine marriage ceremony was cooked up later by the Hunt family to try to protect Frances's now tarnished honour. It is, after all, supported only by the Hunt family, the mother and the two daughters, and denied by everyone else present; and it makes no sense since it followed so firm a refusal by John. What is agreed, however, is that about two hours later the Prestons and the Leighs were woken up by the noise of revelry in the bedroom, where the younger members of the party were throwing the stocking and publicly making merry on and around the alleged bridal bed.[8]

The next day the party dispersed, and Mrs Hunt took the young couple off to her own house at Heveringham, where they continued to sleep together and treat each other as husband and wife. For the following nine weeks, from 25 March to the end of May, Frances was boarded at the Prestons, presumably because it was only two miles from the Harcourt house, so that John, who was still sleeping with her, could

---

[6] D. 1, 4ᵛ, 9ᵛ, 14.   [7] D. 1ᵛ, 4ᵛ, 5, 6, 6ᵛ, 7ᵛ, 8, 9ᵛ, 11ᵛ, 14ᵛ.

[8] D. 2, 5ᵛ, 8, 9ᵛ, 10, 12; these pagan rituals were taken very seriously by the public at all levels of society.

easily slip over to see her. At that time, according to the Revd Preston, Frances 'did not look upon herself to be a married woman'. Meanwhile, somewhat belatedly, the Hunt family at last approached old Mr Harcourt for his consent to the marriage of his son to their daughter, and negotiated with him over the financial terms. The old man was not enthusiastic about the match, but in the end they agreed that the Hunts were to give with Frances a portion of £500 down, and that the next reversion of the rectory of Heveringham, which was in their gift, would go to John. In return, Mr Harcourt promised to settle a jointure to Frances in her widowhood of £50 a year. These were terms which were equitable to both families. But what is significant is that the old man clearly had no idea that his son and Frances were already perhaps contracted or even married, and certainly sleeping together. As a result he was still talking about the need to obtain their consent before the terms were made final.[9]

Early in May, some five or six weeks after the 25 March marriage episode, for unknown reasons, John left Frances's bed, never to return. Some time during the summer he married his old flame Anne Jermy of Hainford, and by September the Hunts were suing the Harcourts in the Consistory Court of Norwich, accusing John of bigamy and claiming a prior marriage to Frances. What the upshot was we do not know, but on the evidence it seems likely that the Hunts failed to establish proof of a legal marriage. The alleged contract carried out by Mr Baispoole was unsupported by any witnesses (except Mrs Hunt's claim to have seen and heard it all through a convenient hole in the wrong door); and the alleged clandestine marriage service was not mentioned by any of those present except members of the Hunt family.

The most remarkable aspect of the story is the permissive attitude taken by these respectable gentry and parsons of Norfolk in about 1700 towards pre-nuptial intercourse between young people from very respectable families, which they allowed to go on in bedrooms behind locked doors in their own houses without so much as a word of protest. If only for reasons of prudence, such behaviour was folly, and it is possible that Frances became pregnant as a result of it. She certainly seems to have been desperate for a husband, for sometime in late May, only a week or two after John had left her, she asked the Revd Preston whether he could use the old licence obtained for herself and John to marry her to a new suitor—which of course he could not.[10]

---

[9] A; D. 1ᵛ, 12.　　[10] A; D. 2, 12.

In this case, as in so many others, the whole business of courtship seems to have been managed and controlled by the mother of the girl, Mrs Hunt. Her strategy was clearly designed to capture John Harcourt as a husband for her daughter. The two flaws in her tactics were her failure even to try to control her daughter's sexual behaviour before marriage, and her failure to negotiate financial terms at an early stage with John's father, or even to keep him informed and obtain his consent. These errors left the Hunts defenceless when John finally tired of Frances and deserted her bed. Presumably Mrs Hunt hoped first to make John a prisoner of sex, and then to persuade his father to come to terms. But the scheme was destroyed by the ebbing of John's sexual passion after three months of satiety. The methods used by Mrs Hunt, the tolerant attitude towards pre-nuptial sex adopted by all the family friends, and her ultimate failure to marry off her daughter, were at bottom the products of the peculiar moral, customary, and legal ambiguities in the late seventeenth and early eighteenth centuries about just how an indissoluble marriage was formed.

16
Beaumont v. Hurnard, 1706–1712

The complications to which the legal anomaly of the clandestine marriage could lead are well illustrated in the case of the marriage in 1706 of Joseph Beaumont to Catherine May.[1] The Beaumonts were a respectable small gentry family, living in a manor house at Tattingstone near Ipswich in Suffolk. The father, John Beaumont senior, did not have much success in controlling the marriage of his three children, Joseph and John, and one daughter. In about 1702–5, his teenage daughter eloped with one of her father's servants and was married clandestinely without banns or license or her father's consent by the Revd Samuel Gibson, a disreputable parson living at Bures, about fifteen miles away.[2] The latter had been deprived of his office and benefice by the ecclesiastical authorities for some nameless 'enormities committed by him'. Even his widow admitted that he was 'looked upon in the neighborhood to be a lawless priest', and the record bears her out. It was said that 'Mr Samuel Gibson would marry anyone without banns or licence', and this was apparently how he earned his living.[3]

In late 1705 John Beaumont's eldest son Joseph, who was still under age, fell in love with Catherine May, the teenage daughter of an even more marginal gentry family who lived a couple of miles away at Stutton. Joseph visited the Mays' house a number of times, until both families firmly forbade any further pursuit of the courtship. The Beaumonts were presumably unwilling to marry their son and heir downward socially and financially, while the Mays had probably heard something disadvantageous about Joseph's character and behaviour, and probably also thought Catherine too young to marry. At all events, they objected strongly. Joseph quarrelled with his father, and early in January 1706 left the family home and moved a few miles away to the village of Whepstead, where he found some lodgings.[4]

From there he secretly continued his intrigue with Catherine, and on

---

[1] LPCA, D. 384.   [2] Ibid. 102.
[3] Ibid. 93, 115, 139.   [4] Ibid. 102, 119, 125.

14 February she slipped out of her father's house very early in the morning, and the pair galloped some fifteen miles to Bures to find the Revd Gibson. Joseph had already met Gibson and knew his trade, since he had been sent by his father some time before to try 'to prevent the marriage of his sister'. On arrival the Revd Gibson as usual asked no questions, did not demand to see a licence, and immediately took them upstairs, with his wife as a witness, and barred and bolted the door to keep out any possible rescue party. He then performed the marriage service according to the Book of Common Prayer, after which Catherine and Joseph left for the latter's lodgings at Whepstead. Meanwhile Catherine's father had sent a servant in hot pursuit, but he presumably did not know where to look and only reached the Gibson house the next day, far too late to stop the proceedings.[5]

On arrival at their lodgings, Catherine and Joseph had supper and immediately went to bed. The marriage was certainly consummated that night, for Joseph told the landlord it had been done, and Catherine admitted the same to the landlord's wife. It was not, however, an enjoyable night for either of them. All day Joseph had been complaining of a pain in his arm, which was swollen and red from an incision performed to let blood by a doctor three days before. It was clearly turning septic, and in the middle of the night he was in such pain and was groaning so loudly that the landlady got up to find out what was wrong. A message was at once sent to summon a surgeon and a doctor from Ipswich, about two miles away.[6]

Poor Catherine, however, had something even more disturbing to worry about. During the night she had discovered that her new husband was suffering from venereal disease, which had taken such a hold that he had an open ulcer or chancre on his genitals. She confided to the landlady a few days later that she was afraid 'she had received some prejudice from Mr Beaumont and that Dr Brereton advised her not to bed any more with Mr Beaumont'. They had been married on Thursday the 14th and Catherine continued to lie in the same bed with Joseph at least until Monday the 18th. Meanwhile the septicaemia from his arm spread rapidly through Joseph's body, and although attended by a surgeon, a physician, and an apothecary, none of them could do anything to save him. His parents were summoned to his bedside, and on Sunday the 24th, a mere ten days after the marriage, he died.[7]

[5] Ibid. 103, 113, 166–7, 119, 142–3.   [6] Ibid. 119, 126–7, 129.
[7] Ibid. 95, 104, 120, 125, 127, 128–9, 135, 140, 156.

The feelings of Catherine, who could not have been more than 16 or 17, since Joseph—himself a minor—addressed her as a child, were inevitably mixed. The landlady, who seems a reliable witness, said that during Joseph's sickness she appeared 'sometimes a little thoughtful, and sometimes unconcerned, but she wept at his death'. She had experienced a dawn elopement; a squalid clandestine marriage ceremony; defloration by a new husband who turned out to be riddled with venereal disease, and who was in such pain that he was groaning in agony in bed the same night; and his death ten days later. All this would cumulatively have been a severe shock to even the toughest of constitutions. It seems, however, from subsequent events that she was indeed very tough, and that the discovery of her husband's venereal disease almost wholly alienated her affections from him. The surgeon testified that 'I can't say that Catherine showed any great kindness or tenderness for Mr Beaumont in his sickness'.[8]

Immediately after Joseph's death, the Beaumont parents took charge of arrangements. Mrs Beaumont fetched Catherine in her coach and took her back home with her to Tattingstone. Her husband, Mr John Beaumont senior, ordered a painter in Ipswich to make an escutcheon with the name of the Beaumonts and the Mays to hang over the front door—and sent to Mr May to enquire what were the family arms. He was also heard calling Mr May 'Brother May', so that there can be no doubt that he regarded the marriage of Catherine with his late son as perfectly legal, if unfortunate. At the funeral Mr Beaumont escorted Catherine, whose widow's weeds he had paid for, to the grave of her late husband in the family churchyard at Tattingstone, and then took her back with him to his house.[9]

So far, Mr and Mrs Beaumont's behaviour to their suddenly widowed daughter-in-law is open to the interpretation that it was motivated by a desire to do the right thing: to see their son decently buried and to show pity for the lonely and friendless young widow. Their next moves, however, do not lend themselves to such a favourable interpretation. They kept Catherine in the house with them, and a mere ten weeks after the death of her first husband, they had openly and officially married her off to a second, Mr Philip Waldegrave. This was a very extraordinary thing to do, since seventeenth- and eighteenth-century etiquette dictated a year's mourning before a widow could decently remarry. Catherine herself and other witnesses agreed that Philip Waldegrave was more or

8 Ibid. 128, 96, 134.   9 Ibid. 84–7, 120–1, 144.

less forced upon her by the Beaumonts, and after the marriage she and Philip continued to live in the Beaumont house at Tattingstone, presumably at the Beaumonts' expense. One can only speculate about the motives of the Beaumonts for this indecent haste in marrying off their newly widowed daughter-in-law. We do not know whether Philip was a young man or an old one, or what the Beaumonts hoped to get out of him. The match certainly cost them money, for one of the inducements held out to Philip to get him to pay court to Catherine was that Mr Beaumont promised him 'that he would give him no trouble, and that he should in the right of his wife enjoy the thirds or dower due to her out of his son Joseph's estate'. Whatever it was he was after, it seems clear that Mr Beaumont did not get what he expected out of the marriage.

He died soon afterwards, and his son and now heir John junior, Joseph's younger brother, refused to hand over Catherine's dower. There was a family row, and Catherine and Philip left the Beaumont house and began a lawsuit against their brother-in-law John to obtain the dower. Philip hired an Ipswich attorney to prosecute the suit, but died before the matter came to court (leaving the attorney unpaid). Meanwhile, apparently before her second husband's death, Catherine had been caught in bed with one of his servants, a fact which was apparently common knowledge all over the district, for many witnesses at the trial, on both sides, admitted having heard about it.[10]

Despite the blots on her reputation, Catherine promptly managed to attract yet a third husband, Robert Hurnard. In 1711 the Hurnards launched a suit against John Beaumont in the Court of Common Pleas to recover the property due to Catherine as her thirds or dower, to which she was entitled by reason of her marriage with Joseph. John Beaumont countered with a suit in the ecclesiastical courts to declare the marriage invalid, but his arguments were internally inconsistent. It was, therefore, hardly surprising that the Consistory Court rejected Beaumont's case, and that the latter's appeal to the Court of Arches was abandoned long before it came to sentence. Catherine presumably had to be bought off by John Beaumont.

Here the story ends, and the chequered career of young Catherine May, with her three husbands and one or more lovers in five years, sinks back again into the darkness of unrecorded history. It shows how extraordinarily easy it was before 1753 for a young couple in a moment of enthusiasm to run off and get indissolubly married for life in defiance of their parents, and how one of the parties might well regret her action a

---

[10] Ibid. 87–9, 97, 106–7, 134, 141.

few hours later. It also shows the legal and financial tangles such clandestine marriages could cause, which for years on end might tie up the resources and energies of several gentry families, and lucratively occupy many lawyers.

17
Rudd v. *Rudd*, 1720–1730

In October 1720 there lived in the town of Carmarthen a 16-year-old Welsh baronet, Sir John Rudd, who had come there to attend school, accompanied by his mother. Among his schoolfellows were the children of a Mr Phillips, at whose house he met their servant, a poor young woman called Lettice Vaughan, who lodged with a Mrs O'Key, and with whom the young baronet fell in love. Unknown to Lady Rudd, the courtship proceeded for three months from August till October, when the infatuated boy was foolish enough to ask Lettice to marry him secretly. Lettice located a parson three miles away 'who for reward would perform clandestine marriages', found a friend to give her away and another to serve as witness, and arranged for the ceremony to be performed in her room in Mrs O'Key's house at seven in the evening one Saturday—after dark in order to avoid arousing suspicion. The groom had to leave immediately after the ceremony, since 'he must be home by eight o'clock' as a result of which consummation could not take place till some days later.[1]

As might be expected, news of the marriage eventually seeped out, and by January 1721 it had become the talk of the town. Lady Rudd and Sir John's guardian were naturally furious at this clandestine marriage of a boy baronet to a penniless, low-born, and uneducated servant girl. They immediately shipped Sir John off to Utrecht in Holland to get him out of the way. Lettice never saw him or heard from him again, and there is no reason to think he had any lasting feelings for her. He was just an inexperienced rich boy of a good family, who had not only fallen in love with a servant girl, which was common enough, but had been silly enough to marry her. By eighteenth-century standards, this was not only foolish but socially scandalous, as he no doubt was soon made to realize.

After Sir John was removed to Utrecht, Lettice moved back to Swansea to live with her mother. She now called herself Lady Rudd, as she was indeed legally entitled to do. But she lacked the resources to assert her legal claim to maintenance as a wife, and so was obliged to eke

[1] LPCA, D. 1805: 139–46, 153–6, 199.

out a miserable living as a mantua-maker, without any assistance whatever from the Rudds.[2]

In about 1725, when Sir John came of age but was still abroad, the
Rudds mounted a deliberate campaign of deception in order to lure
Lettice into a second, bigamous, marriage, which they planned to use as
a first step to obtain the dissolution of the first. They gave out that Sir
John was dead and had an obituary published in the local newspapers.
His mother, Dame Beatrice, and her other relatives went into mourning
for him, and his younger brother, then at Cambridge University, took the
title of Sir Anthony Rudd, Baronet. Six months later, Lettice went to
Dublin, thinking herself a widow, and the Rudds lost track of her.[3]

In Dublin she was courted by and married a dealer or merchant called
John Blackham, but three years later his business failed and they moved
to London in dismally wretched circumstances. To conceal himself from
his creditors Blackham changed his name to Smith, so that Lettice now
passed as Mrs Smith. While in London, Smith tried to earn a living as a
shoemaker, and Lettice gave birth to two children, while augmenting the
family income by taking in washing. So poor were they that they all lived
and worked in a single room, and yet to make a little more money they
agreed to sublet one of the two beds to a Mrs Steward for 6*d*. a week.
Mrs Steward was an elderly widow who had met Lettice in Covent
Garden Church and, because they were both Welsh, they became
friendly. Mrs Steward stayed with the 'Smiths' for about two months,
during which time she was told by a Welsh footman that Lettice was in
fact the wife of Sir John Rudd, Baronet. People so close to the margin of
absolute poverty cannot afford to put friendship or loyalty before gain, so
as soon as she moved elsewhere Mrs Steward went to Lady Rudd and
informed her of Lettice's whereabouts. She admitted in court that over a
period of three months Lady Rudd gave her 5 guineas 'towards her relief
and support', and there were plausible rumours that she had been hired
by Lady Rudd for £50 to round up witnesses to the bigamous cohabitation of Lettice and Mr Smith. She was thus first befriended by Lettice,
and then betrayed her.[4]

Lettice had never made much of a secret of once having been Lady
Rudd, since she had always believed that Sir John was dead. Her first
knowledge that he was still in fact alive was the citation served on her
from the ecclesiastical court on a suit by Sir John Rudd for separation for
bed and board by reason of her adultery with Mr Smith. As a pious

[2] Ibid. 127, 271, 452–4.   [3] Ibid. 176, 199, 453–8.
[4] Ibid. 101, 104–5, 225–32, 239, 242, 259, 398–9, 458–63.

woman she was very uneasy at the situation she found herself in, and soon afterwards separated herself from Smith.[5]

Oddly enough, she won her case in the Consistory Court in 1730, presumably because of the plausible evidence that the Rudds had tricked her into believing that Sir John was dead, but she inevitably lost it on appeal to the Court of Arches in 1731, for tricked or not she had undoubtedly committed inadvertent adultery (and bigamy). Sir John then used this judgment to clear the way for a private Act of Parliament, which at last in 1734 gave him (and her) a full divorce with freedom to remarry.[6]

This did no good for the Rudd family, however, for Sir John died without issue five years later, his younger brother Anthony also died childless, and the male line, and with it the title, expired. What the story shows, however, is how it was occasionally possible by the 1730s to use the system of full divorce by Act of Parliament, in order to free a young heir to a title from the binding legality of a clandestine marriage. But it could only be done by an elite family with plenty of money, and access to the best legal advice, which was prepared to use a good deal of low cunning, duplicity, and blatant manipulation of the law.

[5] Ibid. 259, 465.   [6] Ibid. B. 15/200; Private Act G. I cap. 21.

18

Griffin v. Griffin, 1712–1714

Normally, the clients of the Fleet parsons were poor persons of no account in the world, and their marriages were of concern only to the Church authorities, anxious to stamp out the scandal of clandestine marriages, and after 1696 to the state, which put a stamp tax on all marriage licences and certificates. The Griffins of Dingley, Northamptonshire, however, were a wealthy aristocratic Roman Catholic landed family. The first Lord Griffin was a loyal supporter of James II, but he timed his affairs so badly that he was raised to the peerage a mere eight days before James fled the country, and so left himself with little choice but to accompany his master into exile.[1] In 1708 he was captured, tried for treason, and condemned to death, but was finally pardoned and allowed to die in the Tower of London two years later, at the advanced age of 80. His title and his much encumbered estates were inherited by the second Lord Griffin, also a Roman Catholic. He was described by Swift as 'a plain drunken fellow', and died in 1715 without leaving any mark on the historical record. He did have the good sense, however, to educate his son and heir Edward as a Protestant Tory, sending him to Rugby School and then to Christ Church, Oxford.

During the three years the boy was at Rugby, from 1707 to 1710, he became close friends of the Harpur brothers, sons of John Harpur, 'a gentleman of good estate and a man of worth and reputation' in Derbyshire. Mr Harpur moved house to Rugby 'for the more convenient and better education of his children'—one of the earliest examples of an elite parent putting his children's education above all other considerations in his choice of a place to live.[2] As a result, Edward Griffin was often in and out of the Harpur house, where he met and became very friendly with Elizabeth, the pretty sister of his two friends. He wrote her love-letters, which he conveyed by slipping them into her prayer book while they were in church. In 1710 Edward left Rugby for Oxford, and the pair did not meet again for over a year, at which time Edward Griffin

---

[1] *Peerage*, vi. 203–4.   [2] LPCA, D. 85: 110–11, 141–2.

was a 19-year-old undergraduate and Elizabeth a woman of 20. They now began courting seriously, but agreed 'to keep the courtship private from their respective parents'.[3]

By early 1712 Edward Griffin had finished his time as a student at Oxford, and was living in London, preparing for the Grand Tour. In March, Elizabeth obtained her father's consent to make a seven-week visit to a London friend she had met in Rugby, the daughter of a well-to-do orange merchant called Peacock, who lived in Billingsgate. While staying in the Peacocks' house, Elizabeth was visited by Edward Griffin almost every day, and by April 1712 they were deeply in love, so much so that they took what was an extremely foolish decision for two under-age children of substantial squire and peerage families: they agreed to get married, 'but withall privately and without the consent of their parents'.[4]

Ignoring the warnings of Elizabeth's friend Mary Peacock about her going out alone with a young man at so late an hour, on the evening of 20 April 1712 Elizabeth jumped into a hackney coach with Edward Griffin and drove away into the night. As they galloped off, Mary shouted after them 'take care what you are going about'. Elizabeth returned an hour later, and when asked where she had been, replied evasively 'I have been doing no harm,' and asked Mary not to tell the rest of the household that she had gone out.[5]

What happened during that hour can be reconstructed from several witnesses, and the story throws a vivid light on the way the Fleet marriage business reacted to the increasing pressures of the law. The couple first drove directly to the Fleet Prison, where they saw Dr Vyse, the well-known marriage parson and now a close prisoner.[6] But he was frightened by the new laws and was taking no chances. He asked the young couple whether they had a licence, and when they said no, he flatly refused to marry them. But he did recommend them to a friend, a Dr Draper, who worked outside the prison in the Rules and so ran fewer risks under the new law. Draper was now 66 years old, and was making a precarious living by performing clandestine marriages, while a prisoner for debt in the Rules of the Fleet, where he had been for two years.[7]

His story was that between 8 and 9 p.m. he was visited in his room in Green Arbour Court by two 'gentlefolk' and a footman, who all came

---

[3] Ibid. 40–1, 111, 143–5.
[4] Ibid. 41–3, 113–14, 174–5, 195–6.
[5] Ibid. 174–87, 188.
[6] Whom we have already met pp. 105–12.
[7] Ibid. 44, 125.

upstairs to see him. The couple proposed that he should marry them, and when asked if he had a licence, Edward replied: 'I come from Dr Vyse of the Fleet, who was well satisfied,' and handed Draper a letter from Vyse, explaining that he was 'a minister and then a close prisoner in the Fleet', and asking him 'to marry them for him, and he would do as much at another time for him'. So Draper obligingly married them on the spot in his room, without a licence. When it came to issuing a certificate he took an unstamped blank and filled it in. Draper later testified in court that the certificate was 'subscribed by his name, though not with his own hand'. He explained that 'he conceived himself, in case he had subscribed this with his own hand, as liable to prosecution for felony under the stamped paper clause in the recent Act of Parliament'. It was an ingenious effort to escape the penalties of the law, but his failure to sign the certificate made it worthless. In order to strengthen the evidence for the marriage, Edward Griffin wrote on the back of the certificate—'The proof: no. 268'—which was the number of the hackney coach in which they had come and which was waiting for them—and gave it to Elizabeth. Draper also made an entry of the marriage in 'his pocket book of all marriages by him solemnized', and also in 'some one or other of the Public Registry books belonging to the Fleet Prison', which was known as 'Dr Draper's Register'.[8]

After it was all over, the couple returned back in the coach to the Peacocks' house, and there parted company. A week later Elizabeth returned to her father's house in Rugby, where she was joined a few days later by Edward, who stayed in the Harpur house for two or three days. During this visit Edward and Elizabeth consummated the marriage in as public a manner as they dared. Elizabeth confessed to the housemaid that she was married to Edward, and asked for her help. On 29 April, the first night of Edward's stay, she ordered the maid to bring a bottle of wine and a preserved orange to Edward's chamber, which was the best room in the house. When the maid brought them to the room, Edward asked her to tell Elizabeth to come to him, and she saw the latter go into the room and lock the door. Half an hour later Elizabeth unlocked the door and invited the maid into the room to see herself and Edward in bed together, naked to their shift and shirt, telling her that she must remember that 'she saw them in bed together, that they might not be parted'. This is one more proof that it was widely believed that a public bedding would give additional validity to a marriage. After the maid left, Elizabeth again locked the door, and she and Edward spent the night together in his

[8] Ibid. 125–38, 46–51.

chamber. The next morning the maid found the imprints of two bodies in the feather bed, and the usual tell-tale stains on the sheets.[9]

One way and another, this was about as legitimate and well documented a Fleet marriage as could be devised at the time: there were three written entries—in the private notebook, the register, and the certificate—and a note of the number of the hackney coach, by which the coachman could be traced to confirm the trip to the Fleet. The Revd Draper and Edward's footman were witnesses to the marriage ceremony, and the maid at Rugby was witness to the consummation.

In May 1712 Edward first returned to London and then went back to his father at Dingley, but the couple kept in close touch by letter. By June rumours of the courtship, but not of the marriage, were beginning to circulate and had reached the ears of the two fathers, Lord Griffin and John Harpur, both of whom took it very badly. In these elevated social and economic circles, young people were not supposed to enter into courtship, much less marriage, without prior parental consent. As Edward explained to Elizabeth, 'if your father knows that we are married, he will not give you what he designed' for her marriage portion. He also reported that because of the rumours merely of the courtship, his own father, Lord Griffin 'is still in a very great passion and swears he will never see me more'.[10] His reaction to the news that a clandestine marriage had taken place could be expected to be even more explosive.

Edward Griffin was sent off to Paris to complete his education, and for the next three months the two ignorant fathers engaged in an elaborate fencing match over the financial terms of a possible marriage, that is the size of Elizabeth's portion and of the jointure which in return Lord Griffin was willing to settle on her in her widowhood. Lord Griffin opened negotiations, through a parson intermediary, seeking to extract the largest possible marriage portion with Elizabeth, his opening demand being for £2,000 in cash down. Mr Harpur retorted that he could not and should not pay such a large sum, since his estate was encumbered with a jointure for his mother, and he still had several other children to provide for. To complicate matters still further, at this critical stage Elizabeth fell very ill, and her father used this as an excuse to argue that it would be folly for him to give her a large portion without strings, since she might die at any moment and he would lose it all for nothing. On behalf of Lord Griffin the parson countered with an offer to return the

---

[9] Ibid. 218–23, 55–6.   [10] Ibid. 85.

portion if Elizabeth should die within a year or childless, and proposed a face-to-face meeting of his Lordship and Mr Harpur to settle the matter—a meeting which in fact never took place.[11]

Elizabeth entered the fray after prodding by letters from Edward in Paris saying: 'I hope that your father will act as he ought to do, that I may return.' She wrote to her mother: 'I beg you to see Mr Griffin hath one thousand pounds, which was to have been my portion.' She followed this up with a letter to her father, urging him: 'if ever you hope your children will prosper in this world, and that souls be saved in the next, I desire that Mr Griffin may have the portion you designed to me given him.'[12] The last proposal Lord Griffin made to Mr Harpur was that he should pay £1,500, of which £1,200 was cash down and £300 payable in two or three years. But the sticking point was whether the money should be returnable if Elizabeth died within a year or childless, and on this issue the negotiations finally collapsed.[13]

While all these negotiations were going on, Edward was first in London and then in Paris with the Earl of Shrewsbury, so that the pair of lovers thereafter kept in touch only by correspondence. At first Edward's letters were full of affection and promises of fidelity, telling Elizabeth that 'though my person is not with you, my heart is', and signing himself 'your everlasting husband'. From London he told her that he had been offered an official position with the new ambassador to France, the Duke of Ormonde, but had refused it 'only upon your account'. When he was asked by the Queen in person in full Council if he wanted to go, he deliberately did not reply. The Queen excused him, he kissed her hand, and left the room. He told Elizabeth: 'I think I may truly say: "Ambition cease to alarm me, Honour and Court adieu".' He boasted that 'this has made a great noise in town, you may be sure, after my denial at Court'. If she had been perceptive, Elizabeth might have detected in this boastfulness signs of inner regret that he had sacrificed a promising political career for love of her. He also told her that he had visited the Revd Draper to make sure that the clandestine marriage was duly entered in the register 'and all is right'.[14]

At first arrival in Paris he wrote enthusiastically: 'I think our joys are now completed, nothing now is wanting but our meeting. And when that is done, I think we have nothing left to do but for ever to love one

---

[11] Ibid. 63–6. [12] Ibid. 108.
[13] Ibid. 66–7. [14] Ibid. 73, 76–8, 82.

another, which part your faithful shall never be wanting in.' It does not seem to have crossed his mind that the really hard part might be 'for ever to love one another'. He proposed that as soon as the money matters were settled, and parental consent was obtained, they should marry again in the face of the church.[15]

By late 1712, however, it had become evident that Edward's attachment to Elizabeth was steadily eroding, thanks to physical separation, relentless parental pressure after the collapse of the financial negotiations, a realization of his dependence on his father for money, remorse about having turned down the job with the Ambassador, and the pleasures of life in Paris. He was beginning to realize that he had made a fool of himself by marrying so precipitously without parental consultation. Meanwhile the story of the clandestine marriage was leaking out, which further enraged both fathers. Edward assured Elizabeth: 'if I go through all the pangs and tortures of this world I will satisfy myself in being yours and yours only. I think you have no reason to doubt what I write, since I have already sacrificed all that I have in the world to you... Your faithful and loving husband, Edward Griffin.' This reiterated stress on his sense of sacrifice should have acted as a red flag to Elizabeth. Other letters referred to the bitter quarrels between the two parents over the money, in which Edward tended to side with his father against Mr Harpur, whom he accused of reneging on a promise of £2,000 with Elizabeth. He warned that 'my Lord is mad, he talks strangely what he will do next'.[16] This seems to suggest that he was afraid that his father might disinherit him altogether.

By the winter of 1712, as negotiations between the fathers still trailed on inconclusively, Edward began writing in a rather different style, now stressing money rather than love: 'The best thing you can do is to spur your father to pay or get ready the two thousand pounds as soon as he can, and I give you my word and honour I will come back as soon as he is ready to pay it... If your father will do anything that we may be together handsomely, I will come back.' He also specifically mentioned the marriage, saying: 'you was pleased to order me not to say anything concerning what was done at Mr Draper's, but I do intend to tell my father, with your consent.' In another letter he concluded ambiguously: 'Paris is a very pleasant place and I doubt must be the place I shall spend the rest of my life.' Finally, in early 1713, as Mr Harpur stuck to his guns

---

[15] Ibid. 83–4.   [16] Ibid. 85–6, 93–8.

and refused to offer more than £1,000, Edward gave up, and wrote Elizabeth one last letter, breaking off the relationship:

Dear Betty,
Forever farewell, from one who wishes you all the happiness in the world. Your father will not let me be the man that is to make you [a husband].

Elizabeth's reply was a melancholy poem about the injustice of life between the sexes, ending:

> Men to new joys and conquests fly
> And yet no hazard run.
> Poor we are left if we deny,
> Or if we yield, undone.

In August 1713 Edward married Mary Welden, the daughter of a rich man, a landed gentleman and former Governor of Bengal, who no doubt provided a large portion with her.[17] So far as he was concerned, the relationship with Elizabeth Harpur was finished, and the clandestine marriage never happened. But she refused to let him go so easily.

Some months later, 'Elizabeth Griffin' sued Edward Griffin in the London Consistory Court for restitution of conjugal rights, a suit designed to prove the validity of their marriage. All Edward's letters were produced and the whole story came out about the Fleet marriage, the consummation, and the subsequent abortive financial negotiations between the parents. The Revd Draper appeared as a witness for the marriage, claiming to have been an ordained clergyman for forty-two years, but neither the court nor the Harpurs were able to locate the only other witness to the marriage, Edward's footman, who had suspiciously vanished.[18] The lawyer hired by the Harpurs testified that he had gone to the Fleet with Mr Peacock, the father of Elizabeth's friend, inspected the entry in the Revd Draper's pocket-book, and made a careful copy of it. He could not find the entry in the first Fleet marriage register he inspected, one kept by a distiller near the prison gate. But on enquiry he learned that after the Act of Parliament had forbidden, under severe penalties, marriages without licences on stamped paper, this register only accepted entries of marriages which had complied with the law, at least in this respect. The distiller told him that 'Mr Draper's Register is kept at the Bull and Garter, next door to the Fleet Prison', and indeed he found

---

[17] Ibid. 93, 100–1, 112; *Peerage*, vi. 204.   [18] LPCA, D. 85: 119.

it there, kept by a woman. Later the lawyer met Mr Draper at an inn, produced from his pocket 'a piece of parchment stamped with a single five shilling stamp', and got him to write out another formal marriage certificate on it, and this time to sign and date it himself.[19]

The Harpurs' evidence thus consisted of the testimony of the clergyman, a copy of the entry in his pocket-book, the original unsigned certificate on unstamped paper, and the new signed certificate on stamped paper. They also had the number of the coach which had taken Edward and Elizabeth from Mr Peacock's house to the Fleet on 20 April 1712, although for some reason they were unable to produce the coachman in court. The former maid of John Harpur at Rugby testified to witnessing the consummation of the marriage in the family home on 29 April, 1712. Moreover Edward had specifically mentioned the Fleet marriage in a letter to Elizabeth. Finally, before the court he flatly refused to answer any questions about either it or indeed about any of the contents of his letters.[20] If ever a Fleet marriage was fully proven, and supported by the negative evidence of Edward's failure in court to deny it, this was surely it.

The only defect in the evidence was that the second witness to the marriage, Edward Griffin's footman, could not be found. It was obvious that the Griffins had deliberately hidden the man, but on this ground of there only being a single witness, the court declared the marriage not proven. In doing so, the court was no doubt heavily influenced by the fact that Edward had already made a socially and financially advantageous second marriage, which a sentence in favour of the earlier Fleet marriage would nullify. The Harpurs appealed the sentence up to the Court of Arches, but then let it drop, so that the case never came to trial in that court.

The legal rejection of the Fleet marriage was disastrous to all parties. Edward Griffin, who assumed the title of Lord Griffin on the death of his father in 1715, had no heirs by Mary Welden, and separated from her, looking elsewhere for companionship and love. As a result, when he died thirty years later in 1742 he had no legitimate heirs, and left his estate of and house of Dingley to an illegitimate son Edward, by his mistress Bridget Taylor, the daughter of a local gentleman. He had held no public office, and his second marriage had clearly been a failure. One way or another, his fleeting love affair with Elizabeth Harpur back in 1712 had ruined his life.

[19] Ibid. 161–71.   [20] Ibid. 114–15, 217–23.   [21] *Peerage*, vi. 6: 204.

Elizabeth never remarried, and despite the failure of her lawsuit to prove the legitimacy of her marriage, until her dying day she insisted on calling herself Baroness Griffin. She died in 1767, over half a century after her clandestine marriage, and in her will she described herself as 'widow of Edward Lord Griffin'.[21] If anything, her life was even more shattered than that of Edward, who in his later years had at least found a mistress to comfort him and produce an heir.

19
Phillips v. *Cresse,* 1738

Apprentices formed a significant proportion, perhaps even a majority, of all men involved in legal disputes about the validity of contract and clandestine marriages in the City of London. This is hardly surprising. These were young men in their late teens and early twenties, who were indentured to serve their masters for seven years, in order to learn a trade and at the end to qualify as Freemen of London, which would enable them to practice that trade. One of the standard conditions of apprenticeship was that no marriage should take place during the seven-year period. But in the crowded workshops and houses of London craftsmen and tradesmen, these young men inevitably came into close daily association with young women—servants, lodgers, fellow apprentices, or neighbours—and equally inevitably fell in love. Each had an urgent desire to sleep with the woman of his choice, but if he did so, she was liable to become pregnant. If he married the woman once she was pregnant in order to save her reputation, the apprentice would forfeit his apprenticeship, and be unable to practice his trade in London without paying a sum far beyond his means to obtain his Freedom of the City. His career would thus be ruined. If, on the other hand, he refused marriage, then his reputation would be tarnished by being cited by the parish authorities as the putative father of a bastard child. Whether he was married or disgraced, his father might very well refuse to supply him with the capital he needed in order to set himself up in business.

As a result, apprentices who fell in love before their term had expired twisted and turned in vain efforts to avoid the inevitable moral crisis, triggered off by the woman getting pregnant. One alternative, to which only a few resorted, was to purchase and give to her some pills designed to induce a miscarriage. But these abortifacients seem rarely to have worked—at any rate we usually only hear of those which failed. And whether they failed or succeeded, they frequently made the woman extremely ill, sometimes endangering her life. If this happened, she was likely in her agony to blurt out the truth about who was the father.

Even if the secret of who was the father was kept, and the woman gave birth, the young man was still faced with fulfilling the promise he had made to her that once his apprenticeship was expired, he would marry her. But the unmarried mother all too often found that once the father was out of apprenticeship, he found new and equally persuasive reasons for delaying the marriage.

The trouble was that by that time, the young man's passion for the woman had often cooled and he no longer wanted to marry her. Furthermore the end of apprenticeship marked a moment of acute financial crisis. The young man had to acquire the capital to rent a house, furnish it, and lay in a stock of raw materials and tools in order to set himself up in business. He also had to build up a clientele, so that he could begin to earn a living. The most obvious source of capital was his father or mother, but they were likely to be enraged to discover that he had made a secret marriage or contract with a poor girl without their knowledge or consent. The other way to raise capital was by marriage with a rich wife, possibly his former master's widow or daughter. But this involved reneging on any previous marriage contract or denying any previous clandestine marriage.

No doubt most young men in this situation either married the woman whom they had impregnated, or worked out some agreement for financial compensation and a small annuity, but in some cases either no offer was made or it was found insufficient, and the whole matter ended up in an ecclesiastical court. Either the woman sued to enforce her claim to a contract or a clandestine marriage, or the man sued to obtain a court order for the woman to cease making such claims.

A classic example of such a situation, remarkable only for the duration of the relationship and the high moral sensibility displayed at first by the apprentice, the woman, and her mother, is the case of Thomas Phillips.[1] In early 1738 he had for two years been an apprentice to a wine-cooper in Seething Lane in the heart of the City. He was only 20 years old, and his apprenticeship still had exactly four years to run, when he was foolish enough to fall in love with Eleanor Cresse, the 18-year-old daughter of a milliner. Without the knowledge of his master, his father, or her mother, the couple decided to get married, if possible in a legal way, but for secrecy in a parish other than that in which they resided. Thomas first applied to the curate of St Catherine's by the Tower, but was refused when he admitted that they were both minors and did not have parental permission.

So he returned to Eleanor, told her of his failed attempt, and urged her to settle instead for a clandestine marriage by a Fleet parson. At first she

---

[1] GLRO, DL/C/170, H. 282–95.

refused, but he assured her that such a marriage 'was as good and would be as firm and valid in the law as a marriage had and solemnised by virtue of any licence whatsoever'. She finally agreed, and they went to a well-known marriage shop near the Fleet Prison, the Sign of the Hand and Pen, where they were married by one of the most notorious of the Fleet parsons, the Revd Walter Wyatt. Wyatt gave her a marriage certificate, drawn up on her insistence immediately after the ceremony. To avoid detection, they had claimed to be resident at Barking, Essex, instead of the London parish of All Hallows, Barking. But when the certificate was produced in court seven years later, the word 'Essex' had been obliterated—presumably by Eleanor's mother—and 'All Hallows' inserted instead. This clumsy attempt to conceal the false residence statement in the certificate cannot have added to its credibility before the court.

On the evening of their wedding-day, Thomas and Eleanor went to the latter's mother, confessed what they had done, fell on their knees, asked for her blessing, and begged her to keep the marriage secret. Thomas explained that if it were known to his master before his apprenticeship had expired 'he should be absolutely ruined', since he would lose his right as Freeman of the City to practice his trade. He also added that it was equally important to keep the marriage secret from his father, from whom he had 'great expectations'. He hoped for 'a handsome fortune', but his father was 'of such a rigid and morose temper and disposition' that if he heard of the marriage made without his consent 'he would not give him one farthing—and would never see him again'.[2] If all this about his father were true, Thomas had behaved with criminal irresponsibility.

Mrs Cresse was no fool, and was uncertain what to do. She was shocked at 'the disreputation of a Fleet marriage' for her daughter, and was not at all sure whether it was legally binding. To put her mind at rest and show her that he had 'no sinister view or design' to debauch her daughter without a legal marriage, Thomas offered to try to see if he could obtain from some other source a licence for an open church wedding. So all three went to another parson, but when Thomas evaded his question whether he was over 21, he refused to marry them. After

---

[2] That these prospects were very real is shown by the case of William Reynolds. An apprentice to a London bookseller, in 1738 he made a Fleet marriage with another apprentice. When the marriage became known, he was promptly discharged by his master, his father refused to give him a penny, and he was forced to abandon his wife and emigrate to Boston, Mass. (GLRO, DL/C/167, H. 294–300).

this set-back, Thomas offered to try somewhere else and to lie about his age, but Mrs Cresse would not hear of him committing perjury.

As a result, deadlock ensued. Thomas could find no parson to marry them by licence, and Mrs Cresse refused to let him consummate the marriage with her daughter without a proper church wedding. Six days after the Fleet marriage, however, Mrs Cresse finally relented and gave the young couple the use of a bedroom in her house. But normal life as a married couple was impossible, for fear of arousing the suspicion of Thomas's master, his father, or the neighbours. So for the five years that Thomas continued his service as an apprentice, he was only occasionally able to sneak off to lie with his wife. This occurred in February 1738, just after the marriage, and in October and November of that year; in April, May, and October 1739; in April, June, and November 1740; in May, June, July, and October, 1741; in February, October, and November 1742; and in May and June 1743.

When Thomas's apprenticeship ended in February 1743, Mrs Cresse and her daughter urged him openly to acknowledge the marriage, but he begged them to wait until his father had settled on him the money to set up in business on his own as a wine-cooper. But further delay was now not possible, since Eleanor had been impregnated in November, and the baby was due in July or August 1743. Thomas admitted the cogency of the argument and agreed to go down to Newbury, Berks. to see his father, tell him about the marriage and pregnancy, and ask for the capital to set up in business. But to protect his right to take up the Freedom of the City, he asked the Cresses to declare falsely that the marriage had only taken place after February 1743, when his apprenticeship had expired. The drawback to this was that it meant that the Cresses would have to pretend—falsely—that their daughter had become pregnant before she was married.

Thomas must have met with a very hostile reception from his father, for he found it prudent to stay in the country, while Eleanor's time of delivery came closer and closer. After waiting in vain for several weeks for him to return from the country or to write, the Cresses went to his brother-in-law, a distiller in Smithfield, and told him the whole sorry story. Eleanor gave birth to a daughter in late July, by which time Thomas was flatly denying in public that there had been any marriage. So in October 1743 Mrs Cresse took legal action, suing Thomas in the Court of Common Pleas for board and lodging for him and his wife Eleanor ever since the Fleet marriage in 1738, and for the expenses for the birth (and burial) of the child. The jury found the evidence of a marriage convincing, and Mrs Cresse was awarded £100 plus costs, to be paid by Thomas.

But in February 1744 Thomas fought back, by launching a suit in the London Consistory Court for jactitation of marriage—that is an order forbidding Eleanor from claiming marriage. By now the court was refusing to accept any written evidence of a Fleet marriage, including a register, much less a marriage certificate which had already been altered by another hand. As a result, the Cresses were ordered by the Consistory Court never again to claim publicly that Eleanor was married to Thomas. Thus, despite the verdict of a jury in a secular court which based its decision on the validity of the marriage, Thomas Phillips was now free to marry another woman. Eleanor Cresse became just one more young London girl who lost her virginity and her reputation by putting too much trust in the promises of a sex-starved apprentice and the dubious records kept by a Fleet parson. It was cases like this which nine years later, in 1753, drove Parliament to pass the Marriage Act, which declared that all marriages by minors without parental consent, all contract marriages, and all clandestine marriages, were henceforth null and void.

20
Osborne v. Williams, 1714–1716

Until the early eighteenth century, domestic relations in many high aristocratic families were characterized by the ruthlessness with which parents exercised control over children in the choice of a spouse. The degree of pressure varied from family to family, as did the resistance put up by the children themselves, the most defenceless being daughters whose marriage portion depended on the good will of their parents. This story provides an example of the lengths to which some elite parents were prepared to go in the first decades of the eighteenth century to enforce such control and to punish any disobedience to their wishes. It provides an extreme example of the twin conflicts generated by the choice of a spouse: a conflict over authority, between patriarchy and individualism; and a conflict over motive, between interest—meaning money, property, influence, and status—and love.

Lady Bridget Osborne was born in 1684, the elder daughter of Peregrine Osborne, later 2nd Duke of Leeds (see Genealogy). The latter had started life as the younger son of a North Country baronet, and at the age of 24 he had married the heiress of another baronet and had settled down on her estates in Hertfordshire to live the life of a country gentleman. Six years later, following of the unexpected death of his elder brother, he found himself the heir to the great fortune that his father, by then Earl of Danby, had been busy accumulating through gross political corruption in his office of Lord Treasurer. Thanks to his father's patronage, Peregrine became an admiral, and in the 1690s had a brief if not very glorious naval career.[1] But he was unreliable, dissolute, and a hopelessly extravagant wastrel, being described by two independent witnesses as 'very rakish and extravagant in his manner of living', and 'wild and loose in his life and conduct'. He was prone to violence, being involved in two duels, and later in life became an ardent Jacobite (Plate 2).[2]

Because he feared that his son and heir might squander much of the

---

[1] R. Clutterbuck, *History and Antiquities of the County of Hertford*, 3 vols. (London, 1815), i. 447; A. Collins, *Peerage of England*, 8 vols. (London, 1779), i. 239–40.
[2] *Peerage*, s.n. Leeds.

family fortune, or perhaps be tried and convicted of treason and so lose everything, the old Duke decided to keep out of his clutches the property he himself had amassed during his tenure of office, and which he was therefore free to dispose of as he chose, unlike his entailed Yorkshire estates. So he decided to by-pass his son Peregrine entirely, and instead leave his unentailed estates directly to his grandson, Peregrine's eldest son and heir, William Henry.[3] Despite the great war with France, between 1706 and 1711 the two boys, William Henry and his younger brother Peregrine-Hyde were sent off on the Grand Tour. Shortly after their return the former died of smallpox, and his brother became the heir to the bulk of the family estates.[4]

On the death of the old Duke in 1712, Kiveton Park in Yorkshire, the grand country seat which Talman had built for him some ten years before (Plate 3), therefore descended not to his son the 2nd Duke, but to his grandson Peregrine-Hyde, now Marquis of Carmarthen (Plate 4).[5] The latter's wife died the following year in childbirth, and for some time thereafter the widower Marquis mostly lived in London, where he had inherited Arlington House in the West End.

Since the house steward of Kiveton was detained on business in London, in September 1714 Carmarthen invited his unmarried sister, the 30-year-old Lady Bridget Osborne, to assume the temporary task of overseeing the housekeeping at Kiveton Park, a heavy administrative responsibility which she accepted.[6] During the winter of 1714 she was joined by her mother, Bridget 2nd Duchess of Leeds, who was by now totally separated from her rackety and unstable husband, and by her younger sister Mary, the recently widowed Dowager Duchess of Beaufort, who lived there till after Christmas (Plates 5 and 6). This household of women was supported and served by a large and complex hierarchy of domestic servants, mostly male. Mrs Emes, the wife of the absent house steward, also lived in the house, and although she ate in the steward's room was on intimate social terms with her superiors. Other persons of similar ambiguous status were the two lady's maids, Mrs Jones for the Duchess of Leeds, and Mrs Davis for Lady Bridget, and the Duchess of Leeds' gentleman, Mr Cuthbert Cornforth.

Last but not least there was the domestic chaplain, William Williams.

---

[3] A. Browning, *Thomas Osborne, Earl of Danby and Duke of Leeds*, 3 vols. (Glasgow, 1944–51), ii. 227–33.

[4] Ibid. ii. 561–2, 567.

[5] K. Downes, *Baroque Architecture in England* (London, 1966), 65, 75, pl. 147; the only trace left of the house today is the name of the Kiveton Park Colliery.

[6] LPCA, D. 1521: 43.

Domestic chaplains occupied a peculiarly equivocal status in a great household. They were treated as gentlemen by virtue of their university education and their clerical profession, and therefore normally dined and sat with the family, and were thus thrown into association with their employers. This intimacy occasionally led to a clandestine marriage between the daughter of the house, or even the widowed mistress of the house, and the domestic chaplain, always to the dismay of the family. One such case had already occurred in the Osborne family. Lady Bridget's aunt, a daughter of the 1st Duke also called Bridget, had been married by her father to the Earl of Plymouth, one of Charles II's illegitimate sons, and retained the title of Countess even after his death. As an independent widow, in 1706 she married her domestic chaplain Dr Philip Bisse—to the no small grief of her ancient father the Duke of Leeds. The latter only relented in 1710, when thanks to Osborne family influence Dr Bisse was elevated first to Bishop of St David's and in 1713 to Bishop of Hereford.[7]

Episodes such as this made elite families very careful in their choice of domestic chaplains, whose morals, breeding, discretion, and sense of place in the household hierarchy mattered as much or more than their learning or piety. The Revd Williams fitted this description perfectly. He was a clever but impecunious Welshman, who had spent eight years at Jesus College, Oxford, obtaining his BA and MA degrees, and in 1710 had been appointed part-time domestic chaplain to Dr Bisse, the new Bishop of St David's.[8] Thanks to the recommendation of the Bishop he was taken into the service of the latter's father-in-law, the 1st Duke of Leeds, 'as tutor in latin for his grandson, and as his domestic chaplain', his principal task being 'to improve the hand of the Marquis of Carmarthen in the latin tongue'.[9]

On the old duke's death in 1712, his grandson the Marquis, retained Williams at Kiveton as domestic chaplain. When Lady Bridget arrived to assume her duties as housekeeper, buying and distributing all the food and other supplies for the huge household, Williams was asked by the Marquis to help her in keeping the accounts, something in which he had had some experience, but she none at all. These tasks he performed to the entire satisfaction of the Osborne family in general, and Lady Bridget in particular.[10]

---

[7] See Genealogy above; M. M. Verney (ed.), *Verney Letters of the Eighteenth Century*, 2 vols. (London, 1930), i. 218; *HMC Portland MSS*, iv. 231–2.
[8] LPCA, D. 1521: 41–2.   [9] Ibid. Eee. 11/259, 261.
[10] Ibid. 11/243, 253, 265, 271, 275, 295.

So in the winter months of late 1714, Lady Bridget Osborne and the Revd Williams were thrown much together, as they worked long hours in the still-room, making up the accounts of the income, supplied by the land steward, and the expenses on purchases and wages for running the great house, gardens, and park. It was not long before Lady Bridget was telling a friend that 'he was an extraordinary good man, and very good company'. As Williams later described it, 'a strict friendship and a mutual respect was contracted between us, and we had the same value for each other that is usual between persons that intend to marry.' Indeed Lady Bridget later confessed that she fell in love with Williams at first sight, when she first arrived in September—which must have been why she told him she was 26, when in fact she was 30. The discrepancy between their ages was small, for he was 33.[11]

This household of women was full of spies, eavesdroppers, and malicious gossips, and it was not long before signs of the mutual attraction were noticed by the servants. For example the coachman, who was made to serve at table when there were dinner-parties, remembered that 'when I have been waiting at table where the Lady Bridget and Mr Williams have been at dinner, I observed that they were very free and familiar together, and smiled at each other as they sat at table'. Others observed that the two were 'generally in company together, playing at cards and tables, when no other person was with them', and that 'they took all opportunities to be alone' especially in the withdrawing-room. What the servants could not decide, however, was whether Bridget was courting Williams, or Williams Bridget. But they strongly suspected that Bridget had decided that she wanted him as a husband. All this gossip was brought to the attention of Lady Bridget's sister, the Duchess of Beaufort. She was indignant that so lowly a person as a penniless Welsh clergyman should dream of associating himself so closely with the daughter and sister of a duke, and she passed her suspicions both to their mother the Duchess of Leeds at Kiveton and to their brother the Marquis in London, urging the latter to discharge Williams at once.[12] Bridget unwittingly intensified the suspicions when, in the course of a casual drawing-room conversation with the two duchesses, she observed of her Aunt Bridget that 'the Countess of Plymouth, by marrying the Bishop of Hereford, is very happy, and I think a lady might be very happy that married a clergyman'.[13] By December the atmosphere in the

---

[11] Ibid. 48, 62, 85; Eee. 11/237.
[12] Ibid. Eee 11/263, 286; D. 1521: 49–50; Ee. 8/218, 265.
[13] Ibid. D. 1521: 49–50.

1. Redgrave Hall, Suffolk

2. Peregrine Osborne, 2nd Duke of Leeds

3. Kivetcn Park, Yorks.

4. Peregrine Hyde-Osborne, Marquis of Carmarthen
and 3rd Duke of Leeds

5. Bridget (Hyde) Osborne, 2nd Duchess of Leeds, and her sister

6. Mary Osborne, 2nd Duchess of Beaufort, later Countess of Dundonald

7. Teresia Constantia Phillips

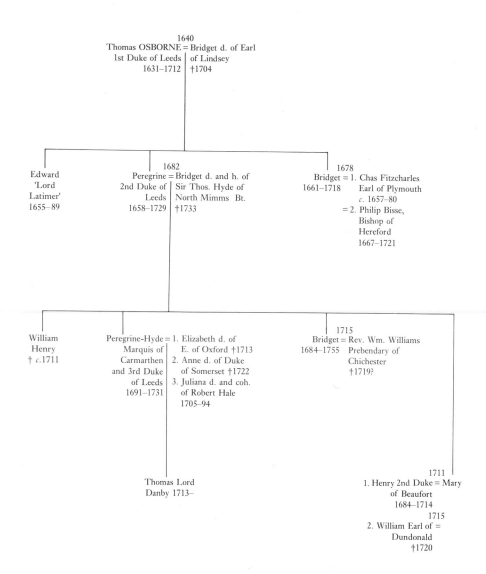

8. Genealogy of the Osbornes

household was so highly charged with suspicion that Lady Bridget no longer dared to be found alone with Williams. Whenever they were together, she was now attended as chaperone by Mrs Davis, her waiting woman, or Mrs Jones, the waiting woman of her mother the Duchess.[14]

Relations between Williams and Lady Bridget reached a climax on New Year's Day 1715, when she made the first approach to him. This was a highly unusual procedure, but the Revd Williams could hardly be expected to make the first move, in view of the huge discrepancy between them in wealth and social rank. On that day she and Williams chanced for once to be alone in the still-room, making up the accounts, she told him she had a present for him, and 'there threw down upon a china plate half a broad piece of gold, which she had almost bent double with her teeth, saying "there's your New Year's gift", and blushed and turned her face from him.' Williams solemnly thanked her, picked it up and wrapped it carefully in paper. Soon afterwards he gave her 'a broken piece of gold which the Marquis of Carmarthen had given me the night before'. This was a gift exchange of great symbolic significance. Indeed, among the lower classes in some parts of the country such as the West, we have already seen how the exchange of broken or bent coins was regarded as a ritual at least as important as an exchange of verbal promises of marriage. By the unwritten conventions of the age, Bridget and Williams had now tentatively engaged themselves to be married, an arrangement they formalized by word of mouth three weeks later, on 22 January.[15]

This was an enormously daring, not to say foolhardy, action on Lady Bridget's part. In the first place, the daughter of a duke was not supposed to commit herself in marriage to anyone without the full knowledge and consent of her family, and she could expect an explosion of anger from her mother, father, sister, and brother, if and when the news of her semi-engagement leaked out. Second, the very idea of a marriage between the daughter of a duke and a penniless clergyman with no means of support whatsoever, except for the patronage of the Osbornes, was by the standards of the day a gross social *mésalliance*. It had been bad enough when her rich aunt, the widowed Countess of Plymouth, had chosen to please herself by marrying, at the age of 45, a handsome young chaplain 12 years her junior. But it was much worse for Lady Bridget secretly to

---

[14] Ibid. 50–3.
[15] Ibid. 54–6, 64; Ee. 8/218; Eee. 11/269, 271, 281, 287. When in early February Williams's possessions were searched, the half-piece of gold was found, carefully wrapped up in a piece of white linen.

contract herself to a low-born clergyman without either a private income or a church living to support him.

To make matters worse, Lady Bridget's own financial situation was almost as precarious as that of Williams. Her grandfather the 1st Duke had left her a huge marriage portion, but with such strings attached to it as to make it almost impossible for her to attract a husband of her own rank and fortune. While her younger sister Mary had been left a portion of £14,000 without strings, Bridget had been left only £10,000. This was a very handsome portion, but it was 'strangely clogged'. The first condition was that she could only marry with 'the consent of her mother the Duchess of Leeds'. The second was that if she married and died without living issue, the portion had to be paid back in full to her brother the Marquis. These were both cripplingly harsh conditions, especially since her mother had already made her attitude absolutely clear, saying to her brutally: 'Biddy, you know your fortune is at my disposal. You shall not marry.' It was not much comfort that she also promised that 'you will have my all at my death'.[16]

Perhaps in order to cause trouble, the Duchess's woman, Mrs Jones, had already warned Williams about Lady Bridget's precarious situation, saying to him 'Surely one would think that the Duke never desired that she should marry at all.' After they became engaged, Williams himself raised the question, to which Lady Bridget replied that 'two lawyers have informed me that although I marry without my Lady's [i.e. mother's] consent, my fortune will not be forfeited'—a statement which encouraged Williams to go ahead with the marriage.[17] The lawyers were presumably referring to the doctrine slowly being formulated through case-law in the ecclesiastical courts, which offered some protection to grown-up children who found themselves in this predicament. The courts ruled that a parent could forbid marriage to a particular person, but not block marriage altogether. But it remained uncertain whether or not if put to the test the courts would in fact give Lady Bridget her portion if she married against her mother's consent.

We do not know why both her grandfather and her mother were so determined that Bridget should spend her life as a spinster, while her younger sister was enabled to make a brilliant marriage with a duke. Perhaps Mary was a beauty and Bridget was plain. At all events, she was already 30 years old, which was seven years more than the age of marriage of most women of her rank at that time, and was financially

[16] Ibid. D. 1521: 64–6; Eee. 11/252–3.
[17] Ibid. Eee. 11/253, 282, 287.

at the mercy of her mother, who did not intend her to marry, no doubt in order to keep her as a companion during her separation from her husband the 2nd Duke.

After they had become formally engaged on 22 January, Williams tried to divert the suspicions of the household about his relationship with Lady Bridget by ostentatiously appearing to court Mrs Jones, but it was a plan that backfired, since it worked only too well. The two duchesses and the marquis became persuaded that Williams was in love with Mrs Jones and 'designed to marry her', and the focus of household gossip now became the sexual play between them, one story being that they were found sitting together alone, with his hand in her pocket. But as a result of all this gossip, Lady Bridget became very jealous, and when Williams next tried to kiss her, she 'told him he was a sad man, and bid him go and kiss Mrs Jones and let her alone'. He finally convinced her that the reports were false, put out by her mother to drive them apart, and offered to get Mrs Jones to swear that nothing had passed between them. But Lady Bridget forbade him to continue to keep company with Mrs Jones as a cover, since 'she is a woman apt to take advantages that way'.[18]

But the abandonment by Williams of his pretended courtship of Mrs Jones greatly increased the chances of discovery of his engagement to Lady Bridget, first because it aroused the active hostility and suspicion of Mrs Jones, and second because the couple no longer had a cover. Williams claimed that they managed to be alone together from time to time, on which occasions Bridget sat on his lap and they kissed. But the suspicions of the servants were such that Williams concluded that it was imperative to arrange a marriage as soon as possible, before the family discovered their intentions. His plan was to persuade and bribe a neighbouring clergyman, the Revd John Hall, to carry out a clandestine marriage, without a licence, in Kiveton Park itself. This was the only possible solution, since he and Lady Bridget were so closely watched by Mrs Davis and Mrs Jones, that any attempt to obtain a licence and go through a public ceremony in a church was out of the question.

The Revd John Hall was a pathetic creature. He had himself made a clandestine marriage with the daughter of Mr Robinet, a neighbouring landowner and the land steward of the Marquis of Carmarthen. He lived with his wife and two children in a rented house and his income was entirely derived from occasional presents from Mr Robinet and a curacy in the gift of the Marquis in the nearby parish of Todwick, which brought in a miserable £21 a year. He was thus wholly dependent for his

[18] Ibid. D. 1521: 57–61; Eee. 11/269, 271, 281, 287.

livelihood on the good will of the Marquis, who could dismiss him from his curacy at any time, and of his wealthy father-in-law, Mr Robinet, who in turn was also dependent on the Marquis. In mid-1715 he confessed that 'he was worth little, his debts paid'. As events were to prove, he was a weak man, whose extreme poverty drove him first to accept a bribe in order to carry out a clandestine marriage, and then to perjure himself by denying it.[19]

Every Sunday, Hall passed through Kiveton Park on his way to perform the morning and afternoon service at Todwick church. On the morning of 30 January 1715, Williams intercepted him and asked him back to dinner at the steward's table, which was appropriate to his rank. When Williams showed him out after dinner, he unexpectedly invited him to come back that evening after prayers, 'to take a glass with him', planning to surprise Hall with a request to marry them on the spot. Lady Bridget was a party to the scheme, and gave Williams a ring with Bristol stones from her finger, given her by her brother 'for a fairing', to use in the ceremony; and 5 guineas to give to Hall as a bribe for marrying them clandestinely.

When Hall returned, Williams led him up to the Marquis of Carmarthen's bedchamber, which he was allowed to use as his own bedroom as long as the Marquis was away in London. After an hour and a half of talk and the consumption of a bottle of wine and another of beer, Williams with great difficulty managed to persuade Hall to agree to marry them. He gave Hall 5 guineas, which for him amounted to three months' income, and also a promissory note for £100 to save him harmless if he should be prosecuted under the Stamp Act for marrying them without a licence, the penalty for which was a £100 fine. Williams then sent a footman to tell Lady Bridget that he wanted to speak to her. When she arrived, he shut the doors of both the antechamber and the bedroom, and told Hall to read the marriage service from the Book of Common Prayer—but to read it quietly, since the bedroom was just above the withdrawing-room where the others were sitting.

The ceremony was soon over, and Williams quickly led Lady Bridget out, suggesting that she tell the Duchess her mother that she had been talking to the under-housekeeper on household business. He then went back into the room, and tried to soothe the anxieties of Hall, who was —with good reason—extremely worried about the possible consequences of what he had just done. Williams assured him of total secrecy, but Hall rightly retorted: 'It's impossible...you cannot refrain from coming

[19] Ibid. Eee. 11/294–5.

together and that will discover you…I wish I may be 100 miles off when the discovery is made.'[20]

It all turned out exactly as Hall had predicted. The day after the marriage, Lady Bridget suggested that it be kept secret until the family had moved back to London. Williams agreed, but remarked that 'as I am your husband, it is my duty to offer myself to you', but left it to her to assess the risk involved. Bridget 'made no answer, but blushed'. That evening he invited her upstairs to his bedroom, and in an anxiety-ridden half-hour the marriage was consummated on a couch in the dressing-room.[21]

The three women attendants in the house, Mrs Emes, the wife of the steward, Mrs Jones, the Duchess of Leeds's woman, and Mrs Davis, Lady Bridget's woman, were by now very suspicious indeed about the intimacy between Williams and Lady Bridget, and they decided to keep a very close watch over them, so that they could never be alone together. They took the view that 'there was a greater familiarity between Lady Bridget Osborne and Mr Williams than there ought to be between two persons where there was so great an inequality in their birth and fortune'.[22]

Given the intense watchfulness of the three women, Williams had been very lucky to have smuggled Lady Bridget up to his bedroom without her being observed. The more difficult problem was how to get her out again, for Mrs Jones had heard sounds of movement in the bedroom over the withdrawing-room, and suspected that Lady Bridget was there.

The door of the bedroom opened on to the long gallery, but Mrs Emes was walking up and down there. Williams went out to join her to try to distract her attention, and they were joined by Mrs Davis. After a while he returned to his room, where Bridget was hiding nervously behind the door. The next time he ventured out into the gallery he found the situation more dangerous than ever. Mrs Emes and Mrs Davis were still walking up and down, but now Mrs Jones was there as well, standing watching his door suspiciously. Williams joined them until Mrs Emes and Mrs Davis had gone away. He then went back into his room, hid Bridget in a closet with a back door to the gallery, and invited Mrs Jones into the bedroom to sit by the fire. But she refused, and continued to keep watch in the gallery.

The couple debated anxiously what to do next. Bridget was in favour of going at once to her mother the Duchess and confessing that they were

---

[20] Ibid. D. 1521: 69–83; Eee. 11/238, 243, 245, 254, 269, 283, 298; Ee. 8/218.
[21] Ibid. D. 1521: 83–4; Eee. 11/288.
[22] Ibid. D. 1521: 86–92; Eee. 11/246.

married, on the grounds that Mrs Jones would certainly betray them anyway. Williams was not so sure, since Mrs Jones had no hard evidence and nothing to gain by disclosing her suspicions. Eventually Mrs Jones went away and Lady Bridget escaped, after agreeing to another rendez-vous in four days' time in 'a place called the great house'.[23]

The next day Mrs Jones 'looked very sullen' on Lady Bridget and 'treated her very roughly'. The latter became so worried that she vomited, which prompted her woman, Mrs Davis, to remark that had she been married she would have concluded she was pregnant. On Wednesday Mrs Davis and Mrs Jones kept up their close watch, and Lady Bridget expressed her fear to Williams that the secret of their marriage would be out in a few days. Williams suggested that he leave the house, to which Lady Bridget replied in alarm: 'What? Will you leave me to be torn in pieces by them?' He reassured her: 'I will perish before I leave you.' Their rendezvous on Thursday morning had to be post-poned, since Mrs Jones never took her eyes off them, but after dinner Bridget thought they would be safe while the Duchess was drinking tea upstairs. They passed through several locked doors, to which Williams had obtained the keys, to arrive at a drawing-room in the unused 'great house', where, in the freezing cold, they once again made love.[24]

So closely were they watched that immediately on their return the storm broke. During their absence the Duchess had twice been to look for Lady Bridget and had also sent others to find her; when she arrived in Mrs Emes's room, where the Duchess was drinking tea, the latter demanded to know where she had been. At first Lady Bridget lied, and said she had been out to buy a fowl, but the Duchess refused to accept that one could buy a fowl at that time in the evening.

DUCHESS. Where have you been?
LADY BRIDGET. In the still room.
DUCHESS. That can't be, for I have been there myself to look for you. Where have you been?
LADY BRIDGET. About the house.
DUCHESS. It is not fit you should go about the house by yourself, when you have your woman and other servants that might go with you.
LADY BRIDGET. I have been in safe hands.
DUCHESS. Who have you been with?
LADY BRIDGET. I have been with Mr Williams.

[23] Ibid. D. 1521: 85–91; Eee. 11/245–6, 253–4, 265–6.
[24] Ibid. D. 1521: 91–100; Eee. 11/247, 266, 273. It would seem that the large and elaborate state rooms in the main block of the huge house were not in use and the family was living in one wing.

DUCHESS. These are not safe hands.
LADY BRIDGET. I am married to him and he is my husband.[25]

The unexpected revelation caused the Duchess to lose all control of herself. She 'fell into a violent passion', started beating Lady Bridget unmercifully and tore off her head clothes. Lady Bridget screamed loudly and ran out of the room into the passage where she met Williams hurrying upstairs to find out what all the uproar was about. Bridget ran to him, crying out 'I am married to him.' He took her by the arm, led her into his bedroom, and locked the door. The houseman, George Bodington, who was carrying candles to the dining-room, also heard the great noise above. At the top of the stairs he found the Duchess of Leeds 'in a terrible passion of grief, and crying very much'. Asked what was the matter, she replied: 'My child, my child…That rogue, that villain Williams has run away with my daughter.' She stood screaming outside the locked door, surrounded by servants who had rushed up to see what was wrong. She ordered them to break open the door, which they did, and she went in. Lady Bridget was so terrified of her mother that she first ran into a corner by the bed, then slipped into a closet and fled through a back door into the gallery and out of the house. A sharp exchange then took place in the bedroom:

DUCHESS. Where is my daughter?
WILLIAMS. Where is my wife?
DUCHESS. Who married you?
WILLIAMS. What is that to you?[26]

Lady Bridget had taken refuge in the bakehouse, from which she sent word by messenger for Williams to join her. When he arrived, she said 'For God's sake carry me away', to which he replied 'I know not how or where to carry you, for it is impossible for you to walk any distance, and if you could nobody hereabouts will dare to receive us'—an admission of the enormous power of the Osbornes in the area. At that moment the Marquis's coachman came by, and they took the risk of asking him to get the chaise ready at once to carry them away. He promised to do so, but instead went to the Duchess and asked if the instructions came from her. This threw the Duchess into another fit of rage and she ordered the coachman 'not to let a horse stir'.[27]

The Duchess, escorted by a group of servants including the coachman,

[25] Ibid. D. 1521: 103; Eee. 11/246, 282, 292.
[26] Ibid. D. 1521: 204–5; Eee. 11/238, 247, 251, 255, 257, 266, 284, 292.
[27] Ibid. D. 1521: 105–7; Eee. 11/263, 252.

Mr Cornforth (her gentleman), and Mrs Jones (her woman), went to the bakehouse, where they found Lady Bridget and Williams. The latter 'opened the door, and bowing very low to the Duchess, her Grace gave him a box on the ear, and then went from him to Lady Bridget, who was sitting by the fire at the other end of the bakehouse and boxed her on the ear'. She then started hurling abuse at the two of them, calling her 'jade' and him 'rogue'—both very opprobrious terms in the eighteenth century. In the face of this onslaught, Williams and Lady Bridget ran together and held each other tightly, with their arms clamped about each other's waist, Lady Bridget saying that she was his wife. The Duchess, still beside herself with fury, retorted ominously 'I will be satisfied of that', meaning that she refused to believe it. She then tried to wrench them apart, shouting: 'Would you rather go away with him than with me, the mother who bore you?' Lady Bridget replied: 'Madam, I'm married to him. He's my husband, and I will go with him. I would rather you would knock me on the head than part me from him.' The Duchess again tried to pull them apart, but failed. She asked 'Do you love him better than me?', to which Lady Bridget replied 'Yes'. The Duchess then tore Williams's periwig off his head, and her gentleman, Mr Cornforth, threw it into the fire. The Duchess ordered her servants to separate the couple by force, but only Mr Cornforth stepped forward to do so, despite the Duchess exclaiming 'Will nobody help me but Mr Cornforth?' The result was an unseemly scuffle, and Williams was only forced to let go of Lady Bridget after Mr Cornforth had bitten him in the arm.

At this point Williams said calmly to the Duchess 'If you will be easy I will go out', and made a more or less dignified retreat from the bakehouse. After he was gone, the Duchess rounded on Bridget, asking: 'How could you behave yourself in that manner to a mother who has brought you up so tenderly and is so fond of you? How could you serve me so as to marry him?' Lady Bridget merely replied: 'It is done and over, and cannot be undone.'[28]

The Duchess left Lady Bridget and a number of servants locked in the bakehouse, and returned to the house, in order to supervise the expulsion of Williams from the premises. On the way the little party met Williams coming back towards the bakehouse, and there followed a short, sharp, verbal exchange:

DUCHESS. Where are you going?
WILLIAMS. To my wife.
DUCHESS. Your wife! Where is your estate?

[28] Ibid. D. 1521: 106–8; Eee. 11/238, 242, 247–8, 252, 264, 284.

WILLIAMS. I have no estate, Madam.

DUCHESS. You are a beggarly rascal, and I will not give you a farthing.

WILLIAMS. What your Grace pleases for that, but I hope you will not deny my going to my wife.

DUCHESS. Go back.[29]

Williams obediently withdrew to the steward's room, where Mr Cornforth tried to lock him in. When he blocked the doorway the Duchess said: 'He is my servant and I command him to lock the door.' Such was her authority that Williams replied 'I will obey your Grace's command', and allowed himself to be locked in.

But the lock was defective and Williams soon got the door open and went back to the bake house. There he found the door locked and the key removed by Mr Cornforth, and the building guarded by the Marquis's gamekeeper, armed with a watchman's staff and under orders to prevent him either getting in or removing Lady Bridget. Inside were not only Lady Bridget but also four male servants, later joined by her woman, Mrs Davis. After Williams pointed out that his orders did not preclude his talking to Bridget, the gamekeeper allowed him to go to a high open window. All he could see was Mrs Davis, who told him that Lady Bridget had fainted away from the stress of what had happened, and was 'just dying'. She told him to go at once to fetch some drops of medicine from her bedroom and a bottle of white wine, which he did. He then fetched a wheelbarrow and stood on it, which allowed him to lean into the window and hold hands with Lady Bridget. By now she had recovered, and whispered to him that an express message was being sent to summon her brother the Marquis. She asked him to fetch her pen, ink, and paper, so that she too could send to the Marquis a letter telling her side of the story. Lady Bridget also urged Williams to write to his patron and her uncle, the Bishop of Hereford, and her aunt the Countess of Plymouth to appeal to them to use their influence with the Duchess to persuade her to be reconciled and to pay Bridget her marriage portion.

By this time there was a crowd of about twenty persons around the bakehouse, and Williams was no doubt speaking for effect when he turned to Mrs Davis, and said: 'Your Lady's marrying of me is without doubt a very great disappointment to you, for doubtless you had designed her for another sort of husband, and perhaps now will hardly think it worth your while to wait upon her. But if you are willing to share with us our fortune, you are heartily welcome to go along with us. If not you are at liberty to go where you please.' He then turned back to

[29] Ibid. D. 1521: 109–16; Eee. 11/252, 284.

187

Lady Bridget and said: 'My dear, all this is as you please, and I beg your pardon for this liberty which I have taken, and though you once promised me to obey me, yet I now promise you before all this company to obey you as long as I live, and will endeavour to make up the great disproportion that is between your fortune and mine by showing myself a most tender and affectionate husband to you, and I hope I shall never give you occasion to repent your having married me.' To which, on cue, Lady Bridget replied: 'I thank you, and don't question that I shall be very happy with you.' All this naturally went down very well with the crowd, who said, according to Williams: 'Pray God bless you. You have spoken well, and God send you well together.'

After about a quarter of an hour, Mr Cornforth came back and ordered Williams to get down from the wheelbarrow and be gone. To hasten his departure, he began to remove the barrow from under Williams's legs, forcing him to let go of Lady Bridget's hands and jump down to the ground, at which she remarked 'Fie, Mr Cornforth, I wonder you can be so rude.' As Williams prepared to leave, so that she could be removed from 'that dirty place', she gave him her purse with about 50 shillings in it. Mr Cornforth, still acting the heavy, said: 'Judas! I hope that will be the last money that ever you will receive of the Lady Bridget.'[30]

Williams found himself lodgings with a yeoman at Todwick Parsonage House about a quarter of a mile from Kiveton Park, whence for several days he carried on a daily correspondence with Lady Bridget by letters and verbal messengers. She sent him a little more money—all she had—and a gift of tea. Williams ended all his smuggled letters to her with 'your most constant and affectionate husband, William Williams'. She began hers with 'My dear dear' and ended with 'I am your tender and affectionate wife till death do us part, B. Williams.' Nor did she show any signs of caving in under family pressure. She reported that 'I am followed by Davis everywhere', and was never let out of sight; but she told Williams defiantly that 'in the house they believe I am breeding and I am glad they think so'. On Friday, she also enclosed a letter to her aunt the Countess of Plymouth, the wife of the Bishop of Hereford, telling her that she was married and bedded by Williams, who had been expelled by her mother, and asking for her help in arranging a family reconciliation.

Altogether, she managed to write and have delivered five letters to Williams between Thursday night when the latter was expelled from the house and Saturday. Although most of the senior servants naturally sided

[30] Ibid. D. 1521: 110–19; Eee. 11/238–9, 242, 252, 266.

with the Duchess against Lady Bridget, there were at least three others of lesser rank, especially George Bodington, the houseman, and Harry Welsh, the footboy, who were willing to smuggle letters and messages for her. Their motive must have been sympathy, since Lady Bridget did not have any money for bribes. On Saturday she warned Williams by message that she was being deprived of pen, ink, and paper, and so could write no more. From then on she communicated partly by notes written in pencil on paper torn out of a pocket-book, and partly by verbal messages via George Bodington and Harry Welsh.[31]

On the morning after his ejection, that is on Friday 4 February, Williams went back to Kiveton Park to collect his belongings. There he met Mr Emes the house steward and Mr Lambert, who were about to set off on orders from the Duchess to go the rounds of the local clergy to find out who it was who had carried out the marriage. They asked him point-blank who had done it, to which he replied: 'Give my duty to the Lady Duchess and let her know that if her Grace desires to be satisfied who was the minister that had married us, I will bring the minister and several witnesses before a Justice of the Peace in order to prove the marriage, if her Grace would think fit.' But he refused to reveal the name of the minister until the Duchess had released Lady Bridget into his custody and the marriage had been verified by a JP—rightly fearing that as soon as they knew who the clergyman was, the agents of the Osborne family would bully or bribe him into denying that he had done it. Mr Emes explained that no decisions could be made until the Marquis arrived from London to take charge. In any case part of Williams's offer was bluff on his part, for there had been no witnesses to the marriage. Even at this early stage, however, suspicion about the identity of the clergyman focused on the Revd John Hall. Three servants had seen him drinking in Williams's bedchamber on 30 January: the houseman George Bodington, who had carried up the candles; the porter John Poole, who had carried up the wine and beer; and William Stacey 'a helper about the house', who had carried up the coals and laid the fire. If it was not to conduct the marriage, why had Hall been invited into Williams's bedchamber in the first place?[32]

The news that the hunt was already on for the minister who had carried out the marriage alarmed Williams, who determined on a bold attempt to smuggle Lady Bridget out of Kiveton Park and the clutches

---

[31] Ibid. D. 1521: 120, 122, 126–7; Eee. 11/239, 243, 248, 297. These letters were later produced in court.

[32] Ibid. Eee. 11/238, 243, 252, 284a, 296.

of her family. On the evening of the same day, Friday, he gave George Bodington a pencilled message to give to Lady Bridget, asking her to be at the closet window next to the garden in the withdrawing-room at two in the morning. He promised to meet her there, presumably with a horse, to receive her and carry her away. Bodington faithfully gave the message to the footboy Harry Welsh to give it to Lady Bridget, with strict instructions to keep the matter secret. Later Lady Bridget instructed him to open the closet window, which he did. At eleven that night Lady Bridget summoned him and gave him a packet of tea and two letters, one to Williams and one to the Countess of Plymouth. Since her woman Mrs Davis was now watching her closely, she was obliged to tell her that she intended to go downstairs soon. Mrs Davis at once told the Duchess's woman, Mrs Jones, who in turn woke Mr Cornforth, and in a few minutes the household was alarmed. From all the commotion in the house, Lady Bridget guessed that Mrs Davis had betrayed her, and therefore told Mrs Jones that she intended merely to go down to the withdrawing-room to speak to Williams. Mrs Jones insisted that she be accompanied, in case Williams intended to help her escape by the window. So half-a-dozen servants lurked outside Lady Bridget's room, and when she emerged, at about one in the morning, they all went with her down to the withdrawing-room. When the Duchess was informed by Mrs Jones of what was going on, she was very angry, and immediately ordered Lady Bridget to be escorted back to her room, and placed under guard all night. This was done, and Mrs Davis accompanied her into her room while the others kept watch outside in the passage until 5 a.m. Meanwhile, at between 1 and 2 a.m., Williams had approached through the garden the closet window in the withdrawing-room only to find the house 'in an uproar', with people running to and fro and lights blazing. He rightly concluded that the escape plan had been betrayed, and the household 'upon their guard and watch', and so beat a hasty retreat.[33]

On Monday 7 February, a mere four days after Lady Bridget had confessed to her marriage, her brother the Marquis arrived from London to deal with the situation. The express message from the Duchess summoning him had reached him on Friday evening, only 24 hours after it was sent from Kiveton. He immediately sent for a lawyer friend, Mr George Bradshaw, and they set off together, presumably by coach, at eleven that night. Travelling day and night, they reached Kiveton on Monday afternoon. The speed of the journey is a measure of how seriously the Osborne family took the news of the alleged marriage of

---

[33] Ibid. D. 1521: 129–31; Eee. 11/239, 244, 252, 255, 267, 284a.

Lady Bridget to a lowly and penniless clergyman. Lady Bridget was seriously afraid that the Marquis might do some physical harm to Williams, and therefore told him to flee at once for protection to the house of his old patron, the Bishop of Hereford. She was wrong in harbouring such suspicions, since her brother seems to have been a decent and fair-minded man, very unlike his irresponsible father the Duke.

The Marquis had a private interview with Lady Bridget soon after his arrival on the Monday, in which she apparently told him that she was married to Williams by Dr Hall in his bedchamber on the evening of Sunday, 20 January. The next day, in the presence of a clergyman and others, the Marquis subjected Bridget to further intense interrogation about her marriage. She replied bravely, even when he told her that her father, the irresponsible and erratic Duke, was coming down and intended 'to take her up with him to Wimbledon and lock her up'. She obstinately stuck to her story, maintaining that she would be torn in pieces before she would deny her marriage to Williams. In the many subsequent interrogations over the coming days and weeks, by the Marquis and Mr Bradshaw, Lady Bridget stuck to her story, besides telling it to her mother the Duchess, her sister the Duchess of Beaufort, and by letter to her aunt the Countess of Plymouth and her uncle the Bishop of Hereford.[34]

The day after his arrival Mr Bradshaw the barrister also subjected Bridget to close but not hostile examination. He was obviously unsure about exactly what had happened, but when he searched Williams's possessions, he found the half of a broad gold piece, which confirmed at least the truth of the story about the exchange of highly symbolic New Year's gifts. After he had expressed his 'very great and friendly concern for her', the following exchange took place:

BRADSHAW. Your brother the Marquis has hazarded his life for you in coming hither to prevent your ruin. I hope his Lordship is not come too late.

LADY BRIDGET. He is too late. I am married. My brother has no reason to be angry with me, for I have by the marriage forfeited my ten thousand pounds. He is very welcome to it, for I would rather beg with my husband from door to door than part with him.

BRADSHAW. You know well enough that your brother has so generous a concern for you that your ten thousand pounds would make but small satisfaction for the blemish which you have brought upon yourself and your family by marrying Mr Williams. The Marquis of Carmarthen is so far from thinking

---

[34] Ibid. D. 1521: 132–4; Eee. 11/218, 239, 252, 267, 271, 287, 292.

your ten thousand pounds to be a recompense, that he is rather desirous to add to it, if he can thereby retrieve your reputation. I hope that you are not married.

LADY BRIDGET. I am married.

BRADSHAW. When were you married?

LADY BRIDGET. In the evening of Sunday 20 January.

BRADSHAW. Where were you married?

LADY BRIDGET. In my brother's bedroom.

BRADSHAW. Who married you?

LADY BRIDGET. Mr Hall.

BRADSHAW. I cannot believe it.

LADY BRIDGET. As I hope for salvation, I am married, and Mr Hall married us.

BRADSHAW. Mr Hall has denied it.

He then showed Lady Bridget a note signed by Hall 'whereby he denied the marriage'. At this news, Lady Bridget became very angry.

LADY BRIDGET. If Hall denies the marriage, he is the greatest villain that ever lived. I desire that he be brought before me. When he sees me, he can't have the impertinence to deny it, for I know him as well as I know you.

Bradshaw expressed disbelief.

LADY BRIDGET. Mr Bradshaw, I am sorry you should think that I would tell a lie. If I am not married then I have done worse, for as I hope to be saved, he has bedded me twice.

Bradshaw then said he did not believe she had been bedded at all.

LADY BRIDGET. On Monday night, 31 January, he lay with me on the green couch in my brother's dressing-room, and on the Thursday following he lay with me in the great house.

BRADSHAW. There might be some engagement between you [he was referring to the exchange of New Year's gifts] which might excuse your lying together, although you have no proof of any legal marriage.

LADY BRIDGET. I do not at all doubt that Mr Williams can prove our marriage. Although I did not see any witnesses, I believe there were some witnesses in the closet.

After this not unfriendly exchange, Lady Bridget trusted Bradshaw sufficiently to show him some of Williams's letters to her, including one which began 'My dearest Life, I am very glad that you are breeding...' and ended with 'your most constant and affectionate husband, William Williams'. This was strong evidence that Lady Bridget was telling the truth when she said that Williams had already bedded her. The reason why Williams was pleased that Lady Bridget was pregnant was that that would make the family very reluctant to deny the marriage, since that would make her the unmarried mother of a bastard. She allowed

Bradshaw to take a copy of this and other letters of Williams, and a few days later, when they had reached St Albans on the journey to London, she was persuaded to destroy the originals.[35]

This interview, which ended inconclusively, highlighted the central role of the Revd Hall, who was in a position to either prove or disprove the alleged clandestine marriage. As Bradshaw had explained to Lady Bridget, he had already been to his house, and interviewed Hall, who admitted that he was in Williams's bedroom, but denied everything else.

HALL. I declare on my salvation, that I never married Mr William Williams and
    Lady Bridget.
BRADSHAW. Will you give me your hand that you have not married them?
HALL. I will.

Hall gave Bradshaw pen and paper, and he drafted two notes denying the marriage, to which Hall put his signature. Thereafter, Hall stuck to his denial, explaining how improbable it was that he should do such a thing, since if he had 'I should have been turned out of my curacy', which was true enough.[36]

The morning after he had signed the note of denial of marriage, Hall was extremely troubled in his conscience, as well as anxious about his future. He was afraid of being ejected from his curacy and his house, since he was still the prime suspect as the minister who had performed the marriage; and also of incurring the wrath of his father-in-law, Mr Robinet, who was naturally suspected of complicity in the marriage plot, if there was one. So first he went to see Mr Williams at the house where he had taken refuge and asked him before witnesses to declare that Mr Robinet knew nothing of a plan for a clandestine marriage with Lady Bridget. Williams frankly declared that neither Robinet nor any other member of the Osborne household and servants knew anything of the marriage plot, adding sardonically: 'I would as soon put my hand in the fire as to trust Mr Robinet with such a secret.' Encouraged by this assurance, Hall asked Williams if he would also publicly declare that it was not he who had married them. But Williams replied sternly 'No Mr Hall, that I cannot do.'[37]

Fearful of exposure at any moment, and feeling acutely guilty about his perjury, the Revd Hall hurried off to consult the leading clergyman in the area. He was a close associate of the Osborne family, Dr Henry Felton, the 36-year-old Rector of Whitwell, just over the Derbyshire border. When Hall arrived, Felton had an appointment, but Hall

---

[35] Ibid. 11/286–8. [36] Ibid. 11/295, 299. [37] Ibid. 11/300.

declared that his business was of the utmost urgency and begged Felton to spare him a few minutes at once. Hall seemed to be verging upon a nervous breakdown, and Felton therefore showed him into an empty room, where the following extraordinary conversation took place:

HALL. What would be the consequences, in reference to my temporal concerns, in case I should have married Mr Williams to Lady Bridget?

FELTON. You was to be prosecuted under the Stamp act [for not procuring a marriage licence] and canonically punished by suspension [for solemnizing a clandestine marriage]. But what need you trouble yourself about that? An innocent man need fear nothing.

HALL. Innocence does not always protect persons, and Mr Williams has threatened to ruin me, and a small prosecution would ruin me, I being in mean circumstances. What would be the consequences if any witness that I do not think of should be produced to swear such a marriage? If Mr Williams produces a witness would it be any use to him, since he has declared there was no one present at the marriage?

FELTON. I am of the opinion that such a witness would be believed and it would be looked on that Mr Williams had denied or concealed the truth.

HALL. What would be the condition of a man in a future state, that had married them, and afterwards denied it on oath?

Felton gave him 'a proper answer' about the danger to his immortal soul.

HALL. In such circumstances, might I expect satisfaction upon repentance?

FELTON. It is my opinion that there would be no hope of pardon without a public confession, and that a private confession would not be sufficient, because the damage that might happen by such a denial may not be repaired without an open acknowledgement. Do not run into any mistake in a matter of this importance. For a private offence against God Almighty, a private repentance might be sufficient, but a public offence requires a public repentance.

HALL. In such circumstances could any good Christian pray for me?

FELTON. It is the duty of every good Christian in that case to pray that you might repent, and God would forgive you on your repentance. There is great villainy on one side or the other.

HALL. I cannot do my duty [i.e. conduct services in church] with any comfort.

FELTON. You must go on in your duty as an honest and innocent man ought to do, and not fear anything.

HALL. I desire you to pray for me.

As Hall got up and went away, he seemed to Dr Felton, and to others present in the house, 'to be in a very great agony and consternation... which gave me great reason to believe that he had married Mr Williams and the Lady Bridget'.[38]

[38] Ibid. 11/275–6, 298–9, 302–3.

Since Dr Felton had nothing to gain by inventing this story, which he repeated twice under oath, and a lot to lose by seriously damaging the case of the Osborne family that there had been no marriage, one has to assume that the conversation took place much as he described it. In any case, Hall's denial of the marriage was so implausible that nobody in the neighbourhood believe it. Indeed Hall's local reputation was thereafter very bad, as shown by a conversation which took place one day some months later, when he and George Bradshaw the barrister, who had drafted his sworn denial, were playing at bowls at Kiveton. Bradshaw complained that he 'had suffered much in his reputation' in the neighbourhood, 'in that it is reported that I bullied you into the denial'. Hall replied: 'My denial of what I had done did not proceed from any threats used towards me by you. I will take an oath to this effect for your justification.'[39]

On Thursday 10 February, the Marquis and Mr Bradshaw transferred Lady Bridget by coach to London, but did not immediately hand her over to the tender mercies of her father the Duke at Wimbledon. Instead they took her to the Marquis's house in Arlington Street, where she was looked after and guarded by her woman Mrs Davis. During the long coach ride the Marquis later claimed that he cross-questioned her closely about her story, in doing so rehearsing all the various implausible scenarios devised by the Osborne family in the coming months to explain it away. He asked her if there was any impediment to marriage, and indeed the Duchess later argued that Williams was already pre-contracted to a Mrs Broughton, a wholly fictitious invention duly repeated by Lady Bridget in her answer before the ecclesiastical court in June 1715, by which time her morale had cracked. The Duchess attributed the story to Dr Felton, but he made no mention of it in his two depositions.[40]

Other suggestions made by the Marquis to Lady Bridget in the coach included whether she was quite sure that it was Mr Hall who married her, and not some other man dressed up to look like a minister; whether the proper form of marriage service had been read in its entirety; and whether she had made all the necessary answers during the service. As for the two consummations, he asked her whether she was sure that Williams had actually penetrated her and ejaculated.[41]

The Marquis was clearly seeking some way to deny that the marriage was legally valid, and over the next few months the Osborne family did

[39] Ibid. 11/302–3.
[40] Ibid. D. 1521: 133–4; Ee. 8/218; Eee. 11/272, 275–6, 281, 302.
[41] Ibid. 11/272–3.

their very best to find or manufacture evidence for one of the other of these objections. Servants in the house in Arlington Street later testified that from February to early May 1715 Lady Bridget held out, obstinately insisting that she was legally married to Williams. The best evidence of her state of mind comes from the depositions of an apothecary who visited her regularly over these months, when she was ill—perhaps under psychological stress; and of Mr Bradshaw, who was now formally counsel to the Marquis of Carmarthen. Like so many of the characters in this story, the apothecary was both loquacious and apparently possessed of a powerful memory for what had been said many months before. His evidence is the more persuasive, since he had been apothecary to the Dukes of Leeds for twenty years, and therefore had every incentive to keep his mouth shut.

He swore that in March or April he often heard Lady Bridget defend her marriage with Williams, but by May he noticed that she was beginning to weaken in her fight. She had now been kept under house arrest and without any contact with Williams for three months. Moreover by now she had learnt that those relatives upon whom she had been relying for support, her aunt and uncle, the Countess of Plymouth and the Bishop of Hereford, had completely washed their hands of her and refused to lift a finger to mediate in the affair on her behalf. The Bishop was clearly afraid that the Osbornes would blame him for having recommended Williams as a suitable candidate for the job of domestic chaplain. The Countess would not even testify to the authenticity of the handwriting of the five letters from Lady Bridget which were produced in court by Williams. As for the Bishop, he was even more craven. He tried to put the blame for recommending Williams on his own domestic chaplain, whom he suggested had been influenced by feelings of Welsh solidarity. He denied that he knew Williams at all well, claiming that he never took him into the house, and that he only 'read prayers some few times to my family'. When the family crisis occurred, he burned unopened all the letters he received from Williams, later telling the court that he had 'resolved to know nothing relating to or to be consulted in the matters of controversy'.[42] Meanwhile, Lady Bridget's mother the Duchess and her other relatives were all pressing her to deny the marriage, while the only witness, the Revd Hall, had already perjured himself on oath, and denied ever having married her.

Under these circumstances, it is hardly surprising that by late May Lady Bridget's morale began to weaken, but when she discussed her

---

[42] Ibid. 11/259–61.

doubts with the apothecary, he reproached her for wavering. He told her: 'marriage is honourable, and if you have been guilty of an indiscreet action in marrying Mr Williams, who is beneath you in quality, yet he is a gentleman by his education and function; and you ought not to depart from the truth, for in doing so you will bring on eternal reproach and dishonour upon yourself.' Lady Bridget acknowledged the validity of these observations and replied: 'If I am ever brought before a court of judication, I will speak the truth.' But she went on to express the doubts that were troubling her.

LADY BRIDGET. If I should live with Mr Williams, I fear that I would have an uneasy life with him.

APOTHECARY. Mr Williams is a good-natured man, and for the sake of her Lady-ship and the rest of the family, as well as in regard to his cloth, he would certainly use you well.[43]

The other key witness as to how Lady Bridget was thinking and feeling in the spring and early summer months of 1715, was the friend and now legal counsel of the Marquis, George Bradshaw, Esq., a barrister of the Middle Temple. He often visited Lady Bridget to advise her about her defence in the lawsuit that Williams had launched against her in the London Consistory Court for 'restitution of conjugal rights', that is, to prove her marriage and obtain her release into his custody. Bradshaw, like the apothecary, was therefore a trusted servant of the Osborne family, and had nothing to gain by supporting Lady Bridget in her struggle to preserve her marriage. It is clear that by now he was fully convinced that she was telling the truth and was indeed legally married and properly bedded.

In his deposition before the court in February 1716, a year after the crisis at Kiveton, he said that during February, March, April, and May, Lady Bridget had insisted that she was married to Williams. He also revealed the internal dissensions within the family by telling the court that Lady Bridget had said to him: 'I fear that my father [the evil 2nd Duke] will murder me in case I will not deny my marriage. I will never deny it. I will suffer any death than damn my soul by forswearing such marriage.' He described how 'with very great agony' she lamented 'what a miserable condition I must be in that I lie under the necessity of perjuring myself by forswearing my marriage, or of being murdered for confessing it.' He testified that he acted as adviser to Lady Bridget in the litigation merely 'as a friend and as one supposed to have knowledge in his profession', and without expectation of any fee or gratuity.

[43] Ibid. 11/249–50.

In late May or early June 1715, however, after she was moved from her brother's house in Arlington Street to her father's house in Wimbledon, Lady Bridget's morale at last collapsed. She told Bradshaw: 'I have promised my mother the Duchess of Leeds that I will marry any man that she should approve of; and I will be married in a very short time.'[44] A common way of short-circuiting litigation about a disputed marriage was for one of the parties publicly to marry another person while the trial was still in progress. The ecclesiastical courts did their best to stop such marriages by issuing injunctions against them. In practice, however, when faced with a litigant's legal marriage in church, and often with a family on the way, they were usually reluctant to break up such a union and would recognize it as valid.

Bradshaw was so morally shocked by Lady Bridget's abject willingness to commit bigamy in order to placate her parents that he refused to advise her any more, saying: 'I will not be concerned with encouraging or countenancing such iniquity.' Despite this principled gesture, Bradshaw remained as legal counsel for the Marquis of Carmarthen, and it must therefore be assumed that by now the latter was also convinced that Lady Bridget's clandestine marriage to Williams was good in law, despite the denials of the Revd Hall. In his later deposition before the court, the Marquis was strikingly mild and ambiguous, especially in comparison with that of his mother the Duchess, which was full of patent lies and evasions. Unlike her he freely admitted that the five letters of Lady Bridget which Williams had submitted to the court as evidence were definitely in her handwriting, while volunteering that he had also seen Williams's letters in reply before they had been destroyed. He conspicuously made no comment one way or another about the validity of the alleged marriage.[45]

The testimony of the Marquis and of Mr Bradford were also very unlike that of the other member of the family deeply involved in the affair, the former Duchess of Beaufort, who by the end of 1715 had remarried and was now Countess of Dundonald. She supported the latest story about the marriage, concocted by her mother and now offered to the court on behalf of Lady Bridget, by which the ceremony had not been properly conducted. In a masterly evasion she said 'I think I heard Lady Bridget tell me' that the clergyman 'read parts of the marriage service and left out some parts of it'. She alleged that Lady Bridget was 'almost sure that she made no answer but that she was in such confusion

---

[44] Ibid. 11/288–9, 290.   [45] Ibid. 11/271–4, 281–5.

that she did not know what she did'. She also alleged that Lady Bridget told her that 'she was in the great house with Mr Williams and that he endeavoured to consummate the marriage, but she was sure he had not his end'.[46] All these were evasive and shifty statements that tried to cast doubt on the legality of the marriage and the consummation without actually committing perjury.

In June the family were sufficiently confident of Lady Bridget's subjection to their wishes that they ventured to confront her with the Revd Hall. He began by asking Lady Bridget to withdraw her accusation that he had married her. Later that summer the Revd Hall and Lady Bridget were alleged to have signed affidavits stating that no marriage had taken place.[47]

The unsolved problem is who it was who provided Williams with enough money to live on, and also to launch not one but two lawsuits, one in the London Consistory Court against Lady Bridget for restitution of conjugal rights, and another against the Revd Hall in the Court of King's Bench, presumably for perjury. All that is known about the latter is that he had Hall arrested on a writ of *qui tam*, but later dropped the suit before it came to trial.[48]

One may surmise from the evidence that there must have been a fearful family quarrel about how to deal with the marriage with Williams. On the one side were Lady Bridget's parents, the Duke and Duchess of Leeds, who agreed about nothing except that the marriage must be invalidated. They were strongly supported by Lady Bridget's sister, the Duchess of Beaufort, who had a personal vendetta against Williams.[49] On the other side was certainly the Marquis of Carmarthen's lawyer, Mr George Bradshaw, and certainly his chief clerical advisor, Dr Felton. It seems plausible that between them Bradshaw and Felton eventually convinced the Marquis that the marriage had indeed taken place and that the Revd Hall was lying. There is evidence that the whole legal business was carefully stage-managed by Bradshaw, in close consultation with the officials of the ecclesiastical court.[50] This would explain why in August 1715 Lady Bridget was not married off to someone else chosen by her mother while the trial was still pending, despite her temporary willingness to do so. It would also explain why, after a period of collapse in June, July, and August 1715, Lady Bridget later recovered her

---

[46] Ibid. 11/271–4, 281–5, 269–70.
[47] Ibid. Ee. 8/216–18; D. 138–46; Eee. 11/290, 299.
[48] Ibid. 11/289, 295, 300.   [49] Ibid. Ee. 8/218.
[50] Ibid. Eee. 11/289, 299.

confidence, helped by encouragement both from the apothecary and Mr Bradshaw.

By early 1716 the family could not trust her to give evidence in person before the court, for fear that she would tell the truth. Her proctor (hired by the family, not by her) told the court that on 6 June 1715, in the presence of witnesses, she had declared that she never was married to Williams. But the court was not satisfied with this bald statement and demanded that Lady Bridget appear in person to give her answer, as was the practice in canon law. Her father the duke was now an active Jacobite plotter, which could not have endeared him to the Hanoverian Whig regime. So when the Osbornes ignored the summons, the court officials nailed a 'peremptory decree' ordering her appearance on the door of the Wimbledon house, and also, since it was not certain where she was being kept, on that of the Arlington Street house as well. Since the Osbornes still refused to produce Lady Bridget, the court, apparently acting after consultation with Mr Bradshaw, gave sentence for Williams, declaring the marriage proven.[51] The family appealed the sentence to the Court of Arches but did not push the case to a conclusion.[52] One can only suppose that even those most hostile to the marriage were finally obliged to recognize that they were beaten.

The end of the story is soon told. In the summer of 1716 Lady Bridget was released from captivity, she and Williams were reunited; she presumably obtained her £10,000 portion, and a prebend at Chichester Cathedral was secured for Williams. But he apparently only held his prebend till 1719 and was never promoted thereafter, so he presumably died four years or so after his marriage to Lady Bridget and barely three years after he was reunited to her.[53] Their married life, if a happy one, was certainly brief, although Bridget lived on as his widow for another thirty-six years. Bridget's sister, the dowager Duchess of Beaufort, who in late 1715 had remarried a Scottish earl, was again widowed in 1720, and died young two years later.

The 2nd Duke lived on until 1729, surrounded in scandal, enmeshed in debt, and busy plotting with the Jacobites. He had long since broken off all relations with his duchess, which is why she was living at Kive-

---

[51] Ibid. D. 1521: 138–46; Eee. 11/289. [52] Ibid. Ee. 8/216, 218.

[53] Foster, *Alumni Oxonienses*, iv. 1647. The most likely candidate for this William Williams is a boy from Anglesea who matriculated at Jesus College in 1698 and left the university with BA and MA degrees in 1705. The prebend is supposed to have been conferred in 1712, but this cannot be correct.

ton Park in 1714–15. But soon afterwards her son the Marquis of Carmarthen must also have quarrelled with her, perhaps over her treatment of his sister Lady Bridget, and turned her out of the house. In 1717 she was petitioning desperately to the government for financial support, saying that she was penniless, had sold all her possessions, and was starving, being 'ruined by her Lord's inhumane usage'.[54] As for Bridget's brother the Marquis of Carmarthen, he lost his first two wives in childbirth in short order, married a very young girl as his third wife, and then died in 1731 at the age of 40, after only two years as 3rd Duke. His widowed duchess lived on for another sixty-three years, during which she enjoyed her huge jointure of £3,000 a year. In all she cost the Osborne family £160,000 less the £30,000 or so of her portion, so that the Marquis's third marriage cost the family vastly more than poor Lady Bridget's love affair.

All but one of those involved in this latter affair, including persons from all walks of life and of very different wealth and status, were disapproving of Lady Bridget's clandestine marriage with a penniless clergyman. The most extreme position was that of her mother, the Duchess of Leeds, who became completely hysterical on hearing the news, screaming and sobbing with rage, and beating both Lady Bridget and Williams. Lady Bridget's brother the Marquis was so upset by the news that at a moment's notice he dropped everything and rushed up from London to Kiveton Park in a 48-hour non-stop journey by coach, which must have been a harrowing experience. The barrister Mr Bradshaw at first talked to Lady Bridget about the Marquis's desire to 'prevent your ruin', and 'retrieve your reputation' by eliminating 'the blemish which you have brought upon yourself and your family'. The sense that such a union was disgraceful, shameful, or at the very least imprudent, was very widespread not only among the family members, but also the upper servants. The three female upper servants, Mrs Emes, Mrs Davis, and Mrs Jones, disapproved of familiarity between two persons 'where there was so great an inequality in their birth and fortune'.[55] The principal male upper servants, such as the Duchess's gentleman Mr Cornforth and the estates steward Mr Robinet, were also very disapproving. On the other hand, it is also true that one day, when Lady Bridget was still confined at Kiveton, the house steward Mr Emes told Williams not unkindly that she 'wants nothing but your company'.[56] Certainly George Bradshaw, Esq., the barrister, started hostile but was in the end won over.

---

[54] *Calendar of Treasury Books, 1714–19*, 323.
[55] LPCA, Eee. 11/246.   [56] Ibid. D. 1571: 132.

In social terms Mr Emes occupied a liminal position between gentleman and upper middling sort—as did Williams himself and the only other man of respectable status who took a more sympathetic view of the marriage. This was the family apothecary, who told Lady Bridget that although beneath her in quality, and without any estate, Williams was nevertheless a gentleman by reason of his university education and his profession as a clergyman.

Amongst the lower servants and the poor, however, the marriage for love seems to have evoked a certain amount of sympathy, as shown by the willingness of the houseman and the footboy to carry letters and messages for Lady Bridget, and by the response of the crowd around the bakehouse to Williams's declaration of affection and obedience.

Despite the weight of opinion against the marriage, this is one of the very few stories in this book with a classic happy ending, in which love triumphed over the most formidable of obstacles. It demonstrates both the extraordinary lengths to which a great aristocratic family was prepared to go in the early eighteenth century to break up what it regarded as an unsuitable marriage, and also the ways in which it could be defeated. It must be said that measures this brutal were by now a rarity. A possible explanation for the savage reaction of the Osbornes to Bridget's marriage is that this was a family dominated by a peculiarly authoritarian ideology of patriarchal power, but peculiarly plagued by clandestine marriages which thwarted its efficacy in practice. Bridget's mother the Duchess had made a scandalous clandestine marriage at the age of 12 with a cousin, and after prolonged attempts to annul it through the law, the cousin had eventually had to be bought off, in return for releasing his claims. Her own ill-fated marriage to Peregrine Osborne in 1682 had also been performed in secret, in the face of family opposition. He too was later accused of having made a clandestine first marriage in his youth, and in 1710 he was struggling to show proof that there was 'no legal marriage to an infamous woman', and was apologizing for living with her to the damage of his wife and father. Finally, only ten years before the events described, Bridget's aunt, the Countess of Plymouth, had made a clandestine second marriage with her domestic chaplain against the wishes of her 75-year-old father. This history of clandestine marriages in the family does much to explain the explosion of rage against Lady Bridget for her relatively innocent matrimonial entanglement.[57]

---

[57] Browning, *Thomas Osborne*, ii. 232–3; *HMC Rutland MSS*, ii. 75; *Peerage*, s.n. Leeds.

(c) A FORGED CLANDESTINE MARRIAGE

21

Bentley v. Bentley, 1715–1727

In 1715 Charles Bentley, the 23-year-old son of a wealthy businessman who lived in Red Lion Square, was a law student at the Inner Temple, having just come down from Oxford where he had spent four years at Queen's College. In January he attended a private dancing party. Looking among the guests for 'a free, forward, good-humoured woman with whom he might converse', his eye fell on Mrs Elizabeth Dent, a 22-year-old widow, the daughter of Richard Wilkinson, a sugar-refiner and member of the Skinner's Company, who had once been a man of substance but whose business was beginning to fail. By the time of the dance Mrs Dent had recovered from her bereavement and was looking for a second husband.[1]

The dance lasted nearly all night, and it was observed that Charles Bentley paid much attention to the vivacious Mrs Dent. They rapidly fell in love, both having powerful reasons to do so. Mrs Dent was lonely in her widowhood and Charles Bentley was desperate to get away from his father, with whom he was living while eating his commons in the Inner Temple. He told Elizabeth that 'no man living had such an ill-tempered father as mine'. He kept Charles very short of money and was always angry if he stayed out late at night. Charles's one desire was to marry, obtain his independence, and get away from home, and he was soon telling Elizabeth that 'you are the only woman capable of making me happy'. According to Charles's later unchivalrous and self-serving account of what happened, Elizabeth was as eager as he was. On his second visit to her lodgings he claimed that he stayed from 4 till 9 p.m. and Elizabeth allowed him 'to use great familiarities with her, too great for a modest woman to allow at second sight'. On the third visit he stayed from 4 till 10 p.m. and did even better. He later alleged contemptuously that he 'believed that a man of address might obtain his purpose from Elizabeth without proposing to marry her'.[2]

It is certainly possible that Elizabeth, as a sex-starved young widow,

---

[1] LPCA, D. 156–7: 248–52, 361–5, 527, 639–43, 647.
[2] Ibid. 253–5, 367–71.

was fairly free with her person, but Charles was undoubtedly lying when he said that there was no talk of marriage. They met all through the spring, and the matter was frequently discussed. Elizabeth asked him how his father would accept a suggestion of marriage, and he explained that he could not even hint of it at present, since he was hoping that his mother would persuade the old man to spend £4,000 to £5,000 to buy him a legal office. Once he had the office, he said that he would then buy a set of chambers in the Inner Temple, and Elizabeth could live nearby. But he claimed to have told her that until his father finally died, they could do no more than marry secretly, since the latter might still disinherit him if he got to hear of it. On the other hand, he said reassuringly that his father was 'ancient and in a bad state of health and I am sure will not live long'.

At this point Elizabeth decided to consult her 20-year-old brother Richard and her younger sister Mary. When Richard Wilkinson junior met Charles in a tavern, the latter declared his love for Elizabeth, but explained that he could not publicize it for fear of infuriating his father, who was about to spend so much money on buying him an office. He offered to give a bond to marry Elizabeth once he got the office. Richard Wilkinson insisted that he also get the permission of his father and mother, but Charles replied that he was certain his father would refuse. But he did bring his mother and sister to visit Elizabeth, to whom they were very affable. After some hesitation, Richard Wilkinson advised Elizabeth to go ahead with the courtship on these terms. Charles sounded out his mother's feelings on the matter by telling her that he had had a dream that 'he was married to and in bed with Mrs Dent'. His mother replied encouragingly that she was indeed 'a very agreable lady'. Another reason for delaying marriage was that Elizabeth was engaged in a lawsuit in Chancery over some copyhold property she had inherited from her late husband. If she married and changed her name to Bentley in the middle of the case, she would have had to start it all over again, such were the procedural technicalities of the English legal system. Each party therefore had a reason either for delaying marriage, or at least for keeping it a close secret.[3]

But their passion for one another grew steadily throughout 1715 despite Elizabeth's landlady's warning that in her opinion Charles did not come 'to look for a wife'. There survives a series of undated love-letters from Charles to Elizabeth which must belong to about this period of their relationship. They appear to be the letters of a young man passion-

---

[3] Ibid. 256–76, 295, 375–81, 456, 610–15, 181–6.

ately in love, and are full of promises, but they make it clear that he is only contemplating marriage some time in the future, after the death of his hated old father, Mr Bentley. On the other hand, he once signed himself 'your affectionate spouse'—an ambiguous word suggesting that they had at least made a contract for marriage in the future.

Until 10 April 1716 there is no proof that they were yet technically lovers. Elizabeth always slept in the same bed with her maid at night, and Charles never spent the night at her lodgings. On the other hand, he rented a bedroom from a Mrs Marston, formerly his mother's chamber-maid, which they used as a place of assignation, at a cost of 2s. 6d. a night. What exactly happened on 10 April is obscure, but after that day they allegedly told one or two close friends whom they could trust, such as Mrs Marston and a fellow-lodger Mrs Middleton, that they had been clandestinely married without a licence in a privileged place, which may or may not be true. All that is certain is that on that day the couple entered into some sort of formal engagement or contract with one another. Charles gave her a gold ring, and from that day they considered themselves committed to one another, as did their families, friends, and neighbours. On the strength of whatever happened on 10 April, Elizabeth consented to become Charles's mistress. In front of Mrs Marston he told her: 'I know my father will not hear of marrying without a great deal of money. But it is now done, Bet, and we are happy, and it is no matter whether they will consent to it or not.'

Charles and Elizabeth were now eager to spend a weekend in the country as a honeymoon after the engagement, and they asked Mrs Marston if she knew of anywhere she could recommend. So six days later Charles and Elizabeth, who was now sporting her gold ring, accompanied by Mrs Marston as her maid, set off in a hired coach and four to Hampton Court, where they spent three days and nights and consummated the union 'several times'. After their return, from 19 April to 17 May, they openly slept in the same bed in Elizabeth's lodgings, while her maid was sent to lie in another room. According to Charles's deposition —not supported by Mrs Marston—the latter asked Elizabeth where they had been married and why she had not been invited. Elizabeth replied that the marriage had been performed by Mr Reid at Clerkenwell Church, without a licence. When Mrs Marston expressed surprise at Mr Reid doing such a thing, Elizabeth replied 'Gold does wonders.' This statement attributed by Charles to Elizabeth must be a complete fabrication, for it is never referred to again.[4]

---

[4] Ibid. 291–7, 476–9, 661–3, 696–700.

On 18 May, the Bentley family, like all other London families who could afford it, withdrew to the country for the summer and Charles had to go along with them. The Bentleys went to Colney Hatch in Essex, and in order not to be parted from Elizabeth, Charles arranged for her and her maid to stay in the nearby village of Hadley, where she lodged for four months. Charles, going under the false name of Butler, contrived to visit Elizabeth almost every other day. Not surprisingly, the neighbours noticed all this coming and going, and Elizabeth got a reputation in the village as 'a loose woman', according to the curate.[5]

In September the Bentleys returned to London, and Charles took fresh lodgings for Elizabeth and her maid in Broad Street, where he visited her daily. By this time the Wilkinson family was in serious financial trouble, and Charles was having to pay for Elizabeth's lodgings, or rather to promise to pay for them. Elizabeth's father's sugar-refining business failed, and he was left owing considerable sums of money to his creditors. They had him arrested and put in the Fleet Prison for a while. When he came out of prison he found it prudent to live for three years within the Verge of the Royal Court, in Downing Street and King Street, Westminster, as protection against rearrest. It was not until 1719 that Mr Wilkinson finally got back on to his feet again, now as a merchant buying and selling sugar, and moved back into the City to Fenchurch Street.

This meant that after late 1716 Elizabeth had very small resources to fall back on. Her late husband's estate to which she was the heir was worth £45 a year, but £16 of it was still in litigation in Chancery, so she only had about £30 a year to live on, and her father was unable to help her. Since Charles was kept extremely short of money by his father, he could only give promises to pay for Elizabeth's board and lodging.[6]

The solution that Charles hit upon to save money and obtain easier access to Elizabeth was to get his mother to invite her to come and live in the Bentley house. The household consisted of the mean and bad-tempered old Mr Bentley; Mrs Bentley, who seems to have been a weak-willed woman, easily bent to his purposes by her son Charles but fearful of her husband; Charles's sister Elizabeth, who was aged 19; his half-sister by his mother's first husband, Anne Weekley, who was then 25; and of course a changing asssortment of female servants. The manoeuvre to get his mother and sisters to invite Elizabeth to the house was carried out in stages. First, Elizabeth insinuated herself into their

<hr />

[5] Ibid. 297–305, 415, 480–2, 982, 1207.
[6] Ibid. 267, 439, 523–4, 567, 676–8, 1559.

company every Sunday, by getting herself placed in the same pew in St George's Chapel, Ormonde Street. Then she was invited to a dance at the Bentleys on 18 December 1716 to celebrate Charles's birthday, a party which lasted until five o'clock in the morning. When Mrs Bentley and the two girls debated whom to invite to stay with them over Christmas, they chose the lonely but lively young widow Elizabeth Dent, who was so friendly and about their own age. Elizabeth came, stayed over the ten-day Christmas festivities, and made herself so agreeable that in February they invited her back for an indefinite period to live with them as one of the family. It was clearly understood among all the women in the house, though not by old Mr Bentley, that Elizabeth and Charles were secretly engaged to be married. According to Elizabeth she frequently spent part of the night in one of the Bentley sisters' beds, where she was supposed to sleep, and part in Charles's. Certainly the neighbours, one of whom was the Bishop of Peterborough, were given to understand that Charles was somehow bound to Elizabeth. The Bishop's daughter-in-law thought 'that they were married or that they would be married to each other at his father's death', while his wife thought that they were secretly married since Elizabeth had told her so.[7]

This curious household held together for three and a half years and survived a move from Red Lion Square in Holborn to St James's Street in Westminster. During all this time Elizabeth was fully accepted as one of the family by Mrs Bentley and by the two girls, with whom she became very close friends. She also helped Charles financially when he was straightened for money because of his father's meanness, as he frequently was. He qualified as a barrister in 1718, but according to one account was put to work for his father in the City, instead of being allowed to pursue a legal career.[8]

Just when Charles grew tired of Elizabeth we do not know, but by late 1719 he was seriously looking elsewhere for a bride, particularly someone wealthier and more socially elevated than she was.[9] By thus repudiating his long-standing and now well-publicized engagement, by the standards of the day Charles behaved perfidiously and was in breach of a moral contract, if not a legal one. But whatever had been said or done four years ago on 10 April, 1715, it had taken place without witnesses, the engagement had been made orally and not in writing, and there had been no marriage service in a church or anywhere else. As a lawyer, Charles

---

[7] Ibid. 312–16, 423–32, 631, 635–7, 718, 799, 947, 1014–16, 1019, 1109, 1117.
[8] Ibid. 317, 322, 349, 353, 440–1, 520, 567, 1000, 1022, 1037.
[9] Ibid. 1047.

must have been aware all along that the contract was legally unenforce-able whenever he chose to deny it.[10]

Two of Charles's closest friends at Queen's College, Oxford, had been Harry and Charles Tyrrell, the 2nd and 3rd sons of a baronet with a seat at Thornton in Buckinghamshire. Their father, the 4th Baronet, had died in 1708, leaving a 35-year-old widow, three young sons Thomas, Harry, and Charles, and a daughter Penelope. The estate was reputed to be worth about £1,500 to £2,000 a year, a comfortable income for a baronet. Sir Thomas and Harry were sent to New College in 1711 and Charles to Queen's College, where Charles Bentley first met them. In 1718 Sir Thomas, the 5th Baronet, died under the age of 25, leaving Harry, Charles Bentley's best friend, as 6th Baronet and heir to the estate. Charles Bentley had visited the Tyrrell family from time to time at Thornton and London, and he and Penelope had become friendly. Thus in October 1719 Charles had accompanied Sir Harry on a trip to Oxford to fetch Penelope and bring her back to the Tyrrells' London house in Red Lion Street. Charles was a frequent visitor to the house throughout that winter, and, unknown to Elizabeth, in May 1720 he asked and received from Lady Tyrrell permission to pay formal court to her daughter Penelope. When on 6 August his father suddenly died, Charles at long last succeeded to the Bentley estate and found himself a free man: his marriage crisis was at hand.[11]

As soon as a decent interval of a couple of weeks had elapsed after his father's death, Elizabeth approached Charles and asked him to fulfil his many promises and publicly marry her. Charles was evasive, said it was too soon after the funeral, and that he would deal with the matter when he got back from another visit to his friend Sir Harry Tyrrell at Thornton. So off he went on 1 September, leaving Elizabeth with 5 guineas to pay for the housekeeping while he was away. Ten days later he wrote Elizabeth a letter in which he announced, in brutal and insult-ing terms, that their relationship was at an end. In order to justify his behaviour, he made a whole series of allegations about her sexual misconduct—all wholly imaginary so far as can be seen, since he never tried to substantiate them. It was, he concluded, 'time to break off the friendship we have enjoyed' and asserted that 'you are sensible that I never intended to marry you'. He ordered her to remove herself from the

---

[10] Ibid. 390, 460–2, 467, 601–7.
[11] G. E. Cokayne, *Complete Baronetage*, 6 vols. (Exeter, 1908–9), iv. 37 n. 7; LPCA, E. 27/58; D. 156–7: 422, 718, 1069–73.

house before he returned and never to come near him again. As can well be imagined, Elizabeth was shattered by this letter and went into shock. She consulted her friend, Charles's sister Elizabeth, saying that Charles 'had used her barbarously and that in his letter he had as good as called her whore'. Elizabeth Bentley advised her to answer it firmly and not to accept it 'like a tame fool'. She told her it was 'the villainousest letter I ever saw', and suggested that Charles was drunk when he wrote it, saying 'I know that both he and Sir Harry go to bed drunk every night.' Charles's half-sister Anne Weekly also took Elizabeth's side, declaring that Charles was 'the vilest creature in the world', and his own mother was also said to be shocked.[12]

On 17 September Elizabeth wrote back to Charles a pathetically incoherent letter. What is most significant about it is that she made no claim either that they were already secretly married or that he had given her a bond to marry her in the future. All she claimed was

above four years engagement as there was between us, and so many vows and promises I had from you, besides under your own hand of your value you always had for me, and what you would do for me when your father was dead. And how often have you said what shall we do if your father did not die? Therefore, this letter is only an excuse to get off what is too far gone to come off so easily. And your hatred had not been of so long standing as you have writ for it's been no longer that since you were last at Thorndon, for it's that family that has led you away. And I suppose Sir Harry and my Lady has made up a match between you and Miss Tyrrell. From thence comes all your hatred, and you think you could get off no other way but by abusing me. As for your carriage to me I thought it only proceeded from your being uneasy with your own family and not anything that I had done to deserve that carriage; and was I guilty of half what you lay to my charge, I do think there would be nothing base enough for me.

She went on to proclaim her complete innocence of his 'accusations', and asked, 'if they were true, how come you writ me so many endearing letters last year from Thorndon when you wished that fortune would favour us in the lottery, that we might meet never to part more, how happy you should think yourself'.

Elizabeth ended by saying that she had been too upset to reply before

for as you must think the affection I have is very great, as I believe you had for me. Therefore the shock is the greater, for it is such a shock I believe I shall never get over it...I desire, Mr Bentley, you would take this whole matter under consideration....How could you sit down and write to me so?...If we must part,

12 Ibid. 319–21, 722–7, 807, 952; E. 27/60a.

I would have you have a better opinion of me first, for I am sure I don't deserve this....

from your humble servant, E.D.

...I neither sleep nor eat but am forced to live upon perfect art. I beg of God to preserve my life to see you once more before I leave this world, for I am sure I never shall get over it, for it's more than I can bear....I haven't eat a bit of meat this week nor I believe I never shall eat much more.[13]

Although this letter was so obviously written in great anguish and from the heart, Elizabeth still made no claim to a marriage, or indeed to anything more than four years of promises. It is also noticeable that she signed herself 'E.D.' (Dent), and not 'E.B.' (Bentley).

A few days later the final blow fell, when a letter arrived from Charles addressed to his mother, who was absent at the time. Elizabeth opened the letter, which announced Charles's engagement to Penelope Tyrrell and their imminent wedding. After she had read it aloud to her friend Elizabeth Bentley, she 'fell into a fit of crying and wept bitterly', saying:

I did not think Mr Bentley would have served me so, for that he promised to have no woman but myself. And now to go down to Thorndon and be married so soon, this will be a blot on my reputation as long as I live....What shall I say to my father, mother, cousin Tryon and the rest of my relations, for I have as good as told them that I was married, which they will soon know to the contrary. My brother is so passionate he will be ready to kill me, and I don't know but that Mr Bentley when he comes to town may say I have been his whore.

When her brother Richard Wilkinson junior was informed of the affair, he did indeed take it very badly. He declared that Charles Bentley 'had done like a villain', claiming that before Elizabeth went to stay in his house he had offered Richard a bond of £20,000 to marry no other woman but Elizabeth. But Richard had 'thought [Charles] was a gentleman and so could take his word, but I find him to be a pitiful rascal, and will stab him wherever I meet him'. Turning to Elizabeth he said: 'You may return God thanks you are rid of such a villain, for if he would use you so beforehand, what might you expect afterwards?'[14]

By this time both Elizabeth Dent and Elizabeth Bentley had left the Bentley house, as ordered for the latter by Charles, and were living with a Mr Holmes. Elizabeth Bentley had left at least partly because Charles was not paying her an allowance, and she was henceforth dependent on hand-outs from the Wilkinsons for money to maintain herself.[15] Within

[13] Ibid. D. 156–7: 350–9.
[14] Ibid. 728–34, 812, 955–8, 1025, 1245.
[15] Ibid. 812–16, 964, 1135.

a week or so Elizabeth Dent had pulled herself together, and perhaps to keep her mother quiet was beginning to claim that she had been secretly married to Charles Bentley on 10 April 1716, near the Fleet Prison, but exactly where, or by whom, or with whom as witnesses she could not at first remember. Meanwhile her father the sugar merchant took action, writing to Lady Tyrrell to warn her that Charles Bentley was already married to his daughter Elizabeth and so was not free to marry Penelope; and that the Wilkinson family was suing Charles in the London Consistory Court to compel him to acknowledge it. Mrs Bentley also wrote to her son Charles, urging delay until the facts of his obligations to Elizabeth could be cleared up. In fact, however, it seems clear that the Wilkinsons were well aware that Elizabeth's claims were no more than moral ones. Elizabeth Bentley later reported a conversation at the Wilkinsons during which a lawyer told them that if they could prove a marriage, Elizabeth would be entitled to separate maintenance. Elizabeth allegedly interjected 'Lord, Sir, you know I cannot prove a marriage', to which Mr Wilkinson retorted: 'then Mr Bentley's father and mother did very well to keep a bawdy house for their son. But we will begin a cause [suit] for it, for it is but dropping it when we please.'[16]

Lady Tyrrell was sufficiently disturbed by the threat of litigation to send up to London her adviser on 'the affairs of the family'. On his return, he told her that so far as he could discover from talking to the Wilkinson's lawyers, they had no hard evidence of either a contract or a clandestine marriage. On the other hand, he strongly advised against rushing Penelope (who was being kept in total ignorance of all these intrigues) into a hasty marriage with Charles Bentley until the matter had been fully cleared up.[17]

But neither Lady Tyrrell, nor her son Sir Harry, nor his friend Charles Bentley paid any attention to this advice, and they immediately proceeded to arrange for a clandestine marriage to be performed in an obscure place where the Wilkinsons could not find them. On the evening of 2 November the clerk of the Church of All Saints, Hertford arrived at the house of the vicar of Bengeo and informed him that 'there was a couple who were to be married and desired him to come to Hertford and to bring with him a matrimonial licence, he being then the surrogate to the Commissary of Huntingdon, and in that capacity had blank matrimonial licences by him from the Commissary'. But the vicar was tired and it was late and the night was cold, so he replied that either he would

---

[16] Ibid. 1089–93, 1191–9, 1250–2; E. 27/60a.
[17] Ibid. D. 156–7: 1309–23.

come to Hertford the next morning, or the couple could come to him. At nine o'clock the next morning Charles Bentley, Penelope, Sir Harry, and Lady Tyrrell arrived on his doorstep, asking for a marriage licence and a marriage on the spot. The vicar was careful to abide by the laws governing the issue of licences. He made each party swear that he or she was free of other ties, obligations, or contracts, that their friends raised no objections, that there were no ties of consanguinity between them, and that there were no lawsuits pending to hinder the marriage. Charles and Penelope swore to all this, Charles blandly perjuring himself on this last point. Lady Tyrrell expressed her consent, Charles and Sir Harry gave bonds for the veracity of their statements, and the licence was duly issued. The marriage service followed immediately, apparently in the parlour of the vicar's house rather than the church, and Charles Bentley and Penelope were made indissolubly man and wife in this hole-and-corner manner. Charles and the Tyrrells had performed a neat end run around the Wilkinsons.[18]

A year later, in the autumn of 1721, by which time Penelope Bentley was already pregnant with her first child, the lawsuit of Elizabeth Dent against Charles Bentley to prove her prior marriage was in full swing in the London Consistory Court. Elizabeth was prosecuting for jactitation of the marriage of Charles and Penelope—that is a court order declaring the marriage to be invalid because of bigamy, and binding both parties to abandon all such claims in the future. In prosecuting the suit, the Wilkinsons were faced with the choice of claiming either a secret marriage between Elizabeth and Charles in 1716, for which they had no witnesses; or a pre-contract based on an alleged bond for £20,000 by Charles to marry Elizabeth in the future, which they were unable to produce. The evidence produced in court indicates that for some time they hesitated between the two options, before finally selecting the first. The trouble with the contract argument was that it depended on a document that no longer existed, if indeed it ever had; and in court the Wilkinsons were not even able to get their stories about it to match. So the Wilkinsons' final plan was to claim that a clandestine Fleet marriage had taken place between Charles and Elizabeth on 10 April 1716. This was the day when Elizabeth had finally consented to become Charles's mistress, on which Charles had given her the ring and in all probability had privately sworn to marry her as soon as he could. There is overwhelming evidence from Elizabeth's letters that it was indeed a day of decision, but none whatever that it was a day of formal marriage. The

[18] Ibid. 1301–5.

Wilkinsons therefore had to improvise the story about the alleged marriage as best they could, and there is evidence that the key witnesses were carefully coached in their lines by the Wilkinsons' proctor over a period of weeks or even months.[19]

Elizabeth's story, as told to the Consistory Court in 1721, and again to the Court of Arches in 1726, was as follows: at 4 p.m. on 10 April 1716, Charles Bentley came to her lodgings in a hackney coach accompanied by a man in a black suit like a parish clerk and 'Revd Dr Henry Gower, then a prisoner in the Fleet Prison'. They proceeded to the Turk's Head Coffee House within the Rules of the Fleet and went upstairs to a room provided with a fire, candles, and some cushions. She and Charles knelt on the cushions while Dr Gower read the marriage service to them from the Prayer Book, and they made the appropriate responses. Charles produced the ring, and the man in black gave her away. The witnesses were Mrs Hollyday, the wife of the landlord of the coffee-house, and 'others'. Charles gave the landlord a crown piece for the use of the room, returned Elizabeth to her lodgings, impressed on her the need for secrecy because of his father, and left her. She explained away the very odd fact that she had not invited along as witness her friend, servant, and confidante Mrs Marston, on the grounds that she was out of town that day, but she could not explain her failure to obtain a certificate of marriage from Dr Gower. Mrs Marston and a fellow-lodger Mrs Middleton were said to have been told about the secret marriage soon afterwards.[20]

Charles flatly denounced the whole of this circumstantial story as a complete fabrication, and both sides set about collecting evidence to support their case. Elizabeth could show that Charles had told several people that they were as good as married. Her young sister Mary testified that that summer at Hadley Charles had said to her 'Now Miss Molly, you are my sister.' Mrs Marston and Mrs Middleton were other witnesses to Charles's acknowledgement that they were married, but whether this meant merely 'married in the sight of God' or in the eyes of the law was never made clear.

Everything turned, therefore, on the quality of the proof of the marriage itself. The star witness was Mrs Hollyday, the wife of the keeper of the Turk's Head Coffee House, who testified on oath that Charles Bentley and Elizabeth Dent had indeed been married in her house in an upstairs room; that she had seen the ceremony through the

[19] Ibid. 276–7, 394, 732–3, 1028, 488, 544–5, 572.
[20] Ibid. 282–8, 295, 560–1, 578.

half-open door; and that the officiating parson was Dr Gower, then a prisoner with freedom to live in the Rules of the Fleet, who had died two years before in 1719. She said she paid particular attention to the bride and groom, since they were very well-dressed and clearly gentlefolk. In any case, since weddings in her house were very rare, only seven or eight a year, she was curious to watch it, which is why she had peered through the door.

Asked how she knew the gentleman was Charles Bentley, she said she had seen him at the bar of her coffee-house the other day, recognized him at once, and whispered to her husband 'That's the gentleman.' Three days later, another customer who knew Charles said to her 'Mr Bentley was here t'other day and you did not know him,' to which she replied 'I knew him well enough, tho' my husband did not.' She deposed that a week later she was sent for to the Oxford Arms Tavern in Ludgate, and found there Charles and the friend who had been in her coffee-house. Charles asked if she could swear to his face, and she said she could. She told him that she had made a long deposition about the marriage. He asked her if she could swear to it, at which she took a glass of wine and said 'as sure as you drink to me and this is wine, so sure will I swear to what I have said'. Charles then asked how she could remember his face after five years, and how she could testify about seeing the marriage ceremony when the door was shut. She replied that she had kept the door ajar on purpose to look in. Finally Charles said 'I can't say, but what you are an honest woman, but I am an undone man.'

It was a plausible performance and was backed up by her maid Hannah Hillman, who was only 12 in 1715 when the marriage allegedly took place. She told the same story, claimed that the officiating clergyman had indeed been 'the Revd Dr Gower, a reputed Dr of Divinity', and claimed that she too had peered in through the door. She identified Charles, since she had walked past his house some weeks ago and seen him at dinner through the window. Henry Hollyday, Mrs Hollyday's husband, was a good deal more cautious in his deposition. He declared that on 10 April, 1716, the Revd Henry Gower had told him that he would be marrying a couple in his house that evening. He denied witnessing the marriage and disclaimed knowing the names of the gentleman and lady.[21]

Charles Bentley's lines of attack were first to destroy Mrs Hollyday's claim to have witnessed the ceremony at the Turk's Head, and second her identification of him. He found two witnesses who said that Mrs

[21] Ibid. 401–2, 507, 534–53, 670–5.

Hollyday had told them that 'no one saw them married'. As for the identification, he proved conclusively that the man Mrs Hollyday picked out as Charles Bentley, first at the Turk's Head Coffee House and then at the Oxford Arms Tavern, was in fact an intimate friend of his from the Inner Temple, George Farewell. Farewell testified that Charles Bentley had asked him to make this impersonation on his behalf to prove that Mrs Hollyday was lying. It could not be a matter of mistaken identity, for Charles was fair, he dark, Charles smooth-faced, he pitted with small-pox, Charles tall, he short. Mrs Hollyday had walked right into the trap so carefully set for her by Charles Bentley, and had been proved to be a perjured witness.[22]

Meanwhile Charles had set an agent to work, and finally by late 1721 or early 1722 the latter discovered evidence which showed that the Hollydays were lying, and that no Fleet marriage had ever taken place on 10 April, 1716. Neighbours testified that the Hollydays were utterly untrustworthy. One called them 'poor, shuffling, and sponging sort of people'. He said that they provided accommodation to prostitutes and acted as receivers for stolen goods, while Mrs Hollyday was reputed to be 'a common night walker...who makes it her business to pick up men in public streets in order to have unlawful conversation with them'. One lodger had been transported for felony, and the maid once put in the Bridewell for robbing her former master, a druggist, of coffee and tea. The neighbours were unanimous in their opinion that the Turk's Head Coffee House was a very unsavoury place, and that its owners were vicious and easily corruptible for money.[23]

This was merely circumstantial evidence that the Hollydays were a thoroughly bad lot, but it was the sort of thing which was taken very seriously by eighteenth-century judges and juries. What clinched the case, however, was hard evidence the agent finally dug up about the Revd Dr Henry Gower, who by now was dead and unable to testify. One witness reported hearing Mrs Hollyday complain: 'This Dr Gower being dead puts them in a confusion. I wish I had said it had been Dr Mottram, for he would have had an opportunity of getting money by it.' But it was Dr Gower whom they already deposed had carried out the marriage, and they were stuck with him.[24]

First the agent searched an entry book of marriages kept in an alehouse just by the Fleet Prison to see whether there was any entry of marriage

---

[22] Ibid. 999, 884, 904, 985.
[23] Ibid. 1429–37, 1455–84.   [24] Ibid. 1445, 1476.

between Charles Bentley and Elizabeth Dent, but found nothing. Next he concentrated on Dr Gower. He searched the register of the Fleet Prison from 1700 onward and could find no trace of admission of a Henry Gower until three months *after* the alleged marriage. From the register he discovered that Gower had been ordered to be transferred from Hereford gaol on a writ of habeas corpus obtained by him, to enable him to enjoy the greater freedom of the Rules of the Fleet (and of course to make a comfortable living by going into the clandestine marriage business). There was a delay, however, and Gower was not transferred from Hereford gaol to the Fleet until 13 July, 1716. There was thus no possibility of him having been in London on 10 April of that year, and the Wilkinsons' case consequently completely collapsed.[25]

The Consistory Court ruled that Elizabeth had not proved her alleged Fleet marriage and dismissed the suit. But the Wilkinsons did not give up so easily, especially since it was obvious that Elizabeth had been shabbily and dishonourably treated by Charles, even if nothing could be proved. Mr Wilkinson senior must by then have been making plenty of money again as a sugar merchant, since after some delay the family appealed the case to the Court of Arches, claiming implausibly that they had mistaken the name of the clergyman in the Fleet. The case dragged on inconclusively into 1726 and early 1727, by which time Charles and Penelope had been married six or seven years and had produced four children, two of whom were already dead. The delay suggests that the court was divided, and so issued no sentence. But the longer the delay, the more impossible it became to break up the Bentley/Tyrrell marriage. For the Wilkinsons, the litigation must by now have had little more than harassment value, its real purpose being to try to extract some monetary compensation for Elizabeth. What happened in the end is not known. Either the Wilkinsons dropped the suit, or the Bentleys and Tyrrells got tired of this endless litigation and settled out of court with a lump-sum payment to Elizabeth.[26]

[25] Ibid. 1039, 1356–1420; Eee. 13/65, 71.
[26] Ibid. D. 156–7: 1573; Ee. 9/132; Eee. 13/65, 67; B. 15/67b.

22

Mordaunt v. Mordaunt, 1707–1711

This story opens in 1706, with the arrival of the Revd George Mordaunt at a London lodging-house frequented by Catholics. He was the younger brother of the 3rd Earl of Anglesea, and a Catholic priest who had just returned from Germany, where he had spent the last eighteen years, first in a Catholic seminary, Lambspring College in Lower Saxony, and later in a college in Westphalia.[1]

The England George found on his return, however, was a very different place from the one from which he had fled in 1688. At that time a Catholic King, James II, had just lost his throne, and George's uncle, the 2nd Earl of Peterborough, a loyal follower of the King and a recent convert to Catholicism, had been briefly locked up in the Tower for attempting to flee the country. By 1706, however, England had been in the hands of Protestants for nearly twenty years, and George's elder brother Charles, who had succeeded their uncle as the 3rd Earl, was an Anglican conformist and an ardent Whig.

As a result, as soon as George returned to England intense pressure was brought to bear on him by his family to make him conform to the Church of England. Within a year, the theological arguments of Bishop William Wake of Lincoln (the future Archbishop of Canterbury), aided by those of the Bishop of Norwich and the Rector of St Bride's, Fleet Street, had persuaded him to abjure his Roman Catholic faith.[2] It is not unlikely that George's abjuration of Catholicism was also encouraged by the seductive blandishments of a fellow-lodger, Susan Forbes, who became his mistress in September 1707, very soon after his renunciation of the Catholic vows of chastity. By January 1708 she was pregnant.

Susan Forbes was 'a bold confident woman'. She was a Roman Catholic but loyal to Queen Anne, as were all her friends. She claimed to be related to Lord Forbes, but in fact came from a humble family in Norfolk, where her grandmother sold ale in a public house at Ashill, and

---

[1] LPCA, D. 1425.
[2] Ibid. 252, 357, 504, 734, 963, 981, 1135–7, 1263–5, 1294–7, 1356–60, 1471; *DNB*, s.n. Mordaunt, Henry, Charles (2nd and 3rd Earls of Peterborough), and John, Lord Mordaunt.

where her parents also lived. She had come to London and somehow contrived to get a good position as a personal maid, first of the Duchess of Richmond and then of the Countess of Sussex.[3]

After this auspicious start, she fell sick, and her career moved steadily downwards. She became servant to the Queen's Pastry Cook, and during the pandemonium caused by the great fire at Whitehall in 1697 she robbed him and ran away with goods worth £12 to £14. The cook prosecuted her, and she fled abroad, where she lived for a while in great poverty. On her return, she seems to have set herself up as a courtesan, while nominally bound apprentice to a milliner. Persons who knew her agreed that she lived 'a lewd and scandalous life'. One of her sexual clients, who put up the money for her apprenticeship, was a Mr Brown, whom she passed off as her uncle, but in fact was a Roman Catholic priest, whose real name was the Revd Wolf. By the time George Mordaunt became her principal client, she had no visible occupation save 'the making and selling of honey water'. She was, however, still regularly visited by several gentlemen, including her 'uncle' Wolf and Sir Edmund Bacon.[4]

When she became pregnant, George persuaded her to keep their liaison and the prospective birth a secret, lest it damage his prospects of patronage and advancement from his brother the Earl. He therefore took new lodgings for them both under the names of Mr and Mrs Morfor (a combination of the first syllable of his and her names). In July 1708 the baby was baptized George Morfor by the Revd Peter Durett, the Roman Catholic chaplain of the Portuguese Ambassador. Although George did not attend the baptism in the Ambassador's Chapel, he gave a small party for a few friends to celebrate the occasion. Three weeks later the infant was put out to nurse, where it shortly afterwards died, to the obvious regret of no one. According to George, Susan had already expressed a wish that the child should die.[5]

Soon afterwards George abandoned Susan. This is hardly surprising since, as a younger son with his way to make in the world, the last thing he wanted was to be saddled with an impecunious lower-class mistress or wife. Unless his elder brother could manage to provide him with a well-endowed church living or a well-paid post in government service, marriage with a rich woman was the best way that he could acquire the money with which to live the idle life of a gentleman. A wealthy

[3] LPCA, D. 1425: 274, 278–9, 369, 885, 1689, 1693.
[4] Ibid. 277, 360, 567–71, 832, 839–44, 932, 986, 1067–8.
[5] Ibid. 114–15, 124–8, 198, 250, 303–6, 344–6, 372–4, 557–9, 1060–5, 1075–80.

middle-aged widow would be particularly attractive, since her expectation of life would not be too long, she would be sexually experienced, and she would bring with her a jointure or inheritance from her previous husband. So on December 3, 1708 he was publicly and officially married in St Bride's Fleet Street, before all his Mordaunt relatives, to Mrs Catherine Dormer, widow of John Dormer of Ascot, Oxon. and co-heiress of Sir John Spencer of Yarnton in the same county.

His relatives may have attended the wedding, but they were none too enthusiastic about the match. George's brother Lewis was reported to have commented 'I would be hanged before I would marry so infamous a strumpet, notwithstanding her estate.' His nephew Charles Mordaunt claimed: 'I have got a ring of that old pocky whore Catherine Dormer, and I believe she had a mind to marry me. Though her money is tempting I durst not venture on her, for she is grown old and might be infectious and kill me, the same way she did Mr Drake.' Susan Forbes described her as 'an old harridan of the town who had got a good estate'.[6] But George did not have to put up with her for more than six years, for she died in 1714.[7] In abandoning Susan Forbes in order to marry the rich if disreputable Catherine Dormer, George had seriously underestimated the anger, greed, resourcefulness, ingenuity, and sheer effrontery of his cast-off mistress. She had once told a friend: 'I wish I could have an intrigue with the Duke of Newcastle or some rich Jew who would keep me handsomely.'[8] Failing this, she seized on George's marriage to the wealthy Mrs Dormer as an opportunity to try to obtain a share of his new-found riches by claiming a prior marriage, and using it to blackmail him into paying for her silence.

But George proved adamant. While it was true that Susan had been his mistress for a few months, that he had impregnated her, and that they had lived together as man and wife under the name of Morfor until the death of the baby, at no time had they gone through any form of marriage. As he stated brutally later: 'having regard to my birth and quality, I never had any thoughts or designs of courting or addressing Susannah in the way of marriage, she being a woman of very mean and obscure extraction, and had been a menial servant to several poor and mean families.'[9]

Susan's problem was that she was attempting blackmail without having any documented proof of a previous marriage with George. Undeterred,

[6] Ibid. 548–9, 619, 963–70, 1011–12.
[7] A. Collins, *The Peerage of England*, 8 vols. (London, 1779), iii. 254.
[8] LPCA, D. 1425: 598.   [9] Ibid. 250.

she resorted to forgery. For this she needed allies and money, and in her search for both she turned to the community of Roman Catholic women and men, living on the bare margins of respectability, to which she belonged. She raised the money 'by my gathering or subscription amongst the Roman Catholics or by money borrowed of Revd Peter Durett or Mrs Clare Cross'. A leading role was evidently played by the latter, a milliner, who may have been the brains behind the plot, and certainly did not disguise her hopes of making a fortune by promoting and financing Susan Forbes's legal battles. She once remarked: 'I would not take £500 for my share of the profits which she [Susan Forbes] will gain out of this cause.' As a result of this fund-raising, Susan Forbes was able to hire five or six proctors and counsel to plead her cases in court, as well as attorneys to prepare the evidence.[10]

The first step in the plot was to arrange for a formal Catholic wedding, which could be backdated. On 6 January 1709, one month after the official Protestant marriage of Catherine Dormer and the real George Mordaunt, Susan Forbes and a man who purported to be George Mordaunt were married in the Portuguese Ambassador's Chapel by the same Catholic priest, the Revd Peter Durett, who had christened George and Susan's baby the year before. They were married privately in the vestry, after a public mass in the chapel. The witnesses were Susan's niece Susan Harvey, Mrs Elizabeth Green, and a man called Edward Barrett. The most suspicious aspect of the groom was that he was dressed in noticeably shabby clothes, and did not carry either the cloak or the sword which were the normal accoutrements of a gentleman. It later turned out that he had been told to put on his best clothes, but he had confessed that they were in pawn for 8 shillings. He therefore borrowed an old wig and some ruffles, and turned up on the day in these and 'a whitish coat, much soiled, with a short wig indifferently combed'—hardly the wedding finery of the brother of an earl. The imposter was very careful to avoid perjury, however, and refused to instruct the Revd Peter Durett to alter the name of the child baptized the previous August, leaving Susan Forbes to do that herself. Durett accordingly altered the item in his memorandum book from 'George Morfor' to 'George Mordaunt'.[11]

A great deal of skilful planning and not a little bribery had gone into stage-managing this fake marriage with a counterfeit bridegroom. There seems little doubt that Peter Durett was personally involved from the

---

[10] Ibid. 1451–60, 1473–7, 1518, 1535, 1542–3, 1567–8, 1571, 1685, 1701.
[11] Ibid. 137, 163, 273, 281, 299, 307–12, 319–21, 342, 426, 602–19, 688–92, 1407–13.

beginning, being an investor in the enterprise, and that the plan was for Durett also to falsify the date of the marriage in his memorandum book, so that it preceded both the birth of the child 'Morfor' and the marriage of George Mordaunt to Catherine Dormer. But this marriage ran into immediate trouble, since somehow or other George Mordaunt got to know about it within a week, and he, the Portuguese Ambassador, and the Earl of Peterborough promptly instituted an intensive interrogation of all the witnesses. What neither the Ambassador nor the Mordaunt family could discover was the crucial question of exactly when the marriage was supposed to have taken place. Durett swore to the facts of the marriage before the Earl and the Ambassador, claimed that the groom was George Mordaunt and not an imposter, but obstinately refused to disclose the date except in a court of law. The Earl staged a line-up of all the Mordaunt brothers, and Durett had no difficulty in picking out George, which temporarily convinced the Earl that he was telling the truth. But the identification was not difficult, since George had come into the chapel the day before to interrogate Durett, and had bumped into Susan Forbes, who had said to the priest 'that's my husband. Don't be baffled, the rogue has come to deny me.'[12]

Encouraged by this preliminary success, Susan Forbes began black-mailing George Mordaunt for money, claiming to be his first and only legitimate wife. She began by demanding fairly large sums of money, either £100 a year for life or £700 in cash. But George Mordaunt refused to give her a penny, so to increase the pressure she had him arrested by a creditor for debts run up by her while she was allegedly living with him as his wife. The case came before the London Sheriff's Court, but her attorney warned her that her case would only stand up if she could prove that she was married to George Mordaunt when the debt was incurred in 1707–8, before the latter's marriage to Catherine Dormer.[13]

The problem of proving the date of the false marriage now became critical. The punishment for a conviction of perjury on oath in court was theoretically severe, but in fact only a handful of the hundreds of perjured witnesses who gave evidence on oath before the London courts every year were ever prosecuted, and virtually all were acquitted.[14] Even so, Susan Forbes's hired witnesses were mostly very reluctant to run this risk. Peter Durett certainly told others that George's marriage to Susan had taken place a year before his marriage with Catherine Dormer, but

---

[12] Ibid. 322–31, 550–1, 622–7.
[13] Ibid. 512, 620, 662, 845–6, 879, 929, 1450.
[14] *OBProc.*, *passim.*

further than that he was not prepared to go. By mid-1709 it was clear to Susan that if Durett was subpoenaed to testify in court, he would play safe and tell the truth, that the marriage had taken place on 6 January 1709, which was too late for her purposes. Her first plot had failed, and the only solution was to invent yet another earlier marriage, this time supported by witnesses with no scruples about perjuring themselves about when it occurred and between whom.

Her first scheme was to find a Fleet parson who would insert a false entry of a marriage in a clandestine marriage register. She told a friend that 'she had been to the Fleet Prison to see if she could get the names of George Mordaunt and Susan Forbes entered in the register as if married there', but found that it could not be done without first performing a marriage, which could then be fairly safely antedated.[15]

So in February 1710 Susan Forbes decided to stage a second fake marriage, in order to allow the witnesses to it truthfully to swear that they had seen it happen. She planned to have it antedated to 29 October 1707, which was the moment when her liaison with Mordaunt was just beginning. So on 23 February 1710 Susan, Susan Harvey, Mrs Green, and a man called Benjamin Hayne trooped up to a room in a tavern called the Hole-in-the-Wall beside St Dunstan's Church. No pretence of disguise was attempted on this occasion, except that Susan Harvey was dressed in men's clothes. When they were all assembled Susan said briskly to Susan Harvey 'you shall be George Mordaunt', and to Benjamin Hayne 'you shall have twenty guineas for marrying me. You shall write a sham letter to me tomorrow…in the name of Vaughan.' There was a moment of confusion when it was discovered that no one had brought a ring for the ceremony, but a piece of orange-peel was found in the fireplace and a ring cut out of it to serve the occasion. Hayne then read the marriage service over Susan Forbes and Susan Harvey (acting as George Mordaunt), who made all the appropriate responses.

After this farce was finished, Susan said with satisfaction 'Now you may really swear you saw me married to Mr Mordaunt,' and Hayne duly sat down and in the name of the Revd Vaughan made out a marriage certificate. He backdated it to 29 October 1707, located it in a tavern called King Harry's Head in Fleet Street near Charing Cross, and cited as witnesses Susan Harvey and a fictitious person named Thomas Blackwell. He also wrote some letters at Susan's dictation in the name of the Revd Vaughan. By nightfall he had became thoroughly frightened by what he had done, and at three o'clock the next morning he fled from his

[15] LPCA, D. 1425: 847.

lodgings with his paper and quill pens, in order to hide from Susan Forbes and the bailiffs. Later he ran into Susan one day in Bloomsbury, when she called him a villain and demanded that he make an affidavit that the certificate of marriage was a true one. He took to his heels and fled from her.[16]

Armed with this evidence, Susan Forbes claimed that a marriage had taken place at the time and place stated in the marriage certificate signed, so she said, by a Catholic priest called the Revd Vaughan. To prove it, she produced the certificate forged by Hayne. But even if this marriage and its alleged date could be proved, this still left the problem of explaining why there had taken place a second marriage in the Portuguese Ambassador's Chapel conducted by Peter Durett on 6 January 1709, a fact which was bound to come out in court.

Susan therefore bribed a Mrs Anne Maynard, alias Le Double, to go to the witness stand and tell a story of going for a walk with Susan in St James's Park and accidentally running into George Mordaunt. According to Mrs Le Double, Susan and George began to quarrel. Susan reproached George for not visiting her as he used to, and George reproached Susan for beginning legal actions against him to prove a marriage with him.

GEORGE. I wonder you will go to ruin yourself and me too, for the marriage between us will not stand good in law, for I was married to you by a priest in a house, and the priest and father are both out of England.

SUSAN. Why, was there not Mrs Green and Mrs Ann Harvey by at our marriage?

GEORGE. What signifies two foolish women's evidence? But to let you see I have no ill design, I will marry you again if you will be easy, and you shall choose by whom and where. I desire you would keep it private, for I have almost made an end of my business with my brother the Earl of Peterborough, and when I have done there, I do not care who knows that I have married you, but if it should be known before I have done with him, it will be a hindrance to me.[17]

This was a cleverly crafted piece of dialogue, which provided an explanation both for the second marriage and for the privacy surrounding it. The only thing wrong was that there was not a word of truth in it.

Meanwhile the Mordaunts were sparing no expense in tracking down and interrogating Susan Forbes's potential witnesses, and threatening and bribing them into changing their stories. Susan Forbes was poor and

[16] Ibid. 168, 437–8, 631–6, 755–63, 776–800, 1431, 1705.
[17] Ibid. 407–10, 1029–30, 1173–9.

could only offer her witnesses bonds for future payment, contingent on her winning her case and extracting large sums from George Mordaunt. The Mordaunts and Catherine Dormer, who personally took an active part in the investigation, had plenty of money and plenty of patronage to offer as counter-inducements. There took place a wholesale auction of witnesses, many of whom sold their testimony to the highest bidder, often changing sides in the process. To stop this, great efforts were made on each sides to prevent key witnesses from being got at by the other.

Susan Forbes had promised various plausible-seeming women £20 or £40 for swearing they were witnesses to her marriage, and lesser sums to totally indigent men for impersonation and forgery of documents. One man was first promised a recommendation to 'a wife who was worth money' for his false evidence, an offer which he managed to push up to £150. A crucial witness, Mrs Maynard alias Le Double, was promised to be set up in a milliner's shop in return for her perjured evidence about the marriage, sworn to in three separate trials. Two witnesses later admitted that they learned their false lines by heart before testifying in court.[18]

On the other side George Mordaunt and Catherine Dormer were even more generous with cash, promises, and threats, spending a lot of money 'taking care of witnesses'. As a result, most of the key figures in Susan Forbes's plot eventually switched sides and testified against her. To make sure that everyone was in line, George Mordaunt summoned all of Susan's witnesses to meet him in a tavern the day before the crucial trial before the Queen's Bench on 6 July 1710. He had hidden some of them away for weeks, paying for their bed and board, for fear lest Susan Forbes should obtain access to them and bribe them back again to her side. Some were flattered and cajoled by personal visits from George or Catherine Dormer. Some were tempted by promises by George of lucrative jobs waiting for them after it was all over. Others were impressed by assurances that at the trial 'my brother Peterborough and all my relations will be there'. Some quite brazenly sold their evidence to the highest bidder, and when one was reproached for his dishonesty, he replied 'I intended no harm, but to try what I could bring them up to.'

Anne Maynard, alias Le Double, stuck loyally by Susan, and to prevent her from testifying George Mordaunt sent out spies to arrest her before the opening of the trial in Westminster Hall. But his agents could

---

[18] Ibid. 575–83, 599–615, 660, 666–7, 790–2, 814, 828, 889–93, 932–3, 1156–8, 1177–9, 1182–3.

not find her, since Susan Forbes kept her hidden with Mrs Cross for a week.[19]

In April 1710 George had collected enough evidence to launch a criminal suit against Susan in the London Assize Court in Hicks Hall for 'hiring people to marry her in his name'. The Grand Jury for Middlesex brought in a true bill, but Susan stalled the proceedings—and upped the stakes—by getting that suit also transferred to the Queen's Bench.[20]

On 23 February 1711, the trial in the Queen's Bench in Westminster Hall at last took place before Chief Justice Parker, and despite the swarm of lawyers with whom Susan surrounded herself, the jury convicted her. She appealed to the judges for a retrial in April, but they rejected her plea out of hand.[21] A year later, in April 1712, two of her key witnesses went before Chief Justice Parker and made an affidavit that they had committed perjury in the earlier trial.[22]

Meanwhile in the Consistory Court in 1711 George countersued Susan for 'jactitation of marriage', that is for an injunction to her to cease claiming herself to be his lawful wife. He won, and although she appealed the sentence to the Court of Arches in 1712, her case collapsed because of confessions of perjury by several of her principal witnesses, who had been persuaded to tell the truth thanks to the larger bribes offered by the Mordaunts.

This one case involved four years of multiple litigation from 1709 to 1712 in three different types of courts, civil, criminal, and ecclesiastical, which gives a good idea of the complexity of the eighteenth-century legal system, and the way it could be manipulated for the purpose of harassment and blackmail by an unscrupulous litigant with sufficient financial resources. Over a period of several years, little by little George Mordaunt and his agents had gradually unravelled the details of the plots contrived against him by Susan Forbes. No fewer than three fake marriages had been planned by her. The first was the nearest to the real thing, the marriage blessed by the Revd Peter Durett in the Portuguese Ambassador's Chapel on 6 January 1709. In this case only the groom was a fake, being a bricklayer called Benjamin Hinsmore. The second was the

---

[19] Ibid. 520, 531–6, 539, 585, 650, 669, 683, 685, 713, 716, 765, 767, 800, 854–6, 927, 1335, 1366–9, 1400–15, 1432, 1498–1503, 1506–8, 1510, 1528–9, 1653–65.
[20] Ibid. 291, 340, 352, 368, 451–2, 801, 1086–90.
[21] Ibid. 412, 453, 628–9, 1057, 1089–90, 1179, 1321, 1445, 1465.
[22] Ibid. 1044, 1171–2.

abortive scheme of Susan to have the backdated entry of a marriage which had never taken place inserted in one of the registers of the Fleet Prison.

Lastly there was the parody of a marriage ceremony which took place in a room in a tavern called the Hole-in-the-Wall near St Dunstan's Church on 23 February 1710. Not only was it falsely backdated to 29 October 1707, and alleged to have taken place in a different tavern, but, as we have seen, most of the principal actors were false. The groom 'George Mordaunt' was a woman called Susan Harvey in men's clothes, and the priest 'the Revd Vaughan' was a scrivener called Benjamin Hayne. Only Susan Forbes the bride was genuine. The sole purpose of this charade was to allow the witnesses to it to swear that they had seen a marriage, without running the risk of perjury.

As George Mordaunt and his agents slowly discovered, all the characters in the plots had three things in common: Roman Catholicism, extreme poverty, and loose morals. Only Susan's financial backer Mrs Cross seems to have had some financial standing, although some neighbours thought little of her moral reputation.[23] But against the money, prestige, and political influence of the Mordaunts and the Dormers, Susan Forbes did not stand a chance. One by one all but one of her hired witnesses were tracked down. Some were flattered and cajoled by personal visits from George Mordaunt or Catherine Dormer. Some were tempted by promises of lucrative jobs waiting for them after it was all over. Others were impressed by assurances that the Earl of Peterborough and other Mordaunt relations would be present at the trial. Many quite brazenly sold their evidence to the highest bidder. Once they had agreed to confess the truth, they were hidden away in safe houses by the Mordaunts, so as to prevent Susan Forbes from getting access to them.

The key actors in the plots of Susan Forbes were Susan Harvey, Anne Maynard, Elizabeth Green, Ann so-called Lady Fitzharris, Edward Barrett, Thomas Hinsmore, and Benjamin Hayne. It was the switching of sides by all seven except Susan Harvey which destroyed Susan Forbes's case and finally led to her conviction for criminal conspiracy. Susan Harvey was a niece of Susan Forbes, and 'a common night walker', who worked out of Beveridge's Dancing School, which was well known as 'a Buttock's Ball, or place of resort of ill women'. She went there dressed up demurely in Quaker costume, in order to add a little religious spice to the pleasure of picking her up and taking her off to a tavern to sleep with her. She lived with a Mr Tasher, to whom she claimed to be married,

[23] Ibid. 1454–7, 1535.

and was a lodger in Mrs Cross's house. In fact she 'was reputed to be kept as a miss or woman for pleasure', and the scandal was heightened by the fact that she and her clients sometimes took Mrs Cross's 12-year-old son to bed with them since 'Sukie would have it so'. In the daytime Susan Harvey was officially a worker in the millinery trade, but this seems to have been merely a cover for her more lucrative evening employments. There was even an ugly story of her acting as a procuress and trying to seduce the young daughter of a blind solicitor. Altogether she seems to have been a thoroughly disreputable character.[24]

Anne Maynard was Susan Harvey's friend and fellow-worker, both in the millinery trade by day and at Beveridge's Dancing School by night, and had an even more unsavory history. Although only 22 in 1711, she had already had one bout of venereal disease and was then pregnant. She was also very quarrelsome and in 1710 was involved in a fight with another woman in a brothel over the favours of a client, for which she was imprisoned for a while in Bridewell. On another occasion she got into a fierce fight over money in a brothel with the keeper, when 'all the women of the house assaulted him'. He called a constable and had Anne arrested and put in the Roundhouse. In revenge she went before a Justice of the Peace and swore that he was the father of the child she was carrying. But at the Quarter Sessions she dropped the charge, and later admitted that in fact the father was the man she was living with, a jeweller named Abraham Le Double.

In 1711 she was arrested for debt, and Susan Forbes took the opportunity to offer to pay for her release if she could find someone prepared to swear that he was the priest who had married her (Susan) to George Mordaunt in 1707. But Anne could not find anyone willing to do this, so Susan left her to rot in prison. It was this episode which, along with monetary inducements and threats from George Mordaunt, induced her to confess before Chief Justice Parker that she had lied in her testimony as witness to both the backdated 1707 marriage and the fraudulent 1710 one. She now retracted her sworn testimony in three separate trials, in Doctors' Commons, Hicks Hall, and Westminster Hall. She confessed that she had learned her story by heart before the trials, being bribed by Susan Forbes with a promise to set her and Susan Harvey up in a business in a milliner's shop.[25]

The other two older women in the plot were neither as impoverished

[24] Ibid. 263, 1126–8, 1220, 1229–30, 1249, 1315–17, 1374, 1380–2, 1385, 1446, 1449, 1478, 1522–4, 1562–4.

[25] Ibid. 406–7, 1126, 1148–53, 1161–3, 1170–1, 1178–83, 1208–10, 1218–20, 1241–8, 1282–3, 1288–90, 1300–1, 1308–19, 1336–6, 1528–9, 1565, 1637–41.

nor as depraved as Susan Harvey and Anne Maynard, nor were they professional prostitutes. Mrs Green (who was 32) first testified for Susan Forbes as witness of her marriage by Durett. But when she saw the plot collapsing, she quickly switched sides and confessed all she knew. When first offered £20 to join the Mordaunt side, she replied that she would 'go out of the way' (i.e. go into hiding) for £100, but was later pressured by Catherine Dormer into confessing to perjury. She claimed to be the widow of an army officer, but in fact had been no more than the mistress of a trooper called Stafford. She eked out a living on her late 'husband's' legacy and her 'mantua making, plain work, quilting of petticoats and other needle-work'. Although distinctly above the poverty line, she was still struggling to keep her head above water.[26]

Far more sinister was her friend, the 50-year-old 'Lady Fitzharris', alias Mrs Magrath, who first drew her into the plot, and then later persuaded her to change sides to the Mordaunts. The widow of a Jacobite conspirator called FitzHarris, who had been convicted of high treason and executed in 1681, she was a procuress and an active lesbian, who tried sexually to assault an unsuspecting bedfellow, who sued her for it. She was a thoroughly unscrupulous woman with a long criminal past, and it was upon her that Susan Forbes placed most reliance to find her witnesses willing to perjure themselves about her fake marriages. But she was 'a dangerous woman to be any ways acquainted with', as Susan Forbes eventually learnt to her cost when 'Lady Fitzharris' double-crossed her and revealed her plots to the Mordaunts.[27]

Three of Susan Forbes's hired conspirators were men. One was Edward Barrett, an Irish Catholic who had joined the French Army, fought under the Duke of Anjou, and been captured. To save his skin he had deserted from the French to the English. He was put on half-pay as a Lieutenant of Foot, but lost his allowance when it was found that he was still a Roman Catholic. He was arrested for debt, upon which Sir Robert Walpole, then Secretary of State for War, paid £30 to release him, as a reward for his desertion from the French. He was now living with a woman in abject poverty in London, while his real wife and child were still in Ireland.

He was hired as one of the witnesses to the marriage in the Portuguese Ambassador's Chapel of Susan Forbes to 'George Mordaunt', whom he claimed (falsely) to have identified, since he had known him for ten years at the Court of the Jacobite Pretender at St Germain. This last statement

---

[26] Ibid. 595–8, 651, 666–71, 1007, 1400–4, 1491–1503, 1553–4.
[27] Ibid. 514–20, 526–8, 884, 900–2, 909, 1421–5, 1521, 1578, 1588–1620.

was what he was paid for, since it was a most damaging accusation. It not only firmly identified the bridegroom as George Mordaunt and not an impostor; but it also cast serious doubt on the latter's political loyalty and the veracity of his account of his life abroad.[28] If the statement were true, it meant that George Mordaunt was probably a Jacobite spy or even a conspirator.

The man who agreed to impersonate George Mordaunt in the January 1709 wedding in the Portuguese Ambassador's Chapel was a 29-year-old bricklayer named Thomas Hinsmore, a man who had long been living with his family 'in most miserable and deplorable circumstances'. He had been contacted by Mrs Green, assured that he only needed to swear to 'a popular marriage'—meaning a verbal contract—and that he would be 'very well rewarded for doing so'. He boasted that 'the cause should not have been lost for lack of swearing', and when accused of giving false testimony retorted: 'False? Who would not swallow any oaths for such a sum of money? So much money would make anyone swear twenty oaths.' When warned he might get into trouble, he retorted 'Damn it, I can never be poorer than I am.' When he was being tempted to switch sides to George Mordaunt and confess the truth, he held out for a long time, saying 'I will bring him up to a greater sum of money before I will do his drudgery for him', and letting it be known that he expected 'some hundreds of pounds' for telling all he knew. Once he had done the switch, Susan Forbes accused him of saying 'who would not forswear himself for so good a friend as Mr Mordaunt, who has put clothes on my back and money in my pocket?' This was a great improvement on his agreement with Susan, to carry out the impersonation in return for a mere 7 shillings and sixpence, paid in advance.[29]

The principal figure in Susan Forbes last plot, which was the false clandestine marriage backdated to 1707, was another seedy character, a 42-year-old self-styled scrivener named Benjamin Hayne, whose career had not been a success. He had started out respectably enough as a writer for a notary public; drifted from there to a temporary job sorting out the army accounts for the widow of a captain; and then got taken on as clerk to Captain Otway's Company. After discharge from the army, he earned a precarious living by writing and selling pens in a poor lodging in a court next to the Bagnio in Long Acre. There he was contacted by Susan Forbes in February 1710 to do a little forgery work for her. First she asked him to alter the end of a letter from George Mordaunt to her from

---

[28] Ibid. 383–401, 1144–7, 1166–9, 1197–1202, 1254–60, 1269–74, 1332.
[29] Ibid. 456–8, 678–9, 745–53, 916–20, 950–7, 963–4.

'your affectionate lover, George Mordaunt' to 'your affectionate husband, George Mordaunt'. He said he could do it, but had doubts because 'I have heard the family of Mordaunts is a very honorable family.' More persuasive was the discovery that he could not satisfactorily imitate George's handwriting.[30]

A little later Susan persuaded him to pretend to be a Fleet parson, and marry her and someone pretending to be George Mordaunt. When she asked him to write a marriage certificate between herself and George Mordaunt in the name of the Revd Vaughan and backdate it to 29 October 1707, he reluctantly agreed, but he flatly refused to go before any court of law and swear an affidavit about its veracity. He also asked for a down payment before attempting to write it, but Susan Forbes could only offer him a note of hand, payable if and when she proved her marriage and got her money out of George Mordaunt.

Hayne having failed her, the resourceful Susan Forbes fell back on Thomas Hinsmore, the first impersonator of George Mordaunt. She got in touch with him again and asked him this time to make an affidavit that he was a priest called Vaughan who had married her to George Mordaunt on 29 October 1707. She threatened to have him indicted for bigamy if he refused, for his private life, like that of all others in the story, was a legal and moral morass. When he refused to make out the affidavit for fear of perjury, Susan ingeniously suggested he merely say in court 'I am the person that married her.' This would have been true but misleading, since in fact he had been impersonating the bridegroom not the priest. But he agreed to do it, and told his false tale to Susan Forbes's proctor, but not under oath. Susan then offered him £20 to swear that he was the priest who had married them, but by now he had cold feet and refused. Instead, he contacted George Mordaunt and told him the whole story. He was well paid for his information, being 'kept a long time at bed and board' in return. But this was not enough to restore his finances, and he was arrested for debt soon after the trial in Westminster Hall in early 1711. His early hopes of getting £40 or £50 out of the business turned out to be wishful thinking.[31]

What is so remarkable about this story is the way a poor but bold and unscrupulous woman could contrive to put a great landed family like the Mordaunts, with great wealth and extensive political connections, through an excruciating legal wringer for nearly four years. This is

[30] Ibid. 773–6.
[31] Ibid. 702–36, 1044–9, 1233, 1396, 1415–17, 1506–12, 1546–7, 1642–54, 1665–6.

especially surprising, since her case was based entirely on perjured testimony, forged documents, and multiple impersonations. No doubt the religious aspect of the story is an important ingredient. The Mordaunts were an old Catholic family, and their recent conversion to Anglicanism and Whiggery was a source of intense resentment among the Catholics of London, who were only too anxious to destroy the reputation of the family. As a recently lapsed Roman Catholic priest, George Mordaunt's liaison with Susan Forbes and subsequent marriage to Mrs Dormer were no doubt particularly offensive to them.

The only explanation for the ample funds Susan had at her disposal for her extensive legal battles was that offered by George Mordaunt in court, namely that she was supported by loans and gifts from a number of well-to-do Catholics.[32] Some of them, like Mrs Cross, were hoping for a share in the hush-money they expected to extract from the Mordaunts, but others were subscribing money merely in the hopes of religious revenge. Edward Barrett's false claim to have known George Mordaunt for ten years at the Court of the Pretender at St Germain is particularly significant in this respect, since it was designed to hint directly at treason.

Few cases in the records are so revealing of both the ease with which perjured testimony could be bought in early eighteenth-century London, and the modest sums that it cost. Fake marriages, involving impersonations, even including transvestism, false testimony, and backdated certificates of marriage, were evidently not too difficult to arrange. Equally impressive are the detective skills of professional investigators at the same period, who were capable of identifying, locating, and building up complete life histories of the obscure impersonators, forgers, and perjurors who populated the underworld of eighteenth-century London.

[32] Ibid. 253.

(d) A BIGAMOUS MARRIAGE

23
Tipping v. *Roberts*, 1704–1733

According to the law of the land bigamy was a serious offence, theoretically punishable in the criminal courts after 1603 by the penalty of death, but in practice mitigated by benefit of clergy to burning in the hand. In reality, however, it seems at least likely that thousands, probably tens of thousands, of English men and women committed bigamy in the seventeenth and eighteenth centuries and went unpunished. Some did it knowingly, as a means of establishing a new family after an old marriage had broken down; some in ignorance; and some on a false presumption of the death of an earlier spouse. Whatever the law might say, there seems little doubt that there was a flourishing practice of self-divorce by bigamy in operation among the lower and lower-middle classes, although it is only from the stories of the few who became entangled with the law that we can obtain a glimpse of this marital underworld.

In 1704 Robert Tipping, the eldest son of a country attorney in Essex, was about 18 years old and serving as an apprentice to a London upholsterer in Fleet Street. He fell in love with and courted Sarah Roberts, a poor young woman but 'of a sober, pious and vertuous life'. Since Robert was not yet free of his apprentice's articles, which strictly forbade any such entanglements, they were married clandestinely by the prison chaplain in the chapel of the Fleet Prison. For a while they lived with Sarah's mother Frances, but after a year they moved out into lodgings on their own. In the course of the next six years three children were born, but only the eldest lived, a daughter named Mary. The upholstery business must have gone badly for Robert Tipping, for in 1711 the pair were obliged to move back with Sarah's mother. There they lived for another four years, and Sarah gave birth to yet another child, who also died. In January 1714, after ten years of marriage, Robert deserted Sarah, who was yet again pregnant.[1]

Robert had fallen in love with a woman called Elizabeth Hughes, and began living with her, giving Sarah and her new baby Francis no support

---

[1] LPCA, D. 2075: 55–72, 82, 140, 150, 168–9.

at all. Sarah's mother therefore had him arrested for fornication and denial of wife support and brought him before the Lord Mayor's Court, when it was discovered, on the evidence of Elizabeth Hughes, that he had also married her. He was therefore put in Newgate Prison to stand trial at the Old Bailey 'for having two wives'. This was presumably at Sarah's instigation, but she had no interest or desire to see her husband burned in the hand for the felony of bigamy. The prosecution was merely a blackmail device to force her husband to settle a maintenance allowance to support herself and her child. Through the mediation of Robert's bachelor brother John, a bargain was therefore easily struck: Sarah agreed to bring no witnesses to the trial to prove her marriage to Robert, thus ensuring his acquittal at the Old Bailey. In return, Robert promised to pay for the costs of the suit and to provide for her future maintenance.[2]

After his acquittal, Robert failed to fulfil his part of the bargain, and Sarah had to sue him in the Court of Common Pleas, where she was awarded £17. After a fresh intervention by Robert's brother, John Tipping, who contributed over half of the award out of his own pocket, Sarah signed a document renouncing any further financial claims on Robert. It was the *de facto* equivalent of a divorce settlement, to demonstrate which Sarah used her maiden name of Sarah Roberts to sign the document. Robert was now therefore free to live in peace in Bristol with his new wife Elizabeth Hughes, while Sarah and the baby remained in London with Mrs Roberts. Neither of them was burdened with support of their oldest child Mary, since as far back as 1709, when she was only 4, she had been adopted by her grandfather the attorney, who brought her up in the country and left her £100 in his will. She was therefore well looked after, and lived and married at a much higher economic level than her mother or father.[3]

For the next ten years, from 1715 to 1725, Sarah and Francis lived with old Mrs Roberts, and Sarah earned money as a 'nurse-keeper', presumably a wet-nurse. But in 1725 Mrs Roberts died, and Sarah was reduced to such straits that she and young Francis were forced to move into the workhouse to live on the charity of the parish. In 1727, at the age of 13, Francis was put out by the parish as apprentice to a fanstick-maker, but he ran away after two years. For the first and last time in her life, Sarah got into trouble with the law, for giving shelter to her runaway child. She was put in Bridewell for a while at hard labour to force her to put him out as apprentice again, which six months later

---

[2] Ibid. 72, 78, 86, 97–8, 112, 142, 151, 188.
[3] Ibid. 81–3, 116, 131, 142–6, 153, 191–3, 215.

she did. By all accounts she thereafter lived quietly on public welfare, a good-hearted and amiable old woman, too much given to drink but otherwise harmless enough.[4]

Nothing more would have been heard of this story if in 1733 Robert Tipping's second wife Elizabeth Hughes had not died, and he presumably wanted to remarry without again running the risk of another charge of bigamy. He therefore sued Sarah in the Consistory Court, claiming that his alleged marriage with her in 1704 had never taken place. He admitted she had been his mistress for a decade but denied marriage, presumably counting on her abject poverty to stop her from collecting the necessary proof of an event which had occurred almost thirty years before.

Here, however, he made a mistake, for their well-to-do daughter Mary, who by now had married and buried two husbands, came to her mother's rescue and financed her legal defence, partly no doubt to prove her own legitimacy. Moreover even his own brother John failed to back him up, and instead testified on Sarah's behalf. The register book from the Fleet Chapel was produced in court by the son of the clerk who had written the entry thirty years before, along with the original certificate of marriage on parchment, which Sarah had carefully kept for all these years, and to the authenticity of which the son of the clerk testified. Robert's brother John described how Robert had only been acquitted years ago at the Old Bailey on a charge of bigamy because Sarah agreed not to bring evidence against him. Robert's case collapsed, but he was obstinate enough to appeal the sentence to the Court of Arches, where he was defeated again.[5]

In theory this presumably left Sarah in a position to renew a claim for support as his wife, despite her written renunciation twenty years before, but there is nothing to suggest that she did so. She clearly regarded her marriage as legitimate but terminated for good in 1715. This story thus provides as clear a case of divorce by mutual consent in the eighteenth century as one could hope to find. It was only Robert Tipping's uneasiness about contracting a third marriage, caused by his earlier brush with the law, which brought the whole business to the surface again. On the other hand, it was only the intervention of the well-to-do daughter Mary which enabled her old mother to mount a successful legal defence against her former husband. The Tippings were a family of the middling sort in which divorce by mutual consent was clearly a morally acceptable way

---

[4] Ibid. 81–9, 107, 122, 131–2, 139, 153, 165–6, 185, 188.
[5] Ibid. 14, 60–1, 108, 148; B. 17/39a, 50.

out of a broken marriage. Clandestine marriage in the Fleet chapel, as conducted in the early years of the eighteenth century, perfectly suited their need for respectability coupled with secrecy, and for a marriage which could be enforced or renounced according to circumstances.

24
Muilman v. *Muilman*, 1722–1748
Con Phillips, serial bigamist

(i) *Introduction*

Teresia Constantia Phillips made herself famous partly by her life, which was sensational enough, what with her five marriages and her position as the successive mistress of at least seven rich and well-connected men. But she was also famous partly because of her scandalous autobiography, entitled *An Apology*, which ran to four editions; and vividly illustrated the defects of the current laws of marriage. Her frank exposure of the chicanery of the law, and the scandalous details of her many matrimonial lawsuits, made her life a paradigm of the abuses of the law in general, and the law of marriage in particular. Her first clandestine marriage to a bigamist, purely in order to obtain protection from her creditors, played some part in changing English law, since it was several times cited by reformers as a prime example of the abuses of the system.

(ii) *Life*

As told in her autobiography, Con Phillips was born in January 1709, the daughter of a well-connected gentleman from an ancient Welsh family, who was then serving as a Captain in the Grenadier Guards. After the end of the war with France in 1713, Lt.-Col. Phillips was discharged from the army, and by 1717 he found himself unable to support his wife and his five children. The children were therefore dispersed among their relations, the 9-year-old Con being taken in by her godmother the Duchess of Bolton, who was an illegitimate daughter of the Duke of Monmouth.

   Given this Whig background, it is surprising that Con appears to have been a Catholic. Some of her many lovers were certainly Catholics, and on three occasions she retreated to a Catholic nunnery at Ghent as a welcome temporary respite from a life of fashionable gaity, extravagance, and sexual excess. It seems quite possible from Con's Christian names, her retreats to the nunnery, and her bilingualism, that her mother had been a French Catholic. But, Con took her religion lightly and could not tolerate pious hypocrisy. Years later she made fun of an extremely devout

Catholic who for a while had been her passionate lover: 'in the midst of an amorous moment, when it is almost out of nature to believe the transport would give time for reflection, he would frequently start and cry out: "Oh! Heavens, my girl, we shall both be damned"'. Con observed coolly that he 'had not less than three or four such vehicles of damnation upon the wheel', and condemned him as 'a damn'd mercenary, designing, hypocrite'.[1]

The Duchess of Bolton sent Con to an elegant girls' boarding-school in Westminster for two years, where she acquired a good polish in the arts and graces of a lady to add to her fluency in French. Meanwhile her father's fortunes revived, and he somehow obtained the reversion of the command of the Company of Invalids at Portsmouth. When his wife died in 1721 he married his servant, and Con was summoned home from the duchess. But she did not get on with her stepmother, and in 1721, at the age of 12, she left home and settled in London, supporting herself and her even younger sister by needlework.[2]

Despite her poverty, Con was stunningly beautiful and evidently sexually irresistible (Plate 7). She also had good connections in high society, which enabled her to spend her Sundays with Mrs Douglas, widow of General Douglas. At the time there lodged with Mrs Douglas young Philip Stanhope, heir to the Earl of Chesterfield, who as a result of the economic crash of the South Sea Bubble was confined to the house for fear of arrest by his creditors. According to Con, Stanhope had a taste for young virgins, and made eager court to her, despite—or because of—her immature age. Con, who was still only 13, rashly accepted his invitation to come to his rooms one evening to watch the fireworks to celebrate King George I's return from Hanover.[3] According to her, Philip Stanhope took advantage of her by first making her drunk, then tying her hands to a chair, after which he stripped and raped her. Decades later, Stanhope, by then the famous moralist Lord Chesterfield, denied the rape but conceded that Con became his mistress for a couple of months. For a while he continued to make her a weekly allowance, but it lapsed when he departed for Portugal.[4]

Left penniless in London, Con Phillips, who was clearly wildly extravagant, soon ran up £500 of debt, and her creditors became increasingly threatening. Since the debts of a married woman were the legal responsibility of her husband, she was advised to protect herself from

---

[1] *An Apology for the Conduct of Mrs Teresia Constantia Phillips*, 3 vols. (London, 1748–9), ii. 223–4; i. 7.
[2] Ibid. i. 19–24.   [3] Ibid. i. 24–36.   [4] Ibid. i. 37–43.

her creditors by marrying a man in full legal manner in church before witnesses. The marriage would be bigamous, since the proposed groom, a man called Delafield, was already married. The marriage took place, and the couple parted immediately after the ceremony, the groom disappearing from sight to avoid arrest by Con's creditors, and Con fleeing to Rouen for a few months to let things blow over. On her return, the certificate of marriage sufficed to keep at bay her creditors, who were unable to find Delafield.[5]

Early in 1723, soon after her return to London, Con met a young Dutchman, Henry Muilman, the son of a very rich Amsterdam merchant, who visited her several times, fell passionately in love with her, and proposed marriage. When Con told him of her previous marriage, Muilman checked the facts, and was assured by expert lawyers that because it was bigamous on Delafield's part, it was therefore automatically null and void. So he went ahead and married Con in early 1724, without telling his Dutch relatives anything about his bride's penurious circumstances or dubious sexual and marital past.[6]

When Muilman's parents discovered all about Con's background, they were furious at this totally unsuitable match for a rising young merchant, and insisted that he get the marriage annulled. Muilman finally succumbed to family pressure, and he bribed Con with a life annuity to leave the country and not to contest a nullity suit. As soon as she had left, he proceeded to have his own marriage declared null and void as bigamous, because of Con's previous marriage with Delafield.[7]

After parting from Muilman, Con, who was still only 16 years old, exerted all her attractions of body and mind to captivate Mr B——, whom she had first met at dancing class when they were both still at school some years before. B——, who was the only son of a general and the heir to a very substantial fortune, fell in love with her and took her on as his mistress. For the next five years the two of them lived a life of frivolous and fashionable excess, by Con's own admission spending money like water, partly in London and partly abroad. They stayed the best part of a year in Paris, where B—— passed her off as his wife. In 1728, however, after a quarrel with B——, Con withdrew to a nunnery at Ghent, where she moved into the opulent quarters of the former mistress of a duke. After some eighteen months at the nunnery, Con returned to England, and again resumed living with B——. But in 1731, after a

<hr/>

[5] Ibid. i. 58–65.   [6] Ibid. i. 65–81; LPCA, D. 1455: 96–104.
[7] *Apology*, i. 82–214.

period of up to two years during which both were being secretly unfaithful to the other, Con and B—— decided to part company for good.[8]

Since B——'s unsettled finances made it impossible for him to make her an annuity after they broke up, Con, who was still only 21, was once more left penniless to live as best she could off her beauty and wits. As long ago as 1727, she had met at a masquerade a young man called Southcote, the second son of Sir John Southcote, and an ostentatiously pious Catholic.[9] At the time, he himself had little money and no hopes of political preferment because of his religion. In her later wicked pen-portrait of Southcote, Con stressed his graceful appearance, his cleanliness 'even to female delicacy', his immaculate and magnificent dress, and the way 'perfumes discover his approach'. He was an early patron of patent leather shoes, 'which particular lustre has also this innocent quality that it leaves no soil, or sign of familiarity, upon the ladies' petticoats: a secret of no trivial consequence to the amorous Tartuffe'. Con describes him as 'of a robust lascivious constitution', but one who 'always preserves an inviolable adherence to his interest'. Consequently 'his addresses were mostly to married ladies. If a child happened to follow,...he chose it should be fathered without any inconvenience or expense to him.' Indeed he was very adept at getting sterile women pregnant, so much so that 'his exploits that way recommended him to many ladies'.[10]

Over a period of four years from 1727 to 1730, Con claimed to have received over 400 love-letters from Southcote, urging her to become his mistress and persuading her that marriage 'is a trick devised only to preserve names and estates...These are contracts we enter into for convenience.' Years later she publicly offered to show the original letters to 'any gentleman of rank or quality she has the honour to be known to'.[11] This liaison was only broken off in 1732, when Southcote left for an extended Grand Tour in Italy with 'the nobleman his patron'.[12] Southcote seems to have been the only man Con ever fell seriously in love with, and he was certainly the only lover she ever paid for. But his later heartless rejection of her in 1746, when he was rich and she had

---

[8] Ibid. i. 301–7, 310–12.

[9] Ibid. ii. 203; Con only called him 'S——te' or 'Tartuffe'; Sir John Bowring identified him as Southgate, but this must be a mistake for Southcote, since there was no knight called Southgate (*The Works of Jeremy Bentham*, ed. J. Bowring, 11 vols. (Edinburgh, 1838–43), x. 47; W. A. Shaw, *Knights of England* (London, 1906).

[10] *Apology*, ii. 119–57.

[11] Ibid. ii. 4–6, 158–91, 238–41.

[12] Ibid. ii. 202–13.

fallen upon hard times, turned that love into a blistering hatred that burns through the pages of the second volume of her *Apology*.[13]

A mere three days after Southcote left for Italy, Con was approached by Sir Herbert Pakington, a rich 31-year-old Worcestershire baronet with a wife and family, and an income of £6,000 a year. He was a Tory MP, who voted consistently for the party line, except on the issue of the removal of Walpole. His father had been a suspected Jacobite and had been arrested briefly in 1715.[14] He invited Con to become his mistress —the renewal of suggestions he had been making for two or three years. Con accepted, in return for the promise of an annuity of £500 a year for life. So Pakington left his wife and four children at his splendid seventeenth-century country seat at Westwood Park in Worcestershire, and for a whole year lived a life of reckless prodigality with Con in London, becoming more and more passionately obsessed with her as time wore on.[15] When Con finally announced her intention of leaving him, Pakington became frenzied with jealousy and made an attempt at suicide with his sword at the dinner-table, which put him into bed for three weeks. A second failed attempt at suicide by the lovelorn Sir Herbert was the last straw, and Con fled in secret with lord F——and settled down happily for the summer of 1732 with him and his brother in a rented house in Hertfordshire, looked after by ten servants.[16] This contented domestic life with Lord F—— lasted right through the winter of 1732–3 and into the spring, when two financially very advantageous marriage offers with women worth £80,000 were made to his Lordship. Con generously offered not to stand in his way, but Lord F——, according to her, was torn. 'What allurements must that fortune have, for which I would barter my Connie?...Why would you force me to be rich and wretched?' But Lord F—— had only a small estate burdened with charges for younger children, while his Tory opinions meant that he 'utterly disdained all dependence on a Court'. A rich marriage was therefore his only salvation.[17]

Con's life during the next few years is somewhat obscure. During the 5-year liaison with B—— from 1727 to 1732 she had clearly accumulated a good deal of money, which she now began spending on extensive litigation about her marriage with Muilman. Her next lover, whom she

---

[13] Ibid.
[14] Ibid. i. 316–19; R. Sedgwick and J. Brook, *History of Parliament, The House of Commons, 1715–1754* (London, 1970), s.n. Pakington.
[15] *Apology*, i. 319–23, 325–47; ii. 11–20.
[16] Ibid. ii. 23–38.   [17] Ibid. ii. 70–9.

picked up in about 1737, she refers to as 'Mr Worthy', the heir to an immensely rich Jamaican planter. He was handsome and Oxford-educated. They were overwhelmed with 'the most violent passion of love', but the affair was soon interrupted in 1739, since mismanagement of his property in Jamaica by his now senile father forced him to return there. Con was broken-hearted, but determined to follow him, despite the discomfort and tedium of the journey and the extreme unhealthiness of the Jamaican climate.[18] After two unhappy trips to try to rejoin 'Worthy', first in Jamaica and then in Boston, in 1740 Con abandoned the relationship and took ship back to England.[19]

This was, as she later admitted, a mistake. First, she fell sick of a fever for the best part of a year, and second, she was hounded by her creditors. The very first day of her return to London she resumed relations with a former surgeon friend, and spent the night in his house. The next morning a bailiff knocked on the door, and as soon as it was opened ran inside the house. Her sister had the presence of mind to lock the parlour door against him, but he threatened to break it down. The surgeon warned him that his action was illegal and that he would be liable to prosecution, but this did not deter the bailiff from forcing his way in. But he was unable to catch Con, who in the mean time had run out into the garden, climbed through the kitchen window, and hidden herself. But bailiffs proceeded to surround the house and set up a round-the-clock watch. Con only managed to escape by using a pruning ladder to scale the garden wall and climb into the next-door house belonging to the Duchess of Marlborough. After this narrow escape, Con found it prudent to come to terms with her creditors. She paid part of her debt, while they repaired the surgeon's parlour door and gave him a haunch of venison for his trouble.[20]

During the early 1740s, while still battling both fever and creditors, Con devoted her energies to her lawsuits against her husband, and had no love affairs in progress save for the rather tepid relationship with her surgeon. She did, however, renew her friendship with the rich Boston merchant Colonel Vassall, whom she had known in Boston and Jamaica, who arrived in London to spend money and tour England. But, alas, in a single year 'the ladies stripped him of his health and the sharpers of his money'. Con, out of pity according to her version of events, lodged him in her house while he recovered from a bout of venereal disease, and lent

---

[18] Ibid. iii. 61–189; ii/4, 9–15.
[19] Ibid. iii. 189–215.   [20] Ibid. ii/4, 16–20.

him money in order to get him home. But he died before he could repay her the money, and so Con lost her loan.

As a result of this loss, the meanness of her surgeon friend, her own reckless extravagance and generosity, and the mounting cost of her lawsuits, she found herself a ruined woman. Between 1742 and 1744 her creditors had her arrested and confined for debt to the Liberties of the King's Bench Prison, and as soon as she obtained release she fled to France for eight months.[21]

Not long after her return to England in 1746, Con began dunning her ex-lovers for help and threatening them with public exposure, and in 1748–9 she finally published her *Apology* in serial parts amid a flurry of printed rebuttals, counter-attacks, and threats of libel suits. Thereafter her life is only hearsay, and all we know are the bare facts. In 1754–5 she returned to Jamaica, and there in Kingston embarked on a new matrimonial and social career. Although her husband Muilman was still alive, she married an Irishman, whom she bullied on his deathbed to assign her all his possessions by deed of gift. In 1757–8 she was appointed Mistress of the Revels in Kingston, her duties being to supervise and organize theatrical and other entertainments, in return for which she was given two benefits a year, worth about 200 guineas.

After two more bigamous marriages, Con Phillips finally died in 1765, in debt as usual and beset with creditors, in particular the apothecary who had tended her in her last illness. It is alleged that in her last hours she expressed her satisfaction at her fortunate timing. By dying on a Saturday, she foiled any attempt on the part of the apothecary to seize her body on the way to the grave as a hostage for the debt, since arrest was prohibited on a Sunday in order to allow debtors to go to church. If the story is true, Con Phillips died as she had lived, witty, extravagant and litigious to the end.[22]

As a person, Con Phillips was clearly a woman of captivating beauty and considerable intelligence, combined with the airs and graces, deportment and skills of a lady. She was perfectly presentable in any company and circulated freely among high aristocrats and even at the royal Court, in both London and Paris. The most prominent of her two weaknesses was a voracious sexual appetite. She made it her business to live off men, and for many years she used her dazzling physical attractions to acquire and spend their wealth. Horace Walpole listed her among the great sexual

[21] Ibid. ii/4, 22–52; iii. 264–5, 272–3.
[22] *DNB*, s.n. Teresia Constantia Phillips.

man-eaters of history, along with Catherine the Great of Russia. In 1751 Henry Fielding saw fit to include her among famous destroyers of men in history such as Delilah, Jezabel, Messalina, Lady Macbeth, and Queen Christina of Sweden, adding in a footnote that she was 'though last, not least'. A late nineteenth-century writer included her in a set of essays about *Twelve Bad Women*, and the Victorian editors of the *Dictionary of National Biography* for some reason gave her an entry.[23]

To place Con in the context of the age in which she lived, she has to be seen as merely the most famous of a small but select army of pretty young ladies of good family and good breeding, but who lacked the money to make a respectable marriage. Their poverty combined with their gentility virtually obliged them to follow careers as mistresses to rich, titled, and powerful men who had lost interest in their wives and were seeking sexually attractive and well-bred companions and bed-mates. From 1769 to 1790 *The Town and Country Magazine* issued monthly articles detailing the careers of some 280 such women and their mostly aristocratic keepers.[24] Con summed up the springs of her own history and that of other such women when she said: 'I was born constitutionally with the greatest share of vivacity and spirits of any woman in the world...but the obligations I had to nature were perverted by my accidental poverty.'[25]

But apart from this amiable fault, Con comes out of the story fairly well. So far as can be seen, she did nothing mean, cruel, or dishon-ourable, according to her lights, although her memoirs were certainly initially intended as blackmail. She was devoted to her younger sister, looked after her when they were driven from home by their step mother, and supported her and her children financially for decades while her husband, an East India merchant, resided in India without remitting a penny to his wife.[26]

She even had pretensions, perhaps not entirely tongue-in-cheek, to be something of a moralist, a feature she displayed in the advice she claimed to have given to her 15-year-old niece, the daughter of her beloved sister. She told her how she had read Cardinal Fénelon's *Télémaque* for French,

---

[23] *Horace Walpole's Correspondence*, ed. W. S. Lewis, 48 vols. (New Haven, Conn., 1937–81), xxv. 35; H. Fielding, *Amelia* [1751], Everyman edn, (London, 1930), i. 28; A. Vincent (ed.), *Twelve Bad Women* (London, 1897); *DNB*, s.n. Teresia Constantia Phillips.

[24] *T & C Mag.*, 1–7 (1769–75); the names of most of the protagonists have been identified by H. Bleakley, 'Tête à Tête Portraits in the "Town and Country Magazine"', *Notes and Queries*, 10: 4 (1905), 241–2, 342–4, 462–4, 522.

[25] T. C. Muilman, *A Letter humbly addressed to the Right Hon. the Earl of Chesterfield* (London, 1750), 9–10.

[26] *Apology*, i. 260.

Archbishop John Tillotson's famous sermons for English, and La Bruyère's *Caractéres* for 'introspection' (meaning insight into character). Furthermore, 'I am not, nor ever in my life ever was, possessed of a novel or romance'—trash that she considered positively dangerous for a young woman to read. She taught her niece religion and virtue—taken in a wider sense than mere chastity. In this, she followed the advice of Montaigne in believing that 'to teach young girls prudery I verily believe may be as pernicious to them as libertinism', on the grounds that it merely encourages hypocrisy.[27]

(iii) An Apology

The three volumes of Con Phillips's *Apology* were written and published in several parts in 1748–9, at the lowest point in her career. She was penniless, had recently spent two years in prison for debt, had temporarily run out of rich lovers and protectors, and had been defeated or frustrated in all her many lawsuits. At the time they created great scandal and generated a number of hostile pamphlets in reply.[28]

The idea of threatening to publish her memoirs as blackmail to extract money from her many lovers had first come to Con in 1737. Eleven years later, in 1748, she was approached by a bookseller, who said 'he would get a proper person to write it, and take the whole upon himself and give her a thousand pounds'. At first Con thought she might make more money from blackmail not to publish than from actual publication.[29] Her plan was to extract from her rich former husband and her now numerous ex-lovers one or more life annuities in return for a promise not to reveal the often disreputable details of their earlier relationships with her. Her prime target was her alleged first lover, who by now had become the famous essayist and moralist Lord Chesterfield.[30]

Her next target was her second husband, the rich merchant Henry Muilman, from whom she also demanded an annuity in return for her silence.[31] But Muilman retorted defiantly: 'I do not care a shilling what

---

[27] *Letter to the Earl of Chesterfield*, 24–31.

[28] *An Apology for the Conduct of Mrs Teresia Constantia Phillips*, 3 vols. (London, 1748–9; 3 more editions 1750–61); it was followed by her *a Letter to the Earl of Chesterfield*. These two libellous broadsides stimulated a barrage of anonymous replies, esp. in defence of the Earl of Chesterfield: *A Defence of the Character of a noble Lord from the scandalous Aspersions contained in a malicious Apology, in a Letter to the supposed Authoress* (London, 1749); *A Counter-Apology: or genuine Confession…containing the secret History, Amours and Intrigues of M—— P——, a famous British Courtesan*, no. 1 (London, 1749); and A Lady, *Remarks on Mrs Muilman's Letter to the Right Hon. the Earl of Chesterfield* (London, 1749).

[29] *Apology*, i. 260–1; for the 1737 scheme, see ibid. iii. 48–58.

[30] Ibid. i. 52–4.   [31] Ibid. ii. 111, 206–8, 216; iii. 306.

she does, nor will give sixpence to hinder it. It is not in her power to expose me more than she has already done...by bringing the affair before all the courts of justice in the nation, as well as in public print.' Later, when the first volume was advertised, he wrote to her sarcastically: 'I think you can't do better to fill up your work than by giving the public a list of those you have ruined from the year 1718 to this time [1749]. Let it be alphabetical, to prevent trouble to those who will look for any particular person. P.S. You may depend, no hush-money will be given, as you flattered yourself.'[32]

A third failed attempt at blackmail explains why in the first volume her relations with one of her lovers, a Mr Southcote, were passed over in a single brief sentence stating that she had met him once, which 'led to a new amour'. In the second volume, however, over a hundred pages were devoted to a scathing analysis of Southcote's character and a blow by blow description of his liaison with her. She explained that she was publishing these details because Southcote had not offered her more than a derisory pension of £10 a year in return for suppressing the story. 'It is evident', she concluded, 'that he loves his money above his reputation.'

Another of Con's purposes for writing her *Apology* was to offer a defence of her sexual conduct. She never attempted to conceal that she made her career as the mistress of a succession of rich men. Her argument was that she was trapped by her gender, her beauty, and her poverty, and that her one moral blemish was to have made her way in the world in the only manner available to a woman in her position.

She observed that men 'usurp the power of making laws to themselves. No wonder, then, if infidelity in men is softened into gallantry, but in the ladies is hardened into infamy.' After all, 'men may be profligate in their amours, and none of you will despise them, being in other respects men of honour.' She came back again and again to the injustice of the double sexual standard, 'this very tyrannic unchristian custom', and constantly stressed the selfish arrogance of rich and well-born males, 'the lords of creation'. She recounted how a nobleman in a public chocolate house, speaking of her *Apology*, remarked: 'Damn'd insolent bitch. How dare she attack people of high rank? The bitch ought to be ducked.'

Apart from this theme of the injustice of the double standard, Con repeatedly complained about the pure lust she aroused in men by her 'extraordinary beauty'. She concluded that: 'All their [men's] purpose is to make women instruments to their vanities and subject to the gratification of their grosser appetites.'[33] She constantly sought from her

---

[32] Ibid. i. 261–7, 303.
[33] *Letter to the Earl of Chesterfield*, 12, 15; *Apology*, ii. 190; i. 252, 313.

lovers a life annuity so that she could have financial independence, but she was never able to obtain one. Nor was she even in a position always to select her lovers, but was more often 'the chosen object of passion than the chooser'. These, she concluded, 'are the disadvantages we labour under from being born women'.[34]

Con also argued that even if her sexual conduct left much to be desired, this did not mean that she was a woman without moral integrity. 'I hope it may be admitted one may be guilty of personal levities, without it following as a necessary consequence that we must also commit the most dishonest and immoral actions.' In other words, chastity is not the one and only virtue in a woman, and lack of it does not mean a lack of full moral integrity in all other areas of life.[35]

Con Phillips's final moral target was the blatant injustices of the legal system. She complained that she had 'buffeted the billows of the law upward of twenty years in search of justice', but that 'in this country of liberty, the means of redress are only found to be an aggravation of the grievance'.[36]

If the motives for publication are clear, the authorship of the work is more problematic. Con admitted that the bookseller offered her the services of a ghost-writer, and Jeremy Bentham's editor Sir John Bowring states flatly that the author of large parts of it was Paul Whitehead.[37] The son of a wealthy London tailor, Whitehead was the author of satirical attacks upon the government, to avoid punishment for which he was obliged to go into hiding in 1739. By 1747 he was a paid writer for the opposition group of Country Whigs around Frederick Prince of Wales. Since Con's *Apology* was dedicated to the 3rd Earl of Scarbrough, who from 1738 to 1757 was the Prince's Treasurer, it seems likely that it was he who recommended Whitehead to her. Whitehead also enjoyed a rich if scandalous social life as secretary and steward to Sir Francis Dashwood's elite libertine group of 'Monks of Medmenham Abbey'.

Thus his literary gifts to sharpen Con's prose, his legal expertise to make sense of her *via dolorosa* through the thickets of litigation, his libertine background to make him tolerant of her sexual promiscuity, and his attachment to the anti-government circle around the Prince of Wales, to which many of her friends and lovers belonged, all made him an ideal

---

[34] *Letter to the Earl of Chesterfield*, 15.
[35] *Apology*, vol. i., pp. xi–xii; ii. 95–8; iii preface, 19, 24, 7–27; iii preface, 11.
[36] Ibid. i. 269; ii. 176; iii. 312, 316–17.
[37] *Works of Jeremy Bentham*, x. 35.

choice to help put Con's story into shape for the printer.[38] According to Sir John Bowring, he was paid 'in kind' for his labours, which presumably means by sexual favours.

How far is Con's story of her life, as retold or reshaped by Paul Whitehead, to be believed? To a considerable extent it bears the ring of truth. Names are given of well-known witnesses to events, such as noblemen, judges, lawyers, and doctors; documents are cited; and Con seems to have been assiduous in keeping copies of legal records, as well as letters from her various lovers and her husband. The stories of what lay behind her endless litigation cannot all be proved, but where legal or other records still survive, her account is exactly corroborated. For example, her description of how William Shirley became Governor of Massachusett thanks to a three-year lobbying campaign with the Duke of Newcastle back home in London turns out to be true; and her description of Sir Herbert Pakington's Toryism is proved by his voting record in the House of Commons.[39]

On the other hand, the most serious charge she made, the alleged rape committed on her as a very young girl by the young Stanhope, future Earl of Chesterfield, naturally cannot be verified. Her account of how her first husband Muilman abducted and then murdered an inconvenient witness seems very unlikely, although she had the audacity to bring it up in open court. Moreover, it is disturbing to discover that the text of her husband Muilman's letters to her, as printed in her autobiography, have been doctored in her favour. In the printed version, she makes him sign off as 'your affectionate husband', but the critical word 'husband' never appears in the court transcripts of the letters.[40] On the other hand, Con's general account of the bribery and counter-bribery of witnesses and of the use of delaying tactics in the courts rings true, since names are given and the events did indeed occur much as she describes them.

(iv) *Matrimonial Litigation*

One of the most frustrating aspects of working from official legal records is that, however detailed and revealing they may seem to be upon the surface, they very rarely allow the observer to uncover what lies behind the evidence presented in the courtroom. The consultations with lawyers, the search for evidence, the detective work to track down witnesses or

---

[38] *DNB* s.n. Paul Whitehead.
[39] G. A. Wood, *William Shirley* (New York, 1920), ch. 4; Sedgwick and Brooke, *History of Parliament*, s.n. Pakington.
[40] Cf. *Apology*, i. 165–96 with copies of the originals in LPCA, D. 1455: 160–90.

observe wrongdoing, the delicate negotiations for an out-of-court settlement, the calculated plans to wear out an opponent by escalating costs,
the corruption, subornation, or concealment of witnesses, and often the
web of complementary and supportive cases in other courts—all these
things are usually more or less unknown. Only very rarely is there a
document of a more private and intimate kind, like Con Phillips's autobiography, which suddenly throws a searchlight upon this hidden world.
Seen from this vantage-point behind the stage, the scandalous and criminal potential uses of the clandestine marriage system are fully exposed,
and its close links to bigamy are proved beyond the shadow of a doubt.
Moreover the judicial scene in the eighteenth century is made to look less
like a quest for truth and justice than a form of ritualized warfare, no less
lethal for being fought with words rather than rapiers and pistols. Con's
story shows how in the long run money and good lawyers could defeat
the ends of justice and force an out-of-court accommodation. It also
shows, as do most of these cases, the critical role of debt in early modern
society, and the part it played in almost all kinds of litigation.

Con's first two marriages were the subject of one of the most complicated and lengthy processes of litigation of the century, involving many
suits in five different lawcourts and stretching over some eighteen years.
The source of most of these legal troubles was her decision in 1722 to
protect herself from arrest for debt by her creditors by going through a
marriage of convenience. She was advised to go to a Mr Morrill 'who for
ten guineas should procure a man (already married) who should marry
her in another name, and the ceremony should be performed before such
witnesses as should, when called upon, prove it, and by that means screen
her from debt'. It was said that 'It is well known to be a common practice at the Fleet; and...there are men there who have each of them,
within the compass of a year, married several women for this wicked
purpose'. The point of such a marriage was to make it impossible for the
woman's creditors to arrest her for debt without first challenging the
validity of the marriage in the ecclesiastical courts and getting it declared
null and void. 'But as the doing of this would be very expensive, and
might perhaps cost them more than their debt, they are hereby put under
the hard necessity of losing their debt, as being the less detrimental
circumstance of the two.'[41]

A willing candidate was found, an enlisted soldier called Francis
Delafield, the impecunious son of the owner of a cookshop; four years

[41] *Apology*, i. 32; H. Gally, *Some Considerations upon Clandestine Marriages* (London,
1750), 13–15.

before in 1718, he had married one Margaret Yeomans, who earned her living in the London silk-mills. Con was nervous about such a step, fearing blackmail, but was assured that Delafield was obliged to keep the fraudulent character of the marriage secret, since otherwise he would be liable to prosecution for the felony of bigamy. A marriage licence was therefore obtained, although it was full of errors: the groom's surname was spelt Devall (to conceal the matter from his wife); Con's first name Teresia was spelt Tresue; and she was falsely stated to be over 21 when in fact she was only 15. They were due to be married on 11 November 1722, by the Rector of St Benet's, Pauls Wharf. Delafield kept them all waiting at the church for two hours, and when he finally turned up was too drunk to stand and had to be supported by Morrill and his landlord, a tailor called Smith. The ceremony was duly performed before several witnesses and entered in the marriage register of the parish. There followed a wedding feast at the Half Moon Tavern in Fleet Street, from which they all proceeded to Morrill's house, where the newly-weds were formally bedded. That is to say Delafield was undressed and put to bed (where he promptly fell into a drunken sleep) and Con lay down beside him under the bedclothes with her clothes on. The witnesses then trooped up to view the scene, so that they could later swear on oath that they had been present at both the marriage and the consummation.

That was the last that Con ever saw of Delafield.[42] Soon after the marriage, the latter, who in about 1721 had enlisted as a soldier in a Grenadier regiment, was posted to the Company of Invalids at Portsmouth, whose commander was now Con's father. There can be little serious doubt that this posting was Delafield's reward for the marriage.[43]

Con fled to Rouen for a while to let things blow over, and it was on her return to London in the spring of 1723 that she met and captivated Henry Muilman, then a young Dutch merchant still not free of his articles, but the son of a very wealthy Amsterdam merchant, with very bright financial prospects. Such was the strength of his passion for Con that he compounded with her creditors and paid them off. He also installed her in style as his mistress in a fully furnished house with a cook-maid, footman, and lady's maid to look after her. He then astonished her by proposing to marry her.

Con claimed that she told him about her previous so-called marriage of convenience (but presumably not about her affair with Stanhope). Muilman investigated the marriage and found that it was bigamous

---

[42] *Apology*, i. 60–4; LPCA, D. 1455: 54–7, 84.
[43] *Apology*, i. 48, 63, 94.

because Delafield had a previous wife who was still alive. He was assured by the two best law firms·in London that the marriage was consequently null and void, so that Con could safely marry him. Muilman was unwilling to have the Delafield marriage formally invalidated by the London Consistory Court, for fear that the publicity would be bad for his business, besides coming to the ears of his father. In September 1723 Con visited Portsmouth and got her father's consent to the marriage, which was needed since she was still under age. In February 1724, only fourteen months after her marriage with Delafield, she was back again at the same church of St Benet's, Paul's Wharf, to be married again by the same clergyman, this time to Henry Muilman.[44]

Muilman was proud of his beautiful and talented new wife, with whom he moved into a fine house in Red Lion Street, Clerkenwell, and whom he introduced to all his friends. Unfortunately, however, the Dutch merchant to whom he was still articled picked up ugly rumours about Con's past. Muilman was placed in a very difficult situation, since he had concealed from his parents in Amsterdam the facts that his 16-year-old Con had no money, had already been married once, had been his mistress before marriage, had a generally bad reputation, and had not converted to Calvinism after the marriage. His master warned him that he would tell his father that 'he had contracted a base marriage with an extravagant abandoned creature, who would infallibly ruin him in a year's time'.

As a pre-emptive strike, Muilman that same evening set off with his bride to Amsterdam, to introduce her to his family before his master arrived with the bad news. According to Con, the visit went well, and she certainly made a close friend of Muilman's sister.[45] But soon after they had returned to England, Muilman's father began hearing more and more ugly rumours about his new daughter-in-law and decided to find out for himself. In July, the whole Muilman family therefore descended upon the house in Red Lion Street and it was not long before the father knew all. He was convinced that his son was living in adultery with a woman who would be the ruin of him, and therefore determined to break the marriage regardless of the cost.[46]

There was a final scene at dinner one day between Con and her father-in-law. Con asked him why he was displeased with her: 'I do not like your character.'

'Pray, sir, what part of my character is it which has so greatly offended you?'

---

[44] Ibid. i. 64–79. [45] Ibid. ii. 97–105. [46] Ibid. i. 80–98, 101.

'Why, I am told you were a common whore before you married my son.'[47] As might be imagined, this exchange resulted in the rapid departure of the Muilman parents from the house and a total breach between them and Con.

Muilman senior demanded that his son at once obtain a nullity of his marriage with Con, on the grounds of her previous marriage with Delafield. Unless he did so, the old man threatened to cut him off completely, which in Dutch law he was legally entitled to do, thus depriving him of the capital essential for starting up in business as a merchant. Muilman was faced with the choice between either a parting with Con or an end to a promising career. After the Muilman parents had returned to Amsterdam, weekly letters poured into the London house, after the receipt of each of which Muilman became more hostile to Con, and sometimes beat her in his frustration. Con secretly abstracted letters from her husband's cabinet and got a Jewish broker to translate them for her from the Dutch, from which she learnt of the enormous financial and emotional pressure the Muilman family were bringing to bear on her husband to break the marriage.[48]

Muilman was torn between his passion for his wife, and the need to obtain a nullity in order to appease his master and his father, and so to save his career as a merchant. His behaviour therefore oscillated wildly from the loving and uxorious to the threatening and cruel. Without informing Con, he launched a suit in the Consistory Court of London to annul their marriage on the grounds that she was already married to Delafield.[49] In order to succeed, he had to ensure first that Con would not seriously defend the suit; second, that she would absent herself so that the court could not examine her on oath; third, that Delafield and the witnesses to *his* marriage with Con would testify to it before the court; and fourth, that they would not breathe a word about the fact that Delafield had already been married four years earlier to Miss Yeomans. If this last fact leaked out, it would mean that the Delafield marriage was itself bigamous and null, which in turn would mean that the Muilman marriage was valid after all.

Muilman's tactics in the autumn and early winter of 1724 to obtain Con's silence and consent began with the stick of economic and moral threats and finally, when these failed, ended with the carrot of financial rewards and promises of remarriage. He warned Con that if she did not

---

[47] Ibid. i. 99.
[48] Ibid i. 103–4; LPCA, D. 1455: 115–17; E. 32/47.
[49] GLRO, DL/C/161, fos. 384–92.

comply with his wishes for an uncontested annulment, he would transfer all his assets in his business to his brother, who was his partner, return to Holland, and leave her to starve in England. Alternatively, he threatened to carry her off to Holland and lock her up in the *Beterhuis*. This was a private place of confinement where, at the request of a member of their family, delinquents of the middle and upper classes—usually licentious sons, adulterous wives, or insane relatives—could be imprisoned by a court order, the cost being born by the family.[50]

Muilman first tightened the screws by carrying out his threat to transfer all his estate in England to his brother, and then by attempting to strip Con of all her personal assets. One day in early September she was visited by a stranger—presumably an enemy of Muilman—who warned her that her husband was planning that very afternoon to seize all her goods and turn her out of the house with nothing but the clothes on her back. Con, who was nothing if not resourceful, immediately threw all her finest clothes, jewelry, and papers into a trunk and had it transported, by hackney coach to a banker in Fleet Street, in whose vaults it was deposited for safety.

Muilman returned for dinner accompanied by three or four 'ruffian fellows', and after a tense meal, curtly demanded that Con surrender all the keys of the house, which she did. One man said to him: 'Damn it, sir, feel her pockets. How do you know what she may have there?' Pale and trembling, Muilman felt her but found nothing. The men searched the house, only to report the absence of all the clothes and jewels—together worth well over £1,000. The men threatened Con, saying 'as we shall be able to prove you are not his wife, and have robbed his house, we shall be obliged, unless you instantly produce them, to send you to Newgate'. Con retorted defiantly 'Pray, sir, who are you?' and turning to her husband told him 'Send me to Newgate if I am not your wife', something which she knew quite well he was not yet prepared to do.[51]

Alarmed by this escalation of the pressure on her, Con took legal advice, going to the very best, Dr Paul, the King's Advocate in Doctors' Commons, who advised her to hire a Dr Farrant as her proctor to defend the nullity suit. Since she was only 16, she had to work through a guardian, whom she appointed to look after her interests. Dr Farrant informed her that everyone in the court had been told that 'it was an amicable

---

[50] LPCA, D. 1455: 117–18; *Apology*, i. 120; *The Emergence of Carceral Institutions: Prisons, Galleys and Lunatic Asylums 1550–1900* (Centrum voor Maatschappijgeshiedenis, 12; Rotterdam, 1984), 43–60; *Het Abdijhospitaal van de Bijloke* (Ghent, 1973). I owe this last reference to the kindness of Prof. H. van der Wee.

[51] LPCA, D. 1455: 119; *Apology*, i 105–12.

affair' which would not be seriously defended. She also discovered that Delafield—presumably in hopes of being well bribed by Muilman to shut up—was suing her for adultery for living with the latter.[52] Delafield added to the pressure on Muilman to buy him off by going to his house and formally demanding his wife back.[53] Con was advised to indict Delafield for bigamy in the Old Bailey, but at the first hint of such action he disappeared, being shipped out to Holland by Muilman, as she later discovered. Even so, this at least forced Delafield to abandon his suit against her for adultery.

So far, the only inducement that Muilman had offered Con not to defend his nullity suit was a promise to keep her as his mistress after the affair had all blown over, and the marriage had been nullified.[54] This was not enough, and she was strongly advised by her lawyers not voluntarily to leave home, but to wait to be ejected, and she therefore went back to Muilman, who continued alternately beating her, entreating her to give way, sleeping with her, and promising her a private marriage later, to be made public when either his father died or he made his fortune, whichever should happen first. The more Con refused his proposals, the more hysterical and desperate Muilman became. On 17 October he finally ejected her from his home, sending her off to the house in Red Lion Street where they had lived when they were first married. But he still could not keep away from her, and kept visiting her at night to sleep with her. When, still on the advice of her counsel, she refused him her bed 'he behaved more like a madman than a rational creature', sometimes in tears, sometimes in a rage, sometimes sitting quietly beside her bed all night. He told her that 'it would be his ruin' if she persisted in defending the nullity suit, but that 'he found it impossible to live without her'.[55]

By now anxiety caused by fear of financial ruin combined with sexual frustration at Con's refusal to sleep with him was driving Muilman out of his mind. At two in the morning one night he came to the house with several men, shouting: 'You damned bitch...Order the door to be opened, or by God I will instantly break it open, and every bone in your skin also.' Con replied that if they did not go away she would shoot them, at which they laughed. So she filled a small pistol with firework powder, bought for the fireworks on Guy Fawkes Day, 5 November, and fired it in their direction. This made a tremendous noise in the confined space of a passage-way and caused the besiegers to flee.

[52] GLRO, DL/C/160, fos. 326–54.   [53] GLRO, DL/C/547.
[54] LPCA, D. 1453: 121–2; E. 32/47; *Apology*, i. 113–15.
[55] LPCA, D. 1455: 124–6; E. 32/47; *Apology*, i. 116–26; 238.

Muilman immediately went to Lord Chief Justice Pratt and swore the peace against Con, claiming that she had tried to murder him. He told the judge 'I so narrowly escaped, I felt the bullet upon my hat'. Summoned before him, Con told what really happened, her story being corroborated by a respectable lady friend, her sister, and all the servants. The judge was much amused and asked why the bullet had not entered Muilman's head if he had felt it, which gave her the opportunity to display her famous wit by instantly replying 'I believe his head is thick enough to be bullet proof.'[56]

After this episode, Con decided that it would be prudent to take lodgings with a landlord who could protect her from these intrusions, and so moved into the house of a grocer, Mr Fox. But Muilman was soon back again, claiming his conjugal rights as a husband, on hearing which Mr Fox felt obliged to let him in. Acting again on the advice of her counsel, Con allowed him back into her bed. Witnessed evidence that Muilman was still sleeping with his wife in the middle of a suit for nullity of their marriage would certainly not help his case, if Con decided to fight it.[57]

Because of the shooting episode in early December Con had to appear before the King's Bench in Westminster Hall to give bail to keep the peace with her husband. She—or more likely Whitehead—gave a vivid, if implausible, account of the occasion. The hard-bitten lawyers and judges were stunned by the appearance of 'the most charming young creature that ever was seen, dressed with all the ornaments that could be invented to set off one that had much less obligation to nature. 'It is not wonderful if such a lovely form commanded respect: the judges rose from their seats to salute her the moment she appeared.'

Unfortunately this personal triumph made her careless. To impress the court, she had withdrawn from the trunk left with the banker all her finest clothes and jewels, and that evening she set off to the playhouse, still dressed up in all this enormously expensive finery. At the end of Downing Street her chair was intercepted by six men led by Muilman. He explained to the chairmen 'This bitch is my wife, and has run away from me with another man', and ordered his men to take her to an alehouse and strip her of all her jewels and clothes. They removed her watch, gold equipage, diamond ear-rings, buckles, finger-rings, lace head and ruffles, gown, petticoat and hoop, quilted coat and pockets. The landlord of the alehouse made no attempt to interfere, as she commented

[56] LPCA, D. 1455: 127–8; *Apology*, i. 127–35.
[57] LPCA, D. 1455: 130–1; E. 32/47; *Apology*, i. 147–60.

bitterly, 'well knowing the dominion that an honest husband ought to have over his domestic drudge, especially if she was such a naughty woman as they described'. This brutal action was indeed entirely within the rights of a husband under existing common law. After she was stripped almost naked, Muilman said to her triumphantly: 'Now, you bitch, go where you please, since I have got your trappings, and see where you will find money to plague me.' He had taken from her jewels upon which she reckoned she could have raised £1,000 to £1,500 with which to fight his lawsuit.[58]

Further to tighten the financial pressure, Muilman cut off her allowance and prevented her from raising money upon his credit by publicly denying that she was his wife, and letting it be known that anyway he was about to leave for Holland or the East Indies. At the same time he kept visiting her at night, sleeping with her, and urging her to agree not to oppose the nullity suit.

Finally Muilman asked for a meeting between the two of them and their legal counsels, a proposal which, in view of her financial straits, Dr Paul advised her to accept. The bargain they finally worked out was as follows: Muilman would give her a bond of £4,000 to secure her an annuity of £200 a year for life 'notwithstanding any marriage had or to be had'; £2,000 in cash; the restoration of her jewels; and plate and furniture to fit up a comfortable house. In return, she would abandon the defence of the nullity suit and go abroad until the sentence was pronounced. She was advised by Dr Paul to accept the deal, whereas Muilman was advised by his counsel, Sergeant Darnell, to reject it since 'he entrusted her with materials in that deed to ruin him', for if ever produced in court the bond would be obvious proof of collusion. Unwritten parts of the deal were that Muilman would pay her proctor and all her counsel to make a sham defence for her; and that the suit of Delafield against her for bigamy and adultery would be dropped.[59]

Muilman ignored Sergeant Darnell's advice to reject the deal, the documents were drawn up, and Muilman invited Con to spend a last weekend with him in the country at St Albans before she left for France. The atmosphere of the weekend was somewhat spoilt, however, by her last-minute discovery that the Latin of the bond to secure her life annuity

---

[58] Ibid. i. 143–7.
[59] LPCA, D. 1455: 131–7; E. 32/47; *Apology*, i. 147–60. The agreement enabled Muilman to obtain the nullity of his marriage, but he was obliged to pay heavily for it. At 16-years-purchase, the life annuity was worth £3,200 and the cash was £2,000. Con later valued her jewels and diamonds at £2,000 and the furniture of the house at £8,000, making a total of over £15,000. Ibid. i. 236–7.

read £400, not £4,000, an error that Muilman disingenuously claimed was an honest mistake.[60]

The story of Con's stay in Paris can be reconstructed from Muilman's letters to her, which she carefully preserved. They harp on three themes: first, his continued devotion to her: 'Take care of yourself, my lovely girl, for without you life would be a burden to your poor Harry...you are the *primum mobile* of all my actions, thoughts and wishes.' The second were warnings and complaints about her extravagant way of life in Paris, and vain admonitions to 'study frugality'. She seems to have been spending money recklessly, and dazzling the high society of Paris with her beauty, wit, and elegant living, being known as 'la belle angloise'.

The third theme in the letters was the progress of the nullity suit. Now that Con was out of the way and could not be cross-examined, and that her proctor was instructed to put up no more than a token defence, all should have gone smoothly. Muilman was not challenged in court when he claimed—quite falsely—that he had never owned her as his wife after he learnt about the 'Devall' (Delafield) marriage; that he had never offered her maintenance, shown affection towards her, promised to pay her proctor and counsel, or had anything to do with her running off to France. The only snag in the proceedings he reported tersely to Con on 20 January: 'I had a damned deal of plague with that fellow Devall since you have been gone; money was the case, which I was forced to give, and now the case goes on.' What had happened was that Delafield and the witnesses to his marriage with Con saw the opportunity to blackmail Muilman heavily in return for their testimony, and he was obliged to buy them off with money, which Con later claimed amounted to £1,000. After payment, all went smoothly, and the sentence of the court nullifying the Muilman marriage was published on 28 February, 1725.[61]

In order to finish the affair, Con's proctor Dr Farrant sent her a 'Renunciation of Appeal in Form' for her to sign. He explained that 'this affair having made a great deal of noise', Muilman's lawyer thought it prudent, in order to avoid suspicions of collusion, for Farrant to lodge an Appeal to the Court of Arches. But this was only for show, so he asked her to sign and return the Renunciation of Appeal form.[62]

Con returned to London in May 1725, and promptly visited Muilman to collect the belongings she had left with Fox the tailor. Muilman was very uneasy to see her, took her off to a tavern, and finally begged her

---

[60] LPCA, D. 1455: 137–8; *Apology*, i. 111–64.
[61] LPCA, D. 1455: 160–90; *Apology*, i. 165–94.
[62] Ibid. i. 194–7.

upon his knees to let him come 'and sleep with you as usual'. Con later claimed that she knew from her lawyers that a renewal of sexual relations after a sentence of nullity would go far to invalidate the sentence if it were ever appealed, so she agreed: after all 'it was not my business to reject his entreaties'. She insisted on going to his house, not hers, since it was already one o'clock in the morning, but he refused since he did not want his brother, who lived with him, to know about her visit. Finally he said he knew somewhere where they could get a room in the middle of the night, and carried her off to 'a private bagnio or bawdy house which he had frequently made use of'.

They slept together regularly for over a month, and in the end Muilman persuaded Con to sign the Renunciation of Appeal. She did so on the assurance of her counsel that it was of no importance, since in civil law 'a marriage was always open', and anyway 'a married woman can do no act or deed to her own prejudice'.[63]

Muilman was now a rich man, for after the nullity his father had invested £16,000 in the business he managed in London with his brother. On the other hand, he was still in his father's power, since the £16,000 could be withdrawn at any moment. He was desperately anxious to keep Con as his mistress, despite her record for wild extravagance and dubious morals, and he offered to increase her allowance to £400 a year, buy her a house, and marry her as soon as his father died. But Con, who already had other irons in the fire, demanded a clandestine marriage at once as the price of agreeing to live with him. When he refused to do it for fear his father should find out, she left him for good.[64]

Before they broke up, however, Con made the greatest mistake of her life. Extravagant as ever, she was soon heavily in debt, and by July 1725 needed £700 in a hurry. She asked Muilman to lend her the money, which he refused to do unless she deposited with him as security for repayment the £4,000 bond for her life annuity of £200 a year. But when she asked for it back four and a half years later, Muilman told her emissary brutally: 'She is a damned impudent bitch. I owe her nothing. I bought that deed for £700 and I will never return it to her.' Con's attempts to force Muilman to return the bond for her annuity were to occupy time in most of the courts of England for the better part of the next twenty years.[65]

In 1728 Muilman announced his own forthcoming marriage with the

---

[63] Ibid. i. 198–210; LPCA, D. 1455: 150–4; E. 32/47.
[64] *Apology*, i. 210–14, 228–30, 236.   [65] Ibid. i. 241–8.

daughter of his lawyer Sergeant Darnell, who was fully informed about his matrimonial situation through his professional dealings on his behalf over the nullity case. Con wrote to Sir John Darnell about 'the illegality of the act', warning him not to marry so rich a co-heiress as his daughter to a man who, however rich, had already been married once. She also wrote to Muilman himself, reproaching him for 'so villainous a fraud', and declaring that 'I am your lawful, married, injured, wife'.

She naturally consulted her legal counsel Dr Paul, who was the official responsible for issuing the marriage licence to Darnell. According to her, Dr Paul told her that he had advised Darnell against it, saying: 'I would not marry a daughter of mine to Mr Muilman, under the circumstances he is in, were he worth five hundred thousand pounds and I could not give my daughter a shilling; for to my certain knowledge he is lawfully the husband of Mrs Phillips. If you insist upon it, I will (notwithstanding my opinion) grant you a licence.' But Darnell replied cheerfully that there was little to fear legally from Mrs Phillips 'when Mr Muilman is to find money and I law,' a combination which he believed—rightly as it turned out—to be invincible.

Con's revenge was to have a little fun at Darnell's expense. The marriage took place shortly before the King's Birthday, and Con was in the royal Drawing Room at St James's Palace at the Birthday reception when the new bride and groom, accompanied by Sir John Darnell, made their appearance. Muilman was so upset by the sight of her that he hastily withdrew, fearing a public scene. The 3rd Duke of Argyle, with whom Con was talking, jumped up, hurried across to Darnell and led him back to where Con sat, saying: 'Pray, Darnell, did you ever see so beautiful a creature? Such a shape! Such a skin! Such eyes! For God's sake do you know her?' Con observed that 'what was mirth to the duke was death to Sir John'. She indignantly denied, however, the story that she went over to the new Mrs Muilman and 'wished her joy of my leavings'.[66]

The legal status of four marriages—Delafield to Miss Yeomans, Delafield to Con Phillips, Muilman to Con Phillips, and Muilman to Miss Darnell—now depended on whether it was possible to find hard evidence to prove the first of them. If so, the second and fourth became bigamous, and the third valid. In May 1733 Con unexpectedly received a letter from Delafield, saying that he had been sick for nine months and was miserably poor. He complained that Muilman had refused to help him any more 'after all his promises and the dirty work he has made me

---

[66] Ibid. i. 236–301, 254; LPCA, D. 1455: 256, 260–9.

do'. The letter concluded by asking pardon for 'a poor miserable wretch who has been persuaded to damn his soul to get a little money', and requesting 'your charity on a poor wretch that is starving'. This was evidently an offer to switch sides and tell all, in return for money. The bearer of the letter, who turned out to be the current Mrs Delafield, explained that after his stint in Portsmouth as a member of the Company of Invalids under Con's father, Muilman had obtained for Delafield a position as out-pensioner at Chelsea Hospital, but that his long sickness had now reduced him to abject poverty.[67]

Con gave the woman half a guinea and rushed off with the news to her former proctor of 1724, Dr Farrant, who immediately sent her to consult her counsel, Drs Paul and Andrews. They advised her to persuade Delafield to appear in the Consistory Court one day and make a public recantation of his false testimony of 1724, and to ask the court to assign a proctor to take down his deposition on oath. The next step was to begin a suit against Delafield to annul his marriage with Con on the grounds of his bigamy; and the third was to bring suit against Muilman to get the court to set aside the sentence of nullity of Con's marriage with him. This would, in turn, lead to the nullification of Muilman's second marriage to Darnell's daughter. Now flush with money and determined on revenge, Con put together a formidable legal team, consisting of her two previous lawyers, together with a high court official Sir Edmund Isham, and Dr Bramston.[68]

Delafield was summoned to appear in court to make his confession. Meanwhile he was very helpful in hunting down the current addresses of the surviving witnesses to his first marriage with Miss Yeomans in 1718. He confessed to Con how Muilman had hidden him for a while in 1724 by shipping him off to Holland; and spoke vaguely of receiving £1,100 at various times over the last nine years from Muilman 'for secret services'. The details of his first marriage were taken down by one of Con's lawyers, and signed by Delafield, and on 2 June he made his confession, in court on oath, about his second marriage with Con which an official took down in writing.[69]

Muilman, however, was swift to respond. Three weeks later, he somehow contrived to have Delafield's court-assigned proctor dismissed and replaced by his own proctor, Mr Trenby. When the court reassembled in November after the summer vacation, Trenby appeared, submitted an

[67] *Apology*, ii. 39–41.   [68] Ibid. ii. 42–4.
[69] Ibid. ii. 44–8; LPCA, D. 1455: 18, 61, 154–5, 252–3.

affidavit that Delafield had died, and claimed that his death put an end to the proceedings against him. Con was stunned, since she was unable to discover where, when, or how Delafield had died, nor even where he was buried. He had vanished into thin air, leaving no trace except Trenby's affidavit of his demise.[70] The court upheld Trenby's claim that 'the suit abated with the death of the party'. Either by accident or as a result of malign intervention, Con's case had stalled.[71]

With the mysterious death of Delafield, Con was left to reconstruct proofs of his first marriage as best she could from his own deposition and from the testimony of those witnesses he had been able to find. Delafield had been married to Magdalen Yeomans on 17 September 1718, in a notorious marriage shop in the Rules of the Fleet, the Sign of the Hand and Pen, by a well-known Fleet parson, the Revd John Draper. The certificate of marriage, copied from the marriage register, falsely described Delafield as 'lawyer and clerk', and was signed with a mark by Thomas Hodgkin, Draper's clerk, in the presence of one male and three female witnesses, two of whom could only make a mark.

As was so often the case with Fleet marriages, however, the evidence was less than perfect. Old Thomas Hodgkin the clerk was blind at the time of the marriage, which is why he had signed the register with a mark, and the entry itself had all been written by his nephew, Thomas Hodgkin junior. By 1733 when Con was assembling her evidence, both Hodgkins were long since dead, as were the Revd Draper and one of the witnesses. The key piece of evidence was therefore the original marriage register itself.[72]

Con produced this register in court, but her account of how she came by it is a story in itself. She alleged that in 1733 or 1734 she learnt that the widow of Hodgkin junior now owned the register, and lived off selling certificates copied from it to people who needed proof of their marriages. She also learnt that Muilman was planning to tamper with or destroy it. First he made 'several attempts to cut a leaf out of the book', but failed due to Mrs Hodgkin's vigilance. Next he made friends with her landlord to whom she owed arrears of rent, and persuaded him to demand that Mrs Hodgkin deposit the book with him as security for payment. But since the register was her only source of income, she refused.

It was only by sheer luck that Con got to hear of what was afoot. The

[70] *Apology*, ii. 48–50; LPCA, D. 1455: 154–5.
[71] *Apology*, ii. 50.   [72] LPCA, D. 1455: 44–50, 75–9; E. 32/47.

maid in the house heard the landlord urging Mrs Hodgkin to give him the register. She had seen Con take a certificate from it, made out by Mrs Hodgkin, and she had heard that there was an important lawsuit depending on the proof of a marriage based upon it. She therefore alerted Con to what was going on by telling her sister, who told her mistress, who passed on the message. Con, who was no fool, made very careful plans to lay hands on the register. She sent her footman to hire a plain suit of clothes, instead of her livery which he normally wore, and sent him off so disguised to Mrs Hodgkin's house to tell her that a lady wanted to search for a marriage dated 1707 (a false date so as not to arouse any suspicion as to the real object of the request). The footman was instructed to ask Mrs Hodgkin to come with him, bringing with her the register, so that the lady could take a copy of it, and in return he offered her the princely sum of 5 guineas. As Con observed, 'the reward was too good a bait to fail of the desired effect', and Mrs Hodgkin picked up the register book and set off with the footman. As they left the house, the footman made a secret signal to a waiting messenger, who rushed off to inform Con. She immediately sent to Doctors' Commons and summoned to her house all the high officials of the court she could contact, including Sir Edmund Isham, her proctor Everard Sayer, and the registrar of the court.

Half an hour later Mrs Hodgkin arrived at the house with the footman, still clutching her precious register book. Con let her in, locked the door behind her, and ushered her into a room full of the court officials. Together they examined the register and found the entry of Delafield's 1718 marriage with Miss Yeomans. They carefully wrapped the book in brown paper and sealed it so that it could not be tampered with. Con gave Mrs Hodgkin 20 guineas and promised to return her the register when the case was over. The next day she handed the register to the judge, who gave it to the Registrar. This time Muilman had been outwitted by Con.[73]

Foiled in his attempt to tamper with the register, Muilman got his proctor to deny its validity as evidence, which forced Con into an expensive search for more details about Mr Hodgkin junior, the clerk who had made the entry. She found that he had died fifteen or sixteen years before, but that he was a relation of Alderman Parsons, who was still alive and willing to swear to Hodgkin's handwriting. The Alderman told her that there were several account books in the City Chamberlain's office in Hodgkin's hand, and when they were compared with the marriage

[73] *Apology*, ii. 79–84.

register the writing was found to be identical. The Alderman also gave Con the address of Hodgkin's nephew, whom he had taught to write, and who still had papers in his handwriting. The handwriting of the papers exactly matched that of the entries in the marriage register, and the nephew swore the latter were in his late uncle's hand. The final proof of the authenticity of the register was that the last entry was 13 December 1720. This was the day before Hodgkin dropped dead—the date being proved by the bill for his funeral.

Moreover it was significant that the entry had been made, and Hodgson had died, three years before Con had even met Muilman, so that there could be no question of a forgery instigated by Con. Her case was now watertight—or so she thought, for she also had a certified copy of the first Mrs Delafield's burial certificate, dated 1724, two years after Con's marriage to Muilman, as well as an eyewitness account of Delafield's visit to his wife's deathbed.[74]

The proof that Delafield had married Miss Yeomans in 1718 and that she had not died before 1724 meant that his second marriage to Con in 1722 was bigamous, and therefore null and void. If this were so, it meant that Con's marriage to Muilman in 1724 was valid after all. And if that were so, then Muilman's marriage to Miss Darnell in 1728 was null and void and their children were illegitimate. Hence the acute anxiety of both Muilman and Sergeant Darnell, whose next step was to attempt to buy off Con. Darnell authorized his proctor to try to reach an accommodation with her, and the proctor and the registrar of the court visited her to see what could be done. First they said they were authorized to offer her £5,000 'to quit all claims to that suit'. When she refused, they raised the offer first to £6,000 and then to £8,000, but Con still refused, for she was by then seeking not so much compensation as revenge.[75]

In the end, this refusal to settle the case out of court turned out to be a catastrophic mistake, for when their generous offer was turned down, the tactics of Muilman and Darnell became very rough indeed. First they ruined her solicitor by aspersing his character to his relatives, so that his mother and aunt changed their wills and left their fortunes away from him. Then they attacked Con's character by publishing a forged poetic love-letter from her to a castrato Italian singer Signor Farinelli, with whom she was supposed to have been living 'in a most ridiculous and abandoned manner'. In 1735 there appeared on the streets of London a 16-page pamphlet, entitled *The Happy Courtesan: An Epistle from Teresia Constantia Phillips to Signor Farinelli*. It was a scurrilous lampoon,

[74] Ibid. ii. 85–8; LPCA, D. 1455: 63, 94; E. 32/47.   [75] *Apology*, ii. 89–90.

designed to show Con as a nymphomaniac courtesan for the elite of Europe:

> All ages, sects and nations have I tried
> But for thy sake, I set them all aside.
> The garter'd knight, the blue, the green, the red,
> Henceforth I ever banish from my bed.
> Entranced in thy embrace, my dear,
> I value neither commoner nor peer.
>
> My trusty Nan can tell what *billet-doux*
> Unopened I've return'd, nay still refuse,
> From Dukes, Earls, Colonels, Captains of renown,
> The courtier gay, prim cit and purse-proud clown;
> Jew merchants too, the richest in the City,
> Have offered settlements exceeding pretty.

The libel went on to explain that Con preferred Signor Farinelli, since:

> Eunuchs can give uninterrupted joys,
> Without the shameful curse of girls or boys.

In rebuttal, Con claimed that she could not have had an affair with Farinelli, since she was so sick with pleurisy that she was spitting blood throughout the whole of his visit to London, a fact attested by her (named) doctor and apothecary, who visited her daily.[76]

Meanwhile Muilman's money and Darnell's legal knowledge and personal contacts were put to work to block every move Con made in the courts of law. As we have seen, her case against Delafield in the Consistory Court for nullity had had to be dropped because of his mysterious death. Con claimed that it was only a year later that she finally discovered what had happened to him, thanks to a confession made by a dissatisfied accomplice. In June 1733, Delafield had been made 'so excessively intoxicated with drink he could scarcely stand on his legs', and in this condition was taken away from where he lived and put to bed in a common lodging-house in the Strand. The persons who removed him were Smith the tailor, his old accomplice in the Delafield–Phillips marriage, and a handsome fair gentleman with a mole on his cheek. Smith told the landlady that he would pay the rent, and that her new guest was 'a sad poor wretch who however was a most material witness in a law cause'. He added that 'he believed he would not live long, for he had been accustomed to fits'.

---

[76] Anon., *The Happy Courtesan*...(London, 1735); *Apology*, ii. 91–2.

The next morning Delafield, who was still insensible, was visited by the gentleman with the mole on his cheek, the encounter being secretly watched by the suspicious landlady who removed a knot in the deal partition in order to peer into the room. The gentleman ordered some tea, added 'some reddish kind of liquor' from a small vial in his pocket, and poured the mixture down Delafield's throat. He searched the latter's pockets, removed all the papers, but left the money untouched. When the landlady looked in a little later, after the gentleman had left, she found Delafield 'in most violent convulsions, his tongue hanging out of his mouth, and his eyes quite starting'. She hastily sent for Smith, who looked at him and remarked calmly: 'Aye, this is one of his fits, and he will certainly never come out of it.' Shortly afterwards Delafield died. Smith sent for an undertaker and gave the now thoroughly suspicious landlady 5 guineas and some wine to keep her mouth shut. But they were still drinking the wine when the undertaker knocked at the door with a coffin, *before* he had had time to received the information from Smith about the death—an event which naturally made the landlady even more suspicious.

According to Con, she had great difficulty coaxing this story out of the landlady, who was afraid to tell all she knew. Con then took her in a coach to the Exchange, to see if any of the merchants going about their business resembled the gentleman with the mole on his cheek. After a long time, the landlady finally spotted a man, went up to him and said 'This is he'. A Captain Ogilvie who was with her asked the man his name, to which he replied 'Muilman'. According to Con, the landlady made a formal deposition of her testimony before the Lord Chief Justice.[77] One may easily believe that Muilman and Smith got Delafield drunk and spirited him out of the way, without necessarily believing the story of murder. After all, there is plenty of evidence that Delafield was a very sick man, and the uncorroborated testimony of what the landlady said she saw through a hole in a door was certainly not enough to put Muilman on trial for murder.

Meanwhile, Con proceeded with her suit against Muilman to revoke the annulment of their marriage in 1724 as procured by fraud, and a second suit against him for restoration of conjugal rights, the point of this being to prepare the way for her claim to maintenance as his legal but deserted wife. The first trial proceeded slowly towards sentence in the Consistory Court of London. By skilful use of his own legal skill and Muilman's money, Darnell fought the case inch by inch, the object being

[77] Ibid. ii. 53–63.

to delay sentence as long as possible and to run up the expense as much as possible, so that Con would eventually be forced to abandon the suit for lack of funds.[78]

During the trial there came a day when Sir Edmund Isham was to read aloud in court all the letters Muilman had sent to Con while she was in Paris back in early 1724. In order to obtain the maximum possible publicity for the reading of these highly embarrassing documents for Muilman's defence, Con advertised the time and day in the newspapers. Muilman used bribery or threats to get the newspapers to refuse the advertisement, so Con instead spent £20, according to her, to have hand-bills distributed all over the City 'which I dare say almost everybody remembers, thirty thousand of them having been dispersed in one day'.[79]

Despite all the delays and legal prevarications used by Darnell, the case in the Consistory Court finally drew to a close. The Judge, Dr Humphrey Henchman, was about to pronounce sentence when Mr Neville, proctor for Mr Muilman, threw upon the table an appeal to the Court of Arches, and insisted that the sentence should not be pronounced. Dr Henchman was furious at being treated in this unprecedently shabby way, being denied the opportunity to pronounce sentence in his own court, as if he were an unjust judge. He uttered a bitter attack in open court on the tactics and ethics of Muilman's lawyer and offered Con his services, free of charge, as one of her legal counsel, a service he continued to perform until his death in 1739.[80]

Muilman's first ploy in the Court of Arches was to ask that his wife Anne Darnell and their two children be admitted as defendants in the case, since they were interested parties. Con claimed that this was merely a trick to spin out the case indefinitely, since the younger child, aged 5, would have to wait for sixteen years until he came of age in order to be in a position to prove his claim. She said she had already 'many thousand pounds buried in Doctors' Commons' and commented bitterly 'how little purpose it is to call a rich man to account', especially a man supported by two counsel learned in the law, a rich father and brother, and a large personal fortune.[81]

The Dean of the Court of Arches eventually issued a complicated decision about what parts of the libel the court would accept, but the decision finally went in favour of Con. Muilman promptly appealed to the ultimate authority, the Court of Delegates. This meant a delay of at

---

[78] Ibid. ii. 51–2.   [79] Ibid. i. 191; ii. 63–4.
[80] Ibid. i. 159; ii. 64–7; *DNB*, s.n. Humphrey Henchman.
[81] *Apology*, ii/5, 248–53.

least two years, since the Delegates were all busy men, consisting as they did of common law and civilian judges. Even if Con won there, her victory would merely send the case back to the Court of Arches for resentencing, where Muilman and Darnell could continue their delaying tactics of 'nursing a cause' and 'splitting points'.[82]

Con was advised that her best tactic was to ask the Delegates to permit her to be a joint appellant. When this request came to be decided by the Court of Delegates, there appeared on each side no fewer than eleven counsel—civilians and common lawyers. Each side presented a brief 40 pages long, and the registrar attended with the exhibits, that is the certificates of marriage and burial of Delafield and Miss Yeomans, the letters of Muilman to Con, etc. The latter wisely decided to hire one of the best shorthand writers in London to take down all the pleadings, as a result of which that single appeal cost her £300.

Her friend Dr Henchman, still acting for her without a fee, opened proceedings as her counsel. He denounced 'a combination, supported with money and great people, against this poor woman'. He admitted that he himself was at first deceived by Muilman's trickery, but finally saw through it. He accused Muilman of subornation of perjury by getting Delafield to testify to his bigamous marriage with Con as if it were genuine—'and to crown it all, murder'—that is the mysterious but convenient death of Delafield. He prophesied that the opposition 'have split this cause into so many points, and made so many unnecessary parties to them' that 'the youngest man here will never live to see it brought to determination'. Moreover, he protested against the appeal by Muilman from the Consistory Court to the Court of Arches 'over a sentence which had never been pronounced' three days before it was due. Finally Henchman asked the obvious question: 'If they have a right, why do they delay so industriously the bringing of that right to proof?' The result was a decision to allow Con and Muilman to stand joint appeal. It was a victory of sorts, but one which promised 'a life of law, misery, and uneasiness'.[83]

The trouble was that the death of Delafield prevented Con from bringing before the ecclesiastical courts conclusive evidence of the bigamous nature of their marriage. Moreover many of the witnesses to Delafield's first marriage were now dead, and the others old and infirm and likely to die before the issue finally came to trial again in the Court of Arches, some two or three years after the conclusion of her first trial there. To make matters worse, the ecclesiastical courts, as well as Lord Hardwicke

---

[82] Ibid. ii/5, 257.   [83] Ibid. ii/5, 257–65.

in Chancery, were beginning to treat Fleet registers as almost worthless as evidence, since they were riddled with false entries, backdated entries, and erasures.[84]

Con was advised by her counsel to arrange for one of her creditors to sue her for debt for necessaries in the civil side of King's Bench; she would then plead marriage to Muilman as a defence; the creditor would challenge the validity of the marriage; and the issue would thus come to trial at common law. She was told that 'this was the only way then practicable by which the testimony of her witnesses could be presented'.[85]

Con therefore persuaded her supplier of beer—certainly a 'necessity' in eighteenth-century England—to sue her for money due. Sergeant Darnell was justifiably alarmed at hearing the news, and concocted a clever defence to block it coming to sentence. He not only moved the court to dismiss the suit on the grounds that it was collusive, which all such suits always were, but also brought suit against Con's agent for subornation of witnesses. The suit was ordered stopped, and Chief Justice Hardwicke summoned Con privately to his chambers. At first she refused to go, but was advised that this was unwise.

She showed up unexpectedly one day at Lord Hardwicke's chambers, to find him in close consultation with Sergeant Darnell. According to Con, as related to Whitehead, there took place the following brisk dialogue between them:

HARDWICKE. Pray who was it that advised you to join issue?
CON. My lord, I won't tell you
HARDWICKE. I'll make you tell me, madam.
CON. You may endeavour it, my lord, but it is above a hundred to one if you succeed....Does your Lordship sit here in your judicial capacity?
HARDWICKE. What is it to do with you, Madam?
CON. Nay, my Lord, no farther than I thought it a pretty unusual thing for a judge to try causes in his chamber.
HARDWICKE. Madam, I shall not give you any further answer.
CON. Nor I ask your lordship any further questions.

Thus ended 'this furious interview, which did not prejudice that great man much in her favour'. Later Con was rash enough to write to Lord Hardwicke an insolent letter in which she said: 'I saw but too plainly that Darnell had a tongue—you an ear; that Muilman had money—you a hand.' It says much for Hardwicke's moderation and good temper that he did not sue Con for slander or commit her to gaol for contempt of court.[86]

---

[84] Ibid. ii/5, 260.   [85] Ibid. ii/5, 267–8.
[86] Ibid. ii/5, 269–77; iii appendix 4.

Con was now faced with two actions to defend in King's Bench, the first against her agent for suborning witnesses, which cost her £400 to have overruled; and the second, more serious one, of 'collusion to try a point'. The upshot was that Con, her attorney and the plaintiff her beer supplier were all committed to stand trial for collusion and ordered to find bail. Con was taken off in prison by a tipstaff, but resolutely refused to apologize. So her counsel went to Lord Hardwicke, apologized for her, and asked for bail, which was granted at £4,000, £2,000 of which was on her own bond.

During the trial Con was cross-questioned to disclose which of her counsel had advised her to launch this collusive suit, something she obstinately refused to reveal, since she regarded it as a plot to discredit 'a great man of the law' (presumably her friend Dr Henchman).[87] She was also subjected to 'some mean low ribaldry' about her private life on the part of one of Muilman's lawyers, which much annoyed her.

In the end she was found guilty of refusing to name the counsel who advised her, and of trying to bring a collusive case before the court, both of which were true. Immediately after the verdict, four or five officers of the court rushed at her and began fighting over who was to have the lucrative privilege of arresting her. She was assured by one of her counsel (later a Master of the Rolls) that she would soon be free, but she remained confined for four or five days until she consented to ask Lord Hardwicke for a sentence. She was fined a mere 13s. 4d. plus assessed costs of £400; in addition she had to pay her own expenses, 'which amounted to a great deal above that sum'. Muilman made the most of this victory by having it reported in the newspapers that Con was found guilty of 'a crime of the most atrocious nature' and imprisoned twice. She complained that as a result her name was blackened before the public.[88]

Con was thus defeated in her suit in King's Bench to establish the validity of her marriage with Muilman. But after 1736 she had another legal iron in the fire, which was a suit in Chancery to recover the bond of £4,000 from Muilman to secure her a £200 annuity for life, which she had so foolishly surrendered to him in 1724 in return for a loan of a mere £700.[89] The presentation of her case gave Con the opportunity of explaining in public just why the bond was given by Muilman in the first place, which was to bribe her not to contest the nullity suit. As Darnell

---

[87] Ibid. ii/5, 277–87.
[88] Ibid. ii/5, 287–94, 300.   [89] Ibid. i. 221–8.

had warned at the time, if ever produced in court, the bond would prove to the world that Muilman's nullity suit was collusive.

At first Con's Chancery case went very well, since in response to her bill Muilman made the mistake of trying to bluster it out, and entered an answer which was a pack of lies. This was too much for the court to swallow, and he was ordered to amplify his answer.[90] Con now had Muilman at her mercy, since she had kept back from the ecclesiastical court two of his letters to her which proved that all that he had said was false. But she made the fatal mistake of boasting of her coming victory, which caused Muilman to panic. He hastily petitioned the court to allow him to withdraw his previous answer as all a mistake, and managed somehow to persuade the Master of the Rolls to expunge the record of what he had said.

Lord Chancellor Talbot was furious when he heard what had happened, and openly sided with Con, advising her in future 'not to pull the line till your fish is hooked'.[91] Muilman then asked the court to force Con to 'make her option of suits', rather than suing him simultaneously in King's Bench, Chancery, and the ecclesiastical courts. Lord Talbot came to Con's help by denying Muilman's petition, observing acidly 'really I think Mr Muilman needs no other advantages against her than those he makes so frequent use of upon the Bible' (i.e. lies).

But it was no good. Muilman delayed and prevaricated, entered a cross-suit against Con, and used his bottomless purse to hire forty lawyers to spin out and obfuscate the case, which dragged on for years. It was bad luck for Con that Lord Talbot died in 1737, to be succeeded by Lord Hardwicke, who was already prejudiced against her from previous experience. Muilman's plan was to prolong the case until Con was financially exhausted and could continue no longer, reckoning that 'there could not be a more effective way of destroying her pretensions than by starving her. That way he might have a chance of killing her.' His chances were augmented by the fact that the ecclesiastical court had relieved him of his obligation to pay Con alimony and court costs during the new trial, on the grounds that the bond for maintenance (although now surrendered) had cancelled out all his obligations. He therefore had an added incentive for not giving the bond back to Con.[92]

After drifting on for two years, the Chancery case fell into abeyance in the period during which Con pursued her new lover 'Worthy' to Jamaica

---

[90] Ibid. i. 231–79.   [91] Ibid. i. 230–3.
[92] Ibid. i. 234–7; ii/5, 295–8.

and Boston. On her return in 1742, however, she started it up again, only to run into the same legal brick wall as before. She complained that Muilman's lawyer 'condescended to play all the tricks and shifts of a Newgate solicitor', so that 'very frequently the modification of a word has been the business of a whole attendance in Masters' Chambers'. Each visit to an old and sleepy Master cost Con counsel's fees, solicitors' fees, the price of a warrant, the hire of a chair, and so on. Things dragged on for two years in this manner, costing Con £600, to pay for which she ran up heavy debts, since for the time being she had run out of rich lovers to support her. In 1744 she at last got a report in her favour from the Master, but the case still had to come to trial.[93]

By now, she was at the end of her tether. If in the long run she lost the Chancery suit and her case was dismissed with costs, she would be arrested for debt and Muilman would have 'the power of keeping her in gaol for her life'. There were already 150 cases on the docket before hers, and no business was done during Parliament time, since the Lord Chancellor was too busy as Speaker in the House of Lords to deal with his judicial responsibilities. Consequently the case was unlikely to come to trial for another year or two. It was probably Whitehead, prompted by Con, who wrote the epitaph upon the legal trap in which she found herself: 'in a country where the best laws that ever were made subsist, they are so corruptly executed that they are become our greatest oppressions, while we are overcome with a swarm of the vermin ministers of it, who loll in their coaches and wallow in the spoils of a ruined people'.[94]

To complete her misery, just before the final hearings Con hired a new solicitor, who turned out to be unscrupulous, greedy and incompetent. He charged her 40 guineas for copying long briefs, and a formal meeting with her counsel cost her almost £100, which is hardly surprising since it consisted of five prominent lawyers, including the Solicitor-General. They all agreed that the solicitor had made serious mistakes: he had claimed that the £700 Muilman had paid for the annuity was inadequate compensation, but had failed to prove his point by getting a deposition from the banker Colonel Duncombe, who had offered £2,000 for the bond. He had also omitted altogether to argue that Con was under age at the time, and therefore not competent to sell the bond. The only solution was to pay the court costs already incurred and to bring in a new bill.

---

[93] Ibid. iii. 215–21.   [94] Ibid. iii. 221–30.

This would add another £1,200 to the expenses and would delay the hearing indefinitely.

Already heavily in debt and in danger of arrest, Con was beaten, and was forced to compromise with Muilman. Since he had her at his mercy, he only offered her a release of claims for costs and £500 in cash, £300 down and £200 after the withdrawal of the case in the Court of Delegates. This £500 was just enough for her to compound with her many creditors. In return Muilman demanded a bond of £1,000 from her never to revive the Chancery suit, and to withdraw the suit still pending in the Court of Delegates. But worse was to come. As Con sat ready to sign the documents and get her money, her crooked solicitor and twelve bailiffs rushed into the room and arrested her for a £300 debt he claimed she owed him. In order to go free, she therefore had no choice but to sign the documents in a hurry, collect the money, and pay off the bailiffs and solicitor.[95]

This unexpected blow left Con still exposed to arrest for debt by her other unsatisfied creditors and forced her still further on the mercy of Muilman. His solicitor's terms for help were that she was to promise never again to pass herself off as Mrs Muilman, in return for which he gave her the remaining £200 with which to flee to France for eight months, leaving her sister to negotiate with her creditors. In Chancery, Muilman asked for the bill to be dismissed since 'he had compromised the affair to her satisfaction', and the Lord Chancellor complied.

In the Court of Delegates, Muilman hired a proctor and counsel 'to make a sham opposition, but in reality to consent to their joint appeal being withdrawn'. The judges at first refused to do so, but were finally convinced that Muilman had satisfied Con. It was still open to her to revive the suit since 'a marriage cause can never be at an end', but she was for the time being barred from doing so by her penniless condition and the £1,000 bond she had given Muilman.

To complete this catalogue of legal disasters, her proctor, to whom she presumably owed money, obtained from the registrar of the Court of Arches all her original exhibits in the case—Muilman's letters, affidavits of persons some now dead, depositions of witnesses, and Con's original libel—documents which she was never able to get hold of again. Her only consolation was that she had retained copies of them all.[96]

When she returned to London in the winter of 1744, she was still

[95] Ibid. iii. 231–55, 302.   [96] Ibid. iii. 256–71.

penniless and utterly dependent on Muilman's charity. She lobbied him through a Jewish broker to give her an annuity of £50 a year, which would enable her to return to live in the nunnery in Ghent. But he refused to help her except on condition that she return to Jamaica— hoping, she suspected, that she would either be captured on the ocean by a privateer, or that she would soon die there from the unhealthy climate. According to Con, this was the one time when her ebullient spirits failed her, and she bought a vial of laudanum to put an end to her life. Next she appealed to her ex-lover Southcote, who sent her a miserable 4 guineas. So she went back again to Muilman, who offered an annuity of £18 if she withdrew to Scotland or Ireland, but she refused this sentence of banishment in return for such a pittance.[97]

This led to the next step in her descent into purgatory: Con was arrested for a debt of £60 she had run up at a public house called Merlin's Cave, and was imprisoned in the Rules of the King's Bench Prison, where she remained for two years. There was, according to her, a dramatic scene as she was arrested by six bailiffs and dragged off to a waiting coach. On her last voyage overseas she had brought two mulatto slave servants back with her from Jamaica. They now fell on their knees before her, begging her to sell them for £100 each to avoid going to prison. To this offer Con claimed to have replied defiantly: 'Sell you, child? No, that I will never do, though it were to prolong my life as well as give me my liberty.'[98]

We should not feel too much sympathy for Con, since her life in the Rules of the King's Bench was far from grim so long as she had money. Con was now such a prominent London figure that Muilman could not let her starve, and so he gave her enough of an allowance to live on, while her two slave servants cost her nothing but their food and clothing. She occupied herself in litigating with her crooked ex-solicitor, who was retaining her papers and still demanding payment of his exorbitant fees. Con fought him all the way, and finally won, but it left her, as usual, out of pocket for legal costs, this time to the tune of £200.[99]

Con was clearly one of the most litigious women in a litigious age, and in 1746, while still in the Rules of the King's Bench Prison, she became involved in another row, this time with the new Marshal of the Prison over his fees. In return for allowing her freedom of the Rules of the Prison, he was demanding £3. 10s. in gaol fees, plus a fee of 5–6 guineas

---

[97] Ibid. iii. 271–86; i preface, 259.
[98] Ibid. iii. 272–88; i. 259.   [99] Ibid. iii. 288–305.

for every £100 of her debt, plus an annual gratuity of 1–2 guineas. Whenever she wanted a day pass to go outside the Rules to visit her legal counsel, he demanded 4s. 2d. for the first day of the law terms and 3s. 2d. for all other days.

A piece of luck was that the old Marshal of the Prison died insolvent without a legal representative, and the new Marshal refused to accept her as a prisoner, since he rejected her sureties never to leave the Rules except with a day pass. Consequently her counsel told her she was free, and not liable to rearrest by a warrant on grounds of escape from prison.[100]

But Muilman was determined not to let her go free, at least in London. So in 1747 he bought up at double its face value a note of hand she had given for a debt, and used it to threaten to have her arrested once more, this time to be closely confined to the Prison Lodge, at the discretion of the Marshal. She promptly moved into the Verge of the royal Court, where she could not be arrested except by the written consent of the Board of Green Cloth. According to her, two days after the publication of the second volume of her *Apology*, Muilman moved to silence her. Having obtained an escape warrant from the Board of Green Cloth, he surrounded the house where she lodged with '13 constables and 50 ruffians'. Con was saved only by the authority of the gentleman whose guest she was, which was sufficient to deter the constables from breaking in.[101]

Since Con's *Apology* included accounts of litigation still in progress, it exposed her to charges of contempt of court. She alleged that Lord Chancellor Talbot raised no objections to her putting the Chancery suit into print, but that Lord Hardwicke, the chief Justice of the King's Bench, was more difficult to handle. First he suggested that Con would do better to compromise the matter:

CON. This could not be a very easy thing, my lord, for I should always insist upon Mr Muilman being hanged, as a preliminary article.

HARDWICKE. My advice is that you should by no means print it. I must consult the rest of my brothers upon this affair.

CON. I don't remember when I was summoned here in August last that I saw any of your brothers (except Sergeant Darnell).

HARDWICKE. Let me tell you, it is not so safe as people think to draw the anger of Courts of Justice upon them.

CON. Alas, my Lord, how lately have I experienced the truth of what you say![102]

---

[100] Ibid. i preface.   [101] Ibid. i preface, 1.   [102] Ibid. iii. 48–59.

Despite this exchange, Con went ahead and published her memoirs, as has already been described. Their publication marked the end of Con Phillips's long career as a litigant, and thereafter she concentrated on picking up more husbands in Jamaica, to which Muilman had finally bribed her to go into exile.

She is not a woman who, once encountered, is easily forgotten, any more than is the story of her five marriages and seven or more lovers, and her Dickensian saga of eighteen years of matrimonial litigation, eventually defeated at every turn by money, duplicity, and legal chicanery. It is fitting that by her self-publicized exploitation of the clandestine marriage system she contributed significantly to its abolition in 1753. Her story was used to great effect in the early 1750s by one of the leading propagandists for the abolition of clandestine marriages, a campaign which culminated in Lord Hardwicke's Marriage Act of 1753.[103] It also was cited by the anonymous author of a tract in defence of the Marriage Act, published in 1761, and again by Lord Mansfield in a speech in the House of Commons in defence of the Act in 1765.[104] Moreover the reading of her *Apology* in 1759 had a profound effect on the young Jeremy Bentham. The story of her sufferings at the hands of the law shocked him into a lifelong passion to reform the English legal system. He described his immediate reactions to her book in vivid, if boastful, terms: 'while reading and musing, the Daemon of Chicanery appeareth to me in all his hideousness. What followed? I abjured his empire. I vowed war against him. My vow has been accomplished. With what effect will be acknowledged when I am no more.'[105]

---

[103] Gally, *Some Considerations upon Clandestine Marriages*, 13–15.
[104] Anon., *Some Observations on the Act for Better Prevention of Clandestine Marriages* (London, 1761), 30; BL MS Add. 35880, fo. 167.
[105] *Works of Jeremy Bentham*, x. 35.

INDEX

Alcester, Warws. 78, 80–1
Amsterdam 238, 249–51
Andrews, Dr 259
Anne, Queen 165, 217
Anjou, Duke of 228
An Apology 236, 240, 242, 244–6, 273–4
Arches, Court of 4, 18, 65, 76, 87, 103, 111, 116, 125, 133, 146, 156, 160, 168, 200, 213, 216, 225, 234, 256, 265–6, 271
Argyle, Duke of, *see* Campbell, Archibald
Ashill, Norfolk 217
Aubrey, John 4
'Ayliffe, Sir John' 129–31
   his daughter Mary 129; *see* Mary Bartlitt
Aylsham, Norfolk 148

B—, Mr 238–9
Bacon, Sir Edmund 218
Bacon, Sir Edward, JP 90
Bacon, Sir Nicholas 138
Bacon, Sir Robert 5th Bt. 136, 138–41, 144, 146
   his daughters Jane 138; and Abigail 138–9
Baispoole, Miles of Aylsham, Norf. 148, 151
Baldock, Sir Robert, of Baldock Hall, Norf 135
   his son Revd John 136–42, 144
Barebones Parliament 20
Barking, Essex 172
Barlow, William 64–6
Barrett, Edward 228, 231
Bartlitt, Barbara 128–30
   her sister Mary alias 'Mary Ayliffe' alias 'Madame Atkinson' alias 'Lady Gerard' 128–34
Barton Turf, Norf. 148–9
Bath, Som. 8, 32, 68–71, 73–4, 77
   Abbey Church 69
   Pump Room 69
Bathwick, Som. 69
Beaumont, John, of Tattingstone, Suff. 153, 155–6
   his sons, John jun. 153, 156; and Joseph 153–5
Belaugh, Norf. 148
Bengeo, Herts. 211
Bennett, Anne 100, 103–4

her sister Ursula 100–4; *see* Mrs Carpenter
Bennett, Sir Levinus 96
Bentham, Jeremy 246, 274
Bentley v. *Bentley* 9
Bentley, Mr and Mrs 205–7, 211
   their son, Charles 203–16; his wife, Penelope, née Tyrrell 208–10, 212, 216
   their daughter, Elizabeth 206, 209–11
Berault, Revd Peter 59, 62–3
Berty, Madame 97
Beterhuis 252
Bewick, Thomas 53–4
Bishop, Catherine 121, 123
Bisse, Philip, Bishop of Hereford 177–78, 187–88, 191, 196
   his wife, Bridget, née Osborne, widow of the Earl of Plymouth, known as 'Countess of Plymouth' 177–9, 187–8, 190–1, 196, 202
Blackham, John, *alias* Smith 159–60
'Blackwell, Thomas' 222
Bloch, Marc 4
Bodington, George 185, 189–90
Book of Common Prayer 17, 19, 22, 139, 148–9, 154, 213
Boston, Mass. 172 n., 241, 270
Bowden, John 68; Bowden, Mrs 69, 71
Bowring, Sir John 239 n., 246–7
Brace, John 79–82
Bradshaw, George 190–3, 195–7, 199–201
Bramston, Dr 259
Breadsall, Derby 37
Breda 126
Brereton, Dr 154
Bridgen v. *Pigeon* 10
Bristol, Som. 233
'Mrs Broughton' 195
Brown, Major 145
Brown, Mr 218
Buck, Edward 88–91
Bures, Suffolk 154
Butler v. *Ingelbright* 18
Butler, James, 2nd Duke of Ormonde 165

Cambridge University 106–7, 147, 159
   Magdalene College 126–7

Campbell, Archibald, 3rd Duke of Argyle 258
canon law 4, 18, 23, 79, 120, 124, 137, 139, 145, 149
  lawyers 21
Canons of 1604 22
Canterbury, Archbishop of 119, 123–4
  province of 4
Carey, Margaret 55–6
Carmarthern 158
  Marquis of, *see* Osborne, Peregrine-Hyde
Carpenter, Mrs 99–101
Cash, James 92–5
  his wife 93
Castlemaine, Mr 61, 64
Catton, Norfolk 148–9
Chamberlain, Dr Hope 59, 62
Chancery, Court of 13, 28, 99, 204, 206, 267–71, 273
Charles II, King 40, 126–8
Cheeke, Thomas 128, 131–2
Chelsea Hospital 259
Chester, 44–6
  Consistory Court 47, 95
Chesterfield, Lord, *see* Stanhope, Philip
Chichester 200
church courts 83–4
  see also ecclesiastical courts
Church of England 17, 20, 23, 118–23, 217
Clerkendown 69
Clewer, William 105 n.
Collier, Arthur 68–77
Colney Hatch, Essex 206
Commission of Appeal 134
common law 18, 23, 267
  courts 15–6
Common Pleas, Court of 156, 173, 233
Commons, House of 20, 31, 247
Convention Parliament 21
Cooke, Richard 109–10
Cooper, Margaret 88–91
Cork, Bishop of 107
Cornforth, Cuthbert 176, 186–8, 190, 201
Cresse, Eleanor 171–4
  her mother, Mrs Cresse 172–4
Cross, Mrs Clare 220, 225, 227, 231
Cudworth, Mary 78–82

Danby, Earl of, *see* Osborne, Thomas
Dancing School, Beveridge's 226–7
Darnell, Sir John, Sergeant-at-Law 255, 258, 262–7
Dashwood, Sir Francis 246
Davis, Mrs 176, 179, 181, 183–4, 187–8, 190, 195, 201

Dean, Revd Bainbrig 148–50
Defoe, Daniel 31–2
Delafield, Francis *alias* Devall 238, 248–51, 253, 255–6, 258–60, 262–4, 266
  his wife Magdalen, née Yeomans 249, 251, 258–60, 262, 266
Delegates, Court of 265–6, 271
Dent, Elizabeth née Wilkinson 203–13, 216
Derby 37–40, 42
Devonshire 119, 121, 123
Dictionary of National Biography 243
Dingley, Northants 161, 164, 168
dissenter 118, 120–1
Dixon, Mr and Mrs 135
Doctors' Commons 30, 68, 227, 252, 261, 265
  see also ecclesiastical courts
Dormer, John, of Ascot, Oxon 219; his widow, *see* Mordaunt, Catherine
Douglas, Mrs, widow of General Douglas 237
Doverdale, Worcs. 79
Draper, Revd John 162–8, 260
Dublin 100, 159
Duncombe, Col. 270
Durett, Revd Peter 218, 220–23, 225, 228

Eccleshall, Staffs. 105
ecclesiastical courts 4, 10, 19, 21, 23, 27–8, 30, 82, 92, 171, 266, 269
  see also church courts; Doctors' Commons
Echard, Revd John 135–46
  his brother Thomas 142–3
Elmes, Henry 113–16
Emes, Mr 189, 201
  his wife 176, 183, 201
England 4, 10, 16, 49
Essex 232
Evesham 78–9
Exeter Consistory Court 21, 124–5

F—, Lord 240
The Fable of the Bees 71
Fairfax, Lady 98
Falmouth, Earl of 132
Farewell, George 215
Farinelli, Signor 262–3
Farrant, Dr 252, 256, 259
Fazas, Jean-Jacques 96–104
Felton, Revd Henry 193–5, 199
Fénelon, Cardinal 243
Fielding, Henry 243
Fitzharris, Ann 'Lady' *alias* Mrs Magrath 228

Fleet 110, 163–4, 167–8
  Chapel 109, 234–5
  marriage 26, 108–9, 111, 162, 168,
    172 n., 173–4, 212, 216, 260
  parson 112, 161, 174, 222
  Prison 27–8, 108–9, 114, 162–3, 167,
    172, 206, 211, 213, 215–16, 222, 232;
    Rules of the 28–9, 105, 110, 117,
    162, 213–14, 216
Forbes, Susan 217–31
Forster, Thomas 54
Fox, Mr 254
France 9, 242, 271
Frederick, Prince of Wales 246
Freud, Sigmund 3
Fuller v. *Sheppard* 18

George I, King 237
Gerard, Sir Gilbert Bt. and Lady 132–4
Ghent 236, 238, 272
Gibson, Revd Samuel 153–4
Gloucester 71
Goddard, Mrs 121–2
Gower, Revd Dr Henry 213–16
Grand Tour 162, 176, 239
Graves v. *Smith* 16
Green, Mrs Elizabeth 220, 222, 226
Green Cloth, Board of 273
Greenhalgh, Ellen 92–5
Greetham, Mrs 121
Gretna Green 30
Griffin, 1st Lord 161
  2nd Lord 161, 164–5
  Edward, later 3rd Lord 109, 161–9; his
    wife, Mary, née Welden 167–8
Gripwell, Mrs 70, 74
Guist, Norf. 91 n.
Gunthorpe, Norf. 91 n.

Hadley, Essex 206, 213
Hall, Revd John 181–3, 189, 191–6,
  198–9
Hanover 237
Harbach, Robert 78–82
  his father 78–9, 81–2
Harcourt v. *Harcourt* 9–10
Harcourt, Mr, senior 151
  his son, John 147–152
Hardwicke, Lord Chancellor, *see* Yorke,
  Philip
  Marriage Act, *see* Marriage Act.
Harpur, John 161, 164–6
  his daughter Elizabeth 161–9
Harris v. *Lingard* 6, 9–11, 18
Harris, Nicholas 86
Harris, René 48–9, 54–6, 60–4, 67
  his wife 6, 48–54, 60, 62–4

  their daughters Abigail 6, 48–67; and
    Clarissa, 48–52, 55, 57–8, 60, 63, 65
Harvey, Mr, JP 89
Harvey, Ann 223
Harvey, Susan 220, 222, 226–8
Hawkins, Mr 105
  his son Edward 107, 110–11
  his daughters Jane 107; and Mary,
    clandestine wife of Revd John Vyse
    105–8, 110–12
Hayne, Benjamin 222–3, 226, 229
Henchman, Dr Henry 265–6, 268
Henworth, William 40–3
Hertford 212
  Church of All Saints 211
Hertfordshire 175
Heveringham, Norf. 148
Hibbert, Mr 85
Hick's Hall 116, 225, 227
Hillman, Hannah 214
Hilton, Captain George 100–1, 103–4
Hingham, Norfolk 88–91
Hinsmore, Thomas 229, 230
Hipsley, Mr 130
Hodgkin, Thomas 260–2
  his widow 260–1
  his nephew, Thomas junior 260–1
Hollyday, Henry 214
  his wife 213–15
Holmes, Mr 210
Holt, Sir John, Lord Chief Justice 103
Hooper v. *Fazas* 16
Hooper, Mrs Lucy 25, 96–104
Houghton, Thomas 92–5
Hughes, Elizabeth 232–4
Hunt, of Heveringham, Norf. Mrs 147–52
  her daughter Frances 147–52
Hurnard, Robert 156
  his wife, Catherine, née May, widow of
    Joseph Beaumont and of Philip
    Waldegrave 153–6

Innocent III, Pope 17
Interregnum 23, 30
Ipswich 153, 155
Ireland 31, 45, 107
Isham, Sir Edmund 259, 261, 265
Italy 239–40

JP 14, 17, 20–1, 23, 42, 83, 85–6, 89–90,
  93–4, 120, 189
Jackson, Robert 39–40
Jacobites 228–9, 240
Jamaica 241–42, 269, 272, 274
James II, King 128, 131, 161, 217
Jermy, Anne 147, 151

Jones, Mrs 176, 179–81, 183–84, 186, 190, 201
Jones, Samuel 44, 46
  his wife 44–7; their daughter, Priscilla 44–7
Jordan, Mrs 113, 116

Keith, Revd Alexander 29
King's Bench 28, 48, 103, 199, 224–5, 254, 267–9, 273
  Prison, Southwark 242; Rules of the 113, 272
Kingston, Jamaica 242
Kinwarton, Warws. 78, 80
Kiveton Park, Yorkshire 176–8, 181–2, 188–9, 190, 195, 201

La Bruyère, Jean de 244
Lacock, Neville 38–9, 42
Lacy, Mary 88
Lambert, Major-General 38, 40
Lambert, Mr 189
Lambspring College, Saxony 217
Larling, Norfolk 88
Le Double, Abraham 227
  see also Maynard, Anne
Leeds;
  Duchess of, *see* Osborne, Bridget (née Hyde)
  Duke of, *see* Osborne, Peregrine, Osborne, Peregrine-Hyde and Osborne, Thomas
Leigh, Mr and Mrs, of Catton, Norfolk 148–50
Lichfield, Staffs. 106, 111
Lingard, John senior 48–9, 59–61, 64
  his wife 49, 59, 62, 64; their son John jr (Jack) 48–56, 58–66
Locke, Leonard 8, 122
  his widow Elizabeth 118–25
London: All Hallows, Barking 172
  Arlington House 176, 195–6, 198, 200
  Bell Tavern in Nicholas Lane 48
  Billingsgate 162
  Blackfriars 109
  'Blue Post' in Haymarket 57
  'Bricklayers' Arms' in the Rules of the Fleet 108
  Bridewell 227, 233
  Broad Street 206
  'Bull and Garter' 109–10, 167
  Clerkenwell Church 205
  Covent Garden 57, 113; Church 159
  Drury Lane 113
  Fenchurch St 206
  Fleet, *see* Fleet
  Globe Tavern in Fleet Street 62

Green Arbour Court 162
Half-Moon Tavern in Fleet Street 249
'Hand and Pen' 172, 260
Hole-in-the-Wall tavern 222
Hyde Park 129; Gate 131
Inner Temple 49, 59, 203
'King Harry's Head' tavern, Fleet St. 222
Knightsbridge 129–30
Lamb's Chapel, *see* St James-on-the-Wall
Leicester Fields 133
Lincoln's Inn Fields 116
Lincoln's Inn Gardens 52
Long Acre 100, 229
Middle Temple 54, 56, 197
Nicholas Lane 49
Old Spring Gardens 129
Oxford Arms Tavern 215
Pall Mall 99–102
Piccadilly 133
Red Lion Square in Holborn 203, 207
Red Lion Street, Clerkenwell 208, 250, 253
'Roebuck' in Suffolk St 57
Rose Street, Covent Garden 113
Roundhouse 227
Russell Street, near Drury Lane 113
St Catherine by the Tower 171
St Clement's Eastcheap 48–9
St Benet's, Paul's Wharf 249–50
St Bride's, Fleet Street 217, 219
St George's Chapel, Ormonde St. 207
St Mary Le Bow 101
St James's 98
St James's Duke's Place 27–8
St James-on-the-Wall *alias* Lamb's Chapel 27
Seething Lane 171
Tower of 161, 217
Turk's Head Coffee House 213–15
Vauxhall 56
White House Yard, Drury Lane 113, 116
White Lyon in Long Acre 100
Wine Office Court 54
London Consistory Court 65, 76, 103, 110–12, 131, 133, 156, 160, 167, 174, 197, 199, 211–12, 225, 234, 250–1, 259, 263–6
London Sheriff's Court 221
Lord Mayor's Court 103, 233
Lords, House of 30–1, 270
Louis XIV, King of France 127
Lumley, Thomas, 3rd Earl of Scarbrough 246
Luttrell, Narcissus 131

Ly, Thomas 113–15
Lycombe Spaw House, near Bath 69

Mandeville, Bernard 71
Mansfield, Lord, *see* Murray, William
Market Harling, Norfolk 143
Marlborough, Wilts. 121–2
Marriage Act 22, 30, 48, 174, 274
Marston, Mrs 205, 213
Matthews, Mary 85–6
Maynard, Anne *alias* Le Double 223–4,
    226–8
Meadows, Ann 109–10
Middleton, Mrs 205, 213
Milner, William 119–20, 123–5
Moll Flanders 31
Monck, George (later 1st Duke of
    Albermarle) 40
Montaigne, Michel de 244
Moody, Revd Alexander 100–1, 103
Mordaunt v. *Mordaunt* 29, 35, 52
Mordaunt, Charles, 3rd Earl of
    Peterborough 217–18
  his brother, George 217–221, 224–7,
    229–31
  his wife Catherine (née Spencer), widow
    of John Dormer 219–21, 224, 226,
    228, 231
  his nephew Charles 219
  his brother Lewis 219
'Mordaunt, George' impersonators 220,
    222, 226, 230
Morland v. *Morland* 15–6, 25
Morland, Sir Samuel Bt. 13, 25, 126–134
Morrill, Mr 248–9
Mortlake 48
Moseley v. *Collier* 8
Moseley, Sir Oswald 1st Bt. 68, 70, 74–6
  his wife *née* Thornhaugh 68, 70
  their daughter, Elizabeth 68–77
Mott, Revd John 41
Mottram, Dr 215
Muilman v. *Muilman* 13, 16, 22
Muilman, Mr senior 250–1
Muilman, Henry 238, 240, 244, 247,
    249–274
  his wife, née Darnell 258, 262, 265
Mundy, Gilbert 43
Murray, William, 1st Earl of Mansfield
    274

Neatishead, Norf. 148
Neech, Revd 89–91
Neville, Mr 265
New Buckingham, Norf. 90
New England 9
Newbury, Berks 173

Newgate Prison 233, 252
Newton St Cyres, Devon 123–5
Norfolk 88, 91 n., 135, 147, 217
Northmore, Edward 118–25
Northumberland 54
Norwich 135, 148–9
  Bishop of 217
  Consistory Court 90, 143, 151
  St Mary's 91 n.
Nottingham 37–8

Ogilvie, Captain 264
Ogle, Revd John 108
O'Key, Mrs 158
Old Bailey 233–4, 253
Ordway, Anne 113–17
  her sisters Ellen and Jane, 113–14
Ormonde, 2nd Duke of *see* Butler, James
Ormskirk, Lancs. 94
Osborne v. *Williams* 5, 8, 12, 19, 35
Osborne, Peregrine, 2nd Duke of Leeds
    175–6, 181, 191, 195, 197–200, 202
  his wife Bridget, née Hyde, Duchess of
    Leeds 176, 178–80, 182–7, 189–90,
    195–6, 198–9, 201–2; their daughter
    Lady Bridget 175–202; their sons
    Peregrine-Hyde, Marquis of
    Carmarthen [later 3rd Duke of Leeds]
    176, 179–82, 187, 189–91, 195–9,
    201, and William Henry 176
Osborne, Thomas, Earl of Danby, 1st
    Duke of Leeds 175–7, 180
Otway, Captain 229
Otway, Thomas 66
Oxford, 118–25, 162
  Bocardo 120
  Carfax 120; Church 123
  Christ Church 161
  George Inn 124–5
  Gloucester Hall 125
  Jesus College 177, 200 n.
  New College 208
  Queen's College 203, 208
  St Giles 119
  Wadham College 118

Packington, Sir Herbert 240, 247
Paradise Lost 71
Paris, 164–6, 234, 256, 265
Parker, Chief Justice 225, 227
Parliament 20
Parsons, Alderman 261–62
Paul, Dr 252, 255, 258–9
Paulet, Henrietta née Scot 2nd wife of
    Charles, 2nd Duke of Bolton 236–7
Peacock, Mr 162, 167–8
  his daughter Mary 162

'Peculiar' 23, 26–8
Pelham-Holles, Thomas, Duke of
    Newcastle 247
Pepys, Samuel 16, 127, 129, 131–2, 134
Peterborough, Bishop of 207
Petty Sessions 92–4
Phillips, Mr 158
Phillips, Lt.-Col. 236–7
    his daughter Constantia 236–74
Phillips, Thomas 171–4
Pierson, Mr 55
Pindar, Reginald 40
Plymouth, Countess of, *see* Bisse, Bridget
Poole, John 189
Poor Law 14
    poor relief 83, 91 n.
Portsmouth 237, 249–50, 259
Portugal 237
Pratt, Lord Chief Justice 254
Preston v. *Matthews* 15, 18
Preston, Revd Charles, of Barton Turf,
    Norf. 148–51
Preston, Richard 85–7

Quarter Sessions 15, 92, 94–5, 120, 227
Queen's Bench, *see* King's Bench

Rawlins, Sergeant, JP 85–6
Redgrave, Norf. 138
    Church 138, 140
    Hall 135–6, 138
Reid, Revd 205
Restoration 20, 27, 40, 118–19
Reynolds, William 172 n.
Richmond 48–9, 54
    Duchess of 218
    Wells 57
Roberts, Frances 232–3
Robinet, Mr 181–2, 193
Robins, Jane, bigamous wife of Revd Vyse,
    108, 111
Rogers, Mr 56, 59–60
Rolleston, Staffs. 68, 70, 73, 77
Rouen 238, 249
Rudd v. *Rudd* 13, 29
Rudd, Sir John Bt. 158–60
    his brother, Anthony 159–60
    his mother Beatrice, Lady Rudd 158–9
    his wife, Lettice née Vaughan, alias Mrs
        Smith 158–60
Rugby 163–4, 168
    School 161
Russia 9
Russell, Sir Francis, JP 86
Ryder v. *Jones* 9, 13
Ryder, George 44–7

St Albans, Herts. 193
Saint Germain, France 228, 231
St James's Palace 258
Salford, Warws. 85–6
Sayer, Dr Everard 261
Scandinavia 9
Scarbrough, Earl of, *see* Lumley
Scotland 9, 31
Sedley, Sir Charles Bt. 57–8, 64–6
Sergeant v. *Sergeant* 22
Settlement, Law of 14, 15, 83–4, 86, 90,
    91 n.
Shadwell, Thomas 66
Shelton, Revd 81
Sheppard, Mrs Frances 64
Shirley, Elizabeth 50
Shirley, William 247
Shrewsbury, Salop 44–5
    Earl (later Duke) of, *see* Talbot, Charles
Smith, Mr 249, 263–4
Smithfield, Middlesex 173
Snettisham, Norfolk 88–91
Somerset, Mary (née Osborne) widow of
    2nd Duke of Beaufort (later Countess
    of Dundonald) 176, 178, 191, 198–200
South Littleton, Warws. 85–6
South Sea Bubble 237
Southcote, Sir John 239
    his 2nd son 239–40, 245, 272
Southwark, Middlesex 113
Spencer, Sir John, of Yarnton, Oxon 219
Stacey, William 189
Stafford, Trooper 228
Stamp Act 28, 163, 182; stamp tax 26,
    161; stamped paper 168
Stanhope, Philip, 4th Earl of Chesterfield
    237, 244, 247, 249
Stenson, Mary 37–43
Steward, Mrs 159
Stone, Staffs. 107
Stourbridge Fair 136
Stow-on-the-Wold, Glos. 113
Stutton, Suffolk 153
Suffolk 153
Sussex, Countess of 218
Swansea 158
Sweden 126
Swift, Jonathan 161
Switzerland 9
Sydenham's Lottery 62

Tacolneston Hall, Norf. 135–7, 145
Talbot, Charles, Lord Chancellor 269, 273
Talbot, Charles, Earl [later Duke] of
    Shrewsbury 165
Talman, William 176

Tasher, Mr 226
Tattingstone, Suffolk 153, 155–6
Taylor, Bridget 168
Tenison, Thomas, Archbishop of
    Canterbury 134
'Thames', *see* Sedley
Thatcher, Mr and Mrs 135–37, 141
Thornton, Bucks. 208
Thurloe, John, Secretary of State 126–7
Tillotson, John 244
Tipping, Robert 232–4
    his wife Sarah, née Hughes 232–4; their
        daughter Mary 232, 234; their son
        Francis 232–3
    his brother John 233–4
Todwick, Yorks. 188
Townsend, Mr 46–7
Townshend, George 135, 142–4
    his daughters Frances 135–9, 141–6;
        and Mary 135–8, 145
Townshend, Lord, of Raynham 135, 144
Trafford, Henry, of Trafford 76
Trenby, Mr 259–60
Trent, Council of 4
Trentham, Staffs. 105–8, 111
Trevor, Thomas, Lord Chief Justice 116
Troope v. *Stenson* 9, 19
Troope, Jonathan 37–40, 42–3
The True Patriot 71
Twelve Bad Women 243
Tyrrell, Charles 208
    his brothers Sir Harry 6th Bt. 208–9,
        211; Sir Thomas 5th Bt. 208
    their mother, Lady— 209, 211–12

Utrecht 158
    Treaty of 88

Vanbrugh, Sir John 66
Vassall, Colonel 241
Vaughan, Lettice 158–60
'Vaughan, Revd' 222–3, 226, 230
Versailles 127
Vyse, Revd John 28, 105–12, 162–3

Wake, William, Bishop of Lincoln 217
Waldegrave, Philip 155–6

Wales 9, 16
Walker, Ellen 39
Walker, Robert 37, 41–2
Walpole, Horace 29, 242
Walpole, Sir Robert 228, 240
Warren, William 109–10
Warwickshire 78, 85
Watts, Revd 130
Weekley, Anne 206, 209
Welsh, Harry 189–90
Westminster, Middlesex
    Assembly 20
    Downing St. 206, 254
    Hall 116, 227, 30
    King St. 206
    St James's St. 207
    Whitehall 218
Westphalia 217
Westwood Park, Worcs. 240
Whepstead, Suff. 154
Whitehead, Paul 246–7, 254, 267, 270
Whitwell, Derby 193
Wigan, Lancs. 93–4
Wilkinson, Richard sen. 203, 206, 211, 216
    his children Mary 204, 213
    Richard Jr. 204, 210; *see also* Dent,
        Elizabeth
Williams, Revd William 176–202, 179 n.
Wimbledon, Middlesex 195, 198, 200
Winchester School 126
Windsor Castle 127
Winwick, Lancs. 92
Wise, Mary 113–17
Wolf, Revd alias Brown 218
Woodward, Mrs Mary 102–3
Worcester 80–1
    Consistory Court 86–7
Worcestershire 240
'Worthy', Mr 241, 269
Wreningham, Norf. 135
Wyatt, Revd Walter 172

Yorke, Philip, 1st Earl of Hardwicke 29,
    266–9, 273–4
Yorkshire 133, 176